MW00991584

The Practice of Correctional Psychology

Marguerite Ternes • Philip R. Magaletta
Marc W. Patry

Editors

The Practice of Correctional Psychology

 Springer

Editors
Marguerite Ternes
Psychology Department
Saint Mary's University
Halifax, NS, Canada

Marc W. Patry
Psychology Department
Saint Mary's University
Halifax, NS, Canada

Philip R. Magaletta
Federal Bureau of Prisons (ret.)
Columbia, MD, USA

George Washington University
Washington, DC, USA

ISBN 978-3-030-00451-4   ISBN 978-3-030-00452-1   (eBook)
https://doi.org/10.1007/978-3-030-00452-1

Library of Congress Control Number: 2018960831

This Springer imprint is published by the registered company Springer Nature Switzerland AG
The registered company address is: Gewerbestrasse 11, 6330 Cham, Switzerland

Acknowledgements

The editors wish to thank Samantha Perry, Ruth Shelton, and Prachi Gaba for reviewing the chapters in this volume. We would also like to thank Sharon Panulla and Sylvana Ruggirello of Springer Science+Business Media for their assistance and support. Finally, a wink of appreciation goes to the spirit of guidance and collaboration that appears when like-minded friends gather together and share their ideas.

Contents

Contributors

Ashley B. Batastini, PhD School of Psychology, University of Southern Mississippi, Hattiesburg, MS, USA

Kelley Blanchette, PhD Department of Psychology, Carleton University, Ottawa, ON, Canada

Douglas P. Boer, PhD Centre for Applied Psychology, Faculty of Health, University of Canberra, Canberra, ACT, Australia

Johann Brink, MB, ChB, BA Hons, FCPsych (SA), FRCPC, RCPSC Forensic Psychiatric Services Commission, BC Mental Health and Substance Use Services, PHSA, Coquitlam, BC, Canada

Division of Forensic Psychiatry, Department of Psychiatry, Faculty of Medicine, University of British Columbia, Vancouver, BC, Canada

Amanda Butler, BA, MA Faculty of Health Sciences, Simon Fraser University, Burnaby, BC, Canada

Joyce P. S. Chan, PhD Centre for Applied Psychology, Faculty of Health, University of Canberra, Canberra, ACT, Australia

Stephanie Goodwin, BSc Psychology Department, Saint Mary's University, Halifax, NS, Canada

Laura M. Gulledge, PhD School of Criminal Justice, University of Southern Mississippi, Hattiesburg, MS, USA

Joshua B. Hill, PhD School of Criminal Justice, University of Southern Mississippi, Hattiesburg, MS, USA

Nancy L. Hogan School of Criminal Justice, Ferris State University, Big Rapids, MI, USA

Robert D. Hoge, PhD Department of Psychology, Carleton University, Ottawa, ON, Canada

Kathleen Hyland, BSc Psychology Department, Saint Mary's University, Halifax, NS, Canada

Roland Jones, PhD, MSc, MB, ChB, BSc, MRCPsych Division of Forensic Psychiatry, Department of Psychiatry, University of Toronto, Toronto, ON, Canada

Forensic Division, Centre for Addiction and Mental Health, Toronto, ON, Canada

Lindsey Kendrick-Koch, BA, MPH Division of Forensic Psychiatry, Department of Psychiatry, Faculty of Medicine, University of British Columbia, Vancouver, BC, Canada

Ashleigh M. Kinlyside, MCP Centre for Applied Psychology, Faculty of Health, University of Canberra, Canberra, ACT, Australia

Eric G. Lambert Department of Criminal Justice, The University of Nevada, Reno, Reno, NV, USA

Matthew R. Labrecque, BA Psychology Department, Saint Mary's University, Halifax, NS, Canada

Zoe K. Livengood, BCJ School of Criminal Justice, University of Southern Mississippi, Hattiesburg, MS, USA

Philip R. Magaletta, PhD Federal Bureau of Prisons (ret.), Columbia, MD, USA

George Washington University, Washington, DC, USA

Donna McDonagh, PhD, CPsych Private Practice, Ottawa, ON, Canada

Jack M. McKnight, MCP Centre for Applied Psychology, Faculty of Health, University of Canberra, Canberra, ACT, Australia

Sarah Moss Psychology Department, Saint Mary's University, Halifax, NS, Canada

Tonia L. Nicholls, BA, MA, PhD Division of Forensic Psychiatry, Department of Psychiatry, Faculty of Medicine, University of British Columbia, Vancouver, BC, Canada

Forensic Psychiatric Services Commission, BC Mental Health and Substance Use Services, PHSA, Coquitlam, BC, Canada

Mark E. Olver, PhD, RD Psych Department of Psychology, University of Saskatchewan, Saskatoon, SK, Canada

Marc W. Patry, PhD Psychology Department, Saint Mary's University, Halifax, NS, Canada

Alexandra Repke, MA School of Psychology, University of Southern Mississippi, Hattiesburg, MS, USA

Maria Simmons, BA Department of Psychiatry, Dalhousie University, Halifax, NS, Canada

Alexander I. F. Simpson, MBChB, BMedSci, FRANZCP Division of Forensic Psychiatry, Department of Psychiatry, University of Toronto, Toronto, ON, Canada
Forensic Division, Centre for Addiction and Mental Health, Toronto, ON, Canada

Skye Stephens, PhD Psychology Department, Saint Mary's University, Halifax, NS, Canada

Keira C. Stockdale, PhD, RD Psych Department of Psychology, University of Saskatchewan, Saskatoon, SK, Canada
Saskatoon Police Service, Saskatoon, SK, Canada

Yvonne Stys, MA Research Branch Correctional Service Canada, Ottawa, ON, Canada

Kelly Taylor, PhD Reintegration Programs Division, Correctional Services Canada, Ottawa, ON, Canada

Marguerite Ternes, PhD Psychology Department, Saint Mary's University, Halifax, NS, Canada

Sydney Trendell, BA Psychology Department, Saint Mary's University, Halifax, NS, Canada

Jennifer Vitale, PhD Hampden-Sydney College, Hampden-Sydney, VA, USA

Chapter 1
The Practice of Correctional Psychology

Philip R. Magaletta

It is an exciting time be practicing correctional psychology—the application of psychological assessment, intervention, and management of offenders in jails, prisons, and other correctional settings. Never before in the history of correctional psychology have practitioners had so many theoretical models and rigorous scientific studies to guide their work. The first two decades of the twenty-first century alone have amassed a literature bursting with valid assessment instruments and psychotherapy and psychoeducational interventions that, with proper implementation and staffing, can be used to advance offender change. Theories, frameworks and research studies are now differentiating between mental illnesses, substance use disorders and criminal lifestyles (Magaletta & Verdeyen, 2005; Skeem, Manchak, & Peterson, 2011). Such differentiation allows for more nuanced strategies and approaches to addressing offender needs through the delivery of psychological services. This differentiation is also reflected in the organizational redesign of criminal justice systems, where the number of court diversion and community reentry programs have proliferated (Fagan & Augustin, 2011). Finally, the differentiation is further validated as community providers expand their clinical repertoires to address criminal lifestyle issues alongside the mental health and substance use disorders they have traditionally addressed in their practice.

In terms of the psychology services workforce, training opportunities in correctional settings are now commonly available and offered within graduate school training programs. Psychologists and students wishing to pursue careers in correctional psychology can easily chart a course to accomplishment. With correctional populations continuing to be characterized by those with mental illnesses, substance use disorders and criminal lifestyles, the demand for psychological services is constant and the need for a workforce of correctional

P. R. Magaletta (✉)
Federal Bureau of Prisons (ret.), Columbia, MD, USA

George Washington University, Washington, DC, USA

© Springer Nature Switzerland AG 2018
M. Ternes et al. (eds.), *The Practice of Correctional Psychology*,
https://doi.org/10.1007/978-3-030-00452-1_1

psychologists who can work with these offenders in the fast paced, challenging correctional environment will remain.

Against this backdrop of progress for contemporary correctional psychologists, we must also note that the complexities of offender problems and the challenges of providing psychological services within the correctional settings remain the same as they have in the past. The need for biopsychosocial interventions to treat offenders with serious mental illness is growing. Yet, staff continue to face challenges finding and organizing interdisciplinary teams that can deliver the range of services required. Offenders with substance use disorders engage in services and initiate their recovery. Yet, the challenge of allowing them to practice coping and other recovery skills in predictable correctional environments evades the full potential of what a psychologist can facilitate in shaping lifestyle change outside the correctional setting. The specific hallmarks of a high-risk criminal lifestyle characterized by irresponsibility, the incessant desire to have one's way no matter the cost, and the use of a power orientation to get it, still collides with the issue of long term treatment engagement required for sustainable lifestyle change (Samenow, 1984; Walters, 1990). The offenders most in need of services (those at highest risk) are still those most likely to refuse services and/or the most difficult to engage (Wormith & Olver, 2002). Finally, such challenges are compounded by the public safety system cycles of constricted funding and staffing, implementation of new or revised legal standards, and the various crises experienced within the correctional system.

To be effective, and fully competent, correctional psychologists must accept and master these complexities and challenges while valuing, formulating, and executing interventions that are responsive to the needs of various clinical offender populations. This clearly requires development of a broad and general set of competencies for use in the correctional setting, and for more than 100 years, psychologists have been developing, defining, and using such competencies (Bartol & Bartol, 2011; Watkins, 1992). Initially researching and assessing intelligence in juveniles and adult offenders, the handful of correctional psychologists from the early 1920s grew in number and the scope as their work expanded (Glueck & Glueck, 1930; Jackson, 1934; Rowland, 1913). Given their versatile, generalist skill set they began contributing to the management and treatment of offenders—delivering a broad array of mental health and substance abuse treatment interventions (Corsini, 1945; Giardini, 1942; Sell, 1955). Finally, given their administrative acumen and skill, some eventually joined the executive ranks of correctional leadership (Cullen, 2005; Hawk, 1997; Silber, 1974; Wicks, 1974).

Overall, these historically developed areas of correctional psychology align with contemporary and mainstream competency definitions of practice such as assessment, intervention, interdisciplinary communication, research, cultural awareness and diversity, and the management and administration of psychological services. Stated in the broadest terms, today's correctional psychologists deliver a wide range of services to an even wider range of offenders. Additionally, they meet the administrative demands and supervisory responsibilities of the correctional setting (Boothby & Clements, 2000, 2002).

In 2002, Epstein and Hundert recommended competence be conceived of as a "statement of the relationship between an ability (in the person), a task (in the world), and the ecology of the health systems and clinical contexts in which these tasks occur" (p. 228). Thus, throughout their development and application of competencies, every correctional psychologist has a responsibility to ask two important questions: what should I do and who should I be? This book answers the first question and does so in a particular way—by critically examining and providing a structured didactic summary of particular offender groups and populations. Such structure allows the authors to address individual points relevant to specific content while simultaneously providing coherence across each chapter. In providing such a structured summary across chapters we address a central challenge of correctional psychology: How to master foundational knowledge of specific and separate offender groups, while knowing that real-life corrections practice requires working with and across an eclectic mix of offender groups, diagnoses and problems.

This central challenge of correctional psychology resonates with the larger specialization movement in healthcare. Specialization dominates the horizon while generalist skills rule the day to day corrections practice world. One must recognize that both perspectives are necessary and there is room for both. Generalists need a global idea of specializations, not to go deep but to remain informed. Specialists need to understand generalist practice and contexts, so they can accurately and effectively provide individual and programmatic level interventions to offenders who will benefit from such services. As such, in this book an array of well-defined specialist viewpoints and broadly focused generalist practices are drawn from the international expertise of leaders in the field. Specifically, chapters consider the unique and common issues related to the assessment of and treatment interventions with distinct groups of offenders e.g., offenders with mental illness, offenders with substance use disorders, offenders with intellectual disabilities, women offenders, young offenders, violent offenders, psychopathic offenders, sexual offenders, and radicalized offenders; and broader issues important to correctional psychology, such as suicidality, self-harm, and correctional staff challenges.

To address this tension between specialist and generalist viewpoints and perspectives, this book employs a narrative structure responsive to the types of knowledge correctional psychologists typically need. What are the key studies in a given area and which theoretical models support the correctional psychologists understanding? What tools do correctional psychologists use to screen for and assess psychopathology? What does the change literature suggest for interventions?

To weave practical coherence and stability into the answers for these questions, each chapter uses the same narrative structure and this begins with an *introduction*. This brief overview of the topic introduces history and a review of key constructs essential for correctional psychologist knowledge and which appear throughout the chapter. Next, *frequency and prevalence* are reviewed. Where available, important studies on the frequency of given phenomena or prevalence of a disorder for male and female offenders within various jurisdictions are reviewed. This helps situate the chapter topic within a public health context by suggesting how many or how often a correctional psychologist might encounter a particular offender problem or diagnostic group. Chapters then consider *theoretical model(s) relevant to service delivery*. In selecting and organizing theories for this volume authors were invited to select the theory most relevant to guide correctional psychology practice. Thus, some chapters briefly review a theory of psychotherapy, others a theory of criminality from criminology. Still others present frameworks on organizing recidivism reduction approaches through a service delivery lens. This allows practitioners and students to learn broadly across various theories in various chapters and reflects the numerous perspectives used by psychologists to understand the full range of offenders and change interventions that they will encounter in their correctional psychology practice (Magaletta, Morgan, Reitzel, & Innes, 2007).

The chapters then move to consider *diagnosis and assessment*. This section reviews the current assessment instruments available for identifying and understanding particular problems or diagnoses. When available, state-of-the-art assessment instruments that are reliable and valid are presented. Distinctions between assessment instruments related to a focus on detecting psychiatric disorders, severity of a problem, or factors that link to recidivism may be highlighted. Many times assessments link back to theories that inform treatment approaches or behavior change. They may also inform how to allocate resources to offenders most in need.

Assessments are often the first step in planning treatment or interventions, which are considered in the next section, *Intervention(s): What Works, What Might Work, and What Doesn't Work*. These classic groupings have been used to organize many contemporary scientific studies, change strategies and techniques. The interventions section is informed by the definition of evidence proposed by American Psychological Association Task Force on Evidence-Based Practice (2006): "Evidence-based practice in psychology is the integration of the best available research with clinical expertise in the context of patient characteristics, culture, and preferences." Sorting the levels of scientific evidence for interventions into the yes, maybe, and no results categories, allows correctional psychologists to look for information they can use. Is the aim of the intervention to reduce or manage symptoms, reduce recidivism, or reduce aggression during incarceration? These are all relevant aims for the practicing correctional psychologist and may be presented.

Moving to *future implications*, chapters then address the question of what remains to be done at the levels of training, practice, research and correctional administration. These are all areas that correctional psychologists contribute to. In addition, given the inevitability of technology's influence upon corrections in the future, authors reflect upon the impact and influence of *technology and innovation*. How will technology and innovation be envisioned to influence the process of knowledge accumulation and dissemination in the service of changing offender behavior? Finally, a brief, summative *conclusion* rounds out each chapter.

This book allows students and other corrections practitioners to broaden perspectives on areas they wish to develop or apply in their daily work—while simultaneously anchoring their understanding in the relevant theories of our day. It can be used to illustrate, organize and animate the burgeoning field of behavioral and social sciences and criminal justice studies. Even with the strength of this broad approach we offer the following reminder. It is the nature of practicing correctional psychology that what is read about in textbooks will trace and outline, but not fill-in and color correctional psychology as it is practiced in the fluid environment of the correctional setting. There are four reasons for this. First, the foundational knowledge required for the multitude of offender populations is ever changing. It requires a mastery of content that is vast, to say the least. Second, the offender population is extremely complex. Many offenders survived neo-natal insults and chemical influences, poverty, and school failures before being involved in the criminal justice system. Comorbid substance use disorders and brain injuries which are common among offender populations may present before the on-set of mental health issues, incarceration, and the establishment and maintenance of a criminal lifestyle. A third reason is that the continual unfolding of challenges evolving from legislative agendas are always influencing correctional settings, missions, and resources. This calls for flexibility and continual correctional psychologist responsiveness. Fourth—the predictable and unpredictable events and influences upon the custodial environment itself can never be adequately captured by a textbook. It has to be experienced, lived, supervised and worked through.

To become proficient, it will always be necessary for correctional psychologists and students to read, practice, re-read and practice some more. The more nuanced features of correctional psychology practice have always been transmitted experientially, through the environment, as opposed to didactically through textbooks and coursework. Whereas theory and research provide the necessary supports and elements for the foundational knowledge required of the practicing correctional psychologist, the integration of the knowledge and its implications in a practice are continually unfolding and best mastered through on-going supervision alongside collegial dialogue and support.

1.1 Conclusion

When it is all boiled down, clinical practice in corrections requires competent generalist skills performed within the specific and unique context of the prison environment. The reciprocal relationship between the offender and the corrections context always influences the practice of correctional psychology. As such, the work of correctional psychologists requires strong partnerships across the interdisciplinary systems that form and sustain the correctional context.

The demands placed upon those who practice correctional psychology; demands on their time and skill, from the offenders, managers, and the communities that expect them to maintain public safety requires the establishment and maintenance of a foundational knowledge base. For over 100 years psychologists have been enlivening this knowledge base by establishing theory, validating and developing assessment instruments, and creating empirically supported interventions that allow correctional systems to best use limited resources. Although the core clinical competencies and duties of correctional psychologists have remained consistent throughout the years, several factors do suggest that contemporary correctional psychologists now function under a greater set of demands.

There are, and will continue to be significant changes in legislation, policy, program offerings, and staffing as the next decade unfolds. Organizational re-design will continue to be a key feature of institution life for those who practice in corrections. New initiatives such as creating staff wellness programs will require training and implementation techniques from correctional psychologists. The needs of the correctional setting will continue to require a public service leadership response characterized by tact and skill; love, and courage. All this accompanied by an exceptional focus on maintaining ethical practices—and all while also caring for oneself and providing services to others. In the pages that follow, correctional psychologists and students who enter this field will find a helpful and hopeful companion for that journey.

References

American Psychological Association Task Force on Evidence-Based Practice. (2006). Evidence-based practice in psychology. *American Psychologist, 61*, 271–285.
Bartol, C. R., & Bartol, A. M. (2011). *Introduction to forensic psychology* (3rd ed.). Thousand Oaks, CA: Sage Publications.
Boothby, J. L., & Clements, C. B. (2000). A national survey of correctional psychologists. *Criminal Justice and Behavior, 27*, 716–732. https://doi.org/10.1177/0093854800027006003
Boothby, J. L., & Clements, C. B. (2002). Job satisfaction and correctional psychologists: Implications for recruitment and retention. *Professional Psychology: Research and Practice, 33*, 310–315. https://doi.org/10.1037/0735-7028.33.3.310
Corsini, R. J. (1945). Functions of a prison psychologist. *Journal of Consulting Psychology, 9*, 101–104. https://doi.org/10.1037/h0059164
Cullen, F. T. (2005). The twelve people who saved rehabilitation: How the science of criminology made a difference – The American Society of Criminology 2004 Presidential address. *Criminology, 43*(1), 1–42.
Epstein, R. M., & Hundert, E. M. (2002). Defining and assessing professional competence. *JAMA: Journal of the American Medical Association, 287*, 226–235. https://doi.org/10.1001/jama.287.2.226
Fagan, T. J., & Augustin, D. (2011). Criminal justice and mental health systems: The new continuum of care system. In T. J. Fagan & R. K. Ax (Eds.), *Correctional mental health* (pp. 7–36). Thousand Oaks, CA: Sage Publications.
Giardini, G. I. (1942). The place of psychology in penal and correctional institutions. *Federal Probation, 29*, 29–33.
Glueck, S., & Glueck, E. T. (1930). *500 Criminal careers*. New York, NY: Alfred A. Knopf.
Hawk, K. M. (1997). Personal reflections on a career in correctional psychology. *Professional Psychology: Research and Practice, 28*, 335–337. https://doi.org/10.1037/0735-7028.28.4.335
Jackson, J. D. (1934). The work of the psychologist in a penal institution: A symposium. *Psychological Exchange, 3*, 49–63.
Magaletta, P. R., Morgan, R. D., Reitzel, L., & Innes, C. (2007). Toward the one: Strengthening behavioral sciences research in corrections. *Criminal Justice and Behavior, 34*, 919–932.
Magaletta, P. R., & Verdeyen, V. (2005). Clinical practice in corrections: A conceptual framework. *Professional Psychology: Research and Practice, 36*, 37–43.

Rowland, E. (1913). Report of experiments at the state reformatory for women at Bedford, New York. *Psychological Review, 20*(3), 245–249. https://doi.org/10.1037/h0075385

Samenow, S. E. (1984). *Inside the criminal mind.* New York, NY: Crown Publishers.

Sell, D. E. (Ed.). (1955). *Manual of applied correctional psychology.* Columbus, OH: Ohio Department of Mental Hygiene and Correction.

Silber, D. E. (1974). Controversy concerning the criminal justice system and its implications for the role of mental health workers. *American Psychologist, 29,* 239–244. https://doi.org/10.1037/h0036266

Skeem, J. L., Manchak, S., & Peterson, J. K. (2011). Correctional policy for offenders with mental illness: Creating a new paradigm for recidivism reduction. *Law and Human Behavior, 35,* 110–126. https://doi.org/10.1007/s10979-010-9223-7

Watkins, R. E. (1992). *A historical review of the role and practice of psychology in the field of corrections. Research Reports, R-28.* Ottowa, ON: Correctional Service Canada.

Walters, G. D. (1990). *The criminal lifestyle: Patterns of serious criminal conduct.* Newbury Park, CA: Sage Publications.

Wicks, R. J. (1974). *Correctional psychology: Themes and problems in correcting the offender.* San Francisco, CA: Canfield Press.

Wormith, J. S., & Olver, M. E. (2002). Offender treatment attrition and its relationship with risk, responsivity, and recidivism. *Criminal Justice and Behavior, 29,* 447–471.

Chapter 2
Assessing and Treating Offenders with Mental Illness

Tonia L. Nicholls, Amanda Butler, Lindsey Kendrick-Koch, Johann Brink, Roland Jones, and Alexander I. F. Simpson

Commentators have long lamented that correctional institutions have become this century's ill-equipped, de facto mental health asylums (e.g., Kirby & Keon, 2006). This is believed to reflect many social drivers including the deinstitutionalization movement and a lack of resources for the care for mentally ill persons in the community (Durbin, Lin, & Zaslavska, 2010; Hartvig & Kjelsberg, 2009; Kirby & Keon, 2006;

T. L. Nicholls (✉) · J. Brink
Division of Forensic Psychiatry, Department of Psychiatry, Faculty of Medicine, University of British Columbia, Vancouver, BC, Canada

Forensic Psychiatric Services Commission, BC Mental Health and Substance Use Services, PHSA, Coquitlam, BC, Canada
e-mail: tnicholls@phsa.ca; johann.brink@ubc.ca

A. Butler
Faculty of Health Sciences, Simon Fraser University, Burnaby, BC, Canada
e-mail: albutler@sfu.ca

L. Kendrick-Koch
Division of Forensic Psychiatry, Department of Psychiatry, Faculty of Medicine, University of British Columbia, Vancouver, BC, Canada
e-mail: Lindsey.kendrick-koc@phsa.ca

R. Jones · A. I. F. Simpson
Division of Forensic Psychiatry, Department of Psychiatry, University of Toronto, Toronto, ON, Canada

Forensic Division, Centre for Addiction and Mental Health, Toronto, ON, Canada
e-mail: Roland.jones@camh.ca; Sandy.simpson@camh.ca

© Springer Nature Switzerland AG 2018
M. Ternes et al. (eds.), *The Practice of Correctional Psychology*,
https://doi.org/10.1007/978-3-030-00452-1_2

Yoon, Domino, Norton, Cuddeback, & Morrissey, 2013); although the independent contribution of bed closures is unclear (e.g., Livingston, Nicholls, & Brink, 2011; Penney, Prosser, Grimbos, Darby, & Simpson, 2017). In turn, this has led to inadequate and fragmented community services in combination with the criminalization of behaviors (e.g., public intoxication) and subsistence strategies (e.g., panhandling; sleeping in public areas) associated with poverty, homelessness, and mental illness (Draine, Salzer, Culhane, & Hadley, 2002; Durbin et al., 2010; Matheson et al., 2005).

In addition to high rates of mental illness among inmates, it is the norm rather than the exception for offenders with mental illnesses to have comorbid health and psychosocial problems. In Canada, it is estimated that among individuals with mental disorders admitted to federal prisons, the majority have more than one disorder (90%; Sapers, 2011) often concurrent substance abuse disorder (80%; Sapers, 2011). Moreover, there is an overrepresentation of other vulnerable populations (Sapers, 2011), with social marginalization (e.g., unemployment, poverty, homelessness) and comorbid infectious as well as chronic disease generally the rule rather than the exception (Kouyoumdjian, Schuler, Matheson, & Hwang, 2016). Further, Aboriginal individuals make up more than one in four federally incarcerated persons in Canada (Sapers, 2016) although they comprise only 4.9% of the Canadian population (Statistics Canada, 2017). Finally, many offenders with mental illness zig-zag between social services, crisis agencies, and criminal justice services at considerable cost to the individual's health and well-being and to society (Baillargeon, Binswanger, Penn, Williams, & Murray, 2009; Somers, Rezansoff, Moniruzzaman, & Zabarauckas, 2015; Sorenson, 2010).

It is also widely recognized that prisoners with serious mental illness (SMI; e.g., depression, schizophrenia, bipolar disorder) are at greater risk of having multiple incarcerations compared to those without SMI (e.g., Baillargeon et al., 2009; Fazel & Seewald, 2012; Scott & Falls, 2015; Skeem, Winter, Kennealy, Louden, & Tatar II, 2014). Of particular concern, many scholars have observed that managing offenders with SMI creates operational, ethical, and safety challenges (for reviews, Nicholls, Roesch, Olley, Ogloff, & Hemphill, 2005; Osher, D'Amora, Plotkin, Jarrett, & Eggleston, 2012; Sapers, 2011), and until radical changes occur, persons with mental illness will continue to occupy correctional beds.

In sum, the evidence demonstrates two primary conclusions. First, this is a population requiring wrap around, holistic services (Livingston, 2009; SAMHSA, 2017); in particular, discharge planning and services that facilitate the inmate's successful transition back into the community (SAMHSA, 2017). Second, although clearly not preferable, admissions to jails and prisons provide an important opportunity to intervene and provide care to a population that is otherwise highly socially marginalized and at risk of continuing to fall through the gaps. This chapter will examine the prevalence of mental illness in correctional populations (prisons vs. jails; men vs. women) and the legal requirements for the provision of mental health services to incarcerated individuals. We then propose a new model for delivering evidence-based care. The STAIR model (also see Forrester, Till, Simpson, & Shaw, 2018; Simpson, Shaw, Forrester, Nicholls, & Martin, 2017) draws together fundamental evidence-based strategies for service provision to offenders with mental health needs, including recommendations for Screening, Triage, Assessment, Intervention, and Reintegration (i.e., STAIR) components, discussed below.

2.1 Prevalence of Mental Illness and Concurrent Disorders in Correctional Populations

Although estimates of the prevalence of mental health problems within prison populations vary, the substantial burden of mental illness among offenders is well documented across international borders (Fazel & Danesh, 2002; Fazel, Hayes, Bartellas, Clerici, & Trestman, 2016; Fazel & Seewald, 2012; Prins, 2014). This includes a wide range of mental illnesses, including anxiety disorders, psychotic disorders, depression, and substance-use disorders, which have been found to be elevated in correctional institutions (Canadian Institute for Health Information, 2008; Fazel, Yoon, & Hayes, 2017). For instance, in Canada, the prevalence of mental illness among inmates exceeds that of the general population (2–3 times higher in federal corrections than in the general population; Sapers, 2011) and despite a long-standing recognition of this issue, has increased in recent years (Correctional Service of Canada (CSC), 2012a).

2.1.1 Federal Prisons

Based on data from a 2011–2012 US survey, approximately 14% of federal prisoners indicated signs of serious psychological distress within the previous month (Bronson & Berzofsky, 2017). Among federal offenders in Canada (i.e., individuals sentenced to 2 years or more), evidence suggests the rates of mental illness have increased substantially in the recent past. Brink, Doherty, and Boer (2001) found that over 30% of newly admitted male inmates in federal penitentiaries in the province of British Columbia qualified as having a current mental disorder. More than a decade later, the Office of the Correctional Investigator (OCI) reported that the proportion of federal offenders with significant, identified mental health needs had more than doubled between 1997 and 2008 (Sapers, 2011). Specifically, in that decade there was a 71% increase in the proportion of offenders diagnosed with mental disorders and an 80% increase in the number of inmates on prescribed medications (Sapers, 2011). In a recent study on the national prevalence of major mental disorders in 1110 new male Canadian federal inmates recruited from March 2012 to September 2014, almost three quarters met criteria for any kind of current mental disorder and more than 50% had a lifetime prevalence of major disorders, even after excluding substance use or alcohol-related disorders and antisocial personality disorder (Beaudette & Stewart, 2016). Despite these findings, there is some evidence from international research (e.g., Fazel & Seewald, 2012) to suggest that the prevalence of mental illness (e.g., psychosis), while high, may not be increasing as a proportion of the standing correctional population worldwide.

2.1.2   State/Provincial Prisons

In some nations, offenders serving short sentences are housed separately from those serving lengthier sentences in what often are referred to as provincial or state prisons. A systematic review of studies from 1989 to 2013 examining the prevalence of different types of mental disorders across prisons in 16 US states revealed that both current and lifetime prevalence of mental disorders was elevated compared to the community, but also highly variable (Prins, 2014). Literature from other nations has also shown high rates of mental disorders in state/provincial prisons (e.g., Butler, Indig, Allnutt, & Mamoon, 2011; Lafortune, 2010) compared to rates in the general population.

2.1.3   Jails/Remand Centres

Given the typically short length of stay (note however, that jails/remand centres may at times hold individuals for lengthy durations during complex trials) and other characteristics common of jail populations (e.g., abrupt incarceration, considerable social disruption and confusion on entry into custody, a range of offences, often a mix of security levels and genders), mental health needs in jails are also a prominent concern (Hayes, 1989; Nicholls, Olley, Ogloff, Roesch, & Felbert Kreis, in press; Ogloff, 2002). Jails often are described as an ideal place to identify risks-needs given they are the 'gateway' into the criminal justice system and an entry point into other societal institutions (Nicholls et al., in press; Ogloff, 2002). The high prevalence of mental health needs in jails is widely noted in the literature, although it is explored relatively less compared to prison populations. James and Glaze (2006) reported on Department of Justice surveys from 2002 and 2004 that 12-month criteria for a mental health 'problem' were met in 64.2% of local jail inmates (compared to 56.2% of state prisons, and 44.8% of federal prisons). In a study based on data from US county jails in Eastern US states in 2002–2003 and 2005–2006, Steadman, Osher, Robbins, Case, and Samuels (2009) found the prevalence of current SMI in US jail inmates to be 14.5% for men and 31% for women. Although engagement in services is a limited indicator of prevalence rates, a report by Romano (2017) revealed that more than 35% of inmates residing in San Francisco jails were engaged with mental health services.

2.1.4   Male vs. Female Inmates

The mental health status of incarcerated women, specifically, remains a pressing challenge (see Taylor, McDonagh, & Blanchette; Chap. 5, this volume), in particular given the expanding population and proportion of women inmates (Glaze & Kaeble, 2014). A 2016 report showed that over 50% of Canadian female inmates compared to 26% of male inmates had some form of identified mental health concern (Sapers, 2016). Steadman et al. (2009) reported the estimated prevalence rates of current SMI among recently received female US jail inmates to be substantially higher than among their male counterparts, regardless of whether current PTSD was included as a SMI or not (cf., Prins, 2014).

In sum, the rates across international borders from multiple studies, including multiple meta-analyses and research across diverse subpopulations, confirms the exemplary burden of mental illness in correctional institutions. Gender comparisons (e.g., as seen in Prins, 2014) and details on the extent to which these rates are increasing or not (e.g., Fazel & Seewald, 2012) suggest a need for further research. Nonetheless, the challenge of caring for mentally ill inmates has led to legal challenges and the necessity to develop national and international standards of care.

2.2 Legal Right to Care, Standards of Care

Despite a longstanding understanding of the negative implications of incarcerating individuals with mental illness and widespread calls for humanitarian and evidence-informed services in the care of individuals with mental illness (World Health Organization & International Committee of the Red Cross, 2005), inmates in the correctional system have historically faced a significant amount of neglect (Penn, 2015). For example, in the US prior to the 1970s there were no standardized health-care policies in jails and prisons (Penn, 2015). The last few decades have seen expansive development in standards regarding the provision of (general) health care in prisons, through international governing bodies such as the UN as well as in nations such as the US, UK, Australia, and Canada (Livingston, 2009; Møller, Stöver, Jürgens, Gatherer, & Nikogosian, 2007; Penn, 2015; Verdun-Jones & Butler, 2016). The UN's *Standard Minimum Rules for Treatment of Prisoners* (adopted 1955), for example, along with legal instruments such as the *International Covenant and Civil and Political Rights* (adopted 1966) provide guidance for medical service provision to prisoners. As a result of the precedent setting US Supreme Court case *Estelle v. Gamble* (1976), incarcerated individuals in the US have the constitutional right to be shielded from cruel and unusual punishment, which has been interpreted as including a legal right to healthcare, including mental health services (Candilis & Huttenbach, 2015).

Standards of care related specifically to mental health for inmates in correctional institutions are also developing across international governing bodies and nations (CSC, 2012b; Hayton & Boyington, 2006; Livingston, 2009; Mental Health America, 2015). Institutions including the American Psychiatric Association (APA), World Health Organization, Correctional Service of Australia, CSC, and Council of Europe have contributed guidelines for improved standards to incarcerated individuals with mental health and substance use needs (Livingston, 2009). The APA asserted, for example, that mental health services in the correctional system should ensure access to the basic amount of mental health programs and medication accessible to individuals residing in the community (Weinstein et al., 2000). As laid out in *Bowring v. Godwin* (1977), inmates should be ensured access to mental health services (Candilis & Huttenbach, 2015). Court cases such as *Ruiz v. Estelle* (1980) also mandate improved standards of care for individuals in correctional settings, advancing limitations to use of seclusion, as well as involvement of trained mental health professionals (Candilis & Huttenbach, 2015).

Other landmark cases such as *Brown v. Plata* (2011) also set standards for the minimum level of care for inmates with mental illness (Mental Health America, 2015). This particular ruling, which concerned inadequate services for over 40,000 prisoners in the US state of California, revealed that there are legal consequences for correctional institutions that fail to implement sufficient mental healthcare services as enshrined in the constitutional right to freedom from cruel and unusual punishment (Mental Health America, 2015). The importance of restricting use of solitary confinement is also growing at the international level (Appelbaum, Trestman, & Metzner, 2015; Verdun-Jones & Butler, 2016). For inmates in segregation, thorough mental health and suicide risk assessments, group and individual psychotherapies, psychiatric medications, and crisis interventions are mandated in most high income countries (Metzner, 2015; Metzner & Dvoskin, 2006; Perrien & O'Keefe, 2015). It is noteworthy that the Attorney General of Canada is presently facing a class action lawsuit alleging systematic over-reliance on solitary confinement and failure to provide adequate health care to individuals with mental illness incarcerated in Federal correctional institutions (Koskie Minsky, n.d.).

In the US, legal requirements to mandate extension of care during transition periods for inmates re-entering the community is limited to case law (Jones, 2015). In the 1989 case of *DeShaney v. Winnebago City Department of Social Sciences*, the US Supreme Court ruled that any constitutional obligation to provide services to people in custody is limited to the period in which they are in custody. However, subsequent cases appeared to extend the legal requirement to include compliance with discharge instructions provided by a healthcare provider (e.g., *Prasad v. County of Sutter*, 2013). In *Brad H v. City of New York* (2000) the court found that failure to provide discharge planning after jail violated the New York State's Mental Hygiene Law which mandates that providers of inpatient health services conduct discharge planning, and a provision of the state's Constitution which prohibits cruel and unusual punishment (Barr, 2003). That landmark class action lawsuit led to the recognition of entitlement of the defendants to discharge planning and the creation of a comprehensive discharge planning system (Jones, 2015).

The principles underlying the settlement agreement were based on New York State and case law, which means *Brad H* has limited precedential value for other states. Nonetheless, the case provides a framework for post-discharge planning litigation and was thus described by Steadman as the "most important case to be litigated on behalf of people with serious mental illness for 20 years" (as cited in Barr, 2003, p. 103) Based on an extensive review of the affidavits and records from *Brad H*, Barr (2003) explained that discharge planning must include housing and social benefits, the patient must understand the plan, and plans must be linguistically and culturally competent. Despite increased awareness and attention to the importance of transition planning, receipt of community-based treatment which links to prison-based treatment is rare (Belenko & Peugh, 2005), and evidence based interventions are not commonly used (Meyer & Altice, 2015).

2.3 The STAIR Model: Screening, Triage, Assessment, Intervention, and Reintegration

In 2004, the CSC outlined a mental health strategy for corrections that included improved assessment, screening, and treatment for offenders with mental illness (Sapers, 2005). This approach is consistent with models recommended internationally including, for example, in the US (SAMHSA, 2017), Australia (Ogloff, Davis, Rivers, & Ross, 2007), and the UK (Forrester et al., 2018). The STAIR model provides a unified, comprehensive strategy for addressing mental health needs in corrections that promotes recovery, and highlights the core components of a comprehensive mental health program including: mental health screening, triage, assessment, intervention, and re-integration (see Forrester et al., 2018; Simpson et al., 2017). We provide details of each aspect of this model below.

Given that mentally ill offenders have both health and criminogenic needs (Harris & Rice, 1997; Skeem et al., 2014), we recommend that correctional mental health professionals generally adhere to the Risk-Need-Responsivity model (RNR; Andrews & Bonta, 2010). As Osher and colleagues (2012) have recommended, the application of this model should reflect an integrated consideration of inmates' mental health, substance abuse, and criminogenic needs. The RNR model (Andrews & Bonta, 2010; Andrews, Bonta, & Hoge, 1990) is particularly relevant to the assessment, intervention and reintegration components of the STAIR model, however, it is covered elsewhere in this volume (e.g., Batastini et al.; Chap. 13, this volume) and thus we will not revisit it here.

2.3.1 Screening

2.3.1.1 Scope of the Issue and the Need for Mental Health Screening in Correctional Settings

Given the prevalence of mental health needs among inmates, universal mental health screening (i.e., all inmates) is widely considered a key component of correctional mental health care (Forrester et al., 2018; Grubin, 2010; SAMHSA, 2017) and is the initial step in the STAIR model. Screening entails an investigation by trained mental health workers using validated tools to identify subpopulations or individuals who have some targeted problem, in this case mental illness, substance disorders, and/or are considered to be at risk of adverse events (e.g., suicide, violence, victimization, non-suicidal self-injury) (Grubin, 2010; Rosenfeld et al., 2017). Screening acts as a referral mechanism to mental health services based on a structured series of questions and/or observations to identify potential mental illness or behavioural challenges that require specialized placement and/or further evaluation or assessment (Grubin, 2010; Rosenfeld et al., 2017). Screening generally involves observing and recording health care concerns or needs of the inmate, past treatment failures/successes, symptoms of psychological distress, withdrawal from alcohol or drugs, suicidal ideation/behaviours, the risk of non-suicidal self-harm, or violence, and the individual's ability to engage in activities/programming (United Nations Office for Project Services, 2016). A key goal of screening is to mitigate the number of false negatives; that is to minimize the number of individuals who are ill but are not accurately identified as having mental health needs (Ogloff et al., 2007).

2.3.1.2 Promising Practices

Screening tools and procedures should be brief (in order to manage the volume of incoming inmates), have clear definitions and criteria, be completed by trained screeners with standardized tools and procedures, be well-documented, and have favourable (i.e., relatively low) false-negative/false-positive rates (Maloney, Dvoskin, & Metzner, 2015). Screening should cover a range of questions, including historical factors (previous diagnoses, medication), current mental state, and symptoms. Although there is relatively limited use of validated instruments and a limited evidence-base overall, a systematic review by Martin, Colman, Simpson, and McKenzie (2013) concluded that five mental health screening tools (including the JSAT, CMHS-W, CMHS-M, EMHS, and BJMHS), ranging from as short as 2–3 min to as long as 30 min, are supported for practice in correctional settings.

   Admission to jails or remand centres, as well as to prison, before inmate triage and placement (within 14 days), are critical times for mental health screening to occur (Maloney et al., 2015; National Institute for Health Care Excellence (NICE), 2017). Continual monitoring throughout incarceration, and at critical time points, such as upon transfer, segregation, and other major events (e.g., anniversary of index offence, legal changes, new case information revealed) represent an essential component of a comprehensive program (NICE, 2017; Nicholls et al., 2005; Ogloff et al., 2007). For example, screening of inmates in segregation/solitary confinement has been identified as a standard of care, in order to divert inmates with SMI to treatment programs (Jones, 2015). This practice gained attention in the 2006 case *Morgan v. Rowland*, which held that offenders placed in segregation should receive mental health screening and evaluation within one day of entering segregation (Jones, 2015). Finally, exiting the criminal justice system (i.e., upon initial release and periodically during parole) is a final key point in time for screening. Monitoring for mental health needs and risks at this time can assist mentally ill offenders with accessing community mental health resources and detect mental health deterioration that could contribute to recidivism (Ogloff et al., 2007; Simpson et al., 2017).

2.3.2 Triage

2.3.2.1 Scope of the Issue and the Need for Triaging in Correctional Settings

According to Martin et al. (2013) and Senior et al. (2013), following screening 25–30% of incarcerated individuals will be in need of additional mental health evaluation. Triage, the second component of the STAIR model, is defined as a strategy for deciding how to prioritize mental health resources (i.e., for assessment, treatments) to those with greatest need/urgency (Rosenfeld et al., 2017), and a key component of mental health services in corrections that can assist in decreasing the cycle of individuals with mental disorders (re-) entering the correctional system (Ogloff et al., 2007).

Although definitions of triage vary, and it remains a relatively unexamined aspect of the STAIR model, there are well-recognized underlying goals. At the initial point of contact following mental health screening, triage processes can help direct offenders with mental disorders to the appropriate type and degree of mental health care based on their needs for particular mental health services or risk to themselves or others (e.g., low, moderate, critical), and in accordance with the urgency of their situation (Victoria Government Department of Health, 2010). Triage is particularly important for directing offenders who are at high risk of self-harm, suicide, violence, victimization or general mental health decompensation, relative to other offenders with low or moderate levels of mental health distress, to the appropriate level of care (Osher, Scott, Steadman, & Robbins, 2006). Triage can also help mitigate the cost of unnecessary mental health assessments, treatments and other harmful outcomes resulting from false positive mental health screens (Martin, Potter, Crocker, Wells, & Colman, 2016).

2.3.2.2 Promising Practices

Triage provides a more comprehensive appraisal of an individual's functioning and level of mental health need, includes use of a validated tool and allocation to appropriate levels of mental health care (Forrester et al., 2018). Institutions such as jails and prisons receive a number of individuals who have diverse types and severity of mental health and substance use needs that require attention for triage (Osher et al., 2006). Simpson et al. (2017) concluded that there is just one known relevant measure to support triage assessments in correctional settings (i.e., the Jail Screening Assessment Tool (JSAT), Nicholls et al., 2005). Triage assessments should be conducted by trained mental health professionals and include a detailed assessment of an offender's functioning and psychiatric needs (Simpson et al., 2017).

2.3.3 Assessment

2.3.3.1 Scope of the Issue and the Need for Assessments in Correctional Settings

Fazel and Seewald (2012) estimated that 15% of inmates will require a comprehensive mental health assessment. Mental health assessment is the next step in the STAIR model, it involves a detailed evaluation by a specialized mental health professional (e.g., psychologist, psychiatrist), a referral to necessary mental health services, and establishment of a detailed treatment plan (also see Forrester et al., 2018;

Simpson et al., 2017). Timely diagnosis permits inmates to be recommended to an appropriate level of psychiatric care and other mental health treatments and social care programs (Simpson et al., 2017).

Clinical presentations of mental disorders in correctional settings are often complex, due to the interplay of significant psychiatric, psychological and social comorbidities, and the correctional environment itself. High levels of substance misuse and withdrawal, personality disorders, neurodevelopmental disorders and acquired brain injuries, as well as high levels of distress due to incarceration can make diagnosis of common psychiatric conditions difficult. As discussed with reference to our guiding theoretical perspective (i.e., RNR), it is essential that clinicians are mindful of the heterogeneity of mentally ill offenders' needs—being attentive to both psychiatric needs and criminogenic needs (Harris & Rice, 1997; Skeem et al., 2014). In addition, the clinician should be aware of the possibility that symptoms are feigned or exaggerated for a perceived gain (such as the desire for medication for abuse or exchange, to be authorized for relocation within the jail, or hospitalization) (Knoll, 2015; Scott & Holoyda, 2015; Walters, 2006). Probably more commonly, symptoms may be minimized if the person perceives an intervention to be undesirable (e.g., placement in a mental health unit and/or the stigma associated with being labelled mentally ill). Given that individuals in this population often have a high level of complexity, a thorough assessment to tease out these issues is required. Also, assessment is needed whenever psychiatric difficulties emerge during incarceration (e.g., decompensation following victimization, new legal developments, family support disappointments). Thus, anticipated mental health trajectories may change during imprisonment requiring renewed assessment and a new or revised treatment plan.

2.3.3.2 Promising Practices

Working within the security and institutional practices of a correctional environment often presents challenges and the mental health practitioner is required to have a degree of tenacity and flexibility. A consultation room that offers privacy and therapeutic space, away from other prisoners and from correctional officers is ideal, but in reality it is often necessary to conduct assessments on the wing or at the cell door, especially for those who are most mentally or behaviorally disturbed. In these circumstances, efforts should be made to maintain confidentiality as far as possible, as well as the need for an awareness and appraisal of immediate risk to one's own safety.

The recommended structure of the assessment in correctional settings is similar to that in hospital and community settings (Silverman et al., 2015). However, unique diagnostic challenges in correctional populations mean that clinicians may need to alter approaches for assessing mental health and substance use disorders. Prior to assessing the patient, it is good practice to obtain and review background information, including speaking to correctional officers as to their observations of the individual. Consideration should also be given to whether an interpreter is required and arrangements made when necessary. The clinical interview includes enquiry into the following elements, though not necessarily in a prescribed order. Whilst there are standardized structured assessment tools that may be used (for example the Structured Clinical Interview for DSM-5 SCID-5 (First, Williams, Karg, & Spitzer, 2015) or Present State Examination (PSE) (Wing, Cooper, & Sartorius, 1974)), they are perhaps more commonly used in settings with greater time and resources. Kamath and Shah (2015) recommend shorter, less time consuming standardized mental health assessment measures in prison environments.

2.3.4 Interventions

2.3.4.1 Scope of the Issue and the Need for Interventions in Correctional Settings

As examined in the introduction (see Sect. 2.1), the need for psychological and psychiatric services in Correctional centres is considerable. Intervention in the STAIR model refers to the variety of treatments and programs that permit an efficient response to diverse mental presentations and should include access to professional mental health support and evidence-based practices comparable to that accessible by members of the general public (Forrester et al., 2018).

2.3.4.2 Promising Practices

Intervention services available to inmates should include the range of culturally competent mental health services designed to treat different levels of mental health needs (e.g., acute mental health services, intermediate level services, and general mental health services for corrections) (Simpson et al., 2017). Intervention decision-making depends on the degree of inmate risk, the extent of the impact of mental illness symptoms on daily functioning, intensity and frequency of mental health support needs, and other social concerns (Simpson et al., 2017; for a review of biological, psychological, and social interventions for psychosis see Brink & Tomita, 2015). Simpson et al. (2017) recommended mental health treatment options in corrections include access to care from professionals including psychiatrists, psychologists and counsellors, nurses, case managers, peer support, and additional evidence-based services (e.g., relapse prevention programs for addiction treatment). Psychological interventions and social support services should be implemented to facilitate continuity of care, when inmates are transferred across correctional institutions or released back into the community (NICE, 2017).

Evidence-based guidelines for the treatment of mental illness in general psychiatric services should be used in correctional settings, although some modification may be necessary (see Table 2.1). Guidelines tend to be syndrome-specific, and there is unlikely to be an evidence-based guideline for the combination of often

Table 2.1 Pharmacotherapy and psychosocial interventions for offenders with mental disorders

	Pharmacotherapy	Psychosocial interventions
Schizophrenia (American Psychiatric Association, 2010)	<u>Initial phase</u> • *Commence antipsychotic without delay.* • *All have similar efficacy (except clozapine, which is reserved for treatment resistant schizophrenia). Choice of antipsychotic guided by side-effect profile, previous response, and patient choice.* • *Dose should be titrated against side effects and efficacy.* <u>Maintenance phase</u> • *Continuation with antipsychotic to prevent relapse (at least 1–2 years).* • *Optimisation of treatment (dose, choice of antipsychotic, treatment for side effects).*	<u>Maintenance phase</u> • *Cognitive Behaviour Therapy (CBT)—to reduce severity of positive symptoms of psychosis, and distress associated with symptoms.* • *Social skills training.*
Bipolar disorder (Goodwin et al., 2016)	<u>Acute manic phase</u> • *Antipsychotic (haloperidol, olanzapine, risperidone, quetiapine particularly effective).* • *Valproate maybe used as an alternative (caution in women if possibility of pregnancy due to risk of teratogenesis).* • *Antidepressive drugs if prescribed should be stopped.* <u>Acute depressive episode</u> • *Quetiapine, lurasidone or olanzapine or lamotrigine.* • *Lithium if symptoms are less severe.* <u>Long-term treatment</u> • *Continuous treatment recommended to reduce relapse. Lithium, olanzapine, quetiapine, risperidone long acting injection and valproate prevent manic relapse.* • *Lamotrigine, lithium, quetiapine and lurasidone prevent depressive relapse.*	<u>Acute depressive episode, maintenance, long term treatment</u> • *In additional to pharmacology—evidence that CBT or Interpersonal Rhythm Therapy can reduce the length of the episode.* <u>Long-term treatment</u> • *Psychoeducation, CBT, Interpersonal Rhythm therapy to reduce residual symptoms and reduce risk of relapse.*

(continued)

Table 2.1 (continued)

	Pharmacotherapy	Psychosocial interventions
Major Depressive Disorder (Nutt et al., 2010)	• *Antidepressant for mild to moderate depression (antidepressants have similar efficacy, choice based on side-effect profile, previous response and patient choice).* • *ECT for severe depression, not responding to antidepressants, or if there are significant catatonic symptoms.* • *Continuation of antipsychotic to prevent relapse for at least 6 months after resolution.*	• *CBT or Interpersonal Psychotherapy for mild to moderate depressive disorder.*
Anxiety Disorders (Katzman et al., 2014)	• *Antidepressants first line treatment. SSRIs and SNRIs safer and better tolerated that TCAs and MAOIs.* • *Antipsychotics considered as second-line treatment, but little supporting evidence for efficacy.*	• *CBT* • *Exposure therapy* • *Mindfulness-based cognitive therapy*
ADHD in adults (Moriyama, Polanczyk, Terzi, Faria, & Rohde, 2013)	• *Strongest evidence of efficacy of stimulants. Short-acting stimulants appear more effective than long-acting.* • *Non-stimulant treatments effective, and have less abuse potential.*	• *Evidence for CBT in reducing symptoms.*
PTSD (American Psychological Association, 2017)	• *Drug treatments are not first-line therapies.* • *Antidepressants paroxetine or mirtazapine in general use, or amitriptyline or phenelzine initiated by mental health specialists if psychological therapies not available.*	• *Psychological therapies are first-line, including CBT, cognitive processing therapy (CPT), cognitive therapy (CT), and prolonged exposure therapy (PE).* • *Eye movement desensitization and reprocessing (EMDR) has some supporting evidence.*

complex clinical problems seen in the heterogeneous prison population. In general, however, good prescribing (Taylor, Barnes, & Yound, 2018) and mental health services practices recommended in general settings also apply in corrections (e.g., see Nicholls & Goossens, 2017) namely the avoidance of polypharmacy, avoidance of high-dose antipsychotic prescribing, the need to undertake frequent reviews of the treatment, therapeutic response and side-effects and the implementation of culturally informed, gender-sensitive, and trauma-informed practices. In addition, medications with high abuse potential or medications that are highly toxic in overdose are to be used with caution in correctional settings.

The main guidelines for treatment of several common psychiatric conditions are summarized in Table 2.1. With respect to schizophrenia, antipsychotic medication is the mainstay of treatment. In most cases, treatment needs to be continuous to treat the acute episode, and subsequently to reduce the risk of relapse. Many antipsychotic medications can be given orally (tablets typically once or twice per day), or by injection (typically every 2–4 weeks) (American Psychiatric Association, 2010). There is also evidence for psychosocial interventions, to improve functioning, the best evidence available being CBT approaches (see Table 2.1).

The treatments of bipolar disorder and major depressive disorder also have well established treatment guidelines (Goodwin et al., 2016) that are applicable in correctional settings. Pharmacotherapy is the primary treatment for bipolar disorder, and generally considered first line for moderate and severe depressive disorders. Psychological therapies and/or medication are effective in mild depressive episodes. One of the key differential diagnoses for mood disorders is an adjustment reaction—the stress response to incarceration, particularly the isolation from family and community support networks, fear and shame, which is particularly important in the early phase of incarceration. The treatment for adjustment reaction is different and may need short-term support or treatment for symptoms such as anxiety or insomnia. Importantly, suicide risk must be carefully considered during this time.

Anxiety disorders form a diverse group, categorized primarily by the underlying cause of the anxiety. Both pharmacological and psychological interventions have proven efficacy (see Table 2.1). Post-traumatic stress disorder especially is common in correctional settings. Recent guidelines suggest that trauma-focused CBT is considered first-line treatment in general settings (American Psychological Association, 2017). Efficacy of antidepressants has also been demonstrated, and should especially be considered when there is a comorbid mood disorder (Katzman et al., 2014). Of the treatments with proven efficacy, SSRIs and mirtazapine are more practical in correctional settings as having low abuse potential and safer in overdose than tricyclic antidepressants and MAOIs.

Treatment of adults with ADHD is controversial. Symptoms that are present in childhood undoubtedly persist into early adulthood for many, and continuation of an effective treatment into adulthood for this group may be appropriate. Assessment of continuation of need is recommended by "drug holidays" (the careful assessment of symptoms upon planned cessation of treatment). It is difficult to diagnose among those who present with symptoms who have not had a prior childhood diagnosis, as much is based on self-report. Despite these challenges, there is evidence of efficacy of medication to reduce symptoms in adults, as well as psychological interventions and psychoeducation (Moriyama et al., 2013; see Table 2.1).

2.3.5   Reintegration

The period of transition from prison to community can be fraught with particular challenges reflecting for instance erosion of social networks, loss of personal belongings, decreased economic mobility, deprivation of security, as well as potential acquisition of self-defeating habits and attitudes (Borzycki & Makkai, 2007;

Liebling & Maruna, 2013; The Pew Centre on the States, 2010). Reintegration, the final component of the STAIR model, refers to activity and programming conducted to prepare a person in custody to return safely to the community. Reintegration is widely acknowledged to be the least well-developed component of correctional service planning despite being recognized as an essential aspect of services, particularly for mentally ill offenders (SAMHSA, 2017).

2.3.5.1 Scope of the Issue and the Need for Re-entry Services and Planning

Nearly all inmates with a mental illness will leave the correctional facility and return to the community (Bureau of Justice Statistics, 2017). In the US, an estimated 650,000 adults are released from prison and 13 million from jails annually (Council of State Governments, 2002). An Australian study found that the number of people released from prison each year is ~25.3% greater than the number in prison on any given day (Avery & Kinner, 2015). The importance of supporting successful community re-entry following incarceration cannot be overstated. In a sample of 30,237 inmates released in the US, Binswanger et al. (2007) found the relative risk of death in the first 2 weeks post-release was nearly 13 times the risk of death in the general population. The same study also found that a returning prisoner's chances of dying from a drug overdose are 129 times that of the general population. These individual, economic, and social costs necessitate efforts to plan for and support successful reintegration of offenders into the community. This transition point presents an underutilized opportunity to address the needs of formerly incarcerated people, to prevent recidivism and improve quality of life among disadvantaged populations (Woods, Lanza, Dyson, & Gordon, 2013).

2.3.5.2 Promising Practices in Re-entry

Studies indicate that discharge planning and re-entry programs which build on success achieved in prison can decrease recidivism. In particular, secure housing, employment aid, and prison-based mental health and substance use treatment have all shown reductions in recidivism (The Pew Centre on the States, 2011). For example, using a sample of 1800 people, Callan and Gardner (2007) demonstrated that a vocational education and training program provided as part of a prisoner rehabilitation program reduced the risk of reoffending from 32% to 23%. Supportive housing models have also shown promise for former prisoners, particularly for people with substance use challenges. One example is the Oxford House, which is peer-led and predicated on principles of self-governance and mutual support (Schlager, 2013). Each house includes 12 residents who agree to pay rent, do maintenance/chores, and refrain from drugs and alcohol. Jason and Ferrari (2010) found that residents of Oxford House are more likely to be employed, and less likely to abuse alcohol or drugs, or engage in criminal activity than usual care patients. Integration of the criminal justice, substance use and mental health systems has the potential to reduce the duplication of administrative functions, and free up scarce resources through appropriate and efficient allocation (Osher, Steadman, & Barr, 2003).

Discharge planning can be thought of as a boundary spanner, connecting institutional and community based services. Consistent with the RNR model (Andrews, 2012), such planning should reflect the assessment of need (SAMHSA, 2017). While there is a dearth of evidence regarding best practices in discharge planning, emerging models can provide guidance. The APIC model, designed by Osher et al. (2003) is a model of transition planning which has strong empirical and conceptual underpinnings, and can be widely implemented and evaluated. The APIC model stands for: Assess, Plan, Identify, and Coordinate. The Substance Abuse and Mental Health Services Administration (SAMHSA, 2017) recently published a set of ten strategic guidelines for the implementation of the APIC model as well as examples of successful/promising programs within each guideline.

2.4   Future Directions

As we have demonstrated, mental health professionals have a solid foundation on which to practice, but considerable work remains to ensure that evidence-informed practice is readily available to individuals with mental illness who become entangled in the criminal justice system. Some of the most prominent challenges include tensions with respect to integrating therapeutic and custodial aspects of care for mentally ill offenders despite evidence that optimal outcomes likely can be achieved only when comprehensive care addressing mental health and criminogenic needs are provided (e.g., Osher et al., 2012; Skeem et al., 2014; for a review see Nicholls & Goossens, 2017). There also remain substantial gaps between what we know and what we deliver in correctional services with respect to basic tenets of good practice (e.g., punitive vs. trauma-informed approaches, also see Dvoskin, Skeem, Novaco, & Douglas, 2012; Nicholls & Goossens, 2017). The challenges of implementing services such the STAIR model into direct care are also well documented (e.g., inadequate training or ongoing support for staff leading to drift and poor fidelity; the need for staff buy-in and engagement; inadequate resources) (e.g., Müller-Isberner, Born, Euker, & Eusterschulte, 2017; Nonstad & Webster, 2011; Viljoen, Cochrane, & Jonnson, 2018). In particular, the need to shift from the identification of needs (i.e., through the Screening, Triage, and Assessment components of the STAIR model) to the management of needs and the prevention of adverse events (e.g., suicide, recidivism; i.e., through Intervention and Triage) remain neglected aspects of research and practice (e.g., via case formulation, risk management). Administrators, clinicians, and researchers alike would do well to focus on translating the results of intake evaluations into care plans, risk management and prevention efforts. As a recent systematic review has demonstrated, the fit between risk assessment and risk management is mixed at best, owing largely to suboptimal integration into practice (Viljoen et al., 2018). In particular, as we discussed here, reintegration efforts are essential but likely the least prominent aspect of assessing and treating mentally ill offenders (or general offenders, for that matter). Finally, systemic issues such as institutional policies, procedures, and negative attitudes regarding individuals with mental illness, and often in particular persons who engage in self-injury and suicide, in correctional settings are also remaining challenges (Zinger, 2017).

2.5 Technology and Innovations

Psychologists working in correctional settings typically provide clinical assessment, treatment, and risk assessment services to a diverse client population. In making a mental health diagnosis, the psychologist relies on a clinical interview, a mental state examination, and multiple questionnaires (Aboraya, France, Young, Curci, & Lepage, 2005). Important diagnostic information may be vulnerable to recall bias (e.g., as it is dependent upon the memory and current mental status of the inmate) and/or interviewer bias (Andreasen, 1995). The need therefore exists for innovative approaches to enhance diagnostic accuracy and assessment of symptom severity, a need exemplified by the harm resulting from erroneously identified recovered memories and over-identification of multiple personality or dissociative disorders (Dorahy et al., 2014; Mazzoni, Loftus, & Kirsch, 2001). To support the objectivity and reliability of a psychiatric diagnosis, a need exists for new and innovative assessment methods. The correctional psychologist also provides treatment using various modalities (e.g., CBT, DBT, dynamic and/or supportive psychotherapy). Virtual Reality and brain-computer interface based treatments such as EEG based biofeedback are examples of such innovation and hold promise for example in the assessment and treatment of populations including individuals who perpetrate sexual offences and offenders with alcohol and illicit substance use disorders.

2.5.1 Virtual Reality

Virtual Reality (VR) is a computer generated environment using sensory stimuli within which to explore and interact (Baus & Bouchard, 2014). The virtual environment, designed to resemble real-life situations, can be extended with standardised, specific stimuli to provoke symptoms (e.g., anxiety, fear, anger, cravings) and computer generated characters or virtual humans (avatars), VR environments are displayed variously on computer screens, head-mounted displays, or visual surround systems. VR thus provides opportunity to study participants in a lifelike, standardized and controlled environment (Meyerbroker & Emmelkamp, 2010; Opris et al., 2012). Reliable correlations have been reported from meta-analytic studies between VR generated scenarios, including various social domains such as shopping streets and virtual cafés in anxiety, social phobias, and paranoid delusions and cognitive impairment in schizophrenia (Valmaggia et al., 2007; van Bennekom, Kasanmoentalib, de Koning, & Denys, 2017). These applications also have potential use with those clients who might be more comfortable with a computerized assessment than a face-to-face clinical assessment (see Mishkind, Norr, Katz, & Reger, 2017; van Bennekom et al., 2017 for detailed reviews).

VR provides the opportunity to expose individuals, including sex offenders (Marschall-Lévesque, Rouleau, & Renaud, 2018; Trottier et al., 2015) and offenders with psychiatric disorders, to potential risky situations in order to evaluate their symptoms, without posing an actual threat to society (Fromberger, Jordan, & Muller, 2014). Additional validated applications for VR include drug and alcohol use disorders (Son et al., 2015), and anxiety and mood disorders (Maples-Keller, Bunnell, Kim, & Rothbaum, 2017; Mishkind et al., 2017). VR in Attention Deficit Disorder (Pollak et al., 2009) and autism spectrum disorder (Fazio, Pietz, & Denney, 2012), afflictions increasingly significant in offender populations, indicates that the inclusion of hyperactivity and neuroimaging parameters contribute to more comprehensive and objective assessments of these disorders (van Bennekom et al., 2017). Although research in VR in correctional populations is scarce and implementation of VR capacity in jails and prisons is in its infancy, it likely will evolve in its application to a range of disorders including PTSD, and obsessive compulsive disorder, all disorders relevant to criminal behaviour (Rizzo & Koenig, 2017; for a review see Benbouriche, Nolet, Trottier, & Renaud (2014).

2.5.2 Neuromodulation and Somatic Therapies

Major depressive disorder is a common and debilitating psychiatric disorder that negatively impacts a large portion of the population, and may be implicated in the commission of an offence. Although a range of psychopharmacological treatments has been developed with intravenous ketamine showing promise in producing rapid improvement in depressive symptoms, many patients do not attain an adequate therapeutic response despite completing several antidepressant medication trials. As a result, neurostimulation treatment modalities, including electroconvulsive treatment, transcranial magnetic stimulation, magnetic seizure therapy, and deep brain stimulation have been developed as alternatives (see Papadimitropoulou, Vossen, Karabis, Donatti, & Kubitz, 2017; Wani, Trevino, Marnell, & Husain, 2013 for detailed reviews).

2.5.3 Precision Medicine

The concept of precision medicine, that is, prevention and treatment strategies that take individual variability into account, is not new. As Collins and Harold (2015) pointed out, blood typing, for instance, has been used to guide blood transfusions for more than a century. However, this concept has been expanded broadly and improved significantly by recent developments such as large-scale biologic databases and characterising patients at the individual level (e.g., the human genome sequence, proteomics, genomics, diverse cellular assays), as well as computational tools for analysing large variable data sets. Regarding mentally ill offenders, the current nosological systems such as International Classification of Diseases and Diagnostic and Statistical Manual of Mental Disorders, were developed to provide a common language based on observable signs and symptoms, and are explicitly agnostic about pathophysiology or treatment response (Insel, 2014). While psychiatric diagnostics can be improved by more precise clustering of symptoms, diagnosis based only on symptoms may never yield the kind of specificity that the rest of medicine has been able to provide. The complex and multi-faceted nature of human behaviour renders difficult a diagnostic approach based only on presenting symptoms, precision medicine will provide for more nuanced approaches to diagnosis. As it stands now, however, the reason for the dearth of biomarker applications to improve the precision of psychiatric diagnosis is that rigorously tested, reproducible, clinically actionable biomarkers for any psychiatric disorder as yet do not exist. Genetic findings are statistical associations of risk, not diagnostic of disease; neuroimaging findings report mean group changes, not individual differences, and metabolic findings are not specific. Improvement in the resolution with each of these modalities may be possible, but we may never have a biomarker for any symptom-based diagnosis because these diagnostic categories were never designed for biological validity.

As an example of developments in mental health, major depressive disorder (MDD) may be described as a heterogeneous illness for which presently no effective methods exist to assess objectively the severity, endophenotypes, or response to treatment. Increasing evidence suggests that circulating levels of peripheral/serum growth factors and cytokines are altered in patients with MDD, and that antidepressant treatments reverse or normalize these effects. In their review of recent studies on the biological markers of MDD, Schmidt, Shelton, and Duman (2011) highlighted the need to develop a biomarker panel for depression that aims to profile diverse peripheral factors that together provide a biological signature of MDD subtypes as well as treatment response (Schmidt et al., 2011). Such a suite of biological markers may include individualised genetic, hormonal, and cytokine profiles predictive of likely response to certain medications. In this manner, patients may respond faster and progress along their recovery pathways differently and predictably such that earlier focus by psychologists on relapse prevention, recovery, and desistance from crime skills could be justified.

2.5.4 Artificial Intelligence, Machine Learning, Big Data, and Bayesian Networks

The nature of mental illness remains a conundrum with traditional models of classification increasingly suspected of misrepresenting the neurological causes underlying mental disorder. Yet, there is reason for optimism as clinical psychologists, psychiatrists, and researchers now have unprecedented opportunity to benefit from complex patterns in brain, behavior, and genes using methods from machine learning (Bzdok & Meyer-Lindenberg, 2018). Innovative methods in machine learning and artificial intelligence include support vector machines, and modern neural network algorithms, including Bayesian networks. Combining these techniques for analysis and classification, with a wealth of data from data repositories has the potential to advance a biologically grounded redefinition of major psychiatric disorders. However, advances in the application of these innovative approaches to health care as well as the appraisal and management of risk for violence, raise ethical questions regarding the use and regulation of robotics in clinical decision making (see Luxton, 2014 for a review). The correctional psychologist would be positioned well in their awareness of, and adjustment to, this fast evolving field by familiarising themselves with the increasing evidence that data-derived subgroups of mentally disordered offenders can predict treatment outcomes better than DSM/ICD diagnoses, and also in the assessment of risk, as these methods may become integrated into regular practice within the next decade (see Bzdok & Meyer-Lindenberg, 2018 for a review).

Presently, the standard models of violence risk prediction typically are based on regression models or some rule-based methods with no statistical composition. Advances in artificial intelligence (AI) and machine learning (ML) using so-called "big data" in the field of violence risk assessment hold particular promise. Constantinou, Fenton, Marsh, and Radlinski (2016) for example, have developed a rigorous and repeatable method for building effective Bayesian network (BN) models for medical decision support from complex, unstructured and incomplete patient questionnaires and interviews. Bayesian networks (BNs) are a well-established graphical formalised algorithm based on the Bayes's Theorem for encoding the conditional probabilistic relationships among uncertain variables of interest. Underpinning BNs is Bayesian probability inference that provides a way for "rational real-world reasoning" (Constantinou et al., 2016; Constantinou, Freestone, Marsh, Fenton, & Coid, 2015).

Fenton and Neil (2011) provided an informative introduction to Bayesian Networks as a means of avoiding the pitfalls of probabilistic reasoning, including in the legal context, where the so-called *prosecutor's fallacy* has demonstrated the difficulty lay persons, including jurors, have in understanding theoretical models of logically correct reasoning. Despite an extensive literature on the issue of probabilistic fallacies, many publications, and the consensus within the statistics community on the means of understanding and avoiding them, probabilistic fallacies continue to proliferate in legal arguments (Fenton & Neil, 2011). Bayes's Theorem provides the definitive explanation for the fallacy; however, as scholars (Tillers, 2007) have pointed out, the usual Bayesian formulation is extremely difficult for non-scholars and lay persons such as jurors to grasp. Hence, it behooves the correctional psychologist who conducts risk appraisals and testifies as an expert in courts of law to be familiar with the basic tenets of Bayes's Theorem, which may be summarised in the following manner: any belief at Time 1 about the uncertainty of some event A occurring at some point in the future is assumed to be provisional upon information or data gained prior to Time 1. Hence, the prior probability assumed about event A is then updated by new experience or data to provide a revised belief about the uncertainty, or posterior probability, of the event B, written P(A|B) (Constantinou et al., 2016). Bayesian Networks (BN) are developed from Bayes's Theorem with the structure and the relationships in BNs relying on both clinical expert knowledge (e.g., identifying risk markers) and relevant statistical data, meaning that they are well suited for enhanced decision making.

2.6 Conclusion

In the year 2000, seven inmates from Rikers Island in New York city brought a class action lawsuit in the Supreme Court of New York for violations of the state constitution and state mental health statutes (*Brad H v. City of New York*). At the time, it was not uncommon for the City of New York to drop off former inmates with mental illness at Queens Plaza with $1.50 in cash and a two-fare Metrocard. Brad H. was a 44-year-old homeless man with schizophrenia who had been treated 26 times in jail for mental illness but never received linkages to services after discharge. As a result of the suit, the City of New York has been required to provide comprehensive discharge planning services to inmates with mental illnesses since 2003. Planning includes assessments and the provision of assistance to ensure that mental health treatment is continued. In 2009, the suit was revisited because the lawyers for the plaintiff said the city was still failing to meet its obligations. Nearly a decade later, Canada is facing significant criticism and legal challenges regarding the treatment of individuals with mental health needs in correctional settings (Koskie Minsky, n.d.).

We have endeavoured to demonstrate that correctional psychologists are well positioned to benefit in their assessment and treatment roles from the promises that standardized psychopharmacological and psychosocial interventions provide (Table 2.1) and the above innovative approaches hold. Clearly, much more research will be required, and practice guidelines established, before some of the technical modalities will be available for general use in correctional settings. The future burns bright for psychologists, including in correctional and forensic psychiatric settings, with comprehensive approaches such as we have outlined here using the STAIR model, and new approaches such as virtual reality available for implementation now and innovative biological technologies likely available within the next decade. Nevertheless, the next generation of correctional psychologists has a heavy burden to bear, as there remain many challenges to ensure the most appropriate services are implemented in Correctional contexts.

References

Aboraya, A., France, C., Young, J., Curci, K., & Lepage, J. (2005). The validity of psychiatric diagnosis revisited: The clinician's guide to improve the validity of psychiatric diagnosis. *Psychiatry (Edgmont)*, 2(9), 48–55.

American Psychiatric Association. (2010). *Practice guideline for the treatment of patients with schizophrenia* (2nd ed.). Washington, DC: Author.

American Psychological Association. (2017). *Clinical practice guideline for the treatment of post-traumatic stress disorder (PTSD) in adults.* Washington, DC: Author.

Andreasen, N. C. (1995). The validation of psychiatric diagnosis: New models and approaches. *American Journal of Psychiatry, 152*(2), 161–162. https://doi.org/10.1176/ajp.152.2.161

Andrews, D. (2012). The Risk-Need-Responsivity Model of correctional assessment and treatment. In J. A. Dvoskin, J. L. Skeen, R. W. Novaco, & K. S. Douglas (Eds.), *Using social science to reduce violent offending.* New York, NY: Oxford University Press.

Andrews, D., & Bonta, J. (2010). *The psychology of criminal conduct* (5th ed.). New Providence, NJ: Anderson Publishing.

Andrews, D., Bonta, J., & Hoge, R. (1990). Classification for effective rehabilitation: Rediscovering psychology. *Criminal Justice and Behavior, 17*(1), 19–52. https://doi.org/10.1177/0093854890017001004

Appelbaum, K. L., Trestman, R. L., & Metzner, J. L. (2015). The future of correctional psychiatry: Evolving and recommended standards. In R. L. Trestman, K. L. Appelbaum, & J. L. Metzner (Eds.), *Oxford textbook of correctional psychiatry* (pp. 404–407). New York, NY: Oxford University Press.

Avery, A., & Kinner, S. A. (2015). A robust estimate of the number and characteristics of persons released from prison in Australia. *Australian and New Zealand Journal of Public Health, 39*(4), 315–318. https://doi.org/10.1111/1753-6405.12346

Baillargeon, J., Binswanger, I. A., Penn, J. V., Williams, B. A., & Murray, O. J. (2009). Psychiatric disorders and repeat incarcerations: The revolving prison door. *American Journal of Psychiatry, 166*(1), 103–109. https://doi.org/10.1176/appi.ajp.2008.08030416

Barr, H. (2003). Transinstitutionalization in the courts: Brad H. v. City of New York, and the fight for discharge planning for people with psychiatric disabilities leaving Rikers Island. *Crime & Delinquency, 49*(1), 97–123. https://doi.org/10.1177/0011128702239238

Baus, O., & Bouchard, S. (2014). Moving from virtual reality exposure-based therapy to augmented reality exposure-based therapy: A review. *Frontiers in Human Neuroscience, 8*, 112. https://doi.org/10.3389/fnhum.2014.00112

Beaudette, J. N., & Stewart, L. A. (2016). National prevalence of mental disorders among incoming Canadian male offenders. *The Canadian Journal of Psychiatry, 61*(10), 624–632. https://doi.org/10.1177/0706743716639929

Belenko, S., & Peugh, J. (2005). Estimating drug treatment needs among state prison inmates. *Drug and Alcohol Dependence, 77*(3), 269–281. https://doi.org/10.1016/j.drugalcdep.2004.08.023

Benbouriche, M., Nolet, K., Trottier, D., & Renaud, P. (2014). *Virtual reality applications in forensic psychiatry.* Paper presented at the Virtual Reality International Conference: Laval Virtual (VRIC'14), Laval, France.

Binswanger, I. A., Stern, M. F., Deyo, R. A., Heagerty, P. J., Cheadle, A., Elmore, J. G., & Koepsell, T. D. (2007). Release from prison—A high risk of death for former inmates. *The New England Journal of Medicine, 356*(2), 157–165. https://doi.org/10.1056/NEJMsa064115

Borzycki, M., & Makkai, T. (2007). *Prisoner reintegration post-release.* Canberra, ACT: Australian Institute of Criminology.

Bowring v. Godwin, 551 F.2d 44 (United States Court of Appeals, Fourth Circuit 1977).

Brad H v. City of New York, 185 Misc 2d 420 (Sup. Ct. N.Y. County 2000).

Brink, J., Doherty, D., & Boer, A. (2001). Mental disorder in federal offenders: A Canadian prevalence study. *International Journal of Law and Psychiatry, 24*(4–5), 339–356. https://doi.org/10.1016/S0160-2527(01)00071-1

Brink, J., & Tomita, T. (2015). Psychotic disorders. In R. L. Trestman, K. L. Appelbaum, & J. L. Metzner (Eds.), *Oxford textbook of correctional psychiatry* (pp. 178–183). New York, NY: Oxford University Press.

Bronson, J., & Berzofsky, M. (2017). *Indicators of mental health problems reported by prisoners and jail inmates, 2011–12.* Washington, DC: Bureau of Justice Statistics, US Department of Justice.

Brown v. Plata, 131 S. Ct. 1910 (2011).
Bureau of Justice Statistics. (2017). *Reentry trends in the US*. Washington, DC: Author.
Butler, T., Indig, D., Allnutt, S., & Mamoon, H. (2011). Co-occurring mental illness and substance use disorder among Australian prisoners. *Drug and Alcohol Review, 30*(2), 188–194. https://doi.org/10.1111/j.1465-3362.2010.00216.x
Bzdok, D., & Meyer-Lindenberg, A. (2018). Machine learning for precision psychiatry: Opportunities and challenges. *Biological Psychiatry: Cognitive Neuroscience and Neuroimaging, 3*(3), 223–230. https://doi.org/10.1016/j.bpsc.2017.11.007
Callan, V., & Gardner, J. (2007). The role of VET in recidivism in Australia. In S. Dawe (Ed.), *Vocational education and training for adult prisoners and offenders in Australia: Research readings* (pp. 34–46). Adelaide, Australia: National Centre for Vocational Education Research.
Canadian Institute for Health Information. (2008). *Improving the health of Canadians: Mental health, delinquency and criminal activity*. Ottawa, ON: CIHI.
Candilis, P. J., & Huttenbach, E. D. (2015). Ethics in correctional health. In R. L. Trestman, K. L. Appelbaum, & J. L. Metzner (Eds.), *Oxford textbook of correctional psychiatry* (pp. 41–45). New York, NY: Oxford University Press.
Collins, F., & Harold, V. (2015). A new initiative on Precision Medicine. *New England Journal of Medicine*, (9), 372, 793–375. https://doi.org/10.1056/NEJMp1500523
Constantinou, A. C., Fenton, N., Marsh, W., & Radlinski, L. (2016). From complex questionnaire and interviewing data to intelligent Bayesian network models for medical decision support. *Artificial Intelligence in Medicine, 67*, 75. https://doi.org/10.1016/j.artmed.2016.01.002
Constantinou, A. C., Freestone, M., Marsh, W., Fenton, N., & Coid, J. (2015). Risk assessment and risk management of violent reoffending among prisoners. *Expert Systems with Applications, 42*(21), 7511–7529. https://doi.org/10.1016/j.eswa.2015.05.025
Correctional Service of Canada. (2012a). *Mental health strategy for corrections in Canada: a Federal-provincial-territorial partnership*. Ottawa, ON: Correctional Service of Canada.
Correctional Service of Canada (CSC). (2012b). *Review of mental health screening at intake*. Retrieved from http://www.csc-scc.gc.ca/publications/005007-2514-eng.shtml
Council of State Governments. (2002). *Criminal Justice/Mental Health Consensus Project*. Washington, DC: Author.
Dorahy, M. J., Brand, B. L., Sar, V., Kruger, C., Stavropoulos, P., Martinez-Taboas, A., … Middleton, W. (2014). Dissociative identity disorder: An empirical overview. *Australian and New Zealand Journal of Psychiatry, 48*(5), 402–417. https://doi.org/10.1177/0004867414527523
Draine, J., Salzer, S., Culhane, D., & Hadley, T. (2002). Role of social disadvantage in crime, joblessness, and homelessness among persons with serious mental illness. *Psychiatric Services, 53*(5), 565–573. https://doi.org/10.1176/appi.ps.53.5.565
Durbin, J., Lin, E., & Zaslavska, N. (2010). Police-citizen encounters that involve mental health concerns: Results of an Ontario Police Services survey. *Canadian Journal of Community Mental Health, 29*(S5), 53–71. https://doi.org/10.7870/cjcmh-2010-0034
Dvoskin, J., Skeem, J. L., Novaco, R. W., & Douglas, K. (2012). *Using social science to reduce violent offending*. New York, NY: Oxford University Press.
Estelle v. Gamble, 429 US 97 (US Supreme Court 1976).
Fazel, S., & Danesh, J. (2002). Serious mental disorder in 23 000 prisoners: A systematic review of 62 surveys. *The Lancet, 359*(9306), 545–550. https://doi.org/10.1016/S0140-6736(02)07740-1
Fazel, S., Hayes, A., Bartellas, K., Clerici, M., & Trestman, R. (2016). Mental health of prisoners: Prevalence, adverse outcomes, and interventions. *The Lancet Psychiatry, 3*(9), 871–881. https://doi.org/10.1016/S2215-0366(16)30142-0
Fazel, S., & Seewald, K. (2012). Severe mental illness in 33 588 prisoners worldwide: Systematic review and meta-regression analysis. *British Journal of Psychiatry, 200*(5), 364–373. https://doi.org/10.1192/bjp.bp.111.096370
Fazel, S., Yoon, I. A., & Hayes, A. J. (2017). Substance use disorders in prisoners: An updated systematic review and meta-regression analysis in recently incarcerated men and women. *Addiction, 112*(10), 1725–1739. https://doi.org/10.1111/add.13877

Fazio, R. L., Pietz, C. A., & Denney, R. L. (2012). An estimate of the prevalence of Autism-Spectrum disorders in an incarcerated population. *Journal of Forensic Psychology, 4*, 69–80.

Fenton, N., & Neil, M. (2011). Avoiding probabilistic reasoning fallacies in legal practice using Bayesian networks. *Australian Journal of Legal Philosophy*, (36), 114–150.

First, M., Williams, J., Karg, R., & Spitzer, R. (2015). *Structured Clinical Interview for DSM-5 Disorders, Clinician Version (SCID-5-CV)*. Arlington, VA: American Psychiatric Association.

Forrester, A., Till, A., Simpson, A., & Shaw, J. (2018). Mental illness and the provision of mental health services in prisons. *British Medical Bulletin, 127*(1), 101–109.

Fromberger, P., Jordan, K., & Muller, J. L. (2014). Use of virtual reality in forensic psychiatry. A new paradigm? *Nervenarzt, 85*(3), 298–303. https://doi.org/10.1007/s00115-013-3904-7

Glaze, L. E., & Kaeble, D. (2014). *Correctional populations in the United States*. Washington, DC: Bureau of Justice Statistics.

Goodwin, G. M., Haddad, P. M., Ferrier, I. N., Aronson, J. K., Barnes, T., Cipriani, A., … Young, A. H. (2016). Evidence-based guidelines for treating bipolar disorder: Revised third edition recommendations from the British Association for Psychopharmacology. *Journal of Psychopharmacology, 30*(6), 495–553. https://doi.org/10.1177/0269881116636545

Grubin, D. (2010). Health screening in prisons. In I. Cumming & S. Wilson (Eds.), *Psychiatry in prisons: A comprehensive handbook* (Vol. 31, pp. 31–39). London, UK: Jessica Kingsley Publishers.

Harris, G., & Rice, M. (1997). Mentally disordered offenders: What research says about effective service. In C. Webster & M. Jackson (Eds.), *Impulsivity: Theory, assessment, and treatment*. New York, NY: The Guilford Press.

Hartvig, P., & Kjelsberg, E. (2009). Penrose's Law revisited: The relationship between mental institution beds, prison population and crime rate. *Nordic Journal of Psychiatry, 63*(1), 51–56.

Hayes, L. M. (1989). National study of jail suicides: Seven years later. *Psychiatric Quarterly, 60*(1), 7–29. https://doi.org/10.1007/bf01064362

Hayton, P., & Boyington, J. (2006). Prisons and health reforms in England and Wales. *American Journal of Public Health, 96*(10), 1730–1733. https://doi.org/10.2105/AJPH.2004.056127

Insel, T. R. (2014). The NIMH Research Domain Criteria (RDoC) Project: Precision medicine for psychiatry. *American Journal of Psychiatry, 171*(4), 395–397. https://doi.org/10.1176/appi. ajp.2014.14020138

James, D. J., & Glaze, L. E. (2006). *Mental health problems of prison and jail inmates*. Washington, DC: Bureau of Justice Statistics, US Department of Justice.

Jason, L. A., & Ferrari, J. R. (2010). Oxford House Recovery Homes: Characteristics and effectiveness. *Psychological Services, 7*(2), 92–102. https://doi.org/10.1037/a0017932

Jones, M. F. (2015). Formative case law and litigation. In R. L. Trestman, K. L. Appelbaum, & J. L. Metzner (Eds.), *Oxford textbook of correctional psychiatry* (pp. 13–17). New York, NY: Oxford University Press.

Kamath, J., & Shah, A. (2015). Mood disorders. In R. L. Trestman, K. L. Appelbaum, & J. L. Metzner (Eds.), *Oxford textbook of correctional psychiatry* (pp. 184–189). New York, NY: Oxford University Press.

Katzman, M. A., Bleau, P., Blier, P., Chokka, P., Kjernisted, K., Van Ameringen, M., … Walker, J. R. (2014). Canadian clinical practice guidelines for the management of anxiety, posttraumatic stress and obsessive-compulsive disorders. *BMC Psychiatry, 14*(Suppl 1), S1. https://doi. org/10.1186/1471-244X-14-S1-S1

Kirby, M. J. L., & Keon, W. J. (2006). *Out of the shadows at last: Transforming mental health, mental illness, and addiction services in Canada*. Final report of the Standing Social Committee on Social Affairs, Science, and Technology.

Knoll, J. (2015). Evaluation of malingering in corrections. In R. L. Trestman, K. L. Appelbaum, & J. L. Metzner (Eds.), *Oxford textbook of correctional psychiatry* (pp. 117–122). New York, NY: Oxford Unviersity Press.

Koskie Minsky. (n.d.). Federal Prisoner Mental Health Class Action. Retrieved March 13, 2018, from https://kmlaw.ca/cases/prisonermentalhealth/

Kouyoumdjian, F., Schuler, A., Matheson, F. I., & Hwang, S. W. (2016). Health status of prisoners in Canada: Narrative review. *Canadian Family Physician, 62*(3), 215–222.

Lafortune, D. (2010). Prevalence and screening of mental disorders in short-term correctional facilities. *International Journal of Law and Psychiatry, 33*(2), 94–100.

Liebling, A., & Maruna, S. (2013). Introduction: The effects of imprisonment revisited. In A. Liebling & S. Maruna (Eds.), *The effects of imprisonment*. New York, NY: Routledge.

Livingston, J. (2009). *Mental health and substance use services in correctional settings: A review of minimum standards and best practices*. Vancouver, BC: The International Centre for Criminal Law Reform and Criminal Justice Policy.

Livingston, J., Nicholls, T. L., & Brink, J. (2011). The impact of realigning a tertiary psychiatric hospital in British Columbia on other institutional sectors. *Psychiatric Services, 62*(2), 200–205. https://doi.org/10.1176/ps.62.2.pss6202_0200

Luxton, D. D. (2014). Recommendations for the ethical use and design of artificial intelligent care providers. *Artificial Intelligence in Medicine, 62*(1), 1–10. https://doi.org/10.1016/j.artmed.2014.06.004

Maloney, M. P., Dvoskin, J., & Metzner, J. L. (2015). Mental health screening and brief assessments. In R. L. Trestman, K. L. Appelbaum, & J. L. Metzner (Eds.), *Oxford textbook of correctional psychiatry* (pp. 57–61). New York, NY: Oxford University Press.

Maples-Keller, J. L., Bunnell, B. E., Kim, S. J., & Rothbaum, B. O. (2017). The use of virtual reality technology in the treatment of anxiety and other psychiatric disorders. *Harvard Review of Psychiatry, 25*(3), 103–113. https://doi.org/10.1097/hrp.0000000000000138

Marschall-Lévesque, S., Rouleau, J.-L., & Renaud, P. (2018). Increasing valid profiles in phallometric assessment of sex offenders with child victims: Combining the strengths of audio stimuli and synthetic characters. *Archives of Sexual Behavior, 47*(2), 417–428. https://doi.org/10.1007/s10508-017-1053-y

Martin, M. S., Colman, I., Simpson, A. I., & McKenzie, K. (2013). Mental health screening tools in correctional institutions: A systematic review. *BMC Psychiatry, 13*(1), 275. https://doi.org/10.1186/1471-244X-13-275

Martin, M. S., Potter, B. K., Crocker, A. G., Wells, G. A., & Colman, I. (2016). Yield and efficiency of mental health screening: A comparison of screening protocols at intake to prison. *PLoS One, 11*(5), e0154106. https://doi.org/10.1371/journal.pone.0154106

Matheson, F. I., Creatore, M. I., Gozdyra, P., Moineddin, R., Rourke, S. B., & Glazier, R. H. (2005). Assessment of police calls for suicidal behavior in a concentrated urban setting. *Psychiatric Services, 56*(12), 1606–1609. https://doi.org/10.1176/appi.ps.56.12.1606

Mazzoni, G. A., Loftus, E. F., & Kirsch, I. (2001). Changing beliefs about implausible autobiographical events: A little plausibility goes a long way. *Journal of Experimental Psychology Applied, 7*(1), 51–59. https://doi.org/10.1037/1076-898X.7.1.51

Mental Health America. (2015). *Position statement 56: Mental health treatment in correctional facilities*. Alexandria, VA: Author.

Metzner, J. L. (2015). *Mental health considerations for segregated inmates*. Chicago, IL: National Commission on Correctional Health Care.

Metzner, J. L., & Dvoskin, J. (2006). An overview of correctional psychiatry. *Psychiatric Clinics of North America, 29*(3), 761–772. https://doi.org/10.1016/j.psc.2006.04.012

Meyer, J. P., & Altice, F. L. (2015). Transition to the community. In R. L. Trestman, K. L. Appelbaum, & J. L. Metzner (Eds.), *Oxford textbook of correctional psychiatry* (pp. 266–274). New York, NY: Oxford University Press.

Meyerbroker, K., & Emmelkamp, P. M. (2010). Virtual reality exposure therapy in anxiety disorders: A systematic review of process-and-outcome studies. *Depression and Anxiety, 27*(10), 933–944. https://doi.org/10.1002/da.20734

Mishkind, M. C., Norr, A. M., Katz, A. C., & Reger, G. M. (2017). Review of virtual reality treatment in psychiatry: Evidence versus current diffusion and use. *Current Psychiatry Reports, 19*(11), 80. https://doi.org/10.1007/s11920-017-0836-0

Møller, L., Stöver, H., Jürgens, R., Gatherer, A., & Nikogosian, H. (2007). *Health in prisons: A WHO guide to the essentials in prison health*. Copenhagen, Denmark: World Health Organization.

Moriyama, T. S., Polanczyk, G. V., Terzi, F. S., Faria, K. M., & Rohde, L. A. (2013). Psychopharmacology and psychotherapy for the treatment of adults with ADHD—A systematic review of available meta-analyses. *CNS Spectrums, 18*(6), 296–306. https://doi.org/10.1017/S109285291300031X

Müller-Isberner, R., Born, P., Euker, S., & Eusterschulte, B. (2017). Implementation of evidence-based practices in forensic mental health services. In R. Roesch & A. N. Cook (Eds.), *Handbook of forensic mental health services* (pp. 443–469). New York, NY: Routledge.

National Institute for Health Care Excellence (NICE). (2017). *Mental health of adults in contact with the criminal justice system.* London, UK: Author.

Nicholls, T. L., & Goossens, I. (2017). Guidelines for improving forensic mental health in inpatient psychiatric settings. In R. Roesch & A. N. Cook (Eds.), *Handbook of forensic mental health services* (pp. 496–542). New York, NY: Routledge.

Nicholls, T. L., Olley, M., Ogloff J., Roesch, R., & Felbert Kreis, M. (in press). Jail Screening Assessment Tool (JSAT). In R. D. Morgan (Ed.), The SAGE encyclopedia of criminal psychology. Thousand Oaks, CA: SAGE Publishing.

Nicholls, T. L., Roesch, R., Olley, M., Ogloff, J., & Hemphill, J. (2005). *Jail Screening Assessment Tool (JSAT): Guidelines for mental health screening in jails.* Burnaby, BC: Mental Health, Law, and Policy Institute, Simon Fraser University.

Nonstad, K., & Webster, C. (2011). How to fail in the implementation of a risk assessment scheme or any other new procedure in your organization. *American Journal of Orthopsychiatry, 8,* 94–99. https://doi.org/10.1111/j.1939-0025.2010.01076.x

Nutt, D. J., Davidson, J. R., Gelenberg, A. J., Higuchi, T., Kanba, S., Karamustafalioglu, O., … Zhang, M. (2010). International consensus statement on major depressive disorder. *Journal of Clinical Psychiatry, 71*(Suppl E1), e08. https://doi.org/10.4088/JCP.9058se1c.08gry

Ogloff, J. (2002). Identifying and accommodating the needs of mentally ill people in gaols and prisons. *Psychiatry, Psychology and Law, 9*(1), 1–33. https://doi.org/10.1375/pplt.2002.9.1.1

Ogloff, J., Davis, M., Rivers, G., & Ross, S. (2007). The identification of mental disorders in the criminal justice system. *Trends & Issues in Crime and Criminal Justice,* (334), 1–6.

Opris, D., Pintea, S., Garcia-Palacios, A., Botella, C., Szamoskozi, S., & David, D. (2012). Virtual reality exposure therapy in anxiety disorders: A quantitative meta-analysis. *Depression and Anxiety, 29*(2), 85–93. https://doi.org/10.1002/da.20910

Osher, F., D'Amora, D., Plotkin, M., Jarrett, N., & Eggleston, A. (2012). *Adults with behavioral health needs under correctional supervision: A shared framework for reducing recidivism and promoting recovery.* New York, NY: Council of State Governments Justice Center.

Osher, F., Scott, J., Steadman, H., & Robbins, P. C. (2006). *Validating a brief jail mental health screen, final technical report.* Washington, D.C: National Institute of Justice. Retrieved from https://www.ncjrs.gov/pdffiles1/nij/grants/213805.pdf

Osher, F., Steadman, H., & Barr, H. (2003). A best practice approach to community reentry from jails for inmates with co-occurring disorders: The Apic Model. *Crime & Delinquency, 49*(1), 79–96. https://doi.org/10.1177/0011128702239237

Papadimitropoulou, K., Vossen, C., Karabis, A., Donatti, C., & Kubitz, N. (2017). Comparative efficacy and tolerability of pharmacological and somatic interventions in adult patients with treatment-resistant depression: A systematic review and network meta-analysis. *Current Medical Research and Opinion, 33*(4), 701–711. https://doi.org/10.1080/03007995.2016.1277201

Penn, J. V. (2015). Standards and accreditation for jails, prisons, and juvenile facilities. In R. L. Trestman, K. L. Appelbaum, & J. L. Metzner (Eds.), *Oxford textbook of correctional psychiatry* (pp. 359–364). New York, NY: Oxford University Press.

Penney, S. R., Prosser, A., Grimbos, T., Darby, P., & Simpson, A. I. F. (2017). Time trends in homicide and mental illness in Ontario from 1987 to 2012: Examining the effects of mental health service provision. *Canadian Journal of Psychiatry, 63*(6), 387–394. https://doi.org/10.1177/0706743717737034

Perrien, M., & O'Keefe, M. L. (2015). Disciplinary infractions and restricted housing. In R. L. Trestman, K. L. Appelbaum, & J. L. Metzner (Eds.), *Oxford textbook of correctional psychiatry* (pp. 71–75). New York, NY: Oxford University Press.

Pollak, Y., Weiss, P. L., Rizzo, A. A., Weizer, M., Shriki, L., Shalev, R. S., & Gross-Tsur, V. (2009). The utility of a continuous performance test embedded in virtual reality in measuring ADHD-related deficits. *Journal of Developmental and Behavioral Pediatrics, 30*(1), 2–6. https://doi.org/10.1097/DBP.0b013e3181969b22

Prasad v. County of Sutter, 958 F. Supp. 2d 1101 (E.D. Cal. 2013).

Prins, S. J. (2014). Prevalence of mental illnesses in US state prisons: A systematic review. *Psychiatric Services, 65*(7), 862–872. https://doi.org/10.1176/appi.ps.201300166

Rizzo, A. S., & Koenig, S. T. (2017). Is clinical virtual reality ready for primetime? *Neuropsychology, 31*(8), 877–899. https://doi.org/10.1037/neu0000405

Romano, M. (2017). *Confronting California's continuing prison crisis: The prevalence and severity of mental illness among California prisoners on the rise.* Stanford Justice Advocacy Project.

Rosenfeld, B., Foellmi, M., Khadivi, A., Wijetunga, C., Howe, J., Nijdam-Jones, A., … Rotter, M. (2017). Determining when to conduct a violence risk assessment: Development and initial validation of the Fordham Risk Screening Tool (FRST). *Law and Human Behavior, 41*(4), 325–332. https://doi.org/10.1037/lhb0000247

Ruiz v. Estelle, 503 F. Supp. 1265 (S.D. Tex. 1980).

SAMHSA. (2017). *Guidelines for successful transition of people with mental or substance use disorders from jail and prison: Implementation guide.* Rockville, MD: Substance Abuse and Mental Health Services Administration.

Sapers, H. (2005). *Annual report of the Office of the Correctional Investigator 2004–2005.* Ottawa, ON: Public Safety and Emergency Preparedness Canada.

Sapers, H. (2011). *Mental health and corrections.* Presentation at the Department of Psychology Colloquium Series. Antigonish, Nova Scotia: Saint Francis Xavier University.

Sapers, H. (2016). *Annual report of the Office of the Correctional Investigator: 2015–2016.* Ottawa, ON: Public Safety and Emergency Preparedness Canada.

Schlager, M. (2013). *Rethinking the reentry paradigm, a blueprint for action.* Durham, NC: Carolina Academic Press.

Schmidt, H. D., Shelton, R. C., & Duman, R. S. (2011). Functional biomarkers of depression: Diagnosis, treatment, and pathophysiology. *Neuropsychopharmacology, 36*(12), 2375–2394. https://doi.org/10.1038/npp.2011.151

Scott, C. L., & Falls, B. (2015). Mental illness management in corrections. In R. L. Trestman, K. L. Appelbaum, & J. L. Metzner (Eds.), *Oxford textbook of correctional psychiatry* (pp. 8–12). New York, NY: Oxford University Press.

Scott, C. L., & Holoyda, B. J. (2015). Role of clinical trainees. In K. L. Appelbaum & J. L. Metzner (Eds.), *Oxford textbook of correctional psychiatry* (pp. 387–391). New York, NY: Oxford University Press.

Senior, J., Birmingham, L., Harty, M., Hassan, L., Hayes, A., Kendall, K., … Mills, A. (2013). Identification and management of prisoners with severe psychiatric illness by specialist mental health services. *Psychological Medicine, 43*(7), 1511–1520. https://doi.org/10.1017/S0033291712002073

Silverman, J. J., Galanter, M., Jackson-Triche, M., Jacobs, D. G., Lomax, J. W., II, Riba, M. B., … Yager, J. (2015). The American Psychiatric Association practice guidelines for the psychiatric evaluation of adults. *American Journal of Psychiatry, 172*(8), 798–802. https://doi.org/10.1176/appi.ajp.2015.1720501

Simpson, A., Shaw, J., Forrester, A., Nicholls, T. L., & Martin, M. (2017). *International Collaboration for Excellence and Innovations Mental Health in Corrections (I-CEIsMIC).* Half-day workshop presented at the annual conference of the International Association of Forensic Mental Health, Split, Croatia.

Skeem, J. L., Winter, E., Kennealy, P. J., Louden, J. E., & Tatar, J. R., II. (2014). Offenders with mental illness have criminogenic needs, too: Toward recidivism reduction. *Law and Human Behavior, 38*(3), 212. https://doi.org/10.1037/lhb0000054

Somers, J. M., Rezansoff, S. N., Moniruzzaman, A., & Zabarauckas, C. (2015). High-frequency use of corrections, health, and social services, and association with mental illness and substance use. *Emerging Themes in Epidemiology, 12*(1), 17. https://doi.org/10.1186%2Fs12982-015-0040-9

Son, J. H., Lee, S. H., Seok, J. W., Kee, B. S., Lee, H. W., Kim, H. J., ... Han, D. H. (2015). Virtual reality therapy for the treatment of alcohol dependence: A preliminary investigation with positron emission tomography/computerized tomography. *Journal of Studies on Alcohol and Drugs, 76*(4), 620–627. https://doi.org/10.15288/jsad.2015.76.620

Sorenson, K. (2010). *Mental health and drug and alcohol addiction in the federal correctional system: Report of the Standing Committee on Public Safety and National Security*. Ottawa, ON: Government of Canada.

Statistics Canada. (2017). *Aboriginal peoples in Canada: Key results from the 2016 Census*. Ottawa, ON: Government of Canada.

Steadman, H., Osher, F., Robbins, P., Case, B., & Samuels, S. (2009). Prevalence of serious mental illness among jail inmates. *Psychiatric Services, 60*(6), 761–765. https://doi.org/10.1176/ps.2009.60.6.761

Taylor, D. M., Barnes, T. R. E., & Yound, A. H. (2018). *The Maudlsey prescribing guidelines* (13th ed.). Chichester, UK: Wiley.

The Pew Centre on the States. (2010). *Collateral costs: Incarceration's effects on economic mobility*. Washington, DC: Author Retrieved from https://repositories.lib.utexas.edu/bitstream/handle/2152/15161/PEW_CollateralCosts.pdf?sequence=2

The Pew Centre on the States. (2011). *State of recidivism, the revolving door of America's prisons*. Washington, DC: Author Retrieved from http://www.pewtrusts.org/-/media/legacy/uploaded-files/wwwpewtrustsorg/reports/sentencing_and_corrections/staterecidivismrevolvingdooramericaprisons20pdf.pdf

Tillers, P. (2007). Introduction: Visualizing evidence and inference in legal settings. *Law, Probability & Risk, 6*(1–4), 1–4. https://doi.org/10.1093/lpr/mgm006

Trottier, D., Renaud, P., Rouleau, J.-L., Goyette, M., Saumur, C., Boukhalfi, T., & Bouchard, S. (2015). Erratum to: Using immersive virtual reality and anatomically correct computer-generated characters in the forensic assessment of deviant sexual preferences. *Virtual Reality, 19*(3), 303. https://doi.org/10.1007/s10055-015-0277-1

United Nations Office for Project Services. (2016). *Technical guidance for prison planning: Technical and operational considerations based on the Nelson Mandela Rules*. Copenhagen, Denmark: Author.

Valmaggia, L. R., Freeman, D., Green, C., Garety, P., Swapp, D., Antley, A., ... McGuire, P. K. (2007). Virtual reality and paranoid ideations in people with an 'at-risk mental state' for psychosis. *British Journal of Psychiatry Supplement, 51*, s63–s68. https://doi.org/10.1192/bjp.191.51.s63

van Bennekom, M. J., Kasanmoentalib, M. S., de Koning, P. P., & Denys, D. (2017). A virtual reality game to assess obsessive-compulsive disorder. *Cyberpsychology, Behavior and Social Networking, 20*(11), 718–722. https://doi.org/10.1089/cyber.2017.0107

Verdun-Jones, S., & Butler, A. (2016). Mental health services in Canadian corrections. In J. A. Chandler & C. M. Flood (Eds.), *Law and mind: Mental health law and policy in Canada* (pp. 345–370). Toronto, ON: LexisNexis Canada Inc.

Victoria Government Department of Health. (2010). *Statewide mental health triage scale: Guidelines*. Melbourne, Australia: Author.

Viljoen, J. L., Cochrane, D. M., & Jonnson, M. R. (2018). Do risk assessment tools help manage and reduce risk of violence and reoffending? A systematic review. *Law and Human Behavior, 42*(3), 181–214. https://doi.org/10.1037/lhb0000280

Walters, G. (2006). Coping with malingering and exaggeration of psychiatric symptomatology in offender populations. *American Journal of Forensic Psychology, 24*(4), 21.

Wani, A., Trevino, K., Marnell, P., & Husain, M. M. (2013). Advances in brain stimulation for depression. *Annals of Clinical Psychiatry, 25*(3), 217–224.

Weinstein, H. C., Burns, K. A., Newkirk, C. F., Zil, J. S., Dvoskin, J. A., & Steadman, H. J. (2000). *Psychiatric services in jails and prisons: A task force report of the American Psychiatric Association* (2nd ed.). Washington, DC: American Psychiatric Association.

Wing, J., Cooper, J., & Sartorius, N. (1974). *Measurement and classification of psychiatric symptoms: An instruction manual for the PSE and CATEGO program*. London, UK: Cambridge University Press.

Woods, L. N., Lanza, A. S., Dyson, W., & Gordon, D. M. (2013). The role of prevention in promoting continuity of health care in prisoner reentry initiatives. *American Journal of Public Health, 103*(5), 830–838. https://doi.org/10.2105/AJPH.2012.300961

World Health Organization, & International Committee of the Red Cross. (2005). *Information sheet: Mental health and prisons*. Geneva, Switzerland: Author.

Yoon, J., Domino, M. E., Norton, E. C., Cuddeback, G. S., & Morrissey, J. P. (2013). The impact of changes in psychiatric bed supply on jail use by persons with severe mental illness. *Journal of Mental Health Policy and Economics, 16*(2), 81–92.

Zinger, I. (2017). *The annual report of the Office of the Correctional Investigator 2016–2017* (44th Annual Report ed.). Ottawa, ON: The Office of the Correctional Investigator of Canada.

Chapter 3
Substance Use Disorders in Correctional Populations

Marguerite Ternes, Stephanie Goodwin, and Kathleen Hyland

Substance use is a major public health problem that affects society on multiple levels. The negative impact of substance use on individual health, family functioning, health care utilization, and offending has been well-established (Kelley & Fals-Stewart, 2004; Lander, Howsare, & Byrne, 2013; Oesterle et al., 2004; Pernanen, Cousineau, Brochu, & Sun, 2002; Rehm et al., 2006). Rates of substance use disorders within incarcerated populations are much higher than those in the general population (Fazel, Bains, & Doll, 2006; Kelly & Farrell MacDonald, 2015b). Moreover, there is a direct link between substance use and criminal behaviour for a significant proportion of incarcerated offenders. For example, approximately 50% of offenders in Canadian or American correctional institutions identified substance use as a contributing factor in their current offences (Bahr, Masters, & Taylor, 2012; Mullins, Ternes, & Farrell Macdonald, 2013; Pernanen et al., 2002). Substance use is also associated with recidivism (e.g., Caudy et al., 2015; Håkansson & Berglund, 2012; Staton-Tindall, Harp, Winston, Webster, & Pangburn, 2015; van der Put, Creemers, & Hoeve, 2013; Wilson, Drane, Hadley, Metraux, & Evans, 2011), with the likelihood of returning to custody increasing as the severity of substance use problems increases (Farrell MacDonald, 2014).

Given the prevalence of substance use among offenders and the importance of effectively dealing with substance use, correctional institutions often offer substance use programs to offenders with problematic drug or alcohol use. Research has shown the programs offered in institutions are effective in reducing reconviction for offenders who complete all sessions (e.g., Doherty, Ternes, & Matheson, 2014; Kunic & Varis, 2009; McMurran & Theodosi, 2007; Ternes, Doherty, & Matheson, 2014). This chapter will review concepts related to substance use disorder among offenders. First, the frequency and prevalence will be discussed. Then, theoretical models related to service delivery will be introduced. Next, methods of diagnosis

M. Ternes (✉) · S. Goodwin · K. Hyland
Psychology Department, Saint Mary's University, Halifax, NS, Canada
e-mail: Meg.ternes@smu.ca

© Springer Nature Switzerland AG 2018
M. Ternes et al. (eds.), *The Practice of Correctional Psychology*,
https://doi.org/10.1007/978-3-030-00452-1_3

and assessment will be introduced. Methods of intervention will follow, including a discussion of which methods are most effective. The chapter will conclude with a discussion of future implications for research and practice, as well as technology and innovation related to the assessment and treatment of substance use disorders.

3.1 Frequency and Prevalence

It is estimated that between 10% and 70% of incarcerated men in North America have a substance use disorder (Kelly & Farrell MacDonald, 2015b; Stewart & Wilton, 2017; Walters, 2012) and approximately 60–77% of women offenders suffer from drug abuse or dependence issues (Farrell MacDonald, Gobeil, Biro, Ritchie, & Curno, 2015; Houser, Belenko, & Brennan, 2012; Kelly & Farrell MacDonald, 2015a). These proportions are nearly 17 times larger than those in the general population (Houser et al., 2012; Tangney et al., 2016).

In addition to elevated drug use rates in the correctional system, substance use disorders tend to co-occur with other mental health disorders. In the inmates considered by Houser et al. (2012), 54% of female inmates and 41% of male inmates had co-occurring substance use and mental health disorders. Additionally, 70–72% of individuals with a severe psychiatric disorder, such as schizophrenia, had a comorbid substance use disorder (Houser et al., 2012; Plourde, Dufour, Brochu, & Gendron, 2013). Similarly, in a Canadian sample of male offenders, over 50% had a substance use disorder, and 68% of these men had co-occurring personality disorders (Stewart & Wilton, 2017). Of those women offenders with dependence on substances, 6–14% were at least moderately dependent on alcohol and 42–59% were at least moderately dependent on illicit drugs (Kelly & Farrell MacDonald, 2015a; Plourde et al., 2013). In comparison, of those men offenders with a substance use issue, approximately 7% were at least moderately dependent on alcohol and about 36% were at least moderately dependent on drugs (Kelly & Farrell MacDonald, 2015a).

Drug use by offenders is not just an issue in North American countries. Fazel et al.'s (2006) review of substance abuse in incarcerated offenders, which considered findings from the United States, England, Ireland, and New Zealand, found that up to 60% of offenders exhibited a drug dependence problem upon intake. Between 70% and 75% of offenders in the United Kingdom reported using illegal substances within 1 year of their incarceration (Jolley & Kerbs, 2010). For those offenders, 32.3% suffered from substance use as their primary disorder while 39.8% had a comorbid psychotic disorder and 2.5% had a comorbid mood or anxiety disorder (Sewell et al., 2015). Additionally, amongst Ugandan prisoners, 65% had used drugs within their lifetime and among Kenyan prisoners at the Eldoret Prison, 66.1% had abused substances within their lifetime (Kinyanjui & Atwoli, 2013). Thirty-eight percent of inmates in Jamaica have substance use as their primary disorder, whereas 39.8% have a comorbid psychotic disorder and 2.5% have a comorbid mood or anxiety disorder (Sewell et al., 2015). In Australia, 62% of female inmates used drugs regularly within the 6 months prior to their incarceration (Plourde et al., 2013).

3.2   Theoretical Models Relevant to Service Delivery

Due to the prevalence and far-reaching effects of substance abuse, it is not surprising that many inter-related theories have been offered to explain substance use disorder, the link between substance use and crime, and ways to reduce substance use. Additionally, the reasons for trying a substance or developing a substance use disorder may be quite different from the reasons why an individual continues to use drugs. Assessment and treatment is based on the assumption that patterns of substance use can have multiple determinants. In this section we will briefly review five overarching models of substance use and treatment: the biopsychological model, the social learning model, the self-medication model, the tripartite conceptual model, the Transtheoretical Model, and the Risk-Needs-Responsivity model.

3.2.1   Biopsychological Model

The biopsychological theory of addiction, also known as the medical or disease model, integrates neurochemistry, motivation, and positive reinforcement to explain why people become addicted to substances (Nutt, Lingford-Hughes, Erritzoe, & Stokes, 2015). This model differentiates between substance dependence, substance misuse, physical dependence, and psychological dependence (National Institute on Drug Abuse [NIDA], 2012; Schug & Fradella, 2015; van Ree, Gerrits, & Vanderschuren, 1999). Substance misuse refers to continued use of a drug despite problems caused by such use (Schug & Fradella, 2015). An individual who is physically dependent on a drug will experience withdrawal symptoms when the substance is taken away and will crave the drug to seek relief of the withdrawal symptoms (NIDA, 2012; Wise & Bozarth, 1987). Psychological dependence is revealed when the user feels that continued drug use is necessary to function or feel optimal (Schug & Fradella, 2015). Substance dependence and addiction refer to substance use disorders, which include physical and psychological dependence, as well as other criteria, such as a persistent desire to cut down use of the substance or recurrent use of the substance resulting in disruption of work or family obligations (NIDA, 2012; van Ree et al., 1999).

The biopsychological theory argues that drugs stimulate the dopamine receptors in the brain, which causes pleasurable or euphoric sensations. Since dopamine is integral for motivating and driving goal-directed behaviour, individuals are motivated to continue using drugs because of the positive reinforcing effects that dopamine activation has on the brain. The biopsychological model sees the initial decision to use drugs as mainly voluntary, although when an individual becomes addicted to a drug, their ability to exert self-control becomes impaired (NIDA, 2012).

Genetics have also been explored as a biological pathway to substance use disorder. Results of twin and adoption studies have shown that genetics play a moderate to strong role in explaining substance use, with heritability estimates for substance use ranging from 50% to 80% (Kendler, Neale, Heath, Kessler, & Eaves, 1994; Prescott et al., 2005). Research on genetics has also found other genetic factors that may make someone more susceptible to developing a substance-related addiction, such as behavioural, temperamental, and personality traits. For example, several genes that control the sensitivity to acute intoxication and alcohol withdrawal have been found to protect against alcoholism (Hinckers et al., 2006; Pihl, 2009).

The biopsychological model has received criticism on a number of issues. For one, not all drugs alter the brain's dopamine neurotransmitter system (Nutt et al., 2015). While it seems evident that stimulants, such as cocaine, activate the brain's dopamine system, it is not clear that cannabis, ketamine, opiates, or alcohol affect the dopamine system. Nutt et al. (2015) also challenge the biopsychosocial theory's basic assumption that dopamine release is the key causal mechanism that directly causes drug addiction due to dopamine's euphoric effects. They posit that dopamine release may lead to increased impulsivity, which then may lead to addiction. Finally, this model has received criticism for completely alleviating the user from responsibility for their problematic substance use and, thus, discouraging professional help-seeking (Schug & Fradella, 2015; Skog, 2000).

3.2.2 Social Learning Model

The social learning model (SLM) puts the responsibility of problematic substance use in the hands of the user by highlighting individual choice. The SLM suggests that substance dependence is the result of a rational choice in which individuals opt for short-term rewards despite the long-term consequences (Lewis, 2015). Social learning theory dictates that the way a person behaves can be attributed to what they learn through the observation of pleasurable or painful consequences of the actions of others (Bandura, 1971). Relating to substance use, the SLM could be interpreted more specifically as individuals observing others engaging in substance use behaviours and either receiving positive feedback or reinforcement for imitating those behaviours or interpreting the consequences for others as positive (Norman & Ford, 2015).

The SLM has been criticized for its concurrence with early models of addiction that regarded those who abuse substances as weak and lacking willpower. Lewis (2015) suggests that while SLM does a good job of explaining why individuals might begin using substances, the biopsychological model does a better job of explaining why individuals continue to use substances.

3.2.3 Self-Medication Model

The self-medication model posits that individuals begin substance use as a coping mechanism, usually to cope with stress and other negative affective and psychological states, often the consequences of trauma and abuse (Lewis, 2015; West, 2005). According to this model, an individual chooses a particular drug to help with a specific problem, such as anxiety or pain (West, 2005). Psychoactive drugs effectively help with negative psychological states, as well as the side-effects of drugs used to treat psychiatric disorder, in the short term (Lewis, 2015; West, 2005). For example, alcohol intoxication can help to calm fears and ease pain, but once the intoxication has worn off, there may be a rebound increase in negative affect (West, 2005). Moreover, repeated intoxication has increased negative effects on the substance user, which serves to increase stress and anxiety (Koob & Le Moal, 2001).

Support for the self-medication model mainly comes from two sources: research on women offenders and research on co-occurring disorders. Research taking the "feminist pathways" perspective on female criminal conduct shows that women offenders commonly experience abuse and trauma, and use substances to cope (Gueta & Chen, 2015; Wattanaporn & Holtfreter, 2014). The high prevalence of co-occurring substance use disorders and issues with mental health also supports the self-medication model. For example, several recent studies of Canadian incarcerated offenders show that most offenders who present with a substance use disorder also have mental health issues such as personality disorders, mood disorders, or anxiety disorders (MacSwain, Cheverie, Farrell MacDonald, & Johnson, 2014; Stewart & Wilton, 2017).

A major limitation of the self-medication model is that it requires that psychological disorders or mental stressors occur prior to the substance use, which is not always the case. This model cannot explain drug use in situations where there are no psychological problems or negative affect to get past (West, 2005). Self-medication and social learning models also fail to consider the compulsive components of substance use disorders, which are better explained by the biopsychological model.

3.2.4 Tripartite Conceptual Model

The tripartite conceptual model was developed to explain the relationship between substance use and crime (Goldstein, 1985). This model suggests three main types of drug-related crime: (1) psychopharmacologically driven crime, (2) systemic crime, and (3) economically compulsive crime. The psychopharmacological aspect of the model suggests that, for some people, substance use changes behaviour, making them more impulsive, excitable, and/or irrational, resulting in violent behaviour. The systemic crime component of the model refers to criminal acts resulting from the drug trade. It includes drug trafficking and distribution, as well as the violence inherent in the enterprise of the drug trade, such as violent disputes over territory, and threats, assaults, and murders committed within and by drug-dealing organizations. Finally, Goldstein's (1985) idea of economically compulsive crime refers to criminal behaviour that supports a drug addiction. A person who has developed an addiction to drugs may engage in criminal acts such as robbery or drug dealing to support his or her addiction.

Support for the latter two aspects of Goldstein's (1985) model comes from research that has found clear links between organized crime, the drug trade, and violence (e.g., Schneider, 2013), as well as links between drug consumption and acquisitive crimes, such as theft or robbery (e.g., Cheverie, Ternes, & Farrell MacDonald, 2014; Ternes & Johnson, 2011). Psychopharmacologically driven crime, on the other hand, is thought to be rare, and more likely to be associated with alcohol rather than illicit drugs (Cheverie, Ternes, & Farrell MacDonald, 2014; MacCoun, Kilmer, & Reuter, 2003). Related to this, several researchers have cautioned that drug or alcohol use is not necessarily causally related to violent crime. Rather, there are many additional risk factors that interact with substance abuse in complex ways to predict criminal conduct (Sinha & Easton, 1999). For example, according to McMurran's (2012) theory regarding the relationship between alcohol and violence, for a person to act violently as a result of alcohol use, the person must already be predisposed to aggression and must have encountered provocation. Alcohol may contribute to violent crime directly through diminished inhibitory control or increased cognitive impairment, or it may be mediated by factors such as personality or social cues. In the former case, treating substance use will reduce violent crime, but in the latter case, a more nuanced treatment approach will be necessary for offenders (McMurran, 2013).

3.2.5 Transtheoretical Model

The Transtheoretical Model (TTM) of behaviour change suggests that recovering from addictive behaviour involves transitioning through various stages (Connors, DiClemente, Velasquez, & Donovan, 2015; Prochaska, Norcross, & DiClemente, 1994; Prochaska & Velicer, 1997). In the *precontemplation* stage, the individual is not actually contemplating change. Often, an individual in the precontemplation stage does not even acknowledge a need to make any behavioural changes. In the *contemplation* stage, the individual is aware of the behavioural problem and is considering change within the next 6 months, but has not made any specific plans to change. The *preparation* stage is a transitory stage, where the individual is making plans to change and may even take some preliminary steps toward change. In the *action* stage, the individual is actively making attempts to change his or her behaviour, experiences, and the environment. Individuals in this stage are committed to making changes and start to put forth effort towards making changes. In the *maintenance* stage, the individual is engaging in the new behaviour pattern. The new pattern of behaviour has replaced the old behaviour, and the threat of relapse is lessened.

Finally, in the *termination* stage, the individual has permanently adopted the new behaviour pattern. Individuals generally move through the stages sequentially, but usually revert to prior stages before achieving maintenance and termination (Prochaska & Velicer, 1997). This model argues that, as different processes are involved in moving through different stages, it is important that behavioural interventions are appropriate to an individual's current stage (Connors et al., 2015; Prochaska & Goldstein, 1991; Prochaska & Velicer, 1997).

Some have criticized the TTM's stages, suggesting that the dividing lines between stages are rather arbitrary (Sutton, 2001). Moreover, it is suggested that the TTM does not actually measure readiness to change (Etter & Sutton, 2002). Others have noted that, although the TTM assumes that individuals typically make stable and coherent plans, most individuals attempting to quit an addictive behaviour do not engage in much planning (Larabie, 2005). TTM also neglects some of the important foundations of human motivation—reward and punishment and associative learning—instead focusing on conscious decision-making and planning processes (Baumeister, Heatherton, & Tice, 1994; Salamone, Correa, Mingote, & Weber, 2003). Empirical support for TTM is relatively weak, with the most supportive studies finding that individuals closer to maintenance at any one time are more likely to have changed their behaviour at follow-up (Reed, Wolf, & Barber, 2005). Despite these limitations, TTM remains popular, possibly due to its ease of use (West, 2005).

3.2.6 Risk-Need-Responsivity Model

The Risk-Need-Responsivity (RNR) model was developed to serve as a guideline for assessing and treating offenders (Andrews & Bonta, 2010; Bonta & Andrews, 2017). Much of correctional programming is based on RNR principles (e.g., Matthews, Feagans, & Kohl, 2015; Ternes et al., 2014). Briefly, correctional programming should match the risk and needs of the offenders, and the mode and style of the program should match the learning style and abilities of the offender (Bonta & Andrews, 2017). Specifically, higher risk offenders require higher intensity programming, which generally means increased program hours. Research suggests that a minimum dosage is required for the program to be effective, and risk seems to moderate the relationship between dosage and recidivism (Makarios, Sperber, & Latessa, 2014). Interestingly, research has also shown that providing programming to lower risk offenders actually increases their risk to reoffend, presumably due to low risk offenders adopting antisocial attitudes when they associate with higher risk offenders during program sessions (Lowenkamp & Latessa, 2004). Additionally, targeting an offender's specific criminogenic needs (e.g., procriminal attitudes, substance abuse) reduces recidivism, while targeting non-criminogenic needs (e.g., self-esteem, physical health) can increase recidivism (Andrews & Bonta, 2010). Since most offenders have several criminogenic needs, programs that target multiple criminogenic needs are the most effective at reducing recidivism (Gendreau, French,

& Taylor, 2002). Finally, RNR's responsivity principle suggests that cognitive social learning methods be used to influence behaviour, specifically behavioural interventions that consider the offenders' strengths, learning style, personality, and motivation (Bonta & Andrews, 2017).

Research has repeatedly demonstrated the effectiveness of rehabilitative programming that considers the RNR model. Indeed, one meta-analysis examining correctional programming reported that when risk, needs, and responsivity principles are followed, recidivism is reduced by 28% (Smith, Gendreau, & Schwartz, 2009). Despite strong empirical support for the RNR model, it has received some criticism. For example, some have suggested that the focus on risk reduction makes it difficult to motivate offenders (Mann, Webster, Schofield, & Marshall, 2004). Others have suggested that the RNR model downplays the importance of the therapeutic alliance and noncriminogenic needs, such as personal distress and low self-esteem, which some have argued are necessary for effectively treating offenders (Marshall et al., 2003; Yates, 2003). Finally, while some researchers do not necessarily object to the model, they do argue that, in practice, RNR is often implemented in a way that does not consider individual values and needs, which ignores the principle of responsivity (Ward, Melser, & Yates, 2007). Andrews, Bonta, and Wormith (2011) maintain that these critiques reflect a cursory understanding of the RNR model. For example, according to the RNR model, motivation and addressing noncriminogenic needs are primary aspects of responsivity that may be very important in treating some offenders.

3.3   Diagnosis and Assessment

In correctional settings, substance use assessments are conducted mainly for general screening purposes (i.e., to detect current or recent substance use) or to diagnose or assess the severity of a substance use disorder for correctional planning purposes (i.e., treatment or relapse prevention). Several different types of instruments exist to assess the presence of substance use disorders, risk for substance use disorders, or the presence of substance use in offenders. These assessments include clinical assessments, self-report assessments, and biological assessments (i.e., urinalysis). Additionally, readiness to change is often assessed in conjunction with correctional planning. These types of assessments are reviewed below.

3.3.1   Clinical Assessments

The Diagnostic and Statistical Manual of Mental Disorders (DSM-5) contains two different diagnoses that are pertinent to the study of substance use in offenders: Alcohol Use Disorder and Substance Use Disorder (American Psychiatric Association [APA], 2013). The DSM-5 describes Alcohol Use Disorder as being either mild, moderate, or severe, depending on the number of criteria the individual being assessed meets (2–3 symptoms, 4–5 symptoms, and 6+ symptoms respectively) out of the 11 possible symptoms (APA, 2013). Symptoms include craving, tolerance, and withdrawal. Substance Use Disorder is also classified as mild, moderate, or severe depending on the number of criteria expressed by the individual (2–3 criteria, 4–5 criteria, or 6+ criteria respectively) out of 11 possible symptoms (APA, 2013). A diagnostic clinical interview is required to diagnose an individual with a Substance Use Disorder or Alcohol Use Disorder. These interviews are typically time consuming to administer, have been normed on psychiatric populations, and assess a broad spectrum of psychological issues, including substance use (Gifford, Kohlenberg, Piasecki, & Webber, 2004). This type of interview may be structured or unstructured. For unstructured interviews, a mental health professional applies the criteria for substance abuse (i.e., substance abuse, intoxication, and withdrawal) to information obtained in a client interview, along with file information (Gifford et al., 2004). Examples of structured interview protocols include the Structured Clinical Interview for DSM-5, the Alcohol Use Disorder and Associated Disabilities Interview Schedule-5, and the Addiction Severity Index; each is briefly summarized below.

3.3.1.1 Structured Clinical Interview for DSM-5

The Structured Clinical Interview for DSM-5 (SCID-5) is a semi-structured interview guide that was developed to be administered by a clinician or trained mental health professional familiar with the DSM-5 classification and diagnostic criteria to make DSM-5 diagnoses (First, Williams, Karg, & Spitzer, 2015). It is a diagnostic interview, meant to be used for a variety of mental health issues, including substance use disorders. The reliability and validity of the SCID-5 has been well-established (e.g., Shankman et al., 2017). Moreover, it has been suggested that the comprehensive nature of this instrument increases its treatment utility, especially when substance use and other co-occurring conditions are being assessed together (Gifford et al., 2004).

3.3.1.2 The Alcohol Use Disorder and Associated Disabilities Interview Schedule-5

The Alcohol Use Disorder and Associated Disabilities Interview Schedule-5 (AUDADIS-5) is a structured diagnostic interview used to assess alcohol and drug use as well as AUD and SUD (Hasin, Carpenter, McCloud, Smith, & Grant, 1997). The AUDADIS-5 takes into consideration how recently and frequently substance use occurs, as well as the overlap between the use of alcohol and other substances in the determination of alcohol and substance use disorders (Hasin et al., 1997).

The AUDADIS-5 was originally designed for use with the general population, but has since been tested and validated for use in clinical populations, such as with offenders with substance use disorders (Grant et al., 2015; Hasin et al., 1997, 2015). The AUDADIS-5 has shown very good concurrent validity (Hasin et al., 1997, 2015) and excellent reliability (Grant et al., 2015).

3.3.1.3   Addiction Severity Index

The Addiction Severity Index (ASI; McLellan, Luborskey, Woody, & O'Brien, 1980) is a standardized structured interview that is widely used to assess substance use. The ASI assesses alcohol and drug use, as well as a variety of life areas that can precipitate substance use or show the impact of substance use, resulting in scores across six life domains: medical, employment/financial, drug/alcohol use, legal/criminal justice involvement, family/social, and psychological/psychiatric. Although the information gathered using this instrument is usually scored on a computer, the authors oppose computer-based administration, placing great importance on clinical judgement (McLellan, Kushner, Metzger, & Peters, 1992). The reliability and validity of this instrument has been well-established, in both clinical and correctional settings (Allen & Columbus, 1995; Breteler, Van den Hurk, Schippers, & Meerkerk, 1996; Casares-López et al., 2013; Leonhard, Mulvey, Gastfriend, & Schwartz, 2000).

3.3.2   Self-Report Assessments

A large variety of self-report assessment instruments have been developed to measure substance use and addiction. Several of those instruments will be highlighted in the subsequent paragraphs, followed by a general discussion of the strengths and limitations of using self-report assessments to measure substance use.

3.3.2.1   Substance Use Risk Profile Scales

The Substance Use Risk Profile Scales (SURPS) consists of 23 items on four scales assessing four different personality traits related to risk of substance use or abuse; hopelessness, anxiety sensitivity, sensation seeking, and impulsivity (Hopley & Brunelle, 2016). SURPS was originally validated using a male offender sample, but has since been validated or assessed for use on individuals of different cultures, ages, and genders (Hopley & Brunelle, 2016; Jurk et al., 2015; Memetovic, Ratner, Gotay, & Richardson, 2016; Omiya, Kobori, Tomoto, Igarashi, & Iyo, 2015; Saliba, Moran, & Yoo, 2014), although certain subscales or items have less validation and more research is still necessary in order to rectify these issues.

3.3.2.2 Alcohol Use Disorders Identification Test

The Alcohol Use Disorders Identification Test (AUDIT; Babor, de la Fuente, Saunders, & Grant, 1992) is a 10-item scale that aims to identify problematic drinking behaviour through an assessment of consumption patterns, dependence symptoms, and the extent to which alcohol use has interfered with life activities. Originally developed for medical settings, the AUDIT has also been used in correctional settings in many different countries, showing strong reliability and validity (e.g., Almarri, Oei, & Amir, 2009; Baltieri, 2014; Coulton et al., 2012), although some researchers have suggested that the AUDIT does not adequately account for incarcerated offender drinking norms, which are very different from the drinking patterns in the general population (Durbeej et al., 2010; Sondhi, Birch, Lynch, Holloway, & Newbury-Birch, 2016).

3.3.2.3 Michigan Alcoholism Screening Test

The Michigan Alcoholism Screening Test (MAST; Selzer, 1971) is a 25-item scale designed to measure a variety of issues related to alcohol abuse, focussing on the extent of psycho-social interference or negative consequences of problematic alcohol use. The MAST has been shown to reliably differentiate between alcoholics and nonalcoholics in a variety of settings, including correctional settings (Boland, Henderson, & Baker, 1998; Kunic, 2006; Kunic & Grant, 2006).

3.3.2.4 Alcohol Dependence Scale

The Alcohol Dependence Scale (ADS; Skinner & Horn, 1984) is a 25-item self-report assessment designed to assess the degree of physiological dependence to alcohol. Specifically, the ADS is meant to measure of the extent to which alcohol use has progressed from psychological involvement to impaired control. The ADS has been established as reliable and valid in a correctional context (Boland et al., 1998; Kunic, 2006; Kunic & Grant, 2006).

3.3.2.5 Drug Abuse Screening Test

Paralleling the MAST, the Drug Abuse Screening Test (DAST; Skinner, 1982) is a 20-item scale that assesses the extent to which drug use has interfered with psycho-social functioning in the recent past. Research on the DAST has established it as a reliable and valid assessment to be used in a correctional context (Boland et al., 1998; Kunic, 2006; Kunic & Grant, 2006).

3.3.2.6   The Severity of Dependence Scale

The Severity of Dependence Scale (SDS; Gossop et al., 1995) measures the psychological dimensions of addiction, such as an individual's preoccupation and anxiety about substance use and impaired control, focusing on the substance used most in the recent past (according to self-report). The SDS shows high reliability and validity with samples of heroin users, cocaine users, and amphetamine users (Gossop et al., 1995), and has been shown to be effective in a correctional context (Kunic, 2006; Kunic & Grant, 2006; Rogerson, Jacups, & Caltabiano, 2016).

3.3.2.7   Summary of Self-Report Assessments

Overall, self-report screening instruments are widely used because of their ease of use, efficiency, cost-effectiveness, and, most importantly, they have been shown to reliably and validly screen for issues related to substance use (Coulton et al., 2012). For example, Correctional Service Canada has used the DAST to establish the severity of drug use for almost 30 years, as part of the intake assessment process (Kunic & Grant, 2006). Using these types of measures helps to correctly match offenders to the appropriate levels of treatment, consistent with the principles of effective correctional treatment (Bonta & Andrews, 2017). However, self-report may not always be truthful or accurate, and thus, these instruments may be most effective when used in conjunction with another assessment of substance abuse that does not rely on self-report (Hopley & Brunelle, 2016).

3.3.3   Biological Assessments

Laboratory tests that detect substances in blood, saliva, perspiration, hair, and urine can be useful for screening and confirming drug and alcohol use, and can support self-report assessments. The most common type of laboratory drug testing in correctional contexts is urinalysis (MacPherson, 2004; Ternes & MacPherson, 2014). Urine testing is commonly used to determine the use of alcohol and drugs by inmates during their incarceration. England randomly tests 10% of their prison population each month, as does the United States in their maximum security institutions. In addition to testing maximum security institutions, the United States also tests 3% of minimum security institution inmates and 5% of the remaining institutions randomly each month. In Canada, 5% of the federally incarcerated inmates are tested via urinalysis each month (MacPherson, 2004; Ternes & MacPherson, 2014).

Depending on where the urinalysis is conducted, urine either goes through an immunoassay, or a gas-chromatography/mass-spectrometry (GC/MS) analysis for each drug group being assessed. In Canada, GC/MS is the method of analysis selected and is the gold standard assessment since it is the most accurate and precise confirmation test for drug presence (MacPherson, 2004). However, agreement between immunoassay and GC/MS is high for adults with drugs use disorders with 93% agreement for cocaine and 98% agreement for methamphetamines, amphetamines, marijuana, and opiates (McDonell et al., 2016).

3.3.4 Assessing Readiness to Change

Assessment instruments focused on readiness to change attempt to measure how motivated a person is to change problematic behaviours, including substance use. A number of questionnaires have been developed to assess readiness or motivation to change over the past several decades, with the most popular being the University of Rhode Island Change Assessment (URICA; McConnaughy, Prochaska, & Velicer, 1983), Stages of Change Readiness and Treatment Eagerness Scale (SOCRATES; Miller & Tonigan, 1996), and the Readiness to Change Questionnaire (RCQ; Rollnick, Heather, Gold, & Hall, 1992). All of these scales were developed to measure how well the respondent fits into each of the stages of change described by Prochaska and DiClemente's (1992) Transtheoretical Model of behavioural change. Each of these measures effectively categorize respondents into groups generally consistent with the stages of change (e.g., Carney & Kivlahan, 1995; DiClemente et al., 1991; Isenhart, 1994; Ko et al., 2009; Willoughby & Edens, 1996). However, none of these measures seems to work effectively for all problematic behaviours, and the various measures do not always classify the same individuals into the same stage of change (Belding, Iguchi, & Lamb, 1997; Carey, Purnine, Maisto, & Carey, 1999). These measures are also limited by the biases always present in self-report questionnaires, namely, they are only effective when the respondent replies accurately and honestly to questions. Additionally, stage status is difficult to assess since it is a dynamic state (Connors et al., 2015). Some researchers have recommended that considering personality characteristics as well as stages of change would improve treatment readiness assessments (D'Sylva, Graffam, Hardcastle, & Shinkfield, 2012).

Despite these limitations, many jurisdictions continue to assess readiness to change substance using behaviours in their incarcerated populations based on its perceived importance for determining treatment match and because motivation to change predicts treatment retention (Brocato & Wagner, 2008; Polaschek, Anstiss, & Wilson, 2010; Ternes & Johnson, 2014). Psychometric research on these measures that focuses on their application to problematic substance use behaviours among correctional samples is scarce, although the limited research does generally support the validity and reliability of the measures (e.g., Ko et al., 2009; Polaschek et al., 2010). Since these measures seem to be used widely in corrections, it is hoped that future researchers further investigate the reliability and validity of these tools among substance using offenders.

3.4   Interventions: What Works, What Might Work, and What Doesn't Work

Correctional substance use treatment programs aim to improve public safety by reducing substance use and crime. Several modes of treatment have shown some success in achieving these goals, including cognitive behavioural therapy, therapeutic communities, opioid substitution therapy, motivational interviewing, and 12-step programs. Each of these treatment methods will be briefly reviewed below, followed by a summary to reflect on which interventions are most effective.

3.4.1   Cognitive Behavioural Therapy

Cognitive behavioural therapy (CBT) is a widely accepted and empirically supported form of psychotherapy, and is used for a variety of disorders and problems. CBT is a process in which maladaptive behaviours or thought patterns are identified, and the client and therapist work towards modifying behaviours or thought patterns in an effort to replace maladaptive thoughts or behaviours with positive ones. Based on SLM's premise that substance use is a learned behaviour, CBT interventions involve identifying the precipitants of habitual substance use and providing the client with effective coping responses (Witkiewitz, Marlatt, & Walker, 2005). The goal is for the individual battling a substance use disorder to use adaptive coping mechanisms learned in CBT in response to high-risk situations (e.g., meeting a friend he or she used to do drugs with), thus increasing self-efficacy and decreasing the probability of relapse (Marlatt & Gordon, 1985). CBT strategies are useful in that they provide clients with self-management skills necessary to avoid relapse, allowing individuals to effectively function independently (Witkiewitz et al., 2005).

Many studies have shown the efficacy of CBT as a treatment option for those with substance use disorder. Several meta-analyses have found a moderate effect size of CBT on a diverse range of substance use disorders (Dutra et al., 2008; Magill & Ray, 2009). Across the studies included in the meta-analysis conducted by Dutra et al. (2008), roughly one-third of participants dropped out prior to completing treatment, showing a lack of strength in retention rates compared to other treatments. Some have suggested that using CBT in conjunction with pharmacotherapy treatments may allow for a more robust result (McHugh, Hearon, & Otto, 2010). For example, Rawson et al. (2002) found that CBT produces long-term management of substance use in a sample of cocaine dependent participants who were receiving methadone maintenance treatment, with 60% of CBT participants providing clean toxicology exams at a 52-week follow-up. Additionally, Moeller et al. (2007) found CBT combined with antidepressant Citalopram successfully treated cocaine dependant individuals.

In a meta-analysis of treatment programs available to offenders completed by Bahr et al. (2012), it was found that participants who received CBT had reduced rates of both drug use and recidivism. Additionally, in a large sample of drug users from both men's and women's federal prisons in the United States, Pelissier et al. (2001) found only 29% of participants who received a CBT intervention showed evidence of substance use 6 months post-release, while only 12.5% of participants were arrested in the 6 months following their release. Evidence shows that CBT seems to be an effective treatment for substance use in corrections, reducing drug use and increasing desistance (McMurran, 2007).

3.4.2 Therapeutic Communities

Therapeutic communities are residential programs occurring within a prison system. Individuals live with a small group of offenders (peers) and facilitators, including psychologists and prison officers, and are isolated from the rest of the prison population (Inciardi, Martin, & Butzin, 2004; Stevens, 2014). In these small groups, individuals undergo unstructured small group therapy focused on resolving issues that may be contributing to their substance use and offending, and are encouraged to confront each other when they observe anti-social, criminal, or substance use behaviours in other participants (Inciardi et al., 2004; Stevens, 2014). The in-prison portion of therapeutic communities lasts approximately 12 months, but may be extended if the individual requires more time, and is followed by transitional or aftercare programs in the community once the offender is released (Inciardi et al., 2004). With an emphasis on community, therapeutic communities are heavily influenced by the SLM of behaviour change.

Therapeutic communities have been found to be effective in many ways. Not only do these communities help decrease recidivism and substance use, they also help to ameliorate the relationships and social functioning of those who participate in the program (Hiller, Knight, Saum, & Simpson, 2006; Hiller, Knight, & Simpson, 1999; Mackenzie & Hickman, 2000). Being given additional responsibilities also helps community members obtain confidence in their abilities, and in turn make them more self-sufficient (Stevens, 2014). These responsibilities also help individuals find stable living conditions and employment post-release and help them to be able to more effectively cope with pressures they may experience after release (Galassi, Mpofu, & Athanasou, 2015; Hiller et al., 1999). Due to the family atmosphere expected within these groups, individuals partaking lose the fear that their weaknesses will be used against them and are challenged in their distrust of authority figures (Stevens, 2014).

In a meta-analysis of the efficacy of four therapeutic communities in the United States, Bullock (2003) found that completing the full program led to a decrease in the rate of recidivism in offenders. Moreover, participating in transitional and aftercare programs, in addition to the in-prison program, led to greater reductions in recidivism and relapse than participating in just the in-prison therapeutic community program (Bullock, 2003; Galassi et al., 2015; Inciardi et al., 2004). In addition, time in the therapeutic community program was negatively associated with risk taking and positively associated with social conformity (Hiller et al., 2006).

Limitations of therapeutic communities include the hostility of individuals towards facilitators and other members of the community in which they live. Hostility is related to dropping out of treatment early, and tends to increase within the first 90 days of treatment as individuals become accustomed to the confrontational approach used in the community (Hiller et al., 2006). Hiller et al. (2006) also determined that women were more likely to drop out earlier than males, perhaps due to their inability to cope with the confrontation that occurs during treatment within the community.

3.4.3 Opioid Substitution Therapy

Opioid substitution treatment (OST) is considered the best practice for treatment of opioid dependency (Oviedo-Joekes et al., 2009), and is currently the most common treatment for opioid users in Canada (Popova, Rehm, & Fischer, 2006; World Health Organization, United Nations Office on Drugs and Crime, & Joint United Nations Programme on HIV/AIDS, 2004). Based mainly on the biopsychological model, OST involves the use of medicinal opioids such as methadone, buprenorphine, or buprenorphine-naloxone under medical supervision, allowing opioid users to better manage detoxification (WHO et al., 2004). Without substitution therapies, opioid users are at a high risk of reverting to opioid use after detoxification, and users who are forced to abstain without OST are vulnerable to overdose, drug emergencies, and death (Kastelic, Pont, & Stöver, 2009; Volkow, Frieden, Hyde, & Cha, 2014; WHO et al., 2004). Opioid substitutions act on the opioid receptors in the brain for long periods of time, reducing withdrawal symptoms and cravings, and avoiding the consequences of illegal opioid use, such as respiratory depression and euphoric responses (Kastelic et al., 2009; WHO, 2004). Typically, opioid users participate in OST with regular doses for more than six months in order to improve brain functioning and prevent craving and withdrawal symptoms. Alternatively, OST can be prescribed over a short period of time using decreasing doses for quick detoxification and treatment of withdrawal symptoms during detoxification (WHO et al., 2004).

The benefits of OST are multi-faceted. Aside from reducing the number of overdoses and opioid related deaths, providing opioid users with substitution therapy increases retention in treatment, improves social-functioning, and lessens the risk of diseases common to intravenous drugs such as Hepatitis C and Human Immunodeficiency Virus (HIV) (Johnson, 2001; Oviedo-Joekes et al., 2009; Volkow et al., 2014). Further, OST provides a safer, more cost-effective solution to opioid dependency for both the opioid user and the community (Warren et al., 2006; WHO et al., 2004).

In terms of correctional use of OST, research has shown that inmates who were provided with OST were less likely to act violently, use illegal drugs during or after incarceration, and were less likely to be re-incarcerated (Johnson, 2001; Johnson, van de Ven, & Grant, 2001; MacSwain, Farrell MacDonald, & Cheverie, 2014; WHO et al., 2004). Further, implementation of OST in prisons has been correlated with improved manageability of inmates: those who were on an OST program were less likely to be placed in segregation during their incarceration period and were more involved in education and employment programs (Cheverie, MacSwain, Farrell MacDonald, & Johnson, 2014; Johnson et al., 2001). The effects of OST are strengthened when combined with counseling and/or contingency management strategies (Epstein et al., 2009; Kinlock, Gordon, Schwartz, & O'Grady, 2008).

3.4.4 Motivational Interviewing

Based on the TTM, motivational interviewing (MI) is described as a client-centred approach to treatment with the intention of strengthening intrinsic motivation to modify maladaptive behaviours (Smedslund et al., 2011). Therapists providing MI are guided by four principles: (1) express empathy, (2) support self-efficacy, (3) roll with resistance, and (4) develop discrepancy. Therapists must show empathy and see their client's point of view, and must support self-efficacy by encouraging clients to take responsibility for actions, whether inhibiting or facilitating change. Further, therapists must roll with resistance, meaning that the therapist must not challenge client resistance, but explore the client's views by allowing resistance to be voiced. Finally, a discrepancy between the client's current behaviour (e.g., substance use) and the goals the client has for the future (e.g., abstaining from substance use) are developed and acknowledged in order to facilitate motivation for change (Smedslund et al., 2011). MI is meant to be a short-term treatment to encourage critical consideration of the client's problem, and is commonly applied in substance use treatment, in particular treatment for alcohol use (e.g., Carroll, Ball, et al., 2006; Carroll, Easton, et al., 2006; Kavanagh et al., 2004; McCambridge & Strang, 2004). In addition, MI has commonly been employed in response to substance use in correctional settings (McMurran, 2009). McMurran (2009) found in her meta-analysis the main purposes for MI use were to improve treatment retention and engagement, enhance motivation for change, and to alter maladaptive behaviours.

While MI seems to improve treatment retention (Carroll, Ball, et al., 2006; Carroll et al., 2009; Kavanagh et al., 2004), evidence regarding its effectiveness at reducing substance use is mixed. For example, Carroll et al. (Carroll, Ball, et al., 2006; Carroll et al., 2009) found that there was no difference in substance use in those who received MI compared to those who received treatment as usual. Alternatively, Kavanagh et al. (2004) found in a small sample of individuals suffering from recent-onset psychosis, those who received MI interventions were able to manage substance use better. Although results seem inconclusive, Smedslund et al.

(2011) conducted a meta-analysis including 59 studies between 1993 and 2010, and found MI had a significant effect in treating substance use in comparison to no treatment. The effect was significant immediately following the MI intervention, as well as during short-term and medium-term follow-up, but there was no significant effect during long-term follow-up (Smedslund et al., 2011).

Similar to MI use in the general population, there are mixed results in terms of behavioural change in response to MI in correctional settings. Some articles show a significant reduction in substance use (Miles, Dutheil, Welsby, & Haider, 2007) and improved attitudes toward crime and substance use (Harper & Hardy, 2000) in response to MI interventions. Alternatively, Carroll, Easton, et al. (2006) found MI only reduced substance use when paired with other treatment such as contingency management (i.e., incentives contingent on producing clean urinalysis or attending sessions) indicating that MI on its own is not effective as a substance use treatment. It is difficult to deduce whether MI is an effective intervention to employ in correctional settings or the general population in order to reduce substance use, as much of the literature is conflicting.

3.4.5   Twelve-Step Approaches

Twelve-step programs are a classic approach to treating addiction and stem from the Alcoholics Anonymous (AA) rehabilitation model (McKay, 2009), which now also includes Narcotics Anonymous (NA), and Cocaine Anonymous (CA). Twelve-step approaches are self-help programs where members are invited to share and listen to personal stories of problems related to substance use. With a cognitive-behavioral orientation and theoretical grounding in SLM, attendees of 12-step programs receive a mentor who has gone through the program before them, and once they have completed enough of the program themselves, have the option to become a mentor for an incoming participant (Magaletta & Leukefeld, 2011; McKay, 2009). As of January 2017, over 1400 AA groups with approximately 35,000 members regularly meet in correctional facilities throughout the U.S. and Canada, making self-help programs the most frequently offered and used criminal justice substance abuse programs (Alcoholics Anonymous, 2017).

These programs require total abstinence from drugs and alcohol, and participants who do not maintain abstinence are either removed from the program or must start the program from the beginning upon resuming abstinence (Donovan, Ingalsbe, Benbow, & Daley, 2013; Martin, Player, & Liriano, 2003). Members are expected to learn and practice the 12 steps of the programs that focus around addiction acceptance and spiritual belief (Center for Substance Abuse Treatment, 1999). Twelve-step approaches are based on the fundamental assumptions that addiction is an incurable illness that may be managed, that addiction is chronic and cumulative, and that recovery is staged and progressive, requiring long-term treatments (Bullock, 2003; McKay, 2009). Moreover, 12-step approaches stress the importance of the spiritual experience to recovery from addiction. It is believed that it is through the spiritual experience that one can take another point of view and do what was previously impossible; that is, change one's whole lifestyle so that substance use is no longer a part of daily life (Magaletta & Leukefeld, 2011).

Twelve-step approaches have been found to be effective for community members who regularly attend meetings and abide by the 12-steps. Donovan et al. (2013), determined that roughly 33% of individuals who participated in AA, NA, or CA 12-step programs remained abstinent for 1–5 years. Individuals who participated in more meetings and who participated more frequently at the meetings they attended were more likely to remain abstinent than those who attended meetings infrequently, or who attended meetings, but did not actively participate in the meetings.

Within the prison system, 12-step approaches may be conducted as intensive programs, lasting between 10 and 12 weeks (Bullock, 2003). Few researchers have examined the efficacy of these approaches in prisons, however, the little scientific evidence that exists suggests mixed results. Some researchers have found that graduates of these programs show reductions in drug use and offending upon release (Fiorentine, 1999; Martin et al., 2003), while others have found that 12-step approaches are less effective than other treatment approaches in reducing drug use and recidivism (Bahr et al., 2012; Carroll, Easton, et al., 2006; Zanis et al., 2003).

One major limitation of 12-step programs is their one-size-fits-all approach to treatment (McKay, 2009), which assumes that all individuals are ready and willing to change, or that those who are not ready may be confronted and convinced to change. Research shows that an unwillingness to change decreases the effectiveness of 12-step approaches (Donovan et al., 2013; Martin et al., 2003). Additionally, those who do not relate to the religious or philosophical aspects of 12-step approaches have a harder time relating to the treatment and have less success completing the program (McKay, 2009). Specific limitations exist in the use of 12-step approaches with youth, who have higher dropout rates than adult attendees, perhaps because they are unable to relate to adult struggles, incomplete brain development, boredom, and difficulty abstaining completely from alcohol or drugs (Donovan et al., 2013). Finally, the high dropout rate for 12-step approaches has limited research in this area, contributing to a selection bias (Bahr et al., 2012). Despite these limitations, the prevalence and continued popularity of 12-step approaches suggest a level of success. For incarcerated offenders, the experience component of 12-step approaches, where individuals review their whole self and their behaviour, has the potential to address problematic lifestyle choices, including criminogenic risk factors (Magaletta & Leukefeld, 2011). There is a need for more research in this area to link the 12-step approach with criminogenic risk-need theories.

3.4.6 Treatment Summary

It seems that cognitive-behavioural treatment, therapeutic communities, motivational interviewing, 12-step approaches, and opioid substitution therapy can effectively help reduce drug use, institutional violence, and recidivism among incarcerated offenders. The most effective method may be combining types of therapy, followed by community maintenance sessions upon release from custody (e.g., Bahr et al., 2012; McHugh et al., 2010; McLellan et al., 1996). For example, in a large-scale study, Doherty et al. (2014) found that incarcerated offenders who completed a substance use program based on social cognitive theory, relapse prevention therapy, and cognitive behavioural therapy showed reductions in institutional misconduct and recidivism. Interestingly, community aftercare upon release was a key component in recidivism reduction for offenders in this study: when participation in community aftercare and release type were considered, the association between program participation and recidivism became nonsignificant. Offenders who did not participate in community aftercare were 45% more likely to return to custody.

3.5 Future Implications

Prison substance abuse treatment primarily aims to reduce recidivism. It seems clear that to achieve that goal, these programs must do more than simply address problematic substance use or addiction; effective substance abuse programs must address the many interacting factors that work with problematic substance use to contribute to crime. Future research should continue to assess for these factors so treatment providers and those developing programs know which factors to address.

It seems that the most effective programs are those that combine intervention techniques and theoretical perspectives to treat addiction, as well as increase treatment readiness and address criminogenic factors (e.g., Bahr et al., 2012). Although some jurisdictions have successfully implemented such programs (e.g., Doherty et al., 2014), other jurisdictions have struggled to meet the needs of offenders with substance use disorders (e.g., Taxman, Perdoni, & Caudy, 2013). It is recommended that correctional administrators expand substance abuse treatment practices by implementing programming matched to offender risk and need (Taxman et al., 2013).

Since it seems that the most effective programs are those that address a variety of problematic factors, some jurisdictions have developed integrated program models to meet various criminogenic needs (Motiuk, 2016). Having one program take the place of multiple programs (e.g., life skills, violence prevention, substance abuse, etc.) should enhance the management and efficiency of correctional programs, as well as allow greater capacity for offenders to access and complete relevant programs (Motiuk & Vuong, 2016). Preliminary research on such programs has found mixed results. While some research suggests that offenders who complete an integrated program are less likely to recidivate than offenders who complete other programs (Motiuk, 2016; Motiuk & Vuong, 2016), other research was less conclusive (Correctional Service Canada [CSC], 2013). Before recommendations can be made regarding implementing programs that target multiple criminogenic needs, more research should be conducted regarding the effectiveness of such programs.

A significant portion of offenders enrolled in a substance abuse program fail to complete the program, which is associated with increased recidivism (e.g., Doherty et al., 2014; McMurran & Theodosi, 2007; Richer, Lemelin, & Ternes, 2014). Interestingly, research shows that mandating offenders to treatment improves treatment completion rates, which reduces illicit drug use and recidivism (e.g., Coviello et al., 2013; McSweeney, Stevens, Hunt, & Turnbill, 2007; Perron & Bright, 2008). Correctional administrators should keep in mind that mandated treatment may improve treatment compliance.

3.6 Technology and Innovation

One of the most influential technological advancements in the management of incarcerated offenders who use substances is the introduction of computerized assessments. Although not necessarily new (i.e., CSC has been using computerized assessments since the late 1980s; CSC, 1990), the use of computerized assessments is efficient and effective. For example, CSC uses the Computerized Assessment of Substance Abuse (CASA) as part of their offender intake assessment to determine substance use within Canadian offenders (Kunic, 2006; Kunic & Grant, 2006). In addition to standardized measures to assess substance use (i.e., ADS, Skinner & Horn, 1984; DAST, Skinner, 1982), it assesses for other factors relevant to understanding substance use among offenders, such as links between substance use and offending, injection drug use, family-related drug use, and history of substance use treatment. During the completion of the online assessment, CASA detects major inconsistencies between answers and where they occur, and gives the offender a chance to rectify the inconsistency by pointing it out. It also gives individuals with reading difficulty an audio option to assist them in the completion of the assessment. At the end of the report, summary scores, severity level, and recommended treatment are automatically generated (Kunic & Grant, 2006). CASA has been used to effectively match treatment intensity with treatment need (e.g., Doherty et al., 2014; Ternes et al., 2014), as well as for profiling substance-using offenders (e.g., Cheverie, MacSwain, et al., 2014; Farrell MacDonald et al., 2015). Although the use of CASA is currently limited to Canada, researchers from other jurisdictions have also looked into computerized assessments for substance use, finding them easy to use and effective (e.g., King et al., 2017; Spear, Shedlin, Gilberti, Fiellin, & McNeely, 2016: Wolff & Shi, 2015).

While computerized assessment practices have been around for a while, computerized treatment practices are relatively new. Recent research suggests that computerized interventions may be as effective as in-person interventions at addressing substance use (Chaple et al., 2014; Schwartz et al., 2014). Additionally, several studies have found that combining OST with computer-delivered CBT was more effective in reducing problematic substance use than OST alone in community samples of drug-dependent individuals (Carroll et al., 2014; Christensen et al., 2014;

Kiluk et al., 2017). Although these results are preliminary and require further validation, this innovation could be promising for the future of treatment delivery among the correctional population, especially for community maintenance.

3.7 Conclusion

Substance use is widespread, especially in the correctional environment, where most incarcerated offenders have substance use disorders. While many theories have been developed to explain problematic substance use, none completely explain substance use or addiction on their own. It seems that the best theories to account for substance use are those that combine biological and psychological theories. Since it takes a combination of theories to best explain substance use, it is intuitive that the most effective interventions are those that draw on a variety of theories to address substance use, as well as the factors that interact with substance use to contribute to criminal behaviour. There has already been a plethora of research on problematic substance use among offenders. As the issues are likely to continue, research will surely continue as well, improving upon treatment and assessment methods to decrease substance use and criminal behaviour.

References

Alcoholics Anonymous. (2017). *Estimates of AA groups and members* [on-line]. Retrieved February 11, 2018, from https://www.aa.org/assets/en_US/smf-53_en.pdf

Allen, J. P., & Columbus, M. (1995). *Assessing alcohol problems: A guide for clinicians and researchers. National Institute on Alcohol Abuse and Alcoholism Treatment Handbook Series 4*. Bethesda, MD: National Institutes of Health.

Almarri, T. S. K., Oei, T. P. S., & Amir, T. (2009). Validation of the Alcohol Use Identification Test in a prison sample living in the Arabian Gulf region. *Substance Use & Misuse, 44*(14), 2001–2013.

American Psychiatric Association. (2013). *Diagnostic and statistical manual of mental disorders* (5th ed.). Arlington, VA: American Psychiatric Association.

Andrews, D. A., & Bonta, J. (2010). Rehabilitating criminal justice policy and practice. *Psychology, Public Policy, and Law, 16*, 39–55.

Andrews, D. A., Bonta, J., & Wormith, J. S. (2011). The Risk-Need-Responsivity (RNR) model: Does adding the Good Lives Model contribute to effective crime prevention? *Criminal Justice and Behavior, 38*(7), 735–755.

Babor, T. F., de la Fuente, J. R., Saunders, J., & Grant, M. (1992). *AUDIT. The Alcohol Use Disorders Identification Test. Guidelines for use in primary health care*. Geneva, Switzerland: World Health Organization.

Bahr, S. J., Masters, A. L., & Taylor, B. M. (2012). What works in substance abuse treatment programs for offenders? *The Prison Journal, 92*(2), 155–174.

Baltieri, D. A. (2014). Predictors of drug use in prison among women convicted of violent crimes. *Criminal Behaviour and Mental Health, 24*, 113–128.

Bandura, A. (1971). *Social learning theory*. New York, NY: General Learning Press.

Baumeister, R. F., Heatherton, T. F., & Tice, D. M. (1994). *Losing control: How and why people fail at self-regulation*. San Diego, CA: Academic Press.

Belding, M., Iguchi, M., & Lamb, R. (1997). Stages and processes of change as predictors of drug use among methadone maintenance patients. *Experimental and Clinical Psychology, 5*, 65–73.

Boland, F. J., Henderson, K., & Baker, J. (1998). *Case needs review: Substance abuse domain* (R-76). Ottawa, ON: Correctional Service Canada.

Bonta, J., & Andrews, D. A. (2017). *The psychology of criminal conduct* (6th ed.). New York, NY: Routledge.

Breteler, M. H., Van den Hurk, A. A., Schippers, G. M., & Meerkerk, G. J. (1996). Enrollment in a drug-free detention program: The prediction of successful behavior change of drug-using inmates. *Addictive Behavior, 21*(5), 665–669.

Brocato, J., & Wagner, E. F. (2008). Predictors of retention in an alternative-to-prison substance abuse treatment program. *Criminal Justice and Behavior, 35*(1), 99–119.

Bullock, T. (2003). Key findings from the literature on the effectiveness of drug treatment in prison. In M. Ramsay (Ed.), *Prisoners' drug use and treatment: Seven research studies* (pp. 71–91). London, UK: Home Office.

Carey, K. B., Purnine, D. M., Maisto, S. A., & Carey, M. P. (1999). Assessing readiness to change substance abuse: A critical review of instruments. *Clinical Psychology: Science and Practice, 6*, 245–266.

Carney, M. M., & Kivlahan, D. R. (1995). Motivational subtypes among veterans seeking substance abuse treatment: Profiles based on stages of change. *Psychology of Addictive Behaviors, 9*(2), 135–142.

Carroll, K. M., Ball, S. A., Nich, C., Martino, S., Frankforter, T. L., Farentinos, C., … Woody, G. E. (2006). Motivational interviewing to improve treatment engagement and outcome in individuals seeking treatment for substance abuse: A multisite effectiveness study. *Drug and Alcohol Dependence, 81*, 301–312.

Carroll, K. M., Easton, C. J., Nich, C., Hunkele, K. A., Neavins, T. M., Sinha, R., … Rounsaville, B. J. (2006). The use of contingency management and motivational/skills-building therapy to treat young adults with marijuana dependence. *Journal of Consulting and Clinical Psychology, 74*(5), 955–966.

Carroll, K. M., Kiluk, B. D., Nich, C., Gordon, M. A., Portney, G. A., Marino, D. R., & Ball, S. A. (2014). Computer-assisted delivery of Cognitive-Behavioral Therapy: Efficacy and durability of CBT4CBT among cocaine-dependent individuals maintained on methadone. *American Journal of Psychiatry, 171*(4), 436–444.

Carroll, K. M., Martino, S., Ball, S. A., Nich, C., Frankforter, T., Anez, L. M., … Farentinos, C. (2009). A multisite randomized trial of motivational enhancement therapy for Spanish-speaking substance users. *Journal of Consulting and Clinical Psychology, 77*(5), 993–999.

Casares-López, M. J., González-Menéndez, A., Festinger, D. S., Fernández-Garcia, P., Fernández-Hermida, J. R., Secades, R., & Matejkowski, J. (2013). Predictors of retention in a drug-free unit/substance abuse treatment in prison. *International Journal of Law & Psychiatry, 36*(3/4), 264–272.

Caudy, M. S., Folk, J. B., Stuewig, J. B., Wooditch, A., Martinez, A., Maass, S., … Taxman, F. S. (2015). Does substance misuse moderate the relationship between criminal thinking and recidivism? *Journal of Criminal Justice, 43*, 12–19.

Center for Substance Abuse Treatment. (1999). *Treatment of adolescents with substance use disorders*. Rockville, MD: Substance Abuse and Mental Health Services Administration (US).

Chaple, M., Sacks, S., McKendrick, K., Marsch, L. A., Belenko, S., Leukefeld, C., … French, M. (2014). Feasibility of a computerized intervention for offenders with substance use disorders: A research note. *Journal of Experimental Criminology, 10*(1), 105–127.

Cheverie, M., MacSwain, M., Farrell MacDonald, S., & Johnson, S. (2014). *Institutional adjustment of methadone maintenance treatment program (MMTP) participants* (R-323). Ottawa, ON: Correctional Service of Canada.

Cheverie, M., Ternes, M, & Farrell MacDonald, S. (2014). *Characteristics, institutional adjustment and post-release success of drug and drug users* (R-299). Ottawa, ON: Correctional Service of Canada.

Christensen, D. R., Landes, R. D., Jackson, L., Marsch, L. A., Mancino, M. J., Chopra, M. P., & Bickel, W. K. (2014). Adding an Internet-delivered treatment to an efficacious treatment package for opioid dependence. *Journal of Consulting and Clinical Psychology, 82*(6), 964–972.

Connors, G. J., DiClemente, C. C., Velasquez, M. M., & Donovan, D. M. (2015). *Substance abuse treatment and the stages of change* (2nd ed.). New York, NY: Guilford Press.

Correctional Service Canada. (1990). Assessing offender substance-abuse problems at reception: Preliminary findings from the computerized lifestyle assessment instrument. *Forum on Corrections Research, 2,* 11–14.

Correctional Service Canada. (2013). *A study of the efficiency and effectiveness of the Integrated Correctional Program Model (ICPM)*. Ottawa, ON: Author.

Coulton, S., Newbury-Birch, D., Cassidy, P., Dale, V., Deluca, P., Gilvarry, E., … Drummond, C. (2012). Screening for alcohol use in criminal justice settings: An exploratory study. *Alcohol and Alcoholism, 47*(4), 423–427.

Coviello, D. M., Zanis, D. A., Wesnoski, S. A., Palman, N., Gur, A., Lynch, K. G., & McKay, J. R. (2013). Does mandating offenders to treatment improve completions rates? *Journal of Substance Abuse Treatment, 44,* 417–425.

D'Sylva, F., Graffam, J., Hardcastle, L., & Shinkfield, A. J. (2012). Analysis of the stages of change model of drug and alcohol treatment readiness among prisoners. *International Journal of Offender Therapy and Comparative Criminology, 56*(2), 265–280.

DiClemente, C. C., Prochaska, J. O., Fairhurst, S. K., Velicer, W. F., Valesquez, M. M., & Rossi, J. S. (1991). The process of smoking cessation: An analysis of precontemplation, contemplation, and preparation stages of change. *Journal of Consulting Clinical Psychology, 59*(2), 295–304.

Doherty, S., Ternes, M., & Matheson, F.I. (2014). *An examination of the effectiveness of the National Substance Abuse Program High Intensity (NSAP-H) on Institutional Adjustment and Post-Release Outcomes* (R-290). Ottawa, ON: Correctional Service of Canada.

Donovan, D. M., Ingalsbe, M. H., Benbow, J., & Daley, D. C. (2013). 12-Step interventions and mutual support programs for substance use disorders: An overview. *Social Work in Public Health, 28*(3–4), 313–332.

Durbeej, N., Berman, A. H., Gumpert, C. H., Palmstierna, T., Kristiansson, M., & Alm, C. (2010). Validation of the Alcohol Use Disorders Identification Test and the Drug Use Disorders Identification Test in a Swedish sample of suspected offenders with signs of mental health problems: Results from the Mental Disorder, Substance Abuse and Crime study. *Journal of Substance Abuse Treatment, 39*(4), 364–377.

Dutra, L., Stathopoulou, G., Basden, S. L., Leyro, T. M., Powers, M. B., & Otto, M. W. (2008). A meta-analytic review of psychosocial interventions for substance use disorders. *American Journal of Psychiatry, 165*(2), 179–187.

Epstein, D. H., Schmittner, J., Umbricht, A., Schroeder, J. R., Moolchan, E. T., & Preston, K. L. (2009). Promoting abstinence from cocaine and heroin with a methadone dose increase and a novel contingency. *Drug and Alcohol Dependence, 101,* 92–100.

Etter, J., & Sutton, S. (2002). Assessing 'stage of change' in current and former smokers. *Addiction, 97*(9), 1171–1182.

Farrell MacDonald, S. (2014). *Severity of substance use, discretionary release, and return to federal custody* (RS-14-19). Ottawa, ON: Correctional Service Canada.

Farrell MacDonald, S., Gobeil, R., Biro, S. M., Ritchie, M. B., & Curno, J. (2015). *Women offenders, substance use, and behaviour* (R-358). Ottawa, ON: Correctional Service of Canada.

Fazel, S., Bains, P., & Doll, H. (2006). Substance abuse and dependence in prisoners: A systematic review. *Addiction, 101,* 181–191.

Fiorentine, R. (2009). After drug treatment: Are 12-Step programs effective in maintaining abstinence?. *The American Journal of Drug and Alcohol Abuse, 25*(1), 93–116.

First, M. B., Williams, J. B. W., Karg, R. S., & Spitzer, R. L. (2015). *Structured Clinical Interview for DSM-5—Research Version (SCID-5 for DSM-5, Research Version; SCID-5-RV)*. Arlington, VA: American Psychiatric Association.

Galassi, A., Mpofu, E., & Athanasou, J. (2015). Therapeutic community treatment of an inmate population with substance use disorders: Post-release trends in re-arrest, re-incarceration, and drug misuse relapse. *International Journal of Environmental Research and Public Health, 12*, 7059–7072.

Gendreau, P., French, S., & Taylor, A. (2002). *What works (what doesn't) revised 2002: The principles of effective correctional treatment.* Unpublished manuscript, University of New Brunswick, Saint John, New Brunswick, Canada.

Gifford, E. V., Kohlenberg, B. S., Piasecki, M. M., & Webber, E. J. (2004). The forensic assessment of substance abuse. In W. O'Donohue & E. Levensky (Eds.), *Handbook of forensic psychology* (pp. 315–345). New York, NY: Elsevier Academic Press.

Goldstein, P. J. (1985). The drugs/violence nexus: A tripartite conceptual framework. *Journal of Drug Issues, 15*, 493–506.

Gossop, M., Darke, S., Griffiths, P., Hando, J., Powis, B., Hall, W., & Strang, J. (1995). The Severity of Dependence Scale (SDS): Psychometric properties of the SDS in English and Australian samples of heroin, cocaine and amphetamine users. *Addiction, 90*(5), 607–614.

Grant, B. F., Goldstein, R. B., Smith, S. M., Jung, J., Zhang, H., Chou, S. P., … Hasin, D. S. (2015). The Alcohol Use Disorder and Associated Disabilities Interview Schedule-5 (AUDADIS-5): Reliability of substance use and psychiatric disorder modules in a general population sample. *Drug and Alcohol Dependence, 148*, 27–33.

Gueta, K., & Chen, G. (2015). "I wanted to rebel, but there they hit me even harder": Discourse analysis of Israeli women offenders' accounts of their pathways to substance abuse and crime. *International Journal of Offender Therapy and Comparative Criminology, 60*(7), 787–807.

Håkansson, A., & Berglund, M. (2012). Risk factors for criminal recidivism—A prospective follow-up study in prisoners with substance abuse. *Bio Med Central Psychiatry, 12*, 111.

Harper, R., & Hardy, S. (2000). An evaluation of motivational interviewing as a method of intervention with clients in a probation setting. *British Journal of Social Work, 30*, 393–400.

Hasin, D., Carpenter, K. M., McCloud, S., Smith, M., & Grant, B. F. (1997). The alcohol use disorder and associated disabilities interview schedule (AUDADIS): Reliability of alcohol and drug modules in a clinical sample. *Drug and Alcohol Dependence, 44*, 133–141.

Hasin, D. S., Greenstein, E., Aivadyan, C., Stohl, M., Aharonovich, E., Saha, T., … Grant, B. F. (2015). The Alcohol Use Disorder and Associated Disabilities Interview Schedule-5 (AUDADIS-5): Procedural validity of substance use disorders modules through clinical reappraisal in a general population sample. *Drug and Alcohol Dependence, 148*, 40–46.

Hiller, M. L., Knight, K., Saum, C. A., & Simpson, D. D. (2006). Social functioning, treatment dropout, and recidivism of probationers mandated to a modified therapeutic community. *Criminal Justice and Behaviour, 33*(6), 739–759.

Hiller, M. L., Knight, K., & Simpson, D. D. (1999). Prison-based substance abuse treatment, residential aftercare and recidivism. *Addiction, 94*(6), 833–842.

Hinckers, A. S., Laucht, M., Schmidt, M. H., Mann, K. F., Schuman, G., Schuckit, M. A., & Heinz, A. (2006). Low level of response to alcohol as associated with serotonin transporter genotype and high alcohol intake in adolescents. *Biological Psychiatry, 60*, 282–287.

Hopley, A. A. B., & Brunelle, C. (2016). Substance use in incarcerated male offenders: Predictive validity of a personality typology of substance misusers. *Addictive Behaviors, 53*, 86–93.

Houser, K. A., Belenko, S., & Brennan, P. K. (2012). The effects of mental health and substance abuse disorders on institutional misconduct among female inmates. *Justice Quarterly, 29*, 799–828.

Inciardi, J. A., Martin, S. S., & Butzin, C. A. (2004). Five-year outcomes of therapeutic community treatment of drug-involved offenders after release from prison. *Crime & Delinquency, 50*, 88–107.

Isenhart, C. E. (1994). Motivational subtypes in an inpatient sample of substance abusers. *Addictive Behaviors, 19*, 463–475.

Johnson, S. L. (2001). Impact of institutional methadone maintenance treatment on release outcome. *Forum on Corrections Research Focusing on Alcohol and Drugs, 13*(3), 51–53.

Johnson, S. L., van de Ven, J. T. C., & Grant, B. A. (2001). *Institutional methadone maintenance treatment: Impact on release outcome and institutional behaviour* (R-119). Ottawa, ON: Correctional Service of Canada.

Jolley, J. M., & Kerbs, J. J. (2010). Risk, need, and responsivity: Unrealized potential for the international delivery of substance abuse treatment in prison. *International Criminal Justice Review, 20*(3), 280–301.

Jurk, S., Kuitunen-Paul, S., Kroemer, N. B., Artiges, E., Banaschewski, T., Bokde, A. L. W., … Smolka, M. N. (2015). Personality and substance use: Psychometric evaluation and validation of the Substance Use Risk Profile Scale (SURPS) in English, Irish, French, and German Adolescents. *Alcoholism: Clinical & Experimental Research, 39*(11), 2234–2248.

Kastelic, A., Pont, J., & Stöver, H. (2009). *Opioid substitution treatment in custodial settings: A practical guide*. Oldenburg, Germany: BIS-Verlag.

Kavanagh, D. J., Young, R., White, A., Saunders, J. B., Wallis, J., Shockley, N., … Clair, A. (2004). A brief motivational intervention for substance misuse in recent-onset psychosis. *Drug and Alcohol Review, 23*, 151–155.

Kelley, M. L., & Fals-Stewart, W. (2004). Psychiatric disorders of children living with drug-abusing, alcohol-abusing, and non-substance-abusing fathers. *Journal of the American Academy of Child & Adolescent Psychiatry, 43*, 621–628.

Kelly, L., & Farrell MacDonald, S. (2015a). *Comparing lifetime substance use patterns of men and women offenders* (RIB 14-44). Ottawa, ON: Correctional Service Canada.

Kelly, L., & Farrell MacDonald, S. (2015b). *Lifetime substance use patterns of men offenders* (RIB 14-43). Ottawa, ON: Correctional Service Canada.

Kendler, K. S., Neale, M. C., Heath, A. C., Kessler, R. C., & Eaves, L. J. (1994). A twin-family study of alcoholism in women. *American Journal of Psychiatry, 151*, 707–715.

Kiluk, B. D., DeVito, E. E., Buck, M. B., Hunkele, K., Nich, C., & Carroll, K. M. (2017). Effect of computerized cognitive behavioral therapy on acquisition of coping skills among cocaine-dependent individuals enrolled in methadone maintenance. *Journal of Substance Abuse Treatment, 82*, 87–92.

King, C. M., Heilbrun, K., Kim, N. Y., McWilliams, K., Phillips, S., Barbera, J., & Fretz, R. (2017). Tablet computers and forensic and correctional psychological assessment: A randomized controlled study. *Law and Human Behavior, 41*(5), 468–477.

Kinlock, T. W., Gordon, M. S., Schwartz, R. P., & O'Grady, K. E. (2008). A study of methadone maintenance for male prisoners: 3-month postrelease outcomes. *Criminal Justice and Behavior, 35*(1), 34–47.

Kinyanjui, D. W. C., & Atwoli, L. (2013). Substance use among inmates at the Eldoret prison in Western Kenya. *BMC Psychiatry, 13*, 53.

Ko, N., Hsu, S., Chen, C., Tsai, C., Chu, P., Huang, C., & Yen, C. (2009). A pilot study of HIV education on readiness to change on substance use, AIDS knowledge, self-efficacy for risk reduction among male drug-dependent inmates. *Substance Use & Misuse, 44*, 322–331.

Koob, G. F., & Le Moal, M. (2001). Drug addiction, dysregulation of reward, and allostasis. *Neuropsychopharmacology, 24*(2), 97–129.

Kunic, D. (2006). The Computerized Assessment of Substance Abuse (CASA). *Forum on Corrections Research, 18*(1), 19–23.

Kunic, D., & Grant, B. A. (2006). *The Computerized Assessment of Substance Abuse (CASA): Results from the demonstration project* (R-173). Ottawa, ON: Correctional Service Canada.

Kunic, D., & Varis, D. D. (2009). *The Aboriginal Offender Substance Abuse Program (AOSAP): Examining the effects of successful completion on post-release outcomes* (R-217). Ottawa, ON: Correctional Service of Canada.

Lander, L., Howsare, J., & Byrne, M. (2013). The impact of substance use disorders on families and children: From theory to practice. *Social Work in Public Health, 28*, 194–205.

Larabie, L. C. (2005). To what extent do smokers plan quit attempts? *Tobacco Control, 14*, 425–428.

Leonhard, C., Mulvey, K., Gastfriend, D. R., & Schwartz, M. (2000). The Addiction Severity Index: A field study of internal consistency and validity. *Journal of Substance Abuse, 18*, 129–135.

Lewis, M. (2015). *The biology of desire: Why addiction is not a disease*. Toronto, ON: Doubleday Canada.

Lowenkamp, C. T., & Latessa, E. J. (2004). Understanding the risk principle: How and why correctional interventions can harm low-risk offenders. *Topics in Community Corrections*, 3–8.

MacCoun, R., Kilmer, B., & Reuter, P. (2003). *Research on drugs-crime linkages: The next generation. NIJ Special Report: Toward a drug and crime research agenda for the 21st century.* Washington, DC: National Institute of Justice.

MacKenzie, D. L., & Hickman, L. J. (2000). The effectiveness of community-based programs for chemically dependent offenders: A review and assessment of the research. *Journal of Substance Abuse Treatment, 19,* 383–393.

MacPherson, P. (2004). *Use of random urinalysis to deter drug use in prison: A review of the issues* (R-149). Ottawa, ON: Correctional Service Canada.

MacSwain, M., Cheverie, M., Farrell MacDonald, S., & Johnson, S. (2014). Characteristics of women participants in the Methadone Maintenance Treatment Program (MMTP). Research Report R307. Ottawa, ON: Correctional Service of Canada.

Magaletta, P. R., & Leukefeld, C. (2011). Self-help. In C. Leukefeld, T. P. Gullotta, & J. Gregrich (Eds.), *Handbook of evidence-based substance abuse treatment in criminal justice settings* (pp. 245–257). New York, NY: Springer.

Magill, M., & Ray, L. A. (2009). Cognitive-behavioral treatment with adult alcohol and illicit drug users: A meta-analysis of randomized control trials. *Journal of Studies on Alcohol and Drugs, 70,* 516–527.

Makarios, M., Sperber, K. G., & Latessa, E. J. (2014). Treatment dosage and the risk principle: A refinement and extension. *Journal of Offender Rehabilitation, 53*(5), 334–350.

Mann, R. E., Webster, S. D., Schofield, C., & Marshall, W. L. (2004). Approach versus avoidance goals in relapse prevention with sexual offenders. *Sexual Abuse: A Journal of Research and Treatment, 16,* 65–76.

Marlatt, G. A., & Gordon, J. R. (1985). *Relapse prevention: Maintenance strategies in the treatment of addictive behaviors.* New York, NY: Guilford.

Marshall, W. L., Fernandez, Y. M., Serran, G. A., Mulloy, R., Thornton, D., Mann, R. E., & Anderson, D. (2003). Process variables in the treatment of sexual offenders: A review of the relevant literature. *Aggression and Violent Behavior, 8*(2), 205–234.

Martin, C., Player, E., & Liriano, S. (2003). Results of evaluations of the RAPt drug treatment programme. In M. Ramsay (Ed.), *Prisoners' drug use and treatment: Seven research studies.* London, UK: Home Office.

Matthews, H. A., Feagans, D., & Kohl, R. (2015). *Massachusetts Department of Correction three-year recidivism study: A descriptive analysis of the January–July 2011 releases and correctional recovery academy participation.* Concord, MA: Massachusetts Department of Correction Strategic Planning & Research.

McCambridge, J., & Strang, J. (2004). The efficacy of single-session motivational interviewing in reducing drug consumption and perceptions of drug-related risk and harm among young people: Results from a multi-site cluster randomized trial. *Addiction, 99,* 39–52.

McConnaughy, E. A., Prochaska, J. O., & Velicer, W. F. (1983). Stages of change in psychotherapy: Measurement and sample profiles. *Psychotherapy: Theory, Research and Practice, 20,* 368–375.

McDonell, M. G., Graves, M. C., West, I. I., Ries, R. K., Donovan, D. M., Bumgardner, K., … Roy-Byrne, P. (2016). Utility of point of care urine drug tests in the treatment of primary care patients with drug use disorders. *Journal of Addiction Medicine, 10*(3), 196–201.

McHugh, R. K., Hearon, B. A., & Otto, M. W. (2010). Cognitive-behavioral therapy for substance use disorders. *Psychiatric Clinics of North America, 33*(3), 511–525.

McKay, J. R. (2009). *Treating substance use disorders with adaptive continuing care.* Washington, DC: American Psychological Association.

McLellan, A. T., Kushner, H., Metzger, D., & Peters, R. (1992). The fifth edition of the Addiction Severity Index. *Journal of Substance Abuse Treatment, 9,* 199–213.

McLellan, A. T., Luborsky, L., Woody, G. E., & O'Brien, C. P. (1980). An improved diagnostic instrument for substance abuse patients: The Addiction Severity Index. *Journal of Nervous and Mental Diseases, 168,* 26–33.

McLellan, A. T., Woody, G. E., Metzger, D., McKay, J., Durell, J., Alterman, A. I., O'Brien, C. P., (1996). Evaluating the effectiveness of addiction treatments: Reasonable expectations, appropriate comparisons. *The Milbank Quarterly, 74*(1), 51

McMurran, M. (2007). What works in substance misuse treatments for offenders? *Criminal Behaviour and Mental Health, 17*, 225–233.

McMurran, M. (2009). Motivational interviewing with offenders: A systematic review. *Legal and Criminological Psychology, 13*, 83–100.

McMurran, M. (2012). Youth, alcohol, and aggression. In F. Losel, A. Bottoms, & D. P. Farrington (Eds.), *Young adult offenders: Lost in transition?* London, UK: Taylor and Francis.

McMurran, M. (2013). Treatment for offenders in prison and in the community. In M. McMurran (Ed.), *Alcohol-related violence: Prevention and treatment, Series in forensic clinical psychology* (pp. 205–225). Malden, MA: Wiley.

McMurran, M., & Theodosi, E. (2007). Is treatment non-completion associated with increased reconviction over no treatment? *Psychology, Crime and Law, 13*(4), 333–343.

MacSwain, M., Farrell MacDonald, S., & Cheverie, M. (2014). Post release outcomes of methadone maintenance treatment program participants: A comparative study. Research Report R322. Ottawa, ON: Correctional Service of Canada.

McSweeney, T., Stevens, A., Hunt, N., & Turnbill, P. J. (2007). Twisting arms or a helping hand? Assessing the impact of "coerced" and comparable "voluntary" drug treatment options. *British Journal of Criminology, 47*, 470–490.

Memetovic, J., Ratner, P. A., Gotay, C., & Richardson, C. G. (2016). Examining the relationship between personality and affect-related attributes and adolescents' intentions to try smoking using the Substance Use Risk Profile Scale. *Addictive Behaviors, 56*, 36–40.

Miles, H., Dutheil, L., Welsby, I., & Haider, D. (2007). 'Just Say No': A preliminary evaluation of a three-stage model of integrated treatment for substance use problems in conditions of medium security. *The Journal of Forensic Psychiatry and Psychology, 18*(2), 141–159.

Miller, W. R., & Tonigan, J. S. (1996). Assessing drinkers' motivation for change: The Stages of Change Readiness and Treatment Eagerness Scale (SOCRATES). *Psychology of Addictive Behaviors, 10*(2), 81–89.

Moeller, F. G., Schmitz, J. M., Steinberg, J. L., Green, C. M., Reist, C., Lai, L. Y., … Grabowski, J. (2007). Citalopram combined with behavioral therapy reduces cocaine use: A double blind, placebo controlled trial. *American Journal of Drug and Alcohol Abuse, 33*, 367–378.

Motiuk, L. (2016). *Performance outcomes in the delivery of the Integrated Correctional Program Model (ICPM) to Federal Offenders* (RIB-16-01). Ottawa, ON: Correctional Service Canada.

Motiuk, L., & Vuong, B. (2016). *Effectiveness of the Integrated Correctional Program Model (ICPM) for federal offenders identified as perpetrators of spousal assault* (RIB-16-02). Ottawa, ON: Correctional Service Canada.

Mullins, P., Ternes, M., & Farrell MacDonald, S. (2013). *Substance use on day of offence in a sample of male federal offenders* (RS 13-01). Ottawa, ON: Correctional Service Canada.

National Institute on Drug Abuse. (2012). *Principles of drug addiction treatment: A research-based guide* (3rd ed.). Bethesda, MD: National Institutes of Health.

Norman, L. B., & Ford, J. A. (2015). Adolescent ecstasy use: A test of social bonds and social learning theory. *Deviant Behaviour, 36*(7), 527–538.

Nutt, D. J., Lingford-Hughes, A., Erritzoe, D., & Stokes, P. R. (2015). The dopamine theory of addiction: 40 years of highs and lows. *Nature Reviews, Neuroscience, 16*(5), 305–312.

Oesterle, S., Hill, K. G., Hawkins, J. D., Guo, J., Catalano, R. F., & Abbott, R. D. (2004). Adolescent heavy episodic drinking trajectories and health in young adulthood. *Journal of Studies on Alcohol, 65*, 204–212.

Omiya, S., Kobori, O., Tomoto, A., Igarashi, Y., & Iyo, M. (2015). Personality and substance use in Japanese adolescents: The Japanese version of Substance Use Risk Profile Scale. *Personality and Individual Differences, 76*, 153–157.

Oviedo-Joekes, E., Brissette, S., Marsh, D. C., Lauzon, P., Guh, D., Anis, A., & Schechter, M. T. (2009). Diacetylmorphine versus methadone for the treatment of opioid addiction. *The New England Journal of Medicine, 361*(8), 777–786.

Pelissier, B., Wallace, S., O'Neil, J. A., Gaes, G. G., Camp, S., Rhodes, W., & Saylor, W. (2001). Federal prison residential drug treatment reduces substance use and arrests after release. *The American Journal of Drug and Alcohol Abuse, 27*(2), 315–337.

Pernanen, K., Cousineau, M.-M., Brochu, S., & Sun, F. (2002). *Proportions of crimes associated with alcohol and other drugs in Canada*. Ottawa, ON: Canadian Centre on Substance Abuse.

Perron, B. E., & Bright, C. L. (2008). The influence of legal coercion on dropout from substance abuse treatment: Results from a national survey. *Drug and Alcohol Dependence, 92*, 123–131.

Pihl, R. O. (2009). Substance abuse: Etiological considerations. In P. H. Blaney & T. Millon (Eds.), *Oxford textbook of psychopathology* (pp. 253–279). New York, NY: Oxford University Press.

Plourde, C., Dufour, N., Brochu, S., & Gendron, A. (2013). Medication use, substance use, and psychological conditions of female inmates in Canadian federal prisons. *International Annals of Criminology, 51*(1–2), 23–37.

Polaschek, D. L. L., Anstiss, B., & Wilson, M. (2010). The assessment of offending-related stage of change in offenders: Psychometric validation of the URICA with male prisoners. *Psychology, Crime & Law, 16*(4), 305–325.

Popova, S., Rehm, J., & Fischer, B. (2006). An overview of illegal opioid use and health services utilization in Canada. *Public Health, 120*, 320–328.

Prescott, C. A., Caldwell, C. B., Carey, G., Vogler, G. P., Trumbetta, S. L., & Gottesman, I. I. (2005). The Washington University twin study of alcoholism. *American Journal of Medical Genetics Part B Neuropsychiatric Genetics, 134B*, 45–55.

Prochaska, J. O., & DiClemente, C. C. (1992). Stages of change in the modification of problem behaviors. *Progress in Behavior Modification, 28*, 183–218.

Prochaska, J. O., & Goldstein, M. (1991). The process of smoking cessation: Implications for clinicians. *Clinics in Chest Medicine, 12*(4), 727–735.

Prochaska, J. O., Norcross, J. C., & DiClemente, C. C. (1994). *Changing for good*. New York, NY: Morrow.

Prochaska, J. O., & Velicer, W. F. (1997). The Transtheoretical Model of health behavior change. *American Journal of Health Promotion, 12*, 38–48.

Rawson, R. A., Huber, A., McCann, M., Shoptaw, S., Farabee, D., Reiber, C., & Ling, W. (2002). A comparison of contingency management and cognitive behavioral approaches during methadone maintenance treatment for cocaine dependence. *Archives of General Psychiatry, 59*, 817–824.

Reed, D. N., Jr., Wolf, B., & Barber, K. R. (2005). The stages of change questionnaire as a predictor of trauma patients most likely to decrease alcohol use. *Journal of the American College of Surgeons, 200*(2), 179–185.

Rehm, J., Baliunas, D., Brochu, S., Fischer, B., Gnam, W., Patra, J. … Taylor, B. In collaboration with Adlaf, E., Recel, M., & Single, E. (2006). *The costs of Substance abuse in Canada 2002: Highlights*. Ottawa, ON: Canadian Centre on Substance Abuse.

Richer, I., Lemelin, M., & Ternes, M. (2014). *Distinguishing characteristics of substance abuse program completers and non-completers* (R-326). Ottawa, ON: Correctional Service Canada.

Rogerson, B., Jacups, S. P., & Caltabiano, N. (2016). Cannabis use, dependence, and withdrawal in indigenous male inmates. *Journal of Substance Use, 21*(1), 65–71.

Rollnick, S., Heather, N., Gold, R., & Hall, W. (1992). Development of a short 'readiness to change' questionnaire for use in brief, opportunistic interventions among excessive drinkers. *British Journal of Addiction, 87*(5), 743–754.

Salamone, J. D., Correa, M., Mingote, S., & Weber, S. M. (2003). Nucleus accumbens dopamine and the regulation of effort in food-seeking behavior: Implications for studies of natural motivation, psychiatry, and drug abuse. *Journal of Pharmacological Experimental Therapy, 305*(1), 1–8.

Saliba, A., Moran, C. C., & Yoo, Y. J. (2014). The Substance Use Risk Profile Scale: Comparison of norms and outcomes for Australian and Korean adults. *International Journal of Mental Health and Addiction, 12*(12), 538–547.

Schneider, S. (2013). Violence, organized crime, and illicit drug markets: A Canadian case study. *Sociologia, 71*, 125–143.

Schug, R. A., & Fradella, H. F. (2015). *Mental illness and crime*. Thousand Oaks, CA: Sage Publications.

Schwartz, R. P., Gryczynski, J., Mitchell, S. G., Gonzales, A., Moseley, A., Peterson, T. R., … O'Grady, K. E. (2014). Computerized versus in-person brief intervention for drug misuse: A randomized clinical trial. Addiction, 109, 1091–1098.

Selzer, M. L. (1971). The Michigan Alcoholism Screening Test: The quest for a new diagnostic instrument. *American Journal of Psychiatry, 127*, 1653–1658.

Sewell, C. A., Hickling, F. W., Abel, W. D., Smith, S., Paisley, V., Martin, J., & Shaw, J. (2015). A comparison of substance abuse and mental illness in male offenders in Jamaica and England and Wales. *WIMJ Open, 2*(1), 36–40.

Shankman, S. A., Funkhouser, C. J., Klein, D. N., Davila, J., Lerner, D., & Hee, D. (2017). Reliability and validity of severity dimensions of psychopathology assessed using the Structured Clinical Interview for DSM-5 (SCID). *International Journal of Methods in Psychiatric Research*. https://doi.org/10.1002/mpr.1590

Sinha, R., & Easton, C. (1999). Substance abuse and criminality. *The Journal of the American Academy of Psychiatry and the Law, 27*, 513–526.

Skinner, H. A. (1982). The Drug Abuse Screening Test. *Addictive Behaviours, 7*, 363–371.

Skinner, H. A., & Horn, J. L. (1984). *Alcohol Dependence Scale (ADS): User's guide*. Toronto, ON: Addiction Research Foundation.

Skog, O. (2000). Addicts' choice. *Addiction, 95*(9), 1309–1314.

Smedslund, G., Berg, R. C., Hammerstrøm, K. T., Steiro, A., Leiknes, K. A., Dahl, H. M., & Karlsen, K. (2011). Motivational interviewing for substance abuse. *Campbell Systematic Reviews, 6*, 1–126.

Smith, P., Gendreau, P., & Schwartz, K. (2009). Validating the principles of effective intervention: A systematic review of the contributions of meta-analysis in the field of corrections. *Victims and Offenders, 4*, 148–169.

Sondhi, A., Birch, J., Lynch, K., Holloway, A., & Newbury-Birch, D. (2016). Exploration of delivering brief interventions in a prison setting: A qualitative study in one English region. *Drugs: Education, Prevention & Policy, 23*(5), 382–387.

Spear, S. E., Shedlin, M., Gilberti, B., Fiellin, M., & McNeely, J. (2016). Feasibility and acceptability of an audio computer-assisted self-interview version of the Alcohol, Smoking and Substance Involvement Screening Test (ASSIST) in primary care patients. *Journal of Substance Abuse, (2)*, 37, 299–305.

Staton-Tindall, M., Harp, K. L. H., Winston, E., Webster, J. M., & Pangburn, K. (2015). Factors associated with recidivism among corrections-based treatment participants in rural and urban areas. *Journal of Substance Abuse Treatment, 56*, 16–22.

Stevens, A. (2014). 'Difference' and desistance in prison-based therapeutic communities. *Prison Service Journal, 213*, 3–9.

Stewart, L. A., & Wilton, G. (2017). *Comorbid mental disorders: Prevalence and impact on institutional outcomes* (R-379). Ottawa, ON: Correctional Service of Canada.

Sutton, S. (2001). Back to the drawing board? A review of applications of the transtheoretical model to substance use. *Addiction, 96*, 175–186.

Tangney, J. P., Folk, J. B., Graham, D. M., Stuewig, J. B., Blalock, D. V., Salatino, A., … Moore, K. E. (2016). Changes in inmates' substance use and dependence from pre-incarceration to one year post-release. *Journal of Criminal Justice, 46*, 228–238.

Taxman, F. S., Perdoni, M. L., & Caudy, M. (2013). The plight of providing substance abuse treatment services to offenders: Modeling the gaps in service delivery. *Victims and Offenders, 8*, 70–93.

Ternes, M., Doherty, S., & Matheson, F. I. (2014). *An examination of the effectiveness of the National Substance Abuse Program Moderate Intensity (NSAP-M) on institutional adjustment and post-release outcomes* (R-291). Ottawa, ON: Correctional Service of Canada.

Ternes, M., & Johnson, S. (2011). *Linking type of substance use and type of crime in male offenders* (RS-11-06). Ottawa, ON: Correctional Service Canada.

Ternes, M., & Johnson, S. (2014). *Substance abuse problem severity, treatment readiness, and response bias among incarcerated men* (RS-13-05). Ottawa, ON: Correctional Service Canada.

Ternes, M., & MacPherson, P. (2014). *Urinalysis results from the 2012/13 Fiscal Year* (RS-14-05). Ottawa, ON: Correctional Service Canada.

van der Put, C. E., Creemers, H. E., & Hoeve, M. (2013). Difference between juvenile offenders with and without substance use problems in the prevalence and impact of risk and protective factors for criminal recidivism. *Drug and Alcohol Dependence, 134*, 267–274.

van Ree, J. M., Gerrits, M. A., & Vanderschuren, L. J. (1999). Opioids, reward and addiction: An encounter of biology, psychology, and medicine. *Pharmacology Review, 51*(2), 341–396.

Volkow, N. D., Frieden, T. R., Hyde, P. S., & Cha, S. S. (2014). Medication-assisted therapies— Tackling the opioid-overdose epidemic. *The New England Journal of Medicine, 370*(22), 2063–2066.

Walters, G. D. (2012). Substance abuse and criminal thinking: Testing the countervailing, mediation, and specificity hypotheses. *Law and Human Behavior, 36*(6), 506–512.

Ward, T., Melser, J., & Yates, P. M. (2007). Reconstructing the risk-need-responsivity model: A theoretical elaboration and evaluation. *Aggression and Violent Behavior, 12*, 208–228.

Warren, E., Viney, R., Shearer, J., Shanahan, M., Wodak, A., & Dolan, K. (2006). Value for money in drug treatment: Economic evaluation of prison methadone. *Drug and Alcohol Dependence, 84*, 160–166.

Wattanaporn, K. A., & Holtfreter, K. (2014). The impact of feminist pathways research on gender-responsive policy and practice. *Feminist Criminology, 9*, 191–207.

West, R. (2005). *Theory of addiction*. Malden, MA: Blackwell Publishing Ltd.

Willoughby, F. W., & Edens, J. F. (1996). Construct validity and predictive utility of the stages of change for alcoholics. *Journal of Substance Abuse, 8*(3), 275–291.

Wilson, A. B., Drane, J., Hadley, T., Metraux, S., & Evans, A. (2011). Examining the impact of mental illness and substance use on recidivism in a county jail. *International Journal of Law and Psychiatry, 34*, 264–268.

Wise, R. A., & Bozarth, M. A. (1987). A psychomotor stimulant theory of addiction. *Psychology Review, 94*(4), 469–492.

Witkiewitz, K., Marlatt, G. A., & Walker, D. (2005). Mindfulness-based relapse prevention for alcohol and substance use disorders. *Journal of Cognitive Psychotherapy: An International Quarterly, 19*(3), 211–228.

Wolff, N., & Shi, J. (2015). Screening for substance use disorder among incarcerated men with the Alcohol, Smoking, Substance Involvement Screening Test (ASSIST): A comparative analysis of computer-administered and interviewer-administered modalities. *Journal of Substance Abuse Treatment, 53*, 22–32.

World Health Organization, United Nations Office on Drugs and Crime, & Joint United Nations Programme on HIV/AIDS. (2004). WHO/UNODC/UNAIDS position paper: Substitution maintenance therapy in the management of opioid dependence and HIV/AIDS prevention. Retrieved from http://www.who.int/substance_abuse/

Yates, P. M. (2003). Treatment of adult sexual offenders: A therapeutic cognitive-behavioral model of intervention. *Journal of Child Sexual Abuse, 12*, 195–232.

Zanis, D. A., Mulvaney, F., Coviello, D., Alterman, A. I., Savtiz, B., & Thompson, W. (2003). The effectiveness of early parole to substance abuse treatment facilities on 24-month criminal recidivism. *Journal of Drug Issues, 33*(1), 223–236.

Chapter 4
Assessing and Treating Offenders with Intellectual Disabilities

Douglas P. Boer, Jack M. McKnight, Ashleigh M. Kinlyside, and Joyce P. S. Chan

This chapter provides an overview of the assessment and treatment of offenders with intellectual disabilities (OIDs). There is a rich history regarding this topic, well beyond the scope of this chapter and the subject of entire volumes (e.g., Lindsay, Sturmey, & Taylor, 2004). It is hoped that the coverage of the topics within this chapter provides enough of an introduction to the subject to help the reader pursue the various subjects surveyed herein.

This brief chapter begins with an overview of the frequency and prevalence of OIDs in various countries and various sorts of offending behaviour. We then look briefly at various theoretical models relevant to service delivery, review diagnostic and assessment issues as well as relevant interventions in the correctional context, and then finish the chapter with conclusory notes and two short sections first, on future implications and, second, regarding some of the recent efforts in terms of innovative technological applications with OIDs.

4.1 Frequency and Prevalence

The research regarding intellectual disability (ID) and criminality appears to show an increased risk of criminal behaviour in persons with an ID (Hayes, 1997; Holland, Clare, & Mukhopadhyay, 2002; Simpson & Hogg, 2001). However, the accurate

This chapter is dedicated to the memory of William (Bill) R. Lindsay, who was an exemplary scientist and practitioner in the study of forensic disability and a generous friend as well. He passed away suddenly in late March of 2017.

D. P. Boer (✉) · J. M. McKnight · A. M. Kinlyside · J. P. S. Chan
Centre for Applied Psychology, Faculty of Health, University of Canberra,
Canberra, ACT, Australia
e-mail: Douglas.Boer@canberra.edu.au

identification of prevalence rates for OIDs is difficult to discuss in a general sense due to widely divergent estimates in the literature. For example, prevalence rates have been reported between 0.6% (MacEachron, 1979) to 69.6% (Einat & Einat, 2008) between studies globally. This may be in part due to the differences in methodology, classification and sampling of participants.

The American Psychiatric Association (APA, 2013) defines ID as a combination of deficits in intellectual functioning, deficits in adaptive behaviour, and the onset of both of these issues during the developmental period. Despite this, many studies define ID based solely upon intelligence quotient (IQ) assessments with very few using adaptive behavioural measures. Further, the IQ cut-off scores that are used to define significant indicators of ID vary, with some adhering to a strict <70 cut-off while others include cut-offs <80 which can dramatically increase reported prevalence rates (Crocker, Cote, Toupin, & St-Onge, 2007). To exemplify the effect that of differences in diagnostic criteria has upon reported rates, we refer to Hayes, Shackell, Mottram, and Lancaster (2007) who adhered to the APA criteria when defining ID. Based upon cut-off scores of <70 for both IQ and adaptive behaviour measures, Hayes et al. (2007) reported a rate of 2.9%, compared to a rate of 7.1% based upon IQ alone. Interestingly, when those with borderline scores (70–74) were included, rates jumped dramatically to 9.4%, and jumped even higher to 21.7% when scores <79 were included.

Looking generally at prevalence rates globally, Harris (2006) estimated rates of ID to stand between 1% and 3% in the general population. The research indicates that within the criminal justice system (CJS) those with ID are generally over-represented (Holland et al., 2002). A systematic analysis conducted by Fazel, Xenitidis, and Powell (2008) reviewed ten prevalence studies including 11,969 participants from Australia, Dubai, New Zealand, the United Kingdom and the United States between 1966 and 2004. These authors concluded that prevalence rates for prisoners with ID ranged from 0% to 2.9% across these jurisdictions. A recent review of four papers published between 2004 and 2014 by Hellenbach, Karatzias, and Brown (2015) noted that only one (Hassiotis et al., 2011) had found a rate consistent (4%) with those reported by Fazel et al. (2008). The remaining studies indicated prevalence at 3–4 times higher rates, though these were dogged by the methodological and diagnostic process issues discussed above such as a lack of full clinical assessment considering both intellectual and adaptive functioning.

In Australia, the prevalence of ID in the criminal justice system is estimated to be between 2% and 12.5% (Crocker et al., 2007; Hayes, 1997). In New South Wales, Cashin, Butler, Levy, and Potter (2006) administered an intelligence test to 167 inmates, and found that 3% of males and 13% of females scored <70. When those in the borderline range (IQs from 70 to 85) were included, a further 36% of men and 46% of women were identified. Hayes (1997) further reported that up to 24% of persons appearing at a rural court may have had an ID. However, this study, and another showing that Indigenous Australians were identified as having higher rates of ID (65%) when compared to the whole sample (54%) (Baldry, Dowse, & Clarence, 2012), may have suffered from sampling and methodological biases in which the assessment may not have been culturally appropriate (Dingwall, Pinkerton, & Lindeman, 2013).

In the United States, two reviews of the ID prison population reported prevalence rates of between 0.5% to 19.1% (Denkowski & Denkowski, 1985; Noble & Conley, 1992). While a study that reviewed prison records for prevalence of ID reported a rate between 1.5% and 5.6% depending on the measure used (MacEachron, 1979). The rates of persons with ID who are sentenced to capital punishment in the United States is an area of controversy, without clear prevalence estimates available. One study by Hall (2002) reported a spread in estimates between 4% and 20% amongst death row inmates, although the author acknowledged that due to recording difficulties, no reliable estimates were available.

In the United Kingdom, prevalence rates have been reported as being between 2% and 7% in varying contexts (Ali, Ghosh, Strydom, & Hassiotis, 2016; Hayes et al., 2007; Murphy, Gardner, & Freeman, 2015; Murphy, Harnett, & Holland, 1995). In a recent report by Mottram (2007) the author stated that 7.1% of the sampled male inmates at the largest prison in Europe (HMP Liverpool) had an IQ below 70. In a female prison, 8.3% of sampled inmates scored below 70, and 3.3% of young offenders also had an IQ below 70 (Mottram, 2007). In a separate study, the prevalence of young offenders with ID was reported as high as 23% based on IQ (Harrington & Bailey, 2005). However, the assessment tool used in the latter study may have been inadequate at distinguishing between lack of education and intrinsic learning difficulties.

Despite the apparent over-representation of OIDs in the CJS, it is unclear whether this is due to the population committing more criminal acts than the general population, or due to sampling biases in research and procedural disadvantages faced by the ID population. It is impossible to develop an accurate picture of all crime that is committed, therefore we rely on identifying persons in certain contexts (contact with police, courts, prison) to identify prevalence rates. As persons with ID are generally more likely to have their crimes detected, may have difficulty understanding legal rights such as the right to silence, provide false confessions, plead guilty, be represented by public defenders, serve longer sentences and be denied parole (Cloud, Shepherd, Barkoff, & Shur, 2002; Drizin & Leo, 2004; Glaser & Deane, 1999), it is possible that the number of criminal acts committed by persons with ID are simply more visible than more frequent compared to their non-ID peers.

4.1.1 Offending Patterns

Nonsexual aggression and sexual aggression are areas of particular concern due to the impact such acts can have upon victims. Research has suggested that people with ID are at a greater risk of perpetrating and being victims of violent and sexual crimes compared to community samples (Fogden, Thomas, Daffern, & Ogloff, 2016; McBrien, Hodgetts, & Gregory, 2003; Simpson & Hogg, 2001). Various research studies have identified high rates of "challenging behaviour" in populations with ID, with aggressive behaviour featuring prominently. A survey of service providers in the UK found that in a sample of 1362 persons with an ID, there was a documented history of aggressive behaviour in 17.6% of the cases (Harris, 1993). A study conducted in Australia by Sigafoos, Elkins, Kerr, and Attwood (1994) noted that in a sample of 2412 persons with ID, service providers reported an overall prevalence rate of aggression at 11%. In both of these studies, rates of aggression varied between settings, with the lowest occurring in community accommodations and the highest rates of aggression occurring within institutions and hospitals, at 35% and 38.2% respectfully (Harris, 1993; Sigafoos et al., 1994).

In a study reviewing the files of defendants on murder charges in the United States, of the 270 cases reviewed, 6% were diagnosed as ID (Dwyer & Frierson, 2006). In another study of 2600 persons with ID and a comparison community group of 4830 participants, Fogden et al. (2016) reported that the ID sample committed violent offences 1.6 times more frequently and sexually offended 3.6 times more frequently. Nixon, Thomas, Daffern, and Ogloff (2017) reported similar results when comparing a sample of ID persons with a community comparison group. These authors reported that the ID group was 3 times more likely to have been charged with a violent offence and 15 times more likely to have been charged with a sexual offence.

There are interesting gender differences in offending prevalence and patterns of OIDs. While men with ID are generally more likely to violently offend than females (Fogden et al., 2016), this is also the case for the non-disabled population. Females with ID are reported to have a particular level of risk for violent offending when compared to female community samples (Fogden et al., 2016). Two separate studies by Nixon et al. (2017) and Fogden et al. (2016) reported that females with ID offended violently at significantly higher rates of between 5 and 11 times that of their non-disabled peers. Further, Nixon et al. (2017) stated that an examination of the relevant confidence intervals revealed that the relative risk of violence between the total ID group and the comparison was significantly higher for females than for males.

The increased risk of offending in the ID population appears to be exacerbated by comorbid mental illness. Fogden et al. (2016) found that when they separated the ID sample into those with and without comorbid mental illness, the comorbid group committed violent offences at a rate of 6.5 times more frequently that the community sample and offended sexually at a rate of 18.9 times higher. When compared to the ID-only group, the comorbid group offended violently four times more, and sexually five times more frequently. This finding is particularly relevant for rehabilitation following incarceration, given that mental illness can be exacerbated by the incarceration itself (Glaser & Deane, 1999).

4.1.2   Substance Abuse Issues

Taggart and Chaplin (2014) provide a thorough review of current literature on prevalence rates of substance abuse in sample of OIDs. In general, the rate of alcohol and substance abuse in the non-offender ID population has been reported to be comparable to, or lower than in the non-disabled community (Burgard, Donohue,

Azrin, & Teichner, 2000; McGillicuddy, 2006). However, several authors have noted rates of substance abuse in OIDs as high as 79% (Glaser & Deane, 1999). Plant, McDermott, Chester, and Alexander (2011) studied a group of 74 OIDs from the UK who were attending a community forensic ID service. Roughly half of the population were dependent upon, or abusing substances, while 35% had used a drug leading up to their index offence, with no sex differences noted. Alcohol was reported as the most commonly abused substance followed by cannabis, cocaine, stimulants and opiates. Klimecki, Jenkinson, and Wilson (1994) examined the impact of substance abuse upon recidivism. The authors noted an increase in the proportion of offenders with substance abuse issues in those with multiple convicted offences; 45.1% of first-time offenders had a history of substance abuse with this number increasing to 87.5% by the fourth offence.

4.1.3 Potential for Victimisation

With regards to potential for victimisation, Fogden et al. (2016)'s study found that the community sample was more likely to have an official history of victimisation. However, at an offence specific level, the ID group was twice as likely to be victims of violent crime, and three times as likely to be victims of sexual crimes. Further, those with comorbid ID and mental illness were three times more likely than the community to be victims of violent crime and ten times more likely to be victims of sexual crimes. Such statistics highlight the vulnerability of this population to come into contact with the corrective services both as victims and perpetrators. However, due to underreporting of crimes by people with ID, even when they are serious (Glaser & Deane, 1999), these rates may be underestimations.

4.2 Relevant Theoretical Models

4.2.1 General Models

Four general models that have been developed for the understanding, assessment and treatment of offender behaviour, while not necessarily always discussed in terms of the behaviour of OIDS, but are relevant in our opinion, include: the Relapse Prevention (RP) model (Pithers, 1990), the Risk-Need-Responsivity (RNR) model (Andrews, Bonta, & Wormith, 2011), the Good Lives Model (GLM; Ward, 2002), and Desistance theory (McNeill & Weaver, 2010).

The RP model originated in the substance abuse treatment field but was brought into the area sexual offender treatment by Pithers (1990) and into virtually all areas of offender therapy since that time. Basically, RP treatments involve helping offenders learn to self-manage their responses to high risk situations and personal

risk factors as to avoid a new offence or relapse. Helping offenders in the identification of risk factors, learning new coping strategies, dealing with lapses, is very basic
and restricted to risk avoidance or risk management and has been eclipsed over time
by the GLM. Some theorists see advantages to a combination of such approaches
(e.g., Boer, 2017), but there is a polemic in the literature in this area beyond the
scope of this chapter.

The RNR model (Andrews et al., 2011) requires that treatment programmes are
most likely to be successful in reducing recidivism if (a) the programmes are delivered at the highest intensity to those offenders who are the highest risk for the
behaviour of concern; (b) the programmes should address those risk-relevant
dynamic treatment target to reduce the behaviour of concern; and, (c) the programmes need to be delivered in a manner that best suits the learning styles of the
offenders in the programme.

The GLM is a theory that extends the content of programmes from that which is
merely risk relevant to the development of protective features in the offender's life.
The underlying idea is that offenders will cope better and offend less when their
basic human needs are being met through more prosocial means (Ward, 2002). The
GLM model is a very expansive theory looking at life goals and the means by which
those goals are attained which could result in offending or, if positively focused, on
a "Good Life" where the goals themselves are positive and pro-social and are similarly attained through positive and pro-social means. It is the view of some authors
(e.g., Boer, 2017), that some of the basic tenets of the GLM are similar, to some
degree, of the "Old Me/New Me" model of Haaven, Little, and Petre-Miller (1990).
The latter model was focused on helping OIDs who had committed sexual crimes
develop new positive, non-offending, identities (or "New Me") as opposed to the
dysfunctional identity who had committed the crime(s) (the "Old Me").

Finally, Desistance theory (McNeill & Weaver, 2010) examines the broader processes associated with decreased reoffending, including personal factors, environmental, and broader social factors. Chan and Boer (2016) looked at the above
theories in terms of their contribution to their concept of Reintegration Theory, a
discussion beyond the scope of this chapter.

4.2.2   Anger/Nonsexual Violence

The discussion of the commission and treatment of aggression and nonsexual violence invokes the consideration of multiple theories including moral development,
emotional regulation, and social information processing models in addition to the
general models provided in the preceding section. There are very few interventions
and theoretical models that acknowledge both the differing types of aggression and
the wide variety of contributing factors, including communication deficits, emotional dysregulation, hostile attribution biases or distorted interpretative biases.
Langdon and Murphy (2017) provided a brief discussion of theoretical models
guiding the assessment and treatment of violence of OIDs. They drew distinctions

between the types of aggression generally exhibited by persons with ID, based upon the severity of their affliction. For persons with severe developmental disorders, instrumental violence is more common as compared to hostile, angry or affective aggression. The authors stated that a communicative element may be present in the behaviour, although treatment programmes generally have a behavioural focus. For those with more mild ID, Langdon and Murphy (2017) stated that hostile aggression is more common, and while a communicative element may be present, the issues are generally conceptualised within emotional regulation, social information processing or cognitive distortion models.

As each model can explain certain portions of the contributing factors for violence, it may be useful to synthesise theoretical conceptualisations when assessing and treating aggression. For example, it has been suggested that in children with ID, externalising behavioural issues are related to increased encoding of negative cues, generation of aggressive responses and negative evaluation of assertive responses (van Nieuwenjizen, de Castro, Wijnroks, Vermeer, & Matthys, 2009). This suggests a link with social information processing theory, which is described in Crick and Dodge (1994) as a series of mental states and processes that occur during a social interaction. There is an indication that for adults with ID and a history of aggression, there are differences in social information processing styles when compared with non-aggressive persons (Larkin, Jahoda, & MacMahon, 2013). These differences include being more likely to mislabel cues in a negative fashion (Matheson & Jahoda, 2005), a greater propensity to attribute hostile intent (Basquill, Nezu, Nezu, & Klein, 2004; Jahoda, Pert, & Trower, 2006), and an increased belief that aggressive choices would have more positive outcomes when compared to submissive choices (Kirk, Jahoda, & Pert, 2008; Pert & Jahoda, 2008). There is also evidence that aggression is linked to increased levels of cognitive distortions in persons with ID (Langdon, Daniel, & Sadek, 2016; Langdon, Murphy, Clare, Steverson, & Palmer, 2011). This suggests a link to biased information processing functions, which would also present a relevant treatment target.

Novaco (2011) described a theoretical relationship between anger and aggression, with anger being neither deterministic or necessary for aggression, but strongly associated (Novaco, 1994). Anger can be defined as a state of arousal and antagonism towards the perceived cause of some aversive event. A recent meta-analytic study found a strong relationship between anger and violence in a forensic sample (Chereji, Pintea, & David, 2012), and anger has been shown to be predictive of assaultive behaviour in several contexts (Novaco & Taylor, 2004). While anger may not be sufficient for aggression or violence, it does present a salient risk factor and therefore its significance to the management of violence risk presents a relevant treatment target for intervention in forensic ID populations. Novaco (2011) described anger as being a product of threat perception which has the effect of repelling perceived threatening others and energising behavioural responses to threat (aggression). As such, anger can be seen to be a product of hostile biases and insecurity in which one will attribute threat to the surrounding environment. The aggression then contributes to confirmation bias processes in which the behaviour exhibited by the individual elicits responses from others that confirm beliefs of threat. The effect of anger upon interpretation of stimuli, and specifically the impact that anger has upon perception has been demonstrated experimentally by Barazzone and Davey (2009). These authors identified that anger potentiates the reporting of threatening interpretations and does so independently of anxiety. Anger can also act as a self-reinforcing mechanism by which the anger elicits thoughts that support its presence and increase the likelihood of future exhibitions of anger occurring again. Therefore, the anger/aggression relationship is informed by various models such as cue biases, cognitive distortions and emotional dysregulation models.

Current treatment packages attempt to identify and correct the emotional regulation and social skill deficits, processing biases and distortions that increase risk of offending through violence and aggression. Developments in theory should focus upon integrating different theoretical models into a single model.

4.2.3 Sexual Violence

Lindsay (2017) has provided a cogent argument for the use of "inappropriate sexual behaviour" or ISB in his discussion of relevant offence-specific theories regarding sexual aggression by OIDs. Lindsay noted that some of the ISB by persons with an ID is "based on a lack of sexual knowledge, poor understanding of social conventions, and lack of opportunity for appropriate sexual expression" (p. 475). Whilst such behaviour may be observably deviant, it is based on developmental and environmental contingencies as opposed to actual deviant attraction to violent sexuality or underaged persons (hence the moniker "Counterfeit Deviance" (CD) hypothesis, originally coined by Hingsburger, Griffiths, and Quinsey (1991)).

Lindsay, Steptoe, and Beech (2008) and subsequently Lindsay (2009) found evidence supporting an expansion of the CD hypothesis and an integration of the CD model with the Self-Regulation Pathways (SRP) Model by Ward and Hudson (2000). Essentially, the SRP assigns sexual offenders to one of four offence pathways, two with "approach" goals and two with "avoidant" goals, depending on whether the offender's ability to self-regulate his offending behaviour is "active" or "passive". Lindsay (2017) noted that most OIDs utilize approach goals (i.e., are intentionally trying to offend) and do not try to avoid satisfying their sexual goals. Hence, it appears that Lindsay's revision of the CD hypothesis is quite useful: some OIDs do not understand that their ISB is illegal (or inappropriate) but actively seek out opportunities to offend nonetheless.

The revised CD theory (integrated with the SRP Model) by Lindsay is not incompatible with other theories of sexual offending. Comprehensive theories of sexual offending (e.g., RNR model, Andrews et al., 2011; GLM, Ward, 2002; and Desistance theory, McNeill & Weaver, 2010) and the integrated models which are focused on the etiology of sexual offending in general, such as the Integrated Theory of the Etiology of Sexual Offending (ITSO) by Marshall and Barbaree (1990) and the updated/expanded revision of the ITSO by Ward and Beech (2006) provide other levels of analyses for examining the genesis of sexual offending by extrapolation to that committed by OIDs.

The most recent explication of the ITSO was by Ward and Beech in 2017. In that revision of the ITSO, Ward and Beech posited that sexually abusive behaviour occurs as a result of a wide of "interacting causal factors, operating at different levels and occurring in distinct domains of human functioning" (p. 124). Without fully expanding on the factors, Ward and Beech noted that these causal factors included "biological (evolution, genetic variations, and neurobiology), ecological (social and cultural environment, personal environment), core neuropsychological systems, and personal agency" (p. 124).

Lindsay's (2017) specific model of sexual offending by OIDs is not at odds with the more unifying theory of Ward and Beech (2017), or with the general comprehensive theories cited above and at the beginning of this section on relevant theoretical models. All of these levels of analysis provide opportunities for conceptualization of how OIDs come to the point of committing sexual offences and hence are useful for the assessment and treatment of these individuals as well as for the formulation of research questions that pertain to the genesis, commission, cessation, and recovery from sexual offending.

4.3 Diagnosis and Assessment

4.3.1 Diagnostic Issues

As alluded to earlier, according to the Diagnostic and Statistical Manual Fifth Edition (DSM-5; American Psychiatric Association, APA, 2013), the diagnosis of "intellectual disability" (intellectual developmental disability) requires a finding of "deficits in intellectual functioning... and deficits in adaptive functioning" (pp. 33), that restrict the individual becoming an independent adult. Both of these difficulties need to occur before development is complete.

"Specific learning disorder" (DSM-5) is characterised by significant impairment in educational and academic skills as demonstrated by difficulties with reading, writing, comprehension and numeracy. These difficulties need to be significantly below other individuals of their chronological age and cause impairment in several life domains. They need to have occurred during the developmental period and related to other intellectual or biological concerns (APA, 2013).

There has been an increase in research regarding factors that predict recidivism in OIDs, particularly for those who commit sexual or arson offences (Holland et al., 2002). It is reported that antisocial behaviours are one of the largest predictors of recidivism in OIDs alongside "allowances made by staff", an unsupportive maternal relationship (Lindsay, Elliot, & Astell, 2004, p. 302), age, gender and a borderline IQ level (Simpson & Hogg, 2001). Antisocial behaviour is a similar predictor in mainstream offenders (Haut & Brewster, 2010). In a systematic review of the patterns of offending by OIDs, Simpson and Hogg (2001) suggested that more research was needed before the similarities and differences between mainstream offenders and OIDs could be described in a definitive manner. Other predictors of recidivism in ID offenders include a lack of responsibility of their criminal behaviour, not responding to treatment, suffering from low self-esteem and low-assertiveness, issues surrounding staff management and the type of offence they were convicted of (Lindsay, Elliot, & Astell, 2004). Substance use by OIDs further increases the risk of recidivism (McGillivray & Newton, 2016). This finding was mirrored in a study by Fitzgerald, Gray, Taylor, and Snowden (2011) which reported a medium effect size for recidivism with drug use and a small effect size for alcohol use. Early termination of treatment and a lack of response to treatment were also linked to a belief that an individual would reoffend (Lindsay, Elliot, & Astell, 2004). Although there is some overlap with predictors of recidivism in general offenders, interestingly, the following were not found to be a factor for those with ID: previous employment, having committed a range of sexual crimes, previous criminal history/ lifestyle, interactions with other offenders, "deviant victim choice", suffering from mental illness and isolation from others (Lindsay, Elliot, & Astell, 2004). This finding was not congruent with research by Fitzgerald et al. (2011), Simpson and Hogg (2001) and Wheeler, Clare, and Holland (2014). Fitzgerald et al. (2011) found that a previous criminal history including "acquisitive" and bail offences predicted recidivism. Previous criminal history and behavioural conduct issues as a risk factor for offending was reported in a systematic review by Simpson and Hogg (2001). Whereas Wheeler et al. (2014) reported negative peer influences (such as antisocial traits, previous offences), chaotic home environments and a lack of normality/routine were found to have a large effect sizes in predicting recidivism rates.

Furthermore, Holland et al. (2002) summarised research by Day (1988), Farrington (2000), Murphy et al. (1995), Noble and Conley (1992), Richardson, Koller, and Katz (1985), Simons (2000), Thompson and Brown (1997) and Winter, Holland, and Collins (1997) on potential risk factors for offenders with intellectual disabilities. Their review of literature found that the following factors are relevant: young males, low socioeconomic status, familial history of criminal behaviour, behavioural issues in childhood and adulthood. The majority of these risk factors were echoed by Simpson and Hogg (2001). They are also more likely to be unemployed and experience co-morbid mental health issues (Holland et al., 2002). However, Simpson and Hogg (2001) believe that there was not enough evidence to link familial mental health to offending and suggested that further studies should be conducted on those who are or were homeless to determine what extent that has on offending behaviours of those with ID.

By assessing and determining whether an offender experiences or has experienced these issues it can help with early intervention and target treatment better to the individual's needs. By educating health or criminal justice professionals to be aware of early signs of risk factors it could help guide them to correct treatment and early interventions and perhaps prevent recidivism.

There is significant overlap between intellectual disability and poor mental health. Haut and Brewster (2010) estimate that one-third of offenders with intellectual disabilities have a comorbid mental illness. Of particular concern for this population is the dual diagnosis of personality disorder (PD). Individuals who suffer from both ID and PD are more likely to commit serious offences (Rayner, Wood, Beail, & Kaur Nagra, 2015), have higher levels of reoffending and are likely to be more violent than their non-ID counterparts (Hauser, Olson, & Drogin, 2014). OIDs were more likely to suffer from PDs if they were women (Alexander et al., 2010). OIDs who suffered from personality disorders experienced more charges of aggression and violence offences despite violence occurring the same amount in all offenders (Alexander et al., 2010). However, there are issues with the diagnosis of PD in those with ID due to difficulties differentiating symptoms that require cognizance of complex symptoms (e.g., concerning identity or empathy; Pridding & Procter, 2008). Diagnostic criteria that may indicate the occurrence of borderline PD or dependent PD may be instead related to symptoms of ID such as attachment with caregivers, making diagnosis complex (Pridding & Procter, 2008). However, this distinction is important to make due to the risk factors for recidivism that may occur especially when a diagnosis of antisocial PD is applicable (Haut & Brewster, 2010).

Assessment of OIDs is important to determine the dynamic treatment needs of the offender, as well as which treatment methodology should be used based on evidence of treatment efficacy (Keeling, Beech, & Rose, 2007; Lindsay, Elliot, & Astell, 2004). Wheeler et al. (2014) found that protective factors against recidivism could include the quality of relationships, quality of home life and daily activities. If assessments are able to determine these and other protective factors in offenders with intellectual disabilities perhaps treatment and interventions can be more specially targeted for these individuals to help decrease overall recidivism rates.

4.3.2 Assessment Issues

There are many tools that have been developed to assess OIDs. This includes measures purposely built for this population as well as previously developed tools cross-validated for this population. Due to the fact that OIDs suffer from cognitive impairments, caution needs to be taken when administering self-report measures to these individuals, especially those that were not designed for this population. This stresses the importance of determining whether mainstream tools have validity within this population.

Measures designed for mainstream offenders that have been cross validated with OIDs include the Static-99 (Hanson & Thornton, 2000), Static-99R (Hanson & Thornton, 2000; Helmus, Thornton, Hanson, & Babchishin, 2012), Rapid Risk Assessment for Sexual Offence Recidivism (RRASOR; Hanson, 1997), the Violence Risk Appraisal Guide (VRAG; Harris, Rice, & Quinsey, 1993), and Sexual Violence Risk-20 (SVR-20; Boer, Hart, Kropp, & Webster, 1997).

The RRASOR and both versions of the Static-99 were developed to determine a risk of a reoffence of a sexual nature in males only. The RRASOR has four items surrounding victims, offences and age. Higher scores increase likelihood of reoffending (Hanson, Sheahan, & VanZuylen, 2013). The Static-99 and Static-99R have ten-items surrounding offences/victims and personal characteristics. The only difference with the revised version is age weights (Hanson et al., 2013).

The Violence Risk Appraisal Guide (VRAG; Harris et al., 1993) is used to determine the likelihood of violent reoffending. It was designed for use with offenders without an ID, but has been cross-validated for use with OIDs who have been convicted of a violent offence (Gray, Fitzgerald, Taylor, MacCulloch, & Snowden, 2007). The VRAG has 12-items that include questions about victims, mental health, personal information and offences. Risk is then categorised into one of nine categories. Higher numbers indicate higher risk (Lofthouse et al., 2013).

Hanson et al. (2013) conducted a meta-analysis of the RRASOR, Static-99 and Static-99R and found that all three instruments had a moderate effect size in being able to differentiate between those OIDs who were likely to reoffend versus those who were not. The Static-99R was only included in one study therefore further follow-ups may be needed to determine its effectiveness. The RRASOR had variations in effect size throughout the different studies encompassing small to large effect sizes. They also conducted a study on 52 offenders who were developmentally delayed with the RRASOR, Static-99 and Static-99R. They found large effect sizes for all measures in detecting differences between those who reoffended and those who did not (Hanson et al., 2013).

Similarly, Stephens, Newman, Cantor, and Seto (2017) studied the Static-99 in 454 male OIDs who were charged with sexual offences. They reported that the Static-99 was able to predict sexual and violent recidivism however, including IQ did not affect incremental validity. For those with below average IQ, caution should be taken as it predicted recidivism levels as being lower than may actually occur.

The Assessment of Risk and Manageability for Individuals with Developmental and Intellectual Limitations who Offend Sexually (ARMIDILO-S; Boer et al., 2013) is a purpose-built tool for offenders 18-years and over with cognitive impairments. It assists in identifying risk-relevant and protective factors to guide and monitor treatment and risk. It features questions on both the client and the environment.

Lofthouse et al. (2013) studied the ARMIDILO-S, Static-99 and the Violence Risk Appraisal Guide in 64 sexual offenders with intellectual disabilities. They reported that the ARMIDILO-S was able to accurately predict reoffending rates with a large effect size when considering client, offender and total scores. The Static-99 was also able to determine sexual reoffending however, they stated that the ARMIDILO-S was superior in terms of predictive validity, even in those offenders with a borderline IQ. Although the client and offender scores were able to predict reoffence rates, the total score was better at overall prediction than its sub-parts. Similarly, in a study of 88 offenders (44 with intellectual disabilities), the ARMIDILO-S had the best predictive validity of sexual recidivism in sexual offenders with intellectual disabilities when compared to the RRASOR and SVR-20 (Blacker, Beech, Wilcox, & Boer, 2011).

The Dynamic Risk Assessment and Management System (DRAMS) developed by Lindsay, Murphy, et al. (2004) aims to identify dynamic risk factors for OIDs. It consists of different categories to measure risk such as: "mood, antisocial behaviour, substance use, thoughts, psychotic symptoms, self-regulation, therapeutic alliance, compliance with routine, renewal of emotional relationships and opportunity for victim access" (p. 269). Scoring is on a three-point scale and uses a traffic light system to identify least to most problematic behaviours (Steptoe, Lindsay, Murphy, & Young, 2008).

A field trial of the DRAMS conducted by Lindsay, Murphy, et al. (2004) on five participants over a 3-month period found that majority of the categories had moderate or higher reliability which indicates it potential usefulness. The only category that was relevant and not reliable was therapeutic alliance. Similar results were found in a study by Steptoe et al. (2008) that assessed the psychometric properties of a modified version of the DRAMS. They studied 23 males residing at a high-secure hospital over a 6-month period. The predictive validity of the DRAMS appears to have a medium effect size when comparing scores 7 days without incident and 2 or 3 days before an incident. Before an incident occurred, a change was noted in "mood, antisocial behaviour, intolerance/agreeableness and total score" (p. 319). They also found evidence for the convergent validity of the DRAMS with the Ward Anger Rating Scale where a large effect size was reported.

Overall, from the research it appears that purpose-built tools such as the ARMIDILO-S and DRAMS are the most useful in this population for predicting recidivism and determining changes in risk factors. However, the other measures discussed above that were designed for mainstream sexual and other violent offenders and cross-validated for OIDs are also recommended for such purposes.

4.4 Interventions

This section of the chapter focuses on three of the main areas that are the main areas of focus for CJS intervention with OIDs: treatment of anger and nonsexual violence, sexual violence. While there are other intervention areas with OIDs relevant to CJS practitioners (e.g., substance use treatment programmes designed specifically for OIDs, female offenders with intellectual disabilities), we found that these were not commonly reviewed or discussed in the offender literature.

4.4.1 Treatment of Anger and Nonsexual Violence in Offenders with Intellectual Disabilities

Anger, defined as a state of arousal and antagonism towards the perceived cause of some aversive event, has been identified as a being strongly associated with aggression (Novaco, 1994). Novaco (2011) presents a detailed conceptualisation of anger in a forensic context, drawing attention to the cognitive and behavioural components of anger experience and expression. A recent meta-analytic study found a strong relationship between anger and violence in a forensic sample (Chereji et al., 2012), and anger has been shown to be predictive of assaultive behaviour in several contexts (Novaco & Taylor, 2004). While anger is not sufficient for aggression or violence, it does present a salient risk factor and therefore its significance to the management of violence risk presents a relevant treatment target for intervention in forensic ID populations.

Taylor (2002), in their review of treatment literature for anger and aggression for persons with ID, identified three primary areas of treatment: psychopharmacological, behavioural and cognitive-behavioural therapy (CBT). The evidence for these will be briefly outlined below.

4.4.1.1 Psychopharmacological Treatments

Matson et al. (2000) reviewed the use of psychopharmacological interventions (i.e., the clinical use of medication) to alleviate or control behavioural difficulties in persons with ID. They reviewed a total of 72 articles published between 1990 and 1999 and identified only 14 that met partial methodological requirements for inclusion into their study. While each of these studies reported significant reductions in aggressive behaviour as a result of treatment, the authors state that each suffered from significant methodological flaws. Further, Matson et al. state that for the 12 studies that used antipsychotic medication as treatment, the observed effects upon aggressive behaviour were due to the indiscriminate suppression effect that decreased aggression in addition to other adaptive behaviours. As such, despite the widespread use of pharmacological intervention strategies, these authors found little evidence to support the use of psychoactive medication as a first line treatment due to the lack of specificity and negative impact upon adaptive behaviour (Brylewski & Duggan, 2009; Matson et al., 2000).

4.4.1.2 Behavioural Treatments

Behavioural interventions for aggression in persons with ID appear to have reasonable evidence for their efficacy in producing behaviour change in persons with ID (Whitaker, 2001). Lennox, Mitltenberger, Spengler, and Erfanian (1988) reviewed 162 studies of behavioural interventions, noting that quite intrusive behavioural techniques such as time outs and aversion therapy (along with medication, a non-behavioural intervention) were the most commonly behaviour change techniques utilised within the ID population (see Martin & Pear, 2015, for a review of many behaviour change techniques). However, they also noted that these were generally less effective at producing behaviour change when compared to less intrusive, and more constructive techniques such as environmental change and contingency management.

Some research has indicated that behavioural interventions are the most efficacious group of methods for reducing aggressive behaviour (Whitaker, 2001). However, behavioural interventions do not promote self-regulation, and once the contingencies that are implemented during intervention are removed, aggressive behaviours may return. Further, they generally require ongoing assistance from staff, and as most persons with ID do not live in environments that would facilitate this, it is necessary to consider other treatment options. Cognitive behavioural therapy, by comparison seeks to produce enduring change by increasing the individual's self-regulatory processes through targeting the cognitive distortions and behavioural skill deficits to replace old, dysfunctional patterns with new, functional ones.

4.4.1.3 Cognitive Behaviour Therapy Based Programmes

Psychological anger management programmes generally adhere to the principles of cognitive behavioural therapy (CBT) whilst utilizing three core components; (1) cognitive restructuring, (2) arousal reduction and (3) behavioural skills training. In forensic contexts they are generally group-based interventions that follow a similar sequence of psychoeducation (of triggers and the relationship between thoughts and feelings), self-monitoring, relaxation skills, problem solving, cognitive restructuring and conflict resolution training in addition to other CBT-based interventions in social and communication skills (Howells et al., 2002; Taylor & Novaco, 2005).

The psychological treatment of anger through this conceptual paradigm has been utilized in general offender populations without intellectual disabilities with significant positive effect. In a meta-analysis by Henwood, Chou, and Browne (2015), the authors noted a reduction in risk of violent crimes as high as 56% in a general offender population following anger management treatment packages. However, in considering OIDs, there is a paucity of research evaluating anger management programmes for the population, with the majority of what little research is available focusing upon persons with ID in other, non-forensic settings. The majority of research has been conducted using case and case-series studies, some of which provide promising indications of potential efficacy. Whitaker (2001) and Taylor (2002) both provide narrative reviews of the current literature regarding cognitive interventions for anger and aggression in persons with ID. None of the cases reviewed in these articles were current clients of corrective services, however much of the behaviour being targeted in the anger management packages would be considered risk-relevant when working with aggressive offenders. Whitaker (2001) reviewed 16 studies of anger interventions, concluding that despite some evidence to support the efficacy of certain aspects of the interventions reviewed, the experimental evidence of interventions efficacy was weak. Taylor (2002) identified six studies of anger management interventions for persons with intellectual disability and despite methodological issues, reported promising improvements for clients following group intervention (King, Lancaster, Wynne, Nettleton, & Davis, 1999; Moore, Adams, Elsworth, & Lewis, 1997; Rose, 1996). Both of these papers describe the mechanisms of change as being unclear, although they do note that certain components of treatment appear to have some treatment efficacy. For example, participants appeared to benefit most from non-cognitive components of the treatment packages such as relaxation, self-monitoring and skills training through role play (Rose, 1996; Rose, West, & Clifford, 2000; Whitaker, 2001).

In a meta-analysis by Hamelin, Travis, and Sturmey (2013) the authors reviewed two randomised controlled trials and six pre-test, post-test trials of anger management programmes with ID persons in which medium to large effect sizes were noted. However, none of the reviewed studies were well-controlled, so the efficacy of anger management could not be empirically supported. A recent randomised controlled-trial by Willner et al. (2013) reviewed the efficacy of a manualised, 12-week CBT-based intervention (see Willner et al. (2011) for a description) for people with ID, which was administered in day services by care staff supervised by a clinical psychologist. The study included several notable modifications for persons with ID, including frequent homework, a lack of written material in favour of pictorial material and functional analysis, which is complimented through the use of a pictorial workbook. The programme is reported to have reduced anger and challenging behaviours as rated by keyworkers and carers. However, there was no significant effect when specifically measuring aggression, and the effect was not maintained at follow up (Willner et al., 2013).

It may be that the relative lack of efficacy of cognitive techniques in the research above could be due to the difficulties persons with ID have in comprehending or utilising complex cognitive techniques. However, there is no research that has evaluated the individual cognitive components of anger management interventions, and therefore it is difficult to determine whether these are necessarily problematic. It may be that persons with ID are capable of comprehending such topics when they are properly supported in doing so through modifications in the way the techniques are presented. Taylor, Novaco, Gillmer, and Thorne (2002) have shown that ID persons can benefit from cognitive interventions by developing a cognitive-behavioural intervention for anger management that resulted in lower levels post-intervention.

The majority of the available research on anger management and the reduction of aggression focuses on persons with ID within the community, or in outpatient contexts. Very little research has considered programmes for OIDs who are incarcerated. This is despite the previously discussed high rate of aggressive behaviour and over-representation of intellectual disability within the CJS.

A study by Taylor, Novaco, et al. (2002) study is one of the few studies that evaluated the use of a CBT-based anger management group programme package for OIDs. The authors evaluated a pilot anger treatment programme in a sample of males with intellectual disabilities ($n = 9$) currently in detention, who had convictions for violent crimes and compared them to a waitlist control ($n = 10$). The treatment protocol was based upon the CBT approach developed by Novaco (1993) with a total of 18, 1-h sessions conducted twice weekly when possible. The authors utilised a 6-session preparatory phase aimed at desensitising participants to anxieties related to intervention and the building of rapport. The treatment phase consisted of 12-sessions focused upon the core components of cognitive restructuring, arousal reduction and behavioural skills training. Within these core components were interventions such as (a) self-monitoring of anger, (b) analysis and formulation of anger issues, (c) construction of a personalised anger hierarchy, (d) the challenging and modification of cognitive distortions and schemas, (e) arousal reduction techniques such as relaxation (breathing, progressive muscle relaxation and calming imagery), (f) the training of problem solving skills and communication through role play and (g) use of stress inoculation practices (Meichenbaum, 1985) to the anger hierarchy items through role play and imaginal exposure. The study's results indicated that participants reported significantly less feelings of anger intensity compared to the waitlist condition. Although, when the staff reports of anger were analysed there was no improvement. The authors state that this may be due to either a floor effect on the variable, or by the period of time between assessments being too short for effects to be observable. Nevertheless, the study provides an indication that persons with ID may benefit from a standardised, structured approach to anger treatment.

A recent case series study by Lindsay, Allan, MacLeod, Smart, and Smith (2003) involved the implementation of a treatment package to six men with assault convictions. The intervention took place over a total of 40 sessions, including a preparatory and arousal reduction phase in which psychoeducation was provided and relaxation methods were developed. Participants then engaged in stress inoculation (Meichenbaum, 1985) by developing hierarchies of anger-provoking situations before engaging in imaginal exposure to the provoking situations. The results indicated that there was generally no reduction in anger or aggression exhibited by the participants. However, there were reductions to the extent to which the men acted in an aggressive fashion. Specifically, among participants there was only one further assault recorded at follow-up in 4.5–10 years later.

Taylor and Novaco (2005) also developed an individually administered treatment programme for anger management for ID persons. Like their earlier group programme, this programme was also based on the work of Novaco (1975) and follows the 'stress inoculation' approach (Meichenbaum, 1985) which utilizes exposure based therapy to provoking situations. The programme begins with a 6-session "preparatory phase" to build engagement and motivation to participate, a necessary inclusion as those with anger issues generally deny that the anger is problematic (DiGiuseppe, Tafrate, & Eckhardt, 1994). This is then followed by a 12-week intervention course with the core components of cognitive restructuring, arousal reduction and behavioural skills training. The reader is directed to Taylor and Novaco (2005) for a detailed description of this treatment package. This manualised programme was evaluated by Novaco and Taylor (2015) in a population of 50 patients at a forensic hospital in the United Kingdom who had previously completed individual treatment for anger management. The results indicated a significant decrease in physical assaults in the 12-months following intervention when controlling for age, IQ, gender, length of stay in the hospital and severity of assaultive history. This provided some promising indication of efficacy for the programme's effectiveness with both forensic, and ID clients. However, the study did suffer from a small sample size and lack of control group, although this should not detract from the promising results it provides.

The research to date provides an indication that anger management programmes for persons with ID can be efficacious in a range of settings including those within the CJS. CBT-based interventions appear to be the most effective at reducing aggression long-term when compared to medication and behavioural interventions, however the exact mechanisms of change within the CBT-treatment packages reviewed are elusive. It seems apparent that the behavioural components of an intervention are generally the most effective, however there is also some indication that the cognitive aspects can be useful when adapted to the client's individual needs. Many of the treatment packages reviewed have used a preparatory stage to habituate the clients to the process of therapy, reduce anxiety and build rapport prior to beginning intervention. This stage is generally followed by a treatment phase including the core principles of cognitive restructuring, arousal reduction and behavioural skills training. The treatment of aggression in offenders with ID would benefit from further identification of mechanisms through which change can occur, and improvements in the methods through which the cognitive aspects of CBT can be implemented within this population.

4.4.2   Treatment of Sexual Violence

A recent book chapter by Boer (2017) echoed the treatment recommendations provided by the Association for the Treatment of Sexual Abusers (ATSA) in their position paper regarding the assessment, treatment, and supervision of persons with intellectual disabilities and problematic sexual behaviours (PIDPSB; Blasingame, Boer, Guidry, Haaven, & Wilson, 2014). Boer (2017) noted that the ATSA position paper found that most treatment programmes for PIDPSB employed aspects of cognitive-behavioural therapy (CBT), the "Old Me/New Me" model (Haaven et al., 1990), the Self-Regulation Pathways (SRP) Model of Ward and Hudson (2000), and a variety of techniques based on Relapse Prevention (RP model; Pithers, 1990) and the Good Lives Model (GLM; Ward, 2002). Succinct descriptions of all of these models were provided in the theory section of this chapter and are also explicated more broadly by Boer (2017).

The "best practice" treatment suggestions from the ATSA position paper along with the corresponding theoretical bases were described by Boer (2017). The suggested treatment intervention approaches based upon the theoretical bases noted above included: the use of CBT approaches, particularly those that are skill-based; adherence to the principles of RNR; review treatment programs to ensure that the targets of treatment are risk-relevant; ensure that treatment plans are individualized according to the dynamic treatment needs of the individual (risk assessment tests like the ARMIDILO-S, which are composed of dynamic risk issues, are particularly well suited to the identification of such needs); use of motivational enhancement techniques which are attuned to the responsivity needs of the clients; use of intervention targets that were risk-relevant (i.e., based on offending patterns); provide a positive focus in therapy in order to increase self-efficacy, positive personal identity and positive "approach" goals (positive goals that the client can feasibly achieve formulated using the GLM); help offenders develop cognitive strategies related to choosing amongst relevant alternatives (e.g., performing cost-benefit analyses) in their offending pathways; ensure that risk-relevant contextual (i.e., environmental) issues are addressed; increase social skills for better community involvement; and help offenders develop positive supports in the community for helping with risk management. Boer (2013) expanded on the latter few issues in a paper in which he explicated the "SOAPP" model, namely risk-reducing Support, Occupation, Accommodation, and Programs, all integrated in a constantly evolving Plan in a paper about "essential environmental ingredients for sex offender reintegration". The paper by Boer (2013) was an attempt to operationalize some of the features of the GLM, particularly the positive, life-enhancing aspects of the model while not abandoning the risk-reducing focus of the RP model during the reintegration process of OIDs who have been convicted of sexual crimes.

The majority of treatment models for OIDs who have been convicted of sexual crimes are based on the theoretical models described above. Some of the older programmes (e.g., the Northstar Programme (Boer, Dorward, Gauthier, & Watson, 1995) were based primarily on a contextualized RP model with RNR values, where more recent programmes (e.g., Lindsay, 2009) were more clearly based on the GLM and RNR theories, with RP influences. While there are some authors who view the RP and RNR models as being in decline in terms of theoretical value to modern programmes, both are clearly still central to some of the best work being done in the field (e.g., the Sex Offender Treatment Services Collaborative in Intellectual Disabilities or "SOTSEC-ID" programme by Murphy & Sinclair, 2009).

The effectiveness literature for the treatment of OIDs who have committed sexual crimes is not overly convincing at this juncture. As noted by Boer (2017), many of the studies in the literature have small sample sizes and suffer from a variety of shortcomings such as inadequate control groups, confounded samples and designs, differing outcome variables (sometimes not recidivism, but other treatment indicators), and variable follow-up periods that make an overall finding of treatment effectiveness difficult at this time. It is hoped that future programmes will take into consideration the advice of Blasingame et al. (2014) to use the ARMDILO-S by Boer et al. (2013) (or other tools utilizing dynamic risk issues) as a means to identify dynamic client and environmental factors in the construction of both risk management and supervision plans, and by extension to organize treatment plans and interventions on risk-relevant dynamic risk issues. A programme organized around these precepts, utilizing the above theoretical models for guidance, with the ultimate aim of safe reintegration would seem the most probable and efficacious programme for OIDs who have committed sexual offences. That programme is yet to be written, but there are many good programmes to draw on at this time, particularly that of Lindsay (2009) and the SOTSEC-ID group (as described by Murphy & Sinclair, 2009).

4.4.3 Other Intervention Foci and Issues

The majority of the focus on treatments and interventions for OIDs has focused on males (Hellenbach, Brown, Karatzias, & Robinson, 2015). As such, there is a lack of knowledge about what treatment is effective for women. Hellenbach, Brown, et al. (2015) conducted a systematic review of four studies that applied cognitive-behavioural therapy type interventions on women offenders with ID. All treatment was delivered in a group and targeted fire-setting and aggression. These interventions were originally designed for males and therefore may target different issues than are needed for women. The four studies all reported improvements in outcomes measures with no participants terminating groups early (e.g., Taylor, Robertson, Thorne, Belshaw, & Watson, 2006). Taylor, Thorne, Robertson, and Avery (2002) also studied fire-setting in women ID offenders. They aimed to decrease risk factors for fire-setting and included psychoeducation on fire-setting and skills for future stress management. They reported that their intervention appeared to decrease negative attitudes and cognitions surrounding fire-setting, as well as having a positive impact on anger and self-esteem.

Allen, Lindsay, MacLeod, and Smith (2001) studied anger levels in women offenders with ID to determine effectiveness of an anger management intervention and found that although improvements did occur, they did not occur at the same rate for all individuals and therefore concluded that external variables may account for some of the change. Furthermore, arousal reduction did not assist anger management in this programme as it had previously done with males. Lindsay, Allan, et al. (2004) also studied treatment for anger and aggression in mixed groups of male and female offenders and reported that improvements were made in levels of anger and maintained 3 and 9 months post-treatment. Treatment included relaxation, 'stress inoculation,' anger psychoeducation, role-plays and problem-solving. Lindsay, Allan, et al. (2004) followed recidivism rates 1 year after treatment with aggressive offences having decreased. As these interventions were developed for men, it may explain why some interventions or outcome measures did not indicate significant improvements as women may have different and more complex needs than men and, as such, may need specifically designed interventions that better treat the unique and complex needs they present with as offenders.

Research for substance use in offenders with intellectual disabilities is varied. A review of substance abuse programmes designed for OIDs examining was completed by Kerr, Lawrence, Darbyshire, Middleton, and Fitzsimmons (2012). These researchers reviewed alcohol treatment (three studies), tobacco use treatment (four studies), and combined treatment for both tobacco and alcohol (two studies). The interventions which were reviewed focused on psychoeducation or attempts to reduce consumption levels. Kerr et al. (2012) cited methodological issues, including lack of control groups and perhaps inappropriate use of measures that may have affected the interpretation of results. Despite this, groups that targeted both tobacco and alcohol appeared to be more effective. Some studies reported an increase in substance abuse knowledge and participants progressed through the stages of change. However, due to small numbers and other study issues caution must be taken in interpreting these studies.

One specific study that focused on OIDs and substance use was conducted by Mendel and Hipkins (2002). These authors studied a pilot group aimed at enhancing motivation to change their alcohol use. This study employed motivational interviewing and psychoeducation on drinking, goal-setting, empowerment, self-esteem and increasing responsibility. All participants except one experienced a positive increase in motivation to address their alcohol use problems. Four out of seven individuals believed that their self-efficacy increased with one believing it decreased however, it was thought to be related to outside circumstances. The majority of participants in the study were able to recognise the consequences of their alcohol use rather than focusing on benefits of drinking. However, measures in this study had not been validated with ID offenders previously. Substances were also banned from the unit where the individuals in this study resided questioning the applicability of them not using alcohol and wanting to change their alcohol use. Further studies may need to be employed to determine the effectiveness of substance use programme for offenders with intellectual disabilities.

4.5 Future Implications

The future of the assessment and treatment of offenders with intellectual disabilities (OIDs) is one likely filled with a mixture of studies and experimental approaches utilizing some of the newer models (e.g., the GLM) and new technology, as well as a back to first principles approach in other studies of the assessment and treatment of OIDs (e.g., utilizing behaviour modification and social skills training). As noted below, traditional and even newer approaches have not provided convincing data of treatment efficacy despite the hundreds of studies in the field. Basic behaviour modification techniques focused on selected behaviours (e.g., managing social situations where alcohol is offered, or learning to be assertive in confrontations, or learning to manage deviant arousal without offending) may be less comprehensive in terms of a treatment optic, but may be more effective in reducing recidivism than the current comprehensive treatment models. The latter models may be too focused on helping offenders design and achieve personal goals, or understand offence pathways and risk factors, while not rehearsing how to react in each situation with routinized responses and actions that could help the individual avoid offending. Simpler interventions focused on how to facilitate and maintain reintegration, using positive behaviour support, and more focus on behaviour change may be worth exploring to help OIDs change their problematic behaviours. There is a large literature on behaviour modification, dating back many decades, on persons with intellectual disabilities and behaviour change. Perhaps it is time to reconsider the current complex programmes and focus on individual problem behaviours with simple intervention programmes across numerous sites to begin to find effective interventions rather than let complex theory dictate programmes that have yet to be proven effective.

4.6   Technology and Innovation

As technology has progressed and become more widely accessible there has been increasing attention being paid to the use of technology such as computers, phones and the internet to improve therapeutic packages. However, many clinicians either hold negative perceptions about their own abilities, or the capacity of the ID persons they are treating to meaningfully engage with computer-based interventions (Vereenooghe, Gega, & Langdon, 2017). Despite this hesitation, technology is becoming increasingly more a part of everyday life, and the general population is becoming quite computer-literate. Therefore, the utility of computers in intervention is something worthy of consideration, particularly with the ID-population who can often have social and communication deficits that interfere with interpersonal therapy.

Virtual reality is a computer-generated world created in three-dimensions that users view through a monitor or similar device and the subjects of the virtual world can be interacted with by the user. It is within this virtual world that therapeutic benefits may lie for persons with ID. Thus far in the chapter we have discussed the benefits of role plays, problem solving and other similar learning practices to reduce risk of reoffending; advances in virtual reality may present an invaluable opportunity to improve learning opportunities to assist persons with ID to develop skills in an environment in which safety of both the clients and the community can be maintained. Further, clients can avoid the embarrassment and confounding factors that may present in the real-world (Salem-Darrow, 1995).

The nature of the CJS dictates that clients who are incarcerated have reduced contact with the external world. For these persons, the flexibility of virtual reality may present an opportunity to engage in scenarios they may encounter outside of the system and develop appropriate strategies to manage these and adapt to the general population upon release, thereby reducing risk to the community. Importantly, the use of the virtual world as a learning tool is flexible, meaning that it can be modified and adapted to the individuals needs and skills. Within virtual reality, worlds can be created that are as simple, or complex as necessary to allow for personalised learning needs and scaffolding methods can be applied where appropriate. Finally, as persons with ID can often have difficulty with language, the virtual world can communicate complex or abstract concepts without the use of language (Standen & Brown, 2005). Technology may also provide an avenue to overcome some of the communication difficulties encountered in sessions, and may prove more engaging for persons with ID than in-person therapy (Vereenooghe et al., 2017).

A study by Cooke, Laczny, Brown, and Francik (2002) evaluated the use of a virtual courtroom to familiarise persons with ID to court proceedings, reduce their anxiety when appearing and to assist in overcoming some of the disadvantages they face in this context. The authors developed a virtual reality environment in which the participants could explore a courtroom and interact with the persons within, having the roles and procedures explained to them by these virtual entities. Further multimedia scenarios were included to demonstrate the giving of evidence and cross examination proceedings to provide the participants with an understanding of their roles and rights within the system. While the authors report that the participants met the proposed learning (outcomes related to becoming familiar with police procedure and court processes), further assessment is required to evaluate the efficacy of this particular teaching method. It does however provide a good indication of the methods in which VR could be used to benefit persons with ID.

There does not appear to be any published research on the use of VR in the rehabilitation of OIDs. However, the use of VR to develop independent living skills has shown promising evidence with persons with ID in the general population. Standen and Brown (2005) provide a review of the literature to date addressing this topic and identified that VR has been successfully employed to develop independent living skills in person with ID. For example, a grocery shopping study (Standen, Cromby, & Brown, 1998) using a RCT design in a sample of 14–19 year old persons with severe ID evaluated the use of a VR environment to learn a list of items and gather these from a real store following practice within the VR environment. The authors found that participants who were given VR practice were significantly faster and more accurate in their selection of items following intervention in a real supermarket than participants without VR practice. Other studies reviewed by Standen and Brown (2005) found similar benefits of VR practice, although not all findings reached the level of statistical significance (e.g., Brooks, Rose, Attree, & Elliot-Square, 2002; Mendozzi et al., 2000). Standen and Brown (2005) concluded that the studies they had reviewed indicated VR may be a possible treatment option for persons with ID as it provides an opportunity to learn adaptive skills in environments that are not readily accessible while in the CJS.

4.7 Conclusions

A review of the information for this chapter indicates that the "magic bullet" for helping offenders with intellectual disabilities (OIDs) change their problematic behaviours has not yet been found. The studies on helping sexually violent or non-sexually violent OIDs (as well as other problematic behaviours such as substance abuse) show some promising developments, but often the studies are plagued by small sample sizes, small effect sizes and lack of replication by other researchers. There is room for optimism, but it is our opinion that some of the more complex theoretical approaches (see Boer, 2017; Blasingame et al., 2014 for theoretical reviews) may not be well-suited to designing interventions for the problematic behaviours of OIDs. A return to basic behavioural interventions for simple but obviously risk-relevant behaviours is recommended across cooperating sites to allow the accumulation of effectiveness data and eventual relevant theory for the assessment and intervention with OIDs.

References

Alexander, R. T., Green, F. N., O'Mahony, B., Gunaratna, I. J., Gangadharan, S. K., & Hoare, S. (2010). Personality disorders in offenders with intellectual disability: A comparison of clinical, forensic and outcome variables and implications for service provision. *Journal of Intellectual Disability Research, 54*(7), 650–658.

Ali, A., Ghosh, S., Strydom, A., & Hassiotis, A. (2016). Prisoners with intellectual disabilities and detention status. Findings from a UK cross sectional study of prisons. *Research in Developmental Disabilities, 53–54*, 189–197.

Allen, R., Lindsay, W. R., MacLeod, F., & Smith, A. H. W. (2001). Treatment of women with intellectual disabilities who have been involved with the criminal justice system for reasons of aggression. *Journal of Applied Research in Intellectual Disabilities, 14*, 340–347. https://doi.org/10.1046/j.1468-3148.2001.00086.x

American Psychiatric Association. (2013). *Diagnostic and statistical manual of mental disorders* (5th ed.). Arlington, VA: American Psychiatric Publishing.

Andrews, D. A., Bonta, J., & Wormith, J. S. (2011). The risk-need-responsivity (RNR) model: Does adding the good lives model contribute to effective crime prevention? *Criminal Justice and Behavior, 38*(7), 735–755.

Baldry, E., Dowse, L., & Clarence, M. (2012). *People with intellectual and other cognitive disability in the criminal justice system.* Sydney: University of New South Wales.

Barazzone, N., & Davey, G. C. (2009). Anger potentiates the reporting of threatening interpretations: An experimental study. *Journal of Anxiety Disorders, 23*(4), 489–495.

Basquill, M. F., Nezu, C. M., Nezu, A. M., & Klein, T. L. (2004). Aggression-related hostility bias and social problem-solving deficits in adult males with mental retardation. *American Journal of Mental Retardation, 109*(3), 255–263.

Blacker, J., Beech, A. R., Wilcox, D. T., & Boer, D. P. (2011). The assessment of dynamic risk and recidivism in a sample of special needs sexual offenders. *Psychology, Crime & Law, 17*, 75–92. https://doi.org/10.1080/10683160903392376

Blasingame, G. D., Boer, D. P., Guidry, L., Haaven, J., & Wilson, R. J. (2014). *Assessment, treatment, and supervision of individuals with intellectual disabilities and problematic sexual behaviors.* Beaverton, OR: Association for the Treatment of Sexual Abuser Retrieved from www.asta.com

Boer, D., Haaven, J., Lambrick, F., Lindsay, B., McVilly, K., Sakdalan, J., & Frize, M. (2013). *ARMIDILO-S: the Assessment of Risk and Manageability of Individuals with Developmental and Intellectual Limitations who Offend-Sexually.* Retrieved from www.Armidilo.net

Boer, D. P. (2013). Some essential environmental ingredients for sex offender reintegration. *International Journal of Behavioral Consultation and Therapy, 8*, 8–11.

Boer, D. P. (2017). Treatment of persons with intellectual disabilities and problematic sexual behaviours. In D. P. Boer (Editor-in-Chief); L. E. Marshall and W. R. Marshall (Volume Eds.), *The Wiley handbook on the theory, assessment, and treatment of sexual offending (Volume III: Treatment)* (pp. 1285–1297). Chichester, UK: John Wiley & Sons.

Boer, D. P., Dorward, J., Gauthier, C., & Watson, D. (1995). *Northstar program.* Abbotsford, Canada: Regional Treatment Centre (Pacific).

Boer, D. P., Hart, S. D., Kropp, P. R., & Webster, C. D. (1997). *Manual for the Sexual Violence Risk-20: Professional guidelines for assessing risk of sexual violence.* Vancouver, Canada: Mental Health, Law and Policy Institute.

Brooks, B. M., Rose, F. D., Attree, E. A., & Elliot-Square, A. (2002). An evaluation of the efficacy of training people with learning disabilities in a virtual environment. *Disability and Rehabilitation, 15*(24), 622–626.

Brylewski, J., & Duggan, L. (2009). Antipsychotic medication for challenging behaviour in people with learning disability. *Cochrane Database of Systematic Reviews*, (3), CD000377.

Burgard, J. F., Donohue, B., Azrin, N. H., & Teichner, G. (2000). Prevalence and treatment of substance abuse in the mentally retarded population: An empirical review. *Journal of Psychoactive Drugs, 32*(3), 293–298. https://doi.org/10.1080/02791072.2000.10400452

Cashin, A., Butler, T., Levy, M., & Potter, E. (2006). Intellectual disability in the New South Wales inmate population. *International Journal of Prisoner Health, 2*(2), 115–120.

Chan, J. P. S., & Boer, D. P. (2016). Managing offenders and what works in Singapore: Ten Reintegration Assessment Predictors (T.R.A.P.). *Safer Communities, 15*(3), 142–159. https://doi.org/10.1108/SC-04-2016-0008

Chereji, S. V., Pintea, S., & David, D. (2012). The relationship of anger and cognitive distortions with violence in violent offenders' population: A meta-analysis review. *The European Journal of Psychology Applied to Legal Context, 4*(1), 59–77.

Cloud, M., Shepherd, G. B., Barkoff, A. N., & Shur, J. V. (2002). Words without meaning: The constitution, confessions, and mentally retarded suspects. *The University of Chicago Law Review, 69*(2), 495–624.

Cooke, P., Laczny, A., Brown, D. J., & Francik, J. (2002). The virtual courtroom: A view of justice. Project to prepare witnesses or victims with learning disabilities to give evidence. *Disability and Rehabilitation, 34*(11–12), 634–642.

Crick, N. R., & Dodge, K. A. (1994). A review and reformulation of social-information-processing mechanisms in children's social adjustment. *Psychological Bulletin, 115*, 74–101.

Crocker, A. G., Cote, G., Toupin, J., & St-Onge, B. (2007). Rate and characteristics of men with an intellectual disability in pre-trial detention. *Journal of Intellectual and Developmental Disability, 32*(2), 143–152. https://doi.org/10.1080/13668250701314053

Day, K. (1988). A hospital-based treatment programme for male mentally handicapped offenders. *British Journal of Psychiatry, 153*, 635–644. https://doi.org/10.1192/bjp.153.5.635

Denkowski, G. C., & Denkowski, K. M. (1985). The mentally retarded offender in the state prison system. Identification, prevalence, adjustment and rehabilitation. *Criminal Justice and Behaviour, 12*, 53–70.

DiGiuseppe, R., Tafrate, R. T., & Eckhardt, C. (1994). Critical issues in the treatment of anger. *Cognitive and Behavioral Practice, 1*, 111–132.

Dingwall, K. M., Pinkerton, J., & Lindeman, M. A. (2013). "People like numbers": A descriptive study of cognitive assessment methods in clinical practice for Aboriginal Australians in the Northern Territory. *BMC Psychiatry, 13*(42). https://doi.org/10.1186/1471-244X-13-42

Drizin, S. A., & Leo, R. A. (2004). The problem of false confessions in the post-DNA world. *North Carolina Law Review, 82*, 891–1007.

Dwyer, R. G., & Frierson, R. L. (2006). The presence of low IQ and mental retardation among murder defendants referred for pretrial evaluation. *Journal of Forensic Sciences, 51*(3), 678–682.

Einat, T., & Einat, A. (2008). Learning disabilities and delinquency. *International Journal of Offender Therapy and Comparative Criminology, 52*(4), 416–434.

Farrington, D. P. (2000). Psychosocial causes of offending. In M. G. Gender, J. J. Lopez-Ibor, & N. Andersen (Eds.), *New Oxford textbook of psychiatry* (Vol. 2, pp. 2029–2036). Oxford: Oxford University Press.

Fazel, S., Xenitidis, K., & Powell, J. (2008). The prevalence of intellectual disabilities among 12,000 prisoners—A systematic review. *International Journal of Law and Psychiatry, 31*, 369–373.

Fitzgerald, S., Gray, N. S., Taylor, J., & Snowden, R. J. (2011). Risk factors for recidivism in offenders with intellectual disabilities. *Psychology, Crime & Law, 17*, 43–58. https://doi.org/10.1080/10683160903392293

Fogden, B. C., Thomas, S. D. M., Daffern, M., & Ogloff, J. R. P. (2016). Crime and victimisation in people with intellectual disability: A case linkage study. *BMC Psychiatry, 16*, 170. https://doi.org/10.1186/s12888-016-0869-7

Glaser, W., & Deane, K. (1999). Normalisation in an abnormal world: A study of prisoners with an intellectual disability. *International Journal of Offender Therapy and Comparative Criminology, 43*(4), 338–356.

Gray, N. S., Fitzgerald, S., Taylor, J., MacCulloch, M. J., & Snowden, R. J. (2007). Predicting future reconviction in offenders with intellectual disabilities: The predictive efficacy of VRAG, PCL-SV, and the HCR-20. *Psychological Assessment, 19*(4), 474–479. http://dx.doi.org/10.1037/1040-3590.19.4.474

Haaven, J., Little, R., & Petre-Miller, D. (1990). *Treating intellectually disabled sex offenders: A model residential program*. Orwell, VT: Safer Society Press.

Hall, T. S. (2002). Legal fictions and moral reasoning: Capital punishment and the mentally retarded defendant after Penry V. Johnson. *Akron Law Review, 35*(3–4), 327–370.

Hamelin, J., Travis, R., & Sturmey, P. (2013). Anger management and intellectual disabilities: A systematic review. *Journal of Mental Health Research in Intellectual Disabilities, 6*, 60–70.

Hanson, R. K. (1997). *The development of a brief actuarial risk scale for sexual offence recidivism (User Report 97-04)*. Ottawa, ON: Department of the Solicitor General of Canada.

Hanson, R. J., Sheahan, C. L., & VanZuylen, H. (2013). STATIC-99 and RRASOR predict recidivism among developmentally delayed sex offenders: A cumulative meta-analysis. *Sexual Offender Treatment, 8*. Retrieved from http://www.sexual-offender-treatment.org/119.html

Hanson, R. K., & Thornton, D. (2000). Improving risk assessments for sex offenders: A comparison of three actuarial scales. *Law and Human Behaviour, 24*, 119–136. https://doi.org/10.1023/a:1005482921333

Harrington, R., & Bailey, S. (2005). *Mental health needs and effectiveness of provision for young offenders in custody and in the community*. London: Youth Justice Board for England and Wales.

Harris, P. (1993). The nature and extent of aggressive behaviour amongst people with learning difficullties (mental handicap) in a single health district. *Journal of Intellectual Disability Research, 37*(3), 221–242.

Harris, J. C. (2006). *Intellectual disability: Understanding its development, causes, classification, evaluation and treatment*. New York, NY: Oxford University Press.

Harris, G. T., Rice, M. E., & Quinsey, V. L. (1993). Violent recidivism of mentally disordered offenders: The development of a statistical prediction instrument. *Criminal Justice and Behavior, 20*, 315–335.

Hassiotis, A., Gazizova, D., Akinlonu, L., Bebbington, P., Meltzer, H., & Strydom, A. (2011). Psychiatric morbidity in prisoners with ID: Analysis of prison survey data for England and Wales. *The British Journal of Psychiatry, 199*, 156–157.

Hauser, M. J., Olson, E., & Drogin, E. Y. (2014). Psychiatric disorders in people with intellectual disability (intellectual developmental disorder): Forensic aspects. *Current Opinion in Psychiatry, 27*, 117–121. https://doi.org/10.1097/YCO.0000000000000036

Haut, F., & Brewster, E. (2010). Psychiatric illness, pervasive development disorders and risk. In L. A. Craig, W. R. Lindsay, & K. D. Browne (Eds.), *Assessment and treatment of sexual offenders with intellectual disabilities* (pp. 89–110). West Sussex, UK: John Wiley & Sons.

Hayes, S. C. (1997). Prevalence of intellectual disability in local courts. *Journal of Intellectual and Developmental Disability, 22*(2), 71–85.

Hayes, S. C., Shackell, P., Mottram, P., & Lancaster, R. (2007). The prevalence of intellectual disability in a major UK prison. *British Journal of Learning Disabilities, 35*, 162–167.

Hellenbach, M., Brown, M., Karatzias, T., & Robinson, R. (2015). Psychological interventions for women with intellectual disabilities and forensic care needs: A systematic review of the literature. *Journal of Intellectual Disability Research, 59*, 319–331. https://doi.org/10.1111/jir.12133

Hellenbach, M., Karatzias, T., & Brown, M. (2015). Intellectual disabilities among prisoners: Prevalence and mental and physical health comorbidities. *Journal of Applied Research in Intellectual Disabilities, 30*, 230–241.

Helmus, L., Thornton, D., Hanson, R. K., & Babchishin, K. M. (2012). Improving the predictive accuracy of Static-99 and Static-2002 with older sex offenders: Revised age weights. *Sexual Abuse: Journal of Research and Treatment, 24*, 64–101. https://doi.org/10.1177/1079063211409951

Henwood, K. S., Chou, S., & Browne, K. D. (2015). A systematic review and meta-analysis on the effectiveness of CBT informed anger management. *Aggression and Violent Behavior, 25*, 280–292.

Hingsburger, D., Griffiths, D., & Quinsey, V. (1991). Detecting counterfeit deviance: Differentiating sexual deviance from sexual inappropriateness. *Habilitative Mental Health Care Newsletter, 10*, 51–54.

Holland, T., Clare, C. H., & Mukhopadhyay, T. (2002). Prevalence of 'criminal offending' by men and women with intellectual disability and the characteristics of 'offenders': Implications for research and service development. *Journal of Intellectual Disability Research, 46*(1), 6–20. https://doi.org/10.1046/j.1365-2788.2002.00001.x

Howells, K., Day, A., Bubner, S., Jauncey, S., Williamson, P., Parker, A., & Heseltine, K. (2002). *Anger management and violence prevention: Improving effectiveness.* Trends & issues in crime and criminal justice No. 227. Canberra, ACT: Australian Institute of Criminology.

Jahoda, A., Pert, C., & Trower, P. (2006). Frequent aggression and attribution of hostile intent in people with mild to moderate intellectual disabilities: An empirical investigation. *American Journal of Mental Retardation, 111*(2), 90–99.

Keeling, J. A., Beech, A. R., & Rose, J. L. (2007). Assessment of intellectually disabled sexual offenders: The current position. *Aggression and Violent Behaviour, 12*, 229–241. https://doi.org/10.1016/j.avb.2006.08.001

Kerr, S., Lawrence, M., Darbyshire, C., Middleton, A. R., & Fitzsimmons, L. (2012). Tobacco and alcohol-related interventions for people with mild/moderate intellectual disabilities: A systematic review of the literature. *Journal of Intellectual Disability Research, 57*, 393–408. https://doi.org/10.1111/j.1365-2788.2012.01543.x

King, N., Lancaster, N., Wynne, G., Nettleton, N., & Davis, R. (1999). Cognitive-behavioural anger management training for adults with mild intellectual disability. *Scandinavian Journal of Behaviour Therapy, 28*, 19–22.

Kirk, J., Jahoda, A., & Pert, C. (2008). Beliefs about aggression and submissiveness: A comparison of aggressive and nonaggressive individuals with mild intellectual disability. *Journal of Mental Health Research in Intellectual Disabilities, 1*(3), 191–204.

Klimecki, M., Jenkinson, J., & Wilson, L. (1994). A study of recidivism among offenders with an intellectual disability. *Australian and New Zealand Journal of Developmental Disabilities, 19*, 209–219.

Langdon, P. E., Daniel, M. R., & Sadek, S. A. (2016). *The relationship between moral development, distorted cognitions and social problem solving amongst men with intellectual disabilities who have a history of criminal offending.* Paper presented at the International Association for the Scientific Study of Intellectual and Developmental Disabilities World Congress, Melbourne.

Langdon, P. E., & Murphy, G. H. (2017). Treatment of violence and aggression in offenders with developmental disabilities. In P. Sturmey (Ed.), *The Wiley handbook of violence and aggression.* New York, NY: John Wiley & Sons. https://doi.org/10.1002/9781119057574.whbva085

Langdon, P. E., Murphy, G. H., Clare, I. C. H., Steverson, T., & Palmer, E. J. (2011). The relationships between moral reasoning, empathy and distorted cognitions amongst men with and without intellectual disabilities who have a history of criminal offending: A comparison study. *American Journal on Intellectual and Developmental Disabilities, 116*(6), 438–456. https://doi.org/10.1352/1944-7558-116.6.438

Larkin, P., Jahoda, A., & MacMahon, K. (2013). The social information processing model as a framework for explaining frequent aggression. *Journal of Applied Research in Intellectual Disabilities, 26*, 447–465.

Lennox, D. B., Mitltenberger, R. G., Spengler, P., & Erfanian, N. (1988). Decelerative treatment practices with persons who have mental retardation: A review of five years of the literature. *American Journal of Mental Retardation, 92*(6), 492–501.

Lindsay, W. R. (2009). *The treatment of sex offenders with developmental disabilities. A practice manual.* Chichester, UK: John Wiley & Sons.

Lindsay, W. R. (2017). Theoretical approaches for sexual offenders with intellectual and developmental disabilities. In D. P. Boer (Editor-in-Chief); A. R. Beech and T. Ward (Volume Eds.), *The Wiley handbook on the theory, assessment, and treatment of sexual offending (Volume I: Theories)* (pp. 473–495*)*. Chichester, UK: John Wiley & Sons.

Lindsay, W. R., Allan, R., MacLeod, F., Smart, N., & Smith, A. H. (2003). Long-term treatment and management of violent tendencies of men with intellectual disabilities convicted of assault. *Mental Retardation, 41*(1), 47–56.

Lindsay, W. R., Allan, R., Parry, C., MacLeod, F., Cottrell, J., Overend, H., & Smith, A. H. W. (2004). Anger and aggression in people with intellectual disabilities: Treatment and follow-up of consecutive referrals and a waiting list comparison. *Clinical Psychology and Psychotherapy, 11*, 255–264. https://doi.org/10.1002/cpp.415

Lindsay, W. R., Elliot, S. F., & Astell, A. (2004). Predictors of sexual offence recidivism in offenders with intellectual disabilities. *Journal of Applied Research in Intellectual Disabilities, 17*, 299–305. https://doi.org/10.1111/j.1468-3148.2004.00217.x

Lindsay, W. R., Murphy, L., Smith, G., Murphy, D., Edwards, Z., Chittock, C., … Young, S. J. (2004). The Dynamic Risk Assessment and Management System: An assessment of immediate risk of violence for individuals with offending and challenging behaviour. *Journal of Applied Research in Intellectual Disabilities, 17*, 267–274. https://doi.org/10.1111/j.1468-3148.2004.00215.x

Lindsay, W. R., Steptoe, L., & Beech, A. R. (2008). The Ward and Hudson Pathways model of the sexual offence process applied to offenders with intellectual disability. *Sexual Abuse: A Journal of Research and Treatment, 20*, 379–392.

Lindsay, W. R., Sturmey, P., & Taylor, J. L. (2004). Natural history and theories of offending in people with developmental disabilities. In W. L. Lindsay, P. Sturmey, & J. L. Taylor (Eds.), *Offenders with developmental disabilities* (pp. 3–21). Chichester, UK: John Wiley & Sons.

Lofthouse, R. E., Lindsay, W. R., Totsika, V., Hastings, R. P., Boer, D. P., & Haaven, J. L. (2013). Prospective dynamic assessment of risk of sexual reoffending in individuals with an intellectual disability and a history of sexual offending behaviour. *Journal of Applied Research in Intellectual Disabilities, 26*, 394–403. https://doi.org/10.1111/jar.12029

MacEachron, A. E. (1979). Mentally retarded offenders: Prevalence and characteristics. *American Journal of Mental Deficiency, 84*(2), 165–176.

Marshall, W. L., & Barbaree, H. E. (1990). An integrated theory of the etiology of sexual offending. In W. L. Marshall, D. R. Laws, & H. E. Barbaree (Eds.), *Handbook of sexual assault: Issues, theories, and treatment of the offender* (pp. 257–275). New York, NY: Plenum.

Martin, G., & Pear, J. P. (2015). *Behavior modification: What is and how to do it*. New York, NY: Pearson Education, Inc.

Matheson, E., & Jahoda, A. (2005). Emotional understanding in aggressive and nonaggressive individuals with mild or moderate mental retardation. *American Journal of Mental Retardation, 110*(1), 57–67.

Matson, J. L., Bamburg, J. W., Mayville, E. A., Pinkston, J., Bielecki, J., Kuhn, D., … Logan, J. R. (2000). Psychopharmacology and mental retardation: A 10 year review (1990–1999). *Research in Developmental Disabilities, 21*, 263–296.

McBrien, J., Hodgetts, A., & Gregory, J. (2003). Offending and risky behaviour in community services for people with intellectual disabilities in one local authority. *The Journal of Forensic Psychiatry & Psychology, 14*(2), 280–287. https://doi.org/10.1080/1478994031000084828

McGillicuddy, N. B. (2006). A review of substance use research among those with mental retardation. *Mental Retardation and Developmental Disabilities Research Reviews, 12*, 41–47.

McGillivray, J. A., & Newton, D. C. (2016). Self-reported substance use and intervention experience of prisoners with intellectual disability. *Journal of Intellectual and Developmental Disability, 41*, 166–176. https://doi.org/10.3109/13668250.2016.1146944

McNeill, F., & Weaver, B. (2010). *Changing lives? Desistance research and offender management*. Glasgow, UK: Scottish Centre for Crime and Justice Research.

Meichenbaum, D. (1985). *Stress inoculation training*. Oxford, UK: Pergamon Press.

Mendel, E., & Hipkins, J. (2002). Motivating learning disabled offenders with alcohol-related problems: A pilot study. *British Journal of Learning Disabilities, 30*, 153–158. https://doi.org/10.1046/j.1468-3156.2002.00209.x

Mendozzi, L., Pugnetti, L., Barbieri, E., Attree, E. A., Rose, F. D., Moro, W., ... Cutelli, E. (2000). VIRT - factory trainer project. *A generic productive process to train persons with disabilities.* Paper presented at the Third International Conference on Disability Virtual Reality and Associated Technologies, Italy.

Moore, E., Adams, R., Elsworth, J., & Lewis, J. (1997). An anger management group for people with a learning disability. *British Journal of Learning Disabilities, 25*, 53–57.

Mottram, P. G. (2007). *HMP Liverpool, Styal and Hindley study report.* Liverpool: University of Liverpool.

Murphy, G. H., Gardner, J., & Freeman, M. J. (2015). Screening prisoners for intellectual disabilties in three english prisons. *Journal of Applied Research in Intellectual Disabilities, 30*, 198–204.

Murphy, G. H., Harnett, H., & Holland, A. (1995). A survey of intellectual disabilities amongst men on remand in prison. *Mental Handicap Research, 8*, 81–98.

Murphy, G. H., & Sinclair, N. (2009). Treatment for men with ID & sexually abusive behaviour. In A. R. Beech, L. A. Craig, & K. D. Browne (Eds.), *Assessment & treatment of sexual offenders: A handbook* (pp. 369–392). Chichester, England: John Wiley & Sons.

Nixon, M., Thomas, S. D. M., Daffern, M., & Ogloff, J. R. P. (2017). Estimating the risk of crime and victimisation in people with intellectual disability: A data-linkage study. *Social Psychiatry and Psychiatric Epidemiology, 52*, 617–626. https://doi.org/10.1007/s00127-017-1371-3

Noble, J. H., & Conley, R. W. (1992). Toward an epidemiology of relevant attributes. In R. W. Conley, R. Luckasson, & G. N. Bouthilet (Eds.), *The criminal justice system and mental retardation.* Baltimore, MD: Paul Brookes.

Novaco, R. W. (1975). *Anger control: The development and evaluation of an experimental treatment.* Lexington, MA: Heath.

Novaco, R. W. (1993). *Stress inoculation therapy for anger control: A manual for therapists.* Irvine: University of California.

Novaco, R. W. (1994). Anger as a risk factor for violence among the mentally disordered. In J. Monahan & H. J. Steadman (Eds.), *Violence and mental disorder: Developments in risk assessment.* Chicago, IL: Chicago Press.

Novaco, R. W. (2011). Anger dysregulation: Driver of violent offending. *The Journal of Forensic Psychiatry & Psychology, 22*(5), 650–668. https://doi.org/10.1080/14789949.2011.617536

Novaco, R. W., & Taylor, J. L. (2004). Assessment of anger and aggression in male offenders with developmental disabilities. *Psychological Assessment, 16*(1), 42–50.

Novaco, R. W., & Taylor, J. L. (2015). Reduction of assaultive behavior following anger treatment of forensic hospital patients with intellectual disabilities. *Behaviour Research and Therapy, 65*, 52–59.

Pert, C., & Jahoda, A. (2008). Social goals and conflict strategies of individuals with mild to moderate intellectual disabilities who present problems of aggression. *Journal of Intellectual Disability Research, 25*(5), 393–403.

Pithers, W. D. (1990). Relapse prevention. In W. L. Marshall, D. R. Laws, & H. E. Barbaree (Eds.), *Handbook of sexual assault: Issues, theories, and treatment of the offender* (pp. 343–361). New York, NY: Plenum.

Plant, A., McDermott, E., Chester, V., & Alexander, R. T. (2011). Substance misuse among offenders in a forensic intellectual service. *Journal of Learning Disabilities and Offending Behaviour, 2*(3), 127–135.

Pridding, A., & Procter, N. G. (2008). A systematic review of personality disorder amongst people with intellectual disability with implications for the mental health nurse practitioner. *Journal of Clinical Nursing, 17*, 2811–2819. https://doi.org/10.1111/j.1365-2702.2007.02269.x

Rayner, K., Wood, H., Beail, N., & Kaur Nagra, M. (2015). Intellectual disability, personality disorder and offending: A systematic review. *Advances in Mental Health and Intellectual Disabilities, 9*, 50–61. https://doi.org/10.1108/AMHID-04-2014-0007

Richardson, S. A., Koller, H., & Katz, M. (1985). Relationship of upbringing to later behaviour disturbance of mildly mentally retarded young people. *American Journal of Mental Deficiency, 90*, 1–8.

Rose, J. (1996). Anger management: A group treatment program for people with mental retardation. *Journal of Developmental and Physical Disabilities, 12*, 211–224.

Rose, J., West, C., & Clifford, D. (2000). Group interventions for anger in people with intellectual disabilities. *Research in Developmental Disabilities, 21*, 171–181.

Salem-Darrow, M. (1995). *Virtual reality's increasing potential for meeting needs of persons with disabilities: What about cognitive impairments.* Paper presented at the The Third International Conference on Virtual Reality and Persons with Disabilities, Northridge, CA.

Sigafoos, J., Elkins, J., Kerr, M., & Attwood, T. (1994). A survey of aggressive behaviour among a population of persons with intellectual disabiltiy in Queensland. *Journal of Intellectual Disability Research, 38*(4), 369–381.

Simons, K. (2000). *Life on the edge: The experiences of people with a learning disability who do not use specialist services.* Brighton, UK: Pavilion Publishing/Joseph Rowntree Foundation.

Simpson, M. K., & Hogg, J. (2001). Patterns of offending among people with intellectual disability: A systematic review. Part II: Predisposing factors. *Journal of Intellectual Disability Research, 45*, 397–406. https://doi.org/10.1046/j.1365-2788.2001.00356.x

Standen, P. J., & Brown, D. J. (2005). Virtual reality in the rehabilitation of people with intellectual disabilities: Review. *Cyberpsychology & Behavior, 8*(3), 272–282.

Standen, P. J., Cromby, J. J., & Brown, D. J. (1998). Playing for real. *Mental Health Care, 1*, 412–415.

Stephens, S., Newman, J. E., Cantor, J. M., & Seto, M. C. (2017). The Static-99R predicts sexual and violent recidivism for individuals with low intellectual functioning. *Journal of Sexual Aggression, 24*, 1–11. https://doi.org/10.1080/13552600.2017.1372936

Steptoe, L. R., Lindsay, W. R., Murphy, L., & Young, S. J. (2008). Construct validity, reliability and predictive validity of the dynamic risk assessment and management system (DRAMS) in offenders with intellectual disability. *Legal and Criminological Psychology, 13*, 309–321. https://doi.org/10.1348/135532507X218251

Taggart, L., & Chaplin, E. (2014). Substance misuse. In E. Tsakanikos & J. McCarthy (Eds.), *Handbook of psychopathology in intellectual disability*. New York, NY: Springer Science.

Taylor, J. L. (2002). A review of the assessment and treatment of anger and aggression in offenders with intellectual disability. *Journal of Intellectual Disability Research, 46*(1), 57–73.

Taylor, J. L., & Novaco, R. W. (2005). *Anger treatment for people with developmental disabilities: A theory, evidence and manual based approach.* Chichester, UK: John Wiley & Sons.

Taylor, J. L., Novaco, R. W., Gillmer, B., & Thorne, I. (2002). Cognitive-behavioural treatment of anger intensity among offenders with intellectual disabilities. *Journal of Applied Research in Intellectual Disabilities, 15*, 151–165.

Taylor, J. L., Robertson, A., Thorne, I., Belshaw, T., & Watson, A. (2006). Responses of female fire-setters with mild and borderline intellectual disabilities to a group intervention. *Journal of Applied Research in Intellectual Disabilities, 19*, 179–190. https://doi.org/10.1111/j.1468-3148.2005.00260x

Taylor, J. L., Thorne, I., Robertson, A., & Avery, G. (2002). Evaluation of a group intervention for convicted arsonists with mild and borderline intellectual disabilities. *Criminal Behaviour and Mental Health, 12*, 282–293. https://doi.org/10.1002/cbm.506

Thompson, D., & Brown, H. (1997). Men with intellectual disabilities who sexually abuse: A review of the literature. *Journal of Applied Research in Intellectual Disabilities, 10*, 140–158. https://doi.org/10.1111/j.1468-3148.1997.tb00014.x

van Nieuwenjizen, M., de Castro, B. O., Wijnroks, L., Vermeer, A., & Matthys, W. (2009). Social problem-solving and mild-intellectual disabilities: Relations with externalizing behavior and therapeutic context. *American Journal on Intellectual and Developmental Disabilities, 114*(1), 42–51.

Vereenooghe, L., Gega, L., & Langdon, P. E. (2017). Intellectual disability and computers in therapy: Views of service users and clinical psychologists. *Cyberpsychology: Journal of Psychosocial Research on Cyberspace, 11*(1), article 11.

Ward, T. (2002). Good lives and the rehabilitation of offenders: Promises and problems. *Aggression and Violent Behaviour, 7*(5), 513–528.

Ward, T., & Beech, A. (2006). An integrated theory of sexual offending. *Aggression and Violent Behavior, 11*, 44–63.

Ward, T., & Beech, A. (2017). The integrated theory of sexual offending - revised: A multifield perspective. In D. P. Boer (Editor-in-Chief); A. R. Beech and T. Ward (Volume Eds.), *The Wiley handbook on the theory, assessment, and treatment of sexual offending (Volume I: Theories)* (pp. 123–137). Chichester, UK: John Wiley & Sons.

Ward, T., & Hudson, S. M. (2000). A self-regulation model of the relapse prevention process. In D. R. Laws, S. M. Hudson, & T. Ward (Eds.), *Remaking relapse prevention with sex offenders: A source book* (pp. 79–101). Thousand Oaks, CA: Sage.

Wheeler, J. R., Clare, I. C. H., & Holland, A. J. (2014). What can social and environmental factors tell us about the risk of offending by people with intellectual disabilities? *Psychology, Crime & Law, 20*, 636668. https://doi.org/10.1080/1068316X.2013.864789

Whitaker, S. (2001). Anger control for people with learning disabilities: A critical review. *Behavioural and Cognitive Psychotherapy, 29*, 277–293.

Willner, P., Jahoda, A., Rose, J., Stenfert-Kroese, B., Hood, K., Townson, J. K., ... Felce, D. (2011). Anger management for people with mild to moderate learning disabilities: Study protocol for a multi-centre cluster randomised controlled trial of a manualised intervention delivered by day-service staff. *Trials, 12*, 36.

Willner, P., Rose, J., Jahoda, A., Stenfert-Kroese, B., Felce, D., Cohen, D., ... Hood, K. (2013). Group-based cognitive-behavioural anger management for people with mild to moderate intellectual disabilities: Cluster randomised controlled trial. *The British Journal of Psychiatry, 203*, 288–296.

Winter, N., Holland, A. J., & Collins, S. (1997). Factors predisposing to suspected offending by adults with self-reported learning disabilities. *Psychological Medicine, 27*, 595–607. https://doi.org/10.1017/s0033291797004777

Chapter 5
Assessing and Treating Women Offenders

Kelly Taylor, Donna McDonagh, and Kelley Blanchette

Relative to men, women are less likely to commit crime; statistics supporting this statement are robust and internationally applicable and women represent, on average, about 5% of those incarcerated (Blanchette & Brown, 2006). The gender gap is largest when comparing males to females on data pertaining to violent crimes (Federal Bureau of Investigations, 2011; Statistics Canada, n.d.). Researchers have reported that these gender differences hold true, regardless of whether the evidence is gleaned from official statistics, self-report surveys, or victimization studies (e.g., Blanchette & Brown, 2006).

Women also reoffend at much lower rates than their male counterparts (Florida Dept. of Corrections, 2017; National Resource Center on Justice Involved Women, 2016). This is commensurate with their lower assessed risk relative to men. Although women differ from men in their criminal offending behaviour (e.g., criminal history, offence types, relationship to victims), many of the same factors reliably predict offending and reoffending for males and females (Andrews et al., 2012; Andrews & Bonta, 2010). This will be discussed in more detail later in this chapter. It merits mention here, however, that there is some empirical evidence for 'gender specific' risk factors as well (e.g., Blanchette & Brown, 2006). For example, while mainstream research suggests that mental health problems are not predictive of criminal offending generally (Andrews & Bonta, 2010; Bonta, Blais, & Wilson, 2013), a few studies have indicated that some mental health diagnoses are associated with criminality for women in particular (e.g., Salisbury, Van Voorhis, & Spiropoulos, 2009).

K. Taylor (✉)
Reintegration Programs Division, Correctional Services Canada, Ottawa, ON, Canada
e-mail: Kelly.Taylor@cihr-irsc.gc.ca

D. McDonagh
Private Practice, Ottawa, ON, Canada

K. Blanchette
Department of Psychology, Carleton University, Ottawa, ON, Canada
e-mail: Kelley.Blanchette@csc-scc.gc.ca

© Springer Nature Switzerland AG 2018
M. Ternes et al. (eds.), *The Practice of Correctional Psychology*,
https://doi.org/10.1007/978-3-030-00452-1_5

5.1 Frequency and Prevalence of Mental Disorder

Establishing prevalence rates for mental health problems is a complicated task. Issues such as the scope and definition of what is meant by a 'mental health problem', a 'mental disorder', or a 'mental illness' are further complicated by determinations and parameters regarding seriousness (e.g., serious or severe mental illnesses), means of assessment (e.g., self-report, endorsement of symptoms, psychiatric diagnosis), type of service provision and patterns of help seeking (e.g., hospital admissions) and sample selection (e.g., gender, age, race, culture and socioeconomic considerations). Generally speaking, mental disorders or illnesses are characterized by any combination of clinically significant disturbances in thought, emotions and behaviour that reflect a dysfunction in the psychological, biological or developmental processes underlying mental functioning (American Psychiatric Association, 2013).

Gender differences in the lifetime prevalence of mental disorders have long been recognized worldwide (Turcotte, 2011; World Health Organization, WHO, 2006). Gender is also associated with differences in susceptibility, expression, comorbidity and course of illness, diagnosis, treatment and adjustment to mental disorder (Muenzenmaier et al., 2015; WHO, 2002, 2006). Women with serious mental illness experience elevated rates of victimization, trauma, poverty, and homelessness (Padgett, Hawkins, Abrams, & Davis, 2006; WHO, 2006), and the context of women's traditionally disadvantaged social status and vulnerability figures prominently in the feminist analysis of etiology and rates of psychopathology, which also includes analyses of the intersectionality of diverse backgrounds with respect to race, ethnicity, culture, disability and sexual orientation.

It is well established that both men and women with mental disorders are overrepresented in criminal justice systems internationally (Brink, 2005; Bronson & Berzofsky, 2017; Collier & Friedman, 2016; Fazel & Danesh, 2002; Fazel, Hayes, Bartellas, Clerici, & Trestman, 2016; Fazel & Seewald, 2012; Prins, 2014). Regardless of methodological complications including sample selection, statistical models, assessment measures, patterns of incarceration and other factors influencing variations in prevalence rates (Fazel et al., 2016), the rates of documented mental health problems and the prevalence of mental disorders is significantly higher than general population comparisons (Brink, 2005; Fazel & Danesh, 2002; Fazel et al., 2016; Prins, 2014; Steadman, Osher, Robbins, Case, & Samuels, 2009). This global reality is often attributed to the inadequacy and/or decline of appropriate mental health resources in the community over time (Chaimowitz, 2012; Munetz, Grande, & Chambers, 2001).

Insofar as most studies of mental illness within prisons are cross-sectional and thus only collect data at one point in time, it is difficult to assess the degree to which mentally ill individuals are more likely to end up in prisons or whether imprisonment leads to more mental health issues. Research does indicate an increased risk for offenders with mental illness having multiple incarcerations (Baillargeon, Binswanger, Penn, Williams, & Murray, 2009). Confinement is a stressful event in itself. Incarcerated individuals experience stress in reaction to the transition from the outside world to prison life, as evidenced by an increase in blood pressure, anxiety, and depression (Islam-Zwart, Vik, & Rawlins, 2007). Within corrections, offenders with mental illness present challenges to correctional management while incarcerated, for example they average more disciplinary infractions per year than offenders without mental illness (O'keefe & Schnell, 2007). Thus, in treating offenders with mental illness, it is important to integrate the principles of effective corrections (e.g., Risk, Need, and Responsivity (RNR model, discussed later) with the principles of effective mental health treatment.

Women offenders report poorer mental health status than women in the general population (Tye & Mullen, 2006) *and* poorer mental health than incarcerated men (Marcus-Mendoza, 2010; Steadman et al., 2009; Warren et al., 2002). For example, in a seminal prevalence study in the United States, while approximately 12% of women in the general population had symptoms of a mental disorder, it was 60–75% among women prisoners (James & Glaze, 2006). Mental disorders are reported as extremely common among women offenders, with research studies estimating between 30% and 84% of incarcerated women suffering from mental health disorders (Drapalski, Youman, Stuewig, & Tangney, 2009; Steadman et al., 2009; Tye & Mullen, 2006). In England and Wales, one study suggested that 90% of women in prison have at least one of neurosis, psychosis, or personality disorder, alcohol abuse or drug dependence (Palmer in Møller, Stöver, Jürgens, Gatherer, & Nikogosian, 2007). In a systematic review of 62 surveys of prisoners in 12 countries, Fazel and Danesh (2002) reported that of 4260 women, 4% had psychotic illnesses, 12% major depression and 42% had at least one personality disorder (25% had Borderline Personality Disorder and 21% had Antisocial Personality Disorder).

Mental health problems reported by women offenders include, but are not limited to, depression (Fazel & Danesh, 2002; Fazel et al., 2016; James & Glaze, 2006; Steadman et al., 2009), anxiety (Kubiak, Beeble, & Bybee, 2009; Steadman et al., 2009), suicidal thinking and/or self-injurious behaviour (Charles, Abram, McClelland, & Teplin, 2003), Borderline Personality Disorder (Drapalski et al., 2009; Fazel & Danesh, 2002), intellectual disabilities (Lindsay et al., 2004) and Post Traumatic Stress Disorder (PTSD; Kubiak et al., 2009; Lynch et al., 2014; Steadman et al., 2009). Furthermore, comorbidity of mental disorders and substance abuse is especially prevalent among women offenders (James & Glaze, 2006; Nowotny, Belknap, Lynch, & Dehart, 2014; Saxena, Messina, & Grella, 2014).

5.2   Theoretical Models Relevant to Service Delivery

From "nothing works" (Martinson, 1974) to "what works" (Andrews, Bonta, & Hoge, 1990; Andrews, Zinger, et al., 1990) to "but does it work for women" (Blanchette & Brown, 2006) is one way to describe the evolution of thought that has driven theoretical models relevant to service delivery for female offenders. In their award-winning book, Blanchette and Brown (2006), outline the existing theoretical paradigms that represent the integrated perspectives crossing multiple disciplinary boundaries. They frame this review by gender-neutral, female-centred, and hybrid theories and ultimately conclude the following:

1. Women are no longer 'theoretical afterthoughts';
2. Work still needs to be done to adequately explain the base rate differential in offending between men and women;
3. Our capacity to explain female criminal conduct is enhanced when considering gender-informed as opposed to gender-neutral theories;
4. Female-centred theories have not been studied to the same degree as those that are gender-neutral;
5. There is variability in the extent to which theory has been translated into practice; and
6. Seemingly divergent theoretical perspectives which are often highly debated in the literature are in fact complementary to one another.

For an in-depth history of theory driving service delivery for female offenders, it is recommended that the work of Blanchette and Brown be examined. For the purposes of this chapter, the focus will remain on the Risk-Need-Responsivity Model (RNR—emanating from the Personal, Interpersonal and Community-Reinforcement Theory (PIC-R), Andrews, 1982; Andrews & Bonta, 2010) and other prominent female-centred theories including Relational Theory (Miller, 1986), and Feminist Pathways perspectives (e.g., Belknap, 2007; Belknap & Holsinger, 1998; Daly, 1992). Furthermore, some emphasis will be placed on strengths-based perspectives and their applicability with female offenders.

The Risk, Need, and Responsivity Principles (Andrews & Bonta, 2010; Andrews, Bonta, & Hoge, 1990; Andrews, Zinger, et al., 1990) are an output of the PIC-R theory and play a prominent role in treatment efforts in Canadian, American, and European jurisdictions, among others. In brief, the *risk principle* states that those offenders exhibiting the highest levels of risk/the highest likelihood of reoffending should receive the most intensive levels of intervention. The *need* principle states that treatment should target those dynamic needs that have been empirically assessed, and are linked to, reductions in criminal recidivism. Finally, the *responsivity* principle places emphasis on how the intervention should be delivered (e.g., positive reinforcement, prosocial modelling, prosocial skills acquisition, extinction, and cognitive restructuring) and more specifically, interventions need to match the learning style, motivation, aptitude, and abilities of the offender in question. It further outlines the importance of structured behavioural interventions in a warm and empathic manner while simultaneously adopting a firm but fair approach (e.g., Gendreau, French, & Gionet, 2004). Importantly, despite vigorous debate about the applicability of these principles for female offenders, there is substantial theoretical evidence to support their use with this group (e.g., Blanchette & Brown, 2006; Dowden & Andrews, 1999).

In considering the need principle, it is important to recognize that researchers have provided evidence to suggest that some criminogenic needs (i.e., dynamic needs that are empirically linked to criminal behavior) emerge as particularly relevant for women. Hollin and Palmer (2006) provide a critique of the literature noting that common criminogenic needs do not imply that the etiology or importance is the same for men and women but maintain that some factors such as experience of physical or sexual abuse are arguably criminogenic needs for women. Personal/emotional factors (e.g., Bell, Trevethan, & Allegri, 2004; Robinson, Porporino, & Beal, 1998), employment (e.g., Greiner, Law, & Brown, 2015), and substance abuse (e.g., Saxena et al., 2014) all have empirical evidence to support this contention. Furthermore, other researchers have raised mental health, parenting, victimization/abuse, and adverse social conditions as female-focused factors that should be considered, and integrated within interventions for female offenders (e.g., Blanchette & Brown, 2006; Derkzen, Booth, McConnell, & Taylor, 2012; Derkzen, Harris, Wardrop, & Thompson, 2017).

As outlined above, in the application of the Risk, Need and Responsivity principles, and in considering the best treatment strategies for application of the responsivity principle in particular, cognitive behavioural therapy (CBT) and skills acquisition have been emphasized as playing a particularly important role in intervention efforts. For example, in examining treatment programs targeting substance abuse and posttraumatic stress disorder, Zlotnick, Johnson, and Najavits (2009) demonstrated that incarcerated women following CBT driven programs demonstrated improvements on clinician rated PTSD symptoms and continued improvement on psychopathology targets.

Relational Theory (Miller, 1986) argues that healthy human development necessitates that individuals feel connected to one another and that this need is particularly critical in women. Healthy relationships are defined as being empathic, empowering, and mutually influential. This theory has been critical to informing women-centred intervention strategies (as discussed below) but has not focused on explaining female offending behavior. Nevertheless, there is emerging evidence to support relational theory and its impact on recidivism outcomes for women (e.g., Benda, 2005). Related constructs such as social bonds have also been examined in relation to recidivism outcomes providing evidence to suggest that the impact varies by gender (Cobbina, Huebner, & Berg, 2010).

Evidence and literature to date do suggest significant alignment between RNR and relational theory perspectives (Blanchette & Brown, 2006) and there is increasing evidence to support arguments are aligning between gender-responsive and gender-neutral theories sometimes arguing that gender-specific concerns may be best viewed as specific responsivity factors for women (e.g., Rettinger and Andrews, 2010). Furthermore, there is some evidence to support the validity of empowerment as a responsivity factor that assists in developing competencies and enables women to achieve independence (Blanchette & Eldjupovic-Guzina, 1998).

Originating with Daly (1992), Feminist Pathways posits that childhood victimization (e.g., abuse, neglect) plays a central role in girls' criminal trajectories. The theory maintains that the voices of girls and women are critical to our comprehensive understanding of criminal pathways. The theory contends that victimization is a significant contributor to the eventual use of drugs (and ultimately drug abuse) as a coping mechanism. Furthermore, involvement in selling drugs, prostitution and robbery are mechanisms for street survival after girls and women escape these abusive situations. Ultimately, theorists ascribing to this theory argue that women may be 'criminalized' for their survival strategies (Chesney-Lind, 1998) and that such cycles result in emotional distress, low self-esteem, anxiety, depression and aggressive/impulsive behaviours (Zaplin, 2008). Since the original pathways work, other pathway models have been proposed implicating abusive male partners who negatively coerce women into lives of crime (e.g., Belknap & Holsinger, 1998) and a variety of other research supports the relevance, and interest in, pathways perspectives (e.g., Brennan, Breitenbach, Dieterich, Salisbury, & Van Voorhis, 2012; Gannon, Rose, & Ward, 2010; Reisig, Holtfreter, & Morash, 2006; Salisbury & Van Voorhis, 2009; Simpson, Yahner, & Dugan, 2008).

In considering trauma as a contributor to long-term negative outcomes, Messina and Grella (2006) examined childhood trauma and women's health outcomes in a California prison population. Their data suggested that childhood traumatic events have strong and cumulative negative outcomes on health. More specifically, their results suggested that as exposure to childhood traumatic events increased the likelihood of negative health related outcomes increased. They point to early prevention and intervention, along with appropriate trauma treatment, as being critical within correctional treatment settings. Saxena et al. (2014) also provide evidence to support gender-responsive substance abuse treatment (GRT) and its effectiveness with women who have experienced prior abuse given that GRT maximizes the benefits of the trauma-informed, gender-sensitive intervention. As noted by Covington and Bloom (2006), all of the above supports the proposition that the integration of substance abuse treatment and trauma services is critical in the consideration of treatment elements for female offenders.

Strengths-based approaches, such as those proposed by Van Wormer (2001), suggest that the client's strengths need to be recognized and integrated into assessments and interventions in corrections. For example, when developing treatment plans, outcome reports, and risk assessments for girls or women, assessors should consider and leverage the offender's strengths in order to help her heal and re-integrate into the community. Some proponents of strengths-based approaches argue that traditional intervention with incarcerated girls and women is complicated by the oppressive patriarchal structure of the jail/prison system, clients' victimization histories and the various psychosocial problems frequently presented by female clients (Mahoney & Daniel, 2006). Accordingly, strength-based approaches may be particularly salient in the treatment of female correctional clients.

Despite advancements in our theoretical knowledge, it is still valid to argue that integrating women-specific factors only enhances theory and service delivery for women offenders and despite on-going debate around the application of gender-neutral theory, there is overwhelming evidence to support its relevance. In fact, upon in-depth examination and more collaborative approaches in treatment design (see below), it becomes abundantly apparent that these theories are complimentary and collectively build on our capacity to better support female offenders when considered holistically as opposed to independently or antagonistically.

5.3 Diagnosis and Assessment

5.3.1 Risk Assessment

Offender risk assessment has evolved considerably over the past 30 years, as paradigms have moved from 'first generation' assessments to 'third generation' assessments; some even reference 'fourth generation' assessments (Bonta & Wormith, 2008). In brief, first generation assessment relied on unstructured clinical judgement. Second generation assessment improved predictive accuracy by standardizing consideration of static risk factors that have been empirically linked to re-offending. Third generation tools included offenders needs (dynamic risk factors) that are empirically linked to re-offending. Third generation tools have the advantage of considering changes in risk as a result of interventions (e.g., correctional programs). Finally, fourth generation assessment instruments have been described as those that integrate case planning with risk/needs assessment. Few jurisdictions continue to use the first generation assessments, as those using mathematical/actuarial methods (second through fourth) have demonstrated superiority in terms of predictive accuracy (Grove, Zald, Lebow, Snitz, & Nelson, 2000; Swets, Dawes, & Monahan, 2000).

Many risk assessment instruments have been studied and validated with robust empirical results supporting their use. Unfortunately, with few exceptions, the research is based on samples of male offenders (Blanchette & Brown, 2006) and critics argue that the failure to consider gender and diversity issues in risk assessment results in inequitable practices of classification for women and other minority offender populations. Accordingly, they argue that these biases result in the systemic discrimination of these groups, ranging from over classification to failure to provide appropriate services (Bloom & Covington, 2000; Hannah-Moffat & Shaw, 2001).

While there is no widely used (cross-jurisdictional) risk assessment tool developed specifically for women, some measures, although developed as 'gender neutral' tools, show promise in terms of their predictive accuracy for women. Examples include the Level of Service/Case Management Inventory (LS/CMI) and its predecessors (see studies by Andrews et al., 2012; Geraghty & Woodhams, 2015), the HCR-20 (see studies by Coid et al., 2009; Strub, Douglas, & Nicholls, 2016), and the VRAG (see studies by Coid et al., 2009). Notwithstanding these promising results, some still suggest that actuarial tools that are gender-informed and developed from the ground up will bring additional relevance and predictive power to assessments for women (Blanchette & Brown, 2006).

5.3.2   Clinical Diagnosis and Assessment

A significant proportion of incarcerated women has been exposed to trauma and victimization that often began in childhood or adolescence with neglect or physical and sexual abuse and continued into adulthood with intimate partner abuse and sexual assaults (Aday, Dye, & Kaiser, 2014; Clements-Nolle, Wolden, & Bargmann-Losche, 2009; Dehart, Lynch, Belknap, Dass-Brailsford & Green, 2014; Hollin & Palmer, 2006; Kimonis et al., 2010; Nowotny et al., 2014; Messina & Grella, 2006; Warren et al., 2002). When combined with the experience of current or past trauma, and/or substance abuse, mental illness functions to increase a woman's involvement in criminal activity and thus the likelihood of incarceration (Kubiak, Fedock, Kim, & Bybee, 2017; Lewis, 2006; Lynch, DeHart, Belknap, & Green, 2012). These factors can also create additional problems for a woman offender by exerting an effect upon behaviour, reasoning, memory, social and adaptive functioning, and motivation. Further, these issues may lead to difficulties in adjusting to incarceration and have been found to be related to higher rates of prison misconduct (O'keefe & Schnell, 2007). In spite of this research demonstrating the prevalence of cumulative and complex mental health needs, women offenders generally encounter more barriers to accessing services in the community (Staton, Leukefeld, & Logan, 2001).

The WHO describes mental health as more than the absence of mental illness, considering it a "state of well-being" that allows individuals to realize their own abilities, cope with daily life stresses, and make a contribution to their community. Critical tenets of mental health include perceived feelings of well-being, self-efficacy, autonomy and competence as well as the recognition of one's ability to realize their intellectual and emotional potential (WHO, 2016). Not surprisingly, the actualization of such a conceptualization poses significant challenges in the context of incarceration in general, and with incarcerated women in particular.

Given the high rates of incarcerated women's mental health issues and the high comorbidity of these with substance use disorders and histories of trauma, clinical assessment is of critical importance. Within the criminal justice system, assessments essentially fall into two categories: those that address interventions and those that address classification/risk. Blanchette (2002) suggests that factors commonly cited as women-specific criminogenic needs generally fall into the 'personal/emotional' domain, and include low self-esteem, histories of trauma and victimization, and self-injury/attempted suicide. These factors also figure prominently into conceptualizations of mental health. Since criminogenic and mental health needs of women offenders are distinct, it is essential that the approach to assessment and treatment be integrated so that needs are addressed in a way that can assist both the women as well as staff tasked with supporting and managing offenders.

For women offenders, the clinical assessment must take into account gender specific issues, including the assessment of mental health problems, substance abuse, histories of trauma and victimization, self-injurious behaviour and suicidality, violence risk, alongside criminogenic need areas. Indeed, failing to do this compromises the effectiveness of any subsequent planned intervention. Further, if these underlying issues are not addressed and stabilized, mental health problems can be exacerbated and women will be subject to more institutional charges, disciplinary infractions and may be further disadvantaged regarding release (Houser & Belenko, 2015).

We recommend that a comprehensive clinical assessment for women offenders include:

- Encouraging collaboration in the process (e.g., the woman should know the purpose of the screening/assessment).
- Attending to contextual factors of women's lives (inclusive of an exploration of trauma, parental responsibilities, disability, poverty and economic marginalization, and intersections of race, culture, ethnicity and sexual orientation) and incorporating a strength-based approach that considers factors associated with mental wellness.
- Explicitly acknowledging the role of trauma when assigning psychiatric diagnoses; this includes exploring current trauma-related symptoms and functional impairment.
- Use of standardized clinical instruments; particularly for the determination of psychopathology, cognitive capacity and suicidality. Choosing standardized clinical instruments that have been developed for women (preferred) or adapted and tested on women, and validated for race, if relevant.
- Incorporating various methods of gathering information: assessment tools, clinical interview, collateral information, retrospective data including previous evaluations, community assessments, etc.
- Providing a rational framework and formulation for understanding complex needs and strengths associated with mental illness and trauma; highlighting the links between these, criminogenic factors, and a range of emotional/behavioural issues that may otherwise be targeted in isolation.

As an entry point to the clinical assessment process, many correctional jurisdictions (e.g., Canada, United States) start with a mental health screening (Every-Palmer et al., 2014). The purpose of the screening processes is to determine which offenders require further assessment and possible referral to mental health services. The screening protocol should detail the results of the screening, the action taken for positive scores and what (if any) further assessment is required. Mental health screening in a correctional context should include general psychopathology, depression, suicidality, substance abuse and cognitive capacity. Screening should occur early in the correctional system, preferably within weeks of intake (Krespi-Boothby, Mullholland, Cases, Carrington, & Bolger, 2010). Commonly used measures that have demonstrated applicability for women offenders include the eight-item Brief Jail Mental Health Screen (BJMHS; Steadman, Scott, Osher, Agnese, & Robbins, 2005); the Jail Screening Assessment Tool (JSAT; Nicholls, Roesch, Olley, Ogloff, & Hemphill, 2005), which includes the completion of a brief semi-structured mental status interview and a revised version of the Brief Psychiatric Rating Scale (BPRS; Overall & Gorham, 1962); the Kessler Psychological Distress Scale (K6; Kessler et al., 2003); and the Computerized Mental Health Intake Screening System

(CoMHISS; Correctional Service of Canada, 2010). Although mental health screening can be indicative of potential mental health problems, it does not result in diagnosis.

A clinical assessment differs from screening in that it is a much more detailed and extensive process for defining the nature of the problem identified, determining a diagnosis, and developing specific treatment recommendations to address the problem. Generally, a clinical assessment delves into the individual's current experiences and her physical, psychological and sociocultural history. A thorough and comprehensive clinical assessment requires multiple avenues to obtain the necessary clinical information, including self-assessment instruments, clinical records, structured clinical interviews, standardized assessment measures/tools, and collateral information.

Given the prevalence rates of certain mental health issues for women offenders, for a clinical assessment to be viewed as robust it should include standardized measures that consider: (1) psychometric measures to assess clinical syndromes (e.g, Millon Clinical Multiaxial Inventory-III (MCMI-III; Millon, 1997); Minnesota Multiphasic Personality Inventory—Second Revised Edition (MMPI-2; Butcher et al., 2001); Personality Assessment Inventory, (PAI; Morey, 2007); Basic Personality Inventory, (BPI; Jackson, 1996) and personality disorders (e.g., Structured Clinical Interview for DSM-IV Axis II Personality Disorders, (SCID-II; First, Gibon, Spitzer, Williams, & Benjamin, 1997); (2) depression and anxiety measures (e.g., Beck Depression Inventory—II, (BDI-II; Beck, Steer, & Brown, 1996); Beck Anxiety Inventory (BAI; Beck & Steer, 1993); State-Trait Anxiety Inventory (STAI; Spielberger, Gorsuch, Lushene, Vagg, & Jacobs, 1983); (3) suicide risk factors (e.g., Beck Hopelessness Scale (BHS; Beck & Steer, 1988); Depression Hopelessness and Suicide Screening Form (DHS; Mills & Kroner, 2004); and (4) actuarial risk measures (e.g., Level of Service/Case Management Inventory (LSI/CMI (Andrews, Bonta, & Wormith, 2004). As well, the process should include a comprehensive clinical interview that explores trauma, posttraumatic stress disorder, history of substance abuse and interpersonal violence (per the Diagnostic and Statistical Manual of Disorders (DSM-V; American Psychiatric Association, 2013), a diagnosis of PTSD requires a history of exposure to a traumatic event). If cognitive impairments are indicated (either through screening or presentation), further intellectual testing should be conducted. Assessments of intellectual functioning should be obtained using an individually administered, reliable and valid standardized test, such as the Weschler Adult Intelligence Scale (WAIS-III, Wechsler, 1997). Consistent with the WHO perspective on mental wellness, the interview should also focus on determining a woman's strengths and protective factors; familiarity with these can assist in directing treatment to optimize desired outcomes. For instance, research has demonstrated that factors such as relationships with prosocial community supports, involvement in structured activities, accessing mental health services, and personal motivation may help to promote criminal desistance among high risk, high need mentally-disordered offenders (Stewart, Brine, Wilton, Power, & Hnain, 2015).

Finally, in light of the importance of the Risk, Need and Responsivity model with women offenders (Blanchette, 2000), it is essential that characteristics of treatment responsivity be thoroughly examined (e.g., intelligence; learning style; cultural considerations; treatment readiness and motivation; emotional disorder). Furthermore, mental illnesses frequently cause functional impairments that may seriously impact an individual's responsivity to interventions targeting criminogenic risk factors. These need to be identified and addressed. For example, a woman with PTSD may not benefit from participating in treatment or programming for substance abuse until the symptoms of PTSD—such as, depression, excessive worrying, lack of motivation, difficulty concentrating, decreased energy, mood swings—are addressed.

Once the comprehensive assessment material is gathered, the essential task of the clinician is to develop a clinical formulation focused toward treatment and intervention that includes an analysis of the extent to which symptoms of mental illness may be relevant to the understanding and prediction of risk. Mental disorders for women offenders, per se, have not been conclusively linked to recidivism statistics. This could be in part a function of low base rates overall, but is more likely similar to the research on men offenders where aggregate data give very little information to clinicians faced with individual risk assessment. For example, according to Pilgrim (2010, p. 282), "a diagnosis such as 'schizophrenia' tells us virtually nothing about risk to others. It is only by using multifactorial formulations specific to the offender that we move towards improved risk assessment."

Toward that end, symptoms of mental illness that may manifest across a variety of the psychiatric diagnoses common to women offenders (i.e., depression, anxiety, personality disorders, PTSD) include: impulsivity, emotional dysregulation, self-injurious behaviours, difficulties with anger and hostility, pessimism, difficulty concentrating, low self-esteem and problems with self-image, which in turn correspond, in essence, to criminogenic need variables. Given personal histories that include multiple marginalizations, trauma, and substance abuse, and frequent co-morbidities, it may be far more useful to investigate the relationship between psychological variables and offending rather than the relationship of specific diagnoses to recidivism per se. By identifying these variables and addressing them in treatment, with particular attention to stabilization and behavioural change, service providers are better able to treat both the underlying issues and address criminogenic factors. This holistic approach can serve the goals of influencing behaviour while incarcerated as well as improve reintegration success for women.

5.4 Interventions: What Works, What Might Work, and What Doesn't Matter

As referenced above, the "what works" literature is quite comprehensive and there is ample theory to draw from in our efforts to better apply these theoretical constructs within different treatment and service delivery models. Nevertheless, it is important to distinguish the goals of the intervention under examination. An intervention that is successful in addressing symptoms of trauma or mental illness, for example, may not prove effective in efforts to reduce recidivism. In turn, as a starting point, it is important to emphasize that no single intervention is a panacea.

Interventions, and their related goals, may pertain to personality (e.g., addressing antisocial and/or borderline personality disorder), mental health, physical health, cognitive ability, or motivation, to name only a few. As above, the strategy ascribed to may vary in approach and success as a function of the target in question. In turn, there is recognition that although there are common principles that align with all service delivery strategies, there is acceptance and acknowledgement that there is no "one size fits all" assumption while working with female offenders.

Gender-informed programs were first promulgated only about 10–15 years ago; however, meta-analytic studies are now emerging, examining their effectiveness in terms of recidivism reduction. Most recently, Gobeil, Blanchette, and Stewart (2016) were interested in determining whether gender-informed and gender-neutral interventions promote similar treatment effects for women. Despite variability in the treatment targets examined (e.g., substance abuse, self-esteem, anger management), the authors concluded that there is preliminary evidence from high-quality studies that gender-informed programs are more effective at reducing recidivism than gender-neutral approaches. Their results further suggested that interventions focusing primarily on substance use had significantly larger effect sizes than did those focusing in other areas. Equally important, interventions offered in the context of a therapeutic community also demonstrated larger effect sizes. Findings also support the need for interventions that bridge institution and community treatment elements. There is also some research evidence to suggest that girls who follow gendered pathways to crime may be more likely to benefit from the relational approach used in gender-informed programs as compared to girls who did not demonstrate these gendered pathways (Day, Zahn, & Tichavsky, 2014).

In considering the effectiveness of interventions respecting theory on gender-informed programming, the Correctional Service of Canada has provided recent evidence around the effectiveness of Women Offender Correctional Program (WOCP) and Aboriginal Women Offender Correctional Program (AWOCP),[1] both rooted in culture and gender responsive approaches. These programs are also trauma-informed while recognizing factors more prevalent in female offender such as parenting stress and adverse social conditions (Derkzen et al., 2017). Results from Derkzen et al. (2017) suggest that women successfully complete these programs, with recognition that the level of risk, need, and histories of violence do have a negative impact on completion rates. Furthermore, for those women who complete the programs, more positive discretionary release rates are achieved.

Stewart and Gobeil (2015) conducted a rapid evidence assessment which examined features of programs providing the strongest outcomes for female offenders arguing that three key areas contribute to the strongest outcomes for this population:

---

[1] For a more in-depth description of these programs please refer to http://www.csc-scc.gc.ca/correctional-process/002001-2001-eng.shtml#s2.

(1) substance abuse treatment provided in-custody or therapeutic community programs; (2) gender-responsive programs that emphasize strengths and competencies, as well as skills acquisition; and (3) following in-custody treatment with participation in community follow-up sessions (i.e., continuum of care). Ultimately, the authors suggest that these results are critical for guiding program designers and administrators interested in effectively promoting public safety goals and female offender reintegration. The importance of a continuum of care is further echoed by Sacks, McKendrick, and Hamilton (2012) who argue that the ability to sustain, and even improve, behaviour change after a women leaves prison relies heavily on access to community-based continuity of mental health and substance abuse services upon re-entry. Finally, Andrews et al. (2012) used the Level of Service/Case Management Inventory and the Youth version to generate risk need domains that are considered relevant for girls and women ultimately highlighting the exceptional validity of targeting substance abuse for females. Grella and Greenwell (2007) maintain that engaging substance-abusing women offenders in community treatment after parole improves their retention in treatment and reduces the likelihood of recidivism. Ultimately, substance abuse treatment both inside and outside of the institutional environment is demonstrated as critical to successful outcomes (e.g., Kassebaum, 1999).

Bloom and colleagues (e.g., Bloom, Owen, & Covington, 2004) have written extensively on gender-responsive programming, offering guiding principles, policy blueprints, and intervention practices that are critical to program design, interventions, and evaluation. Much of the emerging research supports their efforts and reinforces the need to ensure we continue to meet the unique needs of female offenders in our intervention efforts. It is also critical to ensure that as anticipated by the responsivity principle, we are closely monitoring, and adapting to, the responses of female offenders engaged in intervention efforts.

Earlier we provided a very high level and generic definition of the responsivity principle from the RNR model. In their analysis and overview of the assessment and treatment of female offenders, Blanchette and Brown (2006) proposed a gender-informed responsivity principle, as a tentative reformulation of the original work of Andrews, Bonta, and colleagues. Once again, it is recommended that readers with interests in this area refer to their comprehensive critique of this area; however, in sum, their expressed belief is that the "spirit" of this principle can readily accommodate concepts such as empowerment and mutuality (as advocated for within relational theory) thereby advocating for their inclusion in this reformulation as follows:

> A gender-informed responsivity principle states that in general, optimal treatment response will be achieved when treatment providers deliver structured behavioural interventions (grounded in feminist philosophies as well as social learning theory) in an empathic and empowering manner (strengths-based model) while simultaneously adopting a firm but fair approach. (Blanchette & Brown, 2006, p. 126)

In considering "what **might** work", it is important to cautiously, yet optimistically, continue to apply the risk principle. To date, research in this area exists with some flaws and there is a need to expand upon the research literature in this regard. Furthermore, there is some evidence to suggest that co-educational programs/interventions are of value; however, this literature is in its relative infancy and requires further validation. Finally, there is strong evidence for the prominence of mental health needs for female offenders; however, in terms of a capacity to contribute to reductions in recidivism, additional work is required before researchers can state with confidence that this falls into the "what works" domain.

In considering "what **doesn't** work", ample research exists to confirm that punishment (e.g. 'tough on crime' regimes) fails to influence desired outcomes in a favourable manner. For punishment to work it must be both swift and appropriate to the transgression, the former of which is rarely attainable in criminal justice systems that typically include lengthy court processes. Equally relevant, security responses to mental health needs have not in fact demonstrated to be an appropriate response. Certainly, Canada's Office of the Correctional Investigator (2015) has highlighted significant concerns around the application of mental health strategies in Canadian Prisons. More specifically, this work highlights the challenges with providing effective therapeutic interventions within prisons, and maximum security environments in particular (e.g., John Service Consulting, 2010). These concerns have certainly been echoed in other international jurisdictions (e.g., Gonzalez & Connell, 2014; House of Commons Committee of Public Accounts, 2017).

Research to date has offered varieties of delivery specific elements relevant to effective treatment service delivery. Optimal treatment outcomes are argued to be most often achieved when community-based, as opposed to institutional based treatment is provided (e.g., Andrews, 2001; Kennedy, 2004); however, more recent evidence suggests that for women, there may be a weaker effect for community based treatment (in isolation), possibly related to dosage or format and of course with recognition that previous research was based primarily on male study samples (Gobeil et al., 2016). There is also some evidence to suggest that women are more successful in single- versus mixed-gender formats (e.g., Ashley, Marsden, & Brady, 2003; Lex, 1995). Therapeutic environment, in general, and characteristics of the therapist, in particular, have emerged as critical to consider in treatment efforts (e.g., Bloom, Owen, & Covington, 2003; Pollack, 1986). Client characteristics such as individual strengths, resiliency and/or protective factors should be integrated into offender rehabilitation strategies (e.g., Andrews, 2001; Andrews & Bonta, 2010; Bloom et al., 2003; Ward & Brown, 2004). Women-centred training is also emerging as an increasingly important consideration in the provision of effective support and service delivery to women offenders (e.g., Nolan, Harris, & Derkzen, 2017). Finally, there is increasing evidence to support the advantages of integrated intervention approaches/models (Blanchette & Brown, 2006). That is, interventions that address multiple needs at the same time, treatment that is capable of addressing both substance abuse and emotional regulation simultaneously, for example (e.g., Correctional Service of Canada's Integrated Women Offender Correctional Program; WOCP).

Based on the evidence outlined, we would argue, "what works" in treatment and service delivery interventions include:

1. gender-informed interventions, including the integration of trauma-informed care;
2. targeting criminogenic needs;
3. holistic approaches;

4. highly structured, skills-focused and practical interventions;
5. women-centred training for staff;
6. recognizing the unique needs of women and the context in which offending occurs (i.e., trajectories/pathways); and,
7. the maintenance of prosocial family/community ties.

There have been notable advancements in women-centred corrections in Canada (Robeson Barrett, Allenby, & Taylor, 2010), the United States (Bloom et al., 2003), the United Kingdom (Ministry of Justice - NOMS Women and Equalities Group, 2012), and Australia (Salomone, n.d.; Howells, 2000). Almost 30 years ago, Correctional Service of Canada's Task Force on Federally Sentenced Women (1990) provided recommendations for the improvement of correctional policy and practice for female offenders through basic principles that now guide correctional interventions for women. These principles include empowerment, meaningful and responsible choices, respect and dignity, supportive environments, and shared responsibility. They further spoke to the relevance of holistic programming interventions. As a result of a study conducted by the National Institute of Corrections (NIC) in collaboration with Bloom et al. (2003, 2004), the United States also has guiding principles to promote gender-responsive interventions. These include: gender matters, environment (safety, respect, and dignity), relationships (healthy connections), services and supervision (for substance abuse, trauma and mental health), socio-economic status (education and training), and community (re-entry and collaboration). South Australia fully supports the RNR principles and their application with female offenders. More specifically, Howells (2000) argued that these principles sharpen our thinking on what needs to be done in managing women in prison in a more coherent, effective, and humane way.

With the evolution and establishment of guiding principles around effective gender-specific interventions come advancements in treatment and programming options for female offenders. The Correctional Service of Canada has a long-standing history of programs for female offenders; however, as briefly noted above, their current model is integrated as it targets multiple need areas within one correctional program continuum.

Khilnani (2016) provides brief overviews of some gender-specific interventions such as Seeking Safety, a therapeutic program developed by Lisa Najavits. This intervention is designed to treat both post-traumatic stress disorder and substance abuse. Khilnani also discusses the Systems Training for Emotional Predictability and Problem Solving Program (STEPPS) for incarcerated women struggling with trauma and self-esteem issues related to histories of sexual abuse and unhealthy relationships. This program focuses on behavioural and emotions management regulation strategies and is offered in a psychoeducational group format for those women suffering with borderline personality disorder. Finally, the Ladies Empowerment and Action Program (LEAP) is a Miami-based initiative available to women seeking to improve the likelihood of successful release outcomes. LEAP is designed to empower incarcerated women to make positive life changes and uses a multi-disciplinary approach including entrepreneurship training, education, and mentorship. LEAP partners with a local university to offer business classes to women matching the selection criteria for the program.

5.5   Future Implications

The research evidence is clear: women offenders have different trajectories into the criminal justice system, and gender-informed interventions, including trauma-informed care, maximize the likelihood of successful reintegration. Both gender neutral (e.g., Andrews and colleagues, Andrews, 2001; Andrews & Bonta, 2010); and feminist (e.g., Belknap, 2007) perspectives acknowledge the importance of tailoring interventions to the individual client to capitalize on responsivity to services provided. Despite this, few jurisdictions offer training for front line staff on the provision of gender-responsive services for girls and women. As noted earlier, Correctional Service of Canada offers Women-Centred Training and a recent evaluation of this initiative yielded positive results. This is an important innovation that should be considered in other jurisdictions.

The research on 'what works' for women has been instructive with respect to the applicability of the RNR principles and other important considerations for women. Nonetheless, it is still in its infancy (relative to what is known for their male counterparts), and as more primary studies accumulate, prospective meta-analyses will further inform best practices in interventions for women.

Finally, in an era of quickly evolving technological solutions, it is hoped that correctional jurisdictions will be able to capitalize on innovations such as video visitation and telemedicine. These may be particularly beneficial to women, given that they are a small, often geographically dispersed population with unique needs in terms of family and community connections.

5.6   Technology and Innovation

Technology and innovation poses a very interesting challenge in certain correctional and community based environments where the resource constraints are sometimes quite significant; however, we are seeing some success in these areas and should continue to expand upon these positive outcomes. For example, where feasible, some service delivery environments are capitalizing on telehealth/telepsychiatry and the use of electronic medical records systems (see, for example https://www.techcareehr.com). Video visitation for women with children is proving beneficial to the well-being of women, allowing them to maintain a mother-child bond when in-person visitation is not feasible. For example, Correctional Service of Canada's Mother-Child program now includes a non-residential component entitled 'ChildLink'—a video visitation program which allows women inmates to communicate with their children in the community using video conferencing technology (e.g., WebEx). This is an important innovation that, in line with relational theory, will help women to manage the stress of incarceration *and* because there is empirical evidence demonstrating that the maintenance of prosocial family ties assists with women's adjustment to incarceration (Blanchette, 2005; Jiang & Winfree, 2006).

Finally, through greater inter-agency collaboration and sharing of information, there is growing opportunity to leverage technology in support of reintegration efforts. Specifically, technological advances will assist with inter-agency collaboration so that important information can quickly and easily be shared between service providers as appropriate (e.g., police, courts, corrections, mental health agencies, and other support organizations).

5.7 Conclusions

Women offenders differ from their male counterparts in several important ways. The nature and prevalence of mental disorder varies by gender. The onset or 'triggers' of mental illness and offending behaviour seem to vary by gender as well; there is good emerging evidence to show that women's pathways into the criminal justice system are gendered. Arguably, systemic responses to both mental illness and criminality should also be gender-informed to maximize wellness and desistence from crime. Assessment and treatment services for women should attend to important contextual factors of their lives (e.g., experiences of trauma, parental responsibilities, and economic marginalization) and leverage women's strengths to promote healing and desistence from crime.

The very large proportion of women offenders with significant mental health needs underscores the importance of integrated mental health treatment and correctional case management. Ideally, multidisciplinary teams (including correctional officers, parole officers, health/mental health care providers) should be specially selected and trained in the fundamentals of mental illness and provision of gender-informed care. Effective clinical case coordination should incorporate some form of a dedicated staffing model that assigns particular staff members on a caseload basis. Case coordination in this manner serves to both acknowledge the importance of relational factors for women while also enhancing staff familiarity with the multidimensional needs of each woman and reinforcing an integrated approach that maintains the woman at the centre. Within an institutional context, correctional operations and/or security staff must work in close collaboration with mental health teams to maintain the safety and security of all, to and to optimize both correctional and mental health outcomes for women. In sum, we emphatically support the holistic approach to intervention for women, particularly those with mental health needs.

References

Aday, R. H., Dye, M. H., & Kaiser, A. K. (2014). Examining the traumatic effects of sexual victimization on the health of incarcerated women. *Women and Criminal Justice, 24*(4), 341–361.
American Psychiatric Association. (2013). *Diagnostic and Statistical Manual of Mental Disorders: DSM-5*. Washington, DC: Author.

Andrews, D. A. (1982). *Personal, Interpersonal and Community-Reinforcement on Deviant Behaviour (PIC-R)*. Toronto, ON: Ministry of Correctional Services.

Andrews, D. A. (2001). Principles of effective correctional programs. In L. L. Motiuk & R. C. Serin (Eds.), *Compendium 2000 on effective correctional treatment* (pp. 9–17). Ottawa, ON: Correctional Service of Canada, Research Branch.

Andrews, D. A., & Bonta, J. (2010). *The psychology of criminal conduct* (5th ed.). New Providence, NJ: Mathew Bender & Co..

Andrews, D. A., Bonta, J., & Hoge, R. D. (1990). Classification for effective rehabilitation: Rediscovering psychology. *Criminal Justice and Behaviour, 17*(1), 19–52.

Andrews, D. A., Bonta, J., & Wormith, S. J. (2004). *The level of service/case management inventory (LS/CMI)*. Toronto: Multi-Health Systems.

Andrews, D. A., Guzzo, L., Raynor, P., Rowe, R. C., Rettinger, L. J., Brews, A., & Wormith, J. S. (2012). Are the major risk/need factors predictive of both female and male reoffending? A test with the eight domains of the level of service/case management inventory. *International Journal of Offender Therapy and Comparative Criminology, 56*(1), 113–133.

Andrews, D. A., Zinger, I., Hoge, R. D., Bonta, J., Gendreau, P., & Cullen, F. T. (1990). Does correctional treatment work? A clinically relevant and psychologically informed meta-analysis. *Criminology, 28*(3), 369–404.

Ashley, O. S., Marsden, M. E., & Brady, T. M. (2003). Effectiveness of substance abuse treatment programming for women: A review. *The American Journal of Drug and Alcohol Abuse, 29*(1), 19–53.

Baillargeon, J., Binswanger, I. A., Penn, J., Williams, B. A., & Murray, O. J. (2009). Psychiatric disorders and repeat incarcerations: The revolving prison door. *The American Journal of Psychiatry, 166*(1), 103–109.

Beck, A. T., & Steer, R. A. (1988). *Beck Hopelessness Scale*. San Antonio, TX: Psychological Corporation.

Beck, A. T., & Steer, R. A. (1993). *Beck Anxiety Inventory Manual*. San Antonio, TX: Psychological Corporation.

Beck, A. T., Steer, R. A., & Brown, G. K. (1996). *Manual for the Beck Depression Inventory-II*. San Antonio, TX: Psychological Corporation.

Belknap, J. (2007). *The invisible woman: Gender, crime, and justice* (3rd ed.). Belmont, CA: Wadsworth Publishing Co..

Belknap, J., & Holsinger, K. (1998). An overview of delinquent girls: How theory and practice have failed and the need for innovative changes. In R. T. Zaplin (Ed.), *Female offenders: Critical perspectives and effective interventions* (pp. 31–64). Gaithersburg, MD: Aspen Publishers.

Bell, A., Trevethan, S., & Allegri, N. (2004). *A needs assessment of federal Aboriginal women offenders*. Research Report # 156. Ottawa ON: Correctional Services Canada.

Benda, B. B. (2005). Gender differences in life-course theory of recidivism: A survival analysis. *International Journal of Offender Therapy and Comparative Criminology, 49*(3), 325–342.

Blanchette, K. (2000). Effective correctional practice with women offenders. *Compendium 2000 on Effective Correctional Programming*. Ottawa, ON: Correctional Services of Canada.

Blanchette, K. (2002). Classifying female offenders for effective intervention: Application of the case-based principles or risk and need. *Forum on Correctional Research, 14*(1), 31–35.

Blanchette, K. (2005). *Field-test of a gender-informed security reclassification scale for female offenders*. Unpublished doctoral dissertation, Carleton University, Ottawa, Ontario, Canada.

Blanchette, K., & Brown, S. L. (2006). *The assessment and treatment of women offenders: An integrated perspective*. Chichester, UK: Wiley.

Blanchette, K., & Eldjupovic-Guzina, G. (1998). *Results of a pilot study of the peer support program for women offenders*. Research Report #73. Ottawa, ON: Correctional Service of Canada.

Bloom, B. E., & Covington, S. (2000, November). *Gendered justice: Programming for women in correctional settings*. Paper presented at the Annual Meeting of the American Society of Criminology, San Francisco, CA.

Bloom, B., Owen, B., & Covington, S. S. (2003). *Gender-responsive strategies: Research, practice, and guiding principles.* Retrieved from www.nicic.org

Bloom, B., Owen, B., & Covington, S. (2004). Women offenders and the gendered effects of public policy. *Review of Policy Research, 21*(1), 31–48.

Bonta, J., Blais, J., & Wilson, H. A., (2013). *The prediction of risk for mentally disordered offenders: A quantitative analysis.* User Report 2013-01. Ottawa, ON: Public Safety Canada.

Bonta, J., & Wormith, S. J. (2008). Risk and need assessment. In G. McIvor & P. Raynor (Eds.), *Developments in social work with offenders* (pp. 131–152). London, England: Jessica Kingsley Publishers.

Brennan, T., Breitenbach, M., Dieterich, W., Salisbury, E. J., & Van Voorhis, P. (2012). Women's pathways to serious and habitual crime: A person-centred analysis incorporating gender responsive factors. *Criminal Justice and Behaviour, 39*(11), 1481–1508.

Brink, J. (2005). Epidemiology of mental illness in a correctional system. *Current Opinion in Psychiatry, 18*(5), 536–541.

Bronson, J., & Berzofsky, M. (2017). *Indicators of mental health problems reported by prisoners and jail inmates, 2011–2012,* NCJ 250612.

Butcher, J. N., Graham, J. R., Ben-Porath, Y. S., Tellegen, A., Dahlstrom, W. G., & Kaemmer, B. (2001). *MMPI-2 (Minnesota Multiphasic Personality Inventory-2): Manual for administration, scoring, and interpretation, revised edition.* Minneapolis, MN: University of Minnesota Press.

Carson, A. E., & Anderson, E. (2016). *Prisoners in 2015.* Washington, DC: Bureau of Justice Statistics.

Chaimowitz, G. (2012). *The criminalization of people with mental illness.* Ottawa, ON: Canadian Psychiatric Association.

Charles, D. R., Abram, K. M., McClelland, G. M., & Teplin, L. A. (2003). Suicidal ideation and behavior among women in jail. *Journal of Contemporary Criminal Justice, 19*(1), 65–81.

Chesney-Lind, M. (1998). Women in prison: From partial justice to vengeful equity. *Corrections Today, 60*(7), 66–73.

Clements-Nolle, K., Wolden, M., & Bargmann-Losche, J. (2009). Childhood trauma and risk for past and future suicide attempts among women in prison. *Women's Health Issues, 19*(3), 185–192.

Cobbina, J. E., Huebner, B. M., & Berg, M. T. (2010). Men, women, and postrelease offending: An examination of the nature of the link between relational ties and recidivism. *Crime and Delinquency, 58*(3), 331–361.

Coid, J., Yang, M., Ullrich, S., Sizmur, S., Roberts, C., Farrington, D. P., & Rogers, R. D. (2009). Gender differences in structured risk assessment: Comparing the accuracy of five instruments. *Journal of Consulting and Clinical Psychology, 77*, 337–348.

Collier, S., & Friedman, S. H. (2016). Mental illness among women referred for psychiatric services in a New Zealand women's prison. *Behavioral Sciences and the Law, 34*, 539–550.

Correctional Service of Canada. (2010). *Validating the computerized mental health intake screening system. Emerging research results.* Ottawa, ON: Author.

Correctional Service of Canada. (2017). *Women offenders.* Retrieved from http://www.csc-scc.gc.ca/publications/005007-3012-eng.shtml

Covington, S. S., & Bloom, B. (2006). Gender-responsive treatment and services in correctional settings. *Women and Therapy, 29*(3–4), 9–33.

Daly, K. (1992). Women's pathways to felony court: Feminist theories of lawbreaking and problems of representations. *Southern California Review of Law and Women's Studies, 2*(1), 11–52.

Day, J. C., Zahn, M. A., & Tichavsky, L. P. (2014). What works and for whom? The effects of gender responsive programming on girls and boys in secure detention. *Journal of Research in Crime & Delinquency, 52*, 93–129.

DeHart, D., Lynch, S., Belknap, J., Dass-Brailsford, P., & Green, B. (2014). Life history models of female offending: The roles of serious mental illness and trauma in women's pathways to jail. *Psychology of Women Quarterly, 38*(1), 138–51.

Derkzen, D., Booth, L., McConnell, A., & Taylor, K. (2012). *Mental health needs of federal women offenders*. Research Report #R-267, Ottawa, ON: Correctional Service of Canada.

Derkzen, D., Harris, A., Wardrop, K., & Thompson, J. (2017). Outcomes of Women Offender Correctional Programs. *Advancing Corrections Journal, 3*, 66–83.

Dowden, C., & Andrews, D. A. (1999). What works for female offenders: A meta-analytic review. *Crime and Delinquency, 45*, 438–452.

Drapalski, A. L., Youman, K., Stuewig, J., & Tangney, J. (2009). Gender differences in jail inmates' symptoms of mental illness, treatment history and treatment seeking. *Criminal Behaviour and Mental Health, 19*, 193–206.

Every-Palmer, S., Brink, J., Chern, T. P., Choi, W.-K., Hern-Yee, J. G., Green, B., … Mellsop, G. (2014). Review of psychiatric services to mentally disordered offenders around the Pacific Rim. *Asia-Pacific Psychiatry, 6*, 1–17.

Fazel, S., & Danesh, J. (2002). Serious mental disorder in 23,000 prisoners: A systematic review of 62 surveys. *The Lancet, 359*, 545–550.

Fazel, S., Hayes, A. J., Bartellas, K., Clerici, M., & Trestman, R. (2016). The mental health of prisoners: A review of prevalence, adverse outcomes and interventions. *Lancet Psychiatry, 3*(9), 871–881.

Fazel, S., & Seewald, K. (2012). Severe mental illness in 33588 prisoners worldwide: Systematic review and meta-regression analysis. *British Journal of Psychiatry, 200*(5), 364–373.

Federal Bureau of Investigations. (2011). *Data Table 66*. Retrieved February 23, 2018, from https://www.fbi.gov/about-us/cjis/ucr/crime-in-the-u.s/2011/crime-in-the-u.s.-2011/tables/table_66_arrests_suburban_areas_by_sex_2011.xls

First, M. B., Gibon, M., Spitzer, R. L., Williams, J. B., & Benjamin, L. S. (1997). *Structured Clinical Interview for DSM-IV Axis II Personality Disorders, (SCID-II)*. Washington, DC: American Psychiatric Press.

Florida Dept of Corrections. (2017). Retrieved from http://www.dc.state.fl.us/pub/recidivism/2016/RecidivismReport2017.pdf

Gannon, T., Rose, M., & Ward, T. (2010). Pathways to female sexual offending: Approach or avoidance? *Psychology, Crime, and Law, 16*, 359–380.

Gendreau, P., French, S., & Gionet, A. (2004). What works (What doesn't work): The principles of effective correctional treatment. *Journal of Community Corrections, XIII*(Spring edition), 4–30.

Geraghty, K. A., & Woodhams, J. (2015). The predictive validity of risk assessment tools for female offenders: A systematic review. *Aggression and Violent Behaviour, 21*, 25–38.

Gobeil, R., Blanchette, K., & Stewart, L. (2016). A meta-analytic review of correctional interventions for women offenders: Gender-neutral versus gender-informed approaches. *Criminal Justice and Behavior, 43*(3), 301–322.

Gonzalez, J. M. R., & Connell, N. M. (2014). Mental health of prisoners: Identifying barriers to mental health treatment and medication continuity. *American Journal of Public Health, 104*(12), 2328–2333.

Greiner, L. E., Law, M. A., & Brown, S. L. (2015). Using dynamic factors to predict recidivism among women: A four-wave prospective study. *Criminal Justice and Behaviour, 42*(5), 457–480.

Grella, C. E., & Greenwell, L. (2007). Treatment needs and completion of community-based aftercare among substance-abusing women offenders. *Women's Health Issues, 17*(4), 244–255.

Grove, W. M., Zald, D. H., Lebow, B. S., Snitz, B. E., & Nelson, C. (2000). Clinical versus mechanical prediction: A meta-analysis. *Psychological Assessment, 12*(1), 19–30.

Hannah-Moffat, K., & Shaw, M. (2001). *Taking risks: Incorporating gender and culture into classification and assessment of federally sentenced women in Canada*. Ottawa, ON: Status of Women Canada.

Hollin, C. R., & Palmer, E. J. (2006). Criminogenic need and women offenders: A critique of the literature. *Legal and Criminological Psychology, 11*, 179–195.

House of Commons Committee of Public Accounts. (2017). *Mental health in prisons: Eight report of session 2017–19*. Retrieved February 22, 2018, from https://publications.parliament.uk/pa/cm201719/cmselect/cmpubacc/400/400.pdf

Houser, K., & Belenko, S. (2015). Disciplinary responses to misconduct among female prison inmates with mental illness, substance use disorders, and co-occurring disorders. *Psychiatric Rehabilitation Journal, 38*(1), 24–34.

Howells, K. (2000, November). *Treatment, management and rehabilitation of women in prison: Relevance of rehabilitation principles*. Paper presented at the Women in Corrections: Staff and Clients Conference, Australian Institute of Criminology in conjunction with the Department of Correctional Services South Australia, Adelaide.

Islam-Zwart, K. A., Vik, P. W., & Rawlins, K. S. (2007). Short-term psychological adjustment of female prison inmates on a minimum security unit. *Women's Health Issues, 17*(4), 237–243.

Jackson, D. N. (1996). *Basic Personality Inventory Manual* (2nd ed.). London, ON: Sigma Assessment Systems.

James, D. J., & Glaze, L. E. (2006). *Mental health problems of prison and jail inmates*. Washington, DC: U.S. Department of Justice, Office of Justice Programs, Bureau of Justice Statistics.

Jiang, S. L., & Winfree, L. T. (2006). Social support, gender, and inmate adjustment to prison life: Insights from a national sample. *The Prison Journal, 86*(1), 32–55.

John Service Consulting. (2010). *Under warrant: A review of the implementation of the Correctional Service of Canada's Mental Health Strategy*. Ottawa, ON: Office of the Correctional Investigator.

Kassebaum, P. A. (1999). *Substance abuse treatment for women offenders: Guide to promising practices*. Rockville, MD: Rockwall.

Kennedy, S. M. (2004). A practitioner's guide to responsivity: Maximizing treatment effectiveness. *Journal of Community Corrections, XIII*, 7–9, 22–30.

Kessler, R. C., Barker, P. R., Colpe, L. J., Epstein, J. F., Gfroerer, J. C., Hiripi, E., … Zaslavsky, A. M. (2003). Screening for serious mental illness in the general population. *Archives of General Psychiatry, 60*(2), 184–189.

Khilnani, S. (2016). Gender-specific programming targets females' unique needs. *Correct Care, 30*, 7–11.

Kimonis, E. R., Skeem, J. L., Edens, J. F., Douglas, K. S., Lilienfeld, S. O., & Poythress, N. G. (2010). Suicidal and criminal behavior among female offenders: The role of abuse and psychopathology. *Journal of Personality Disorders, 24*(5), 581–609.

Krespi-Boothby, M. R., Mullholland, I., Cases, A., Carrington, K., & Bolger, T. (2010). Towards mental health promotion in prisons: The role of screening for emotional distress. *Social and Behavioral Sciences, 5*, 90–94.

Kubiak, S. P., Beeble, M. L., & Bybee, D. (2009). Using the K6 to assess the mental health of jailed women. *Journal of Offender Rehabilitation, 48*(4), 296–313.

Kubiak, S. P., Fedock, G., Kim, W. J., & Bybee, D. (2017). Examining perpetration of physical violence by women: The influence of childhood adversity, victimization, mental illness, substance abuse, and anger. *Violence and Victims, 32*(1), 22–45.

Lewis, C. (2006). Treating incarcerated women: Gender matters. *Psychiatric Clinics of North America, 29*(3), 773–789.

Lex, B. W. (1995). Alcohol and other psychoactive substances dependence in women and men. In M. V. Seeman (Ed.), *Gender and psychopathology* (pp. 311–357). Washington, DC: American Psychiatric Press.

Lindsay, W. R., Smith, A. H. W., Quinn, K., Anderson, A., Smith, A., Allan, R., & Law, J. (2004). Women with intellectual disability who have offended: Characteristics and outcome. *Journal of Intellectual Disability Research, 48*(6), 580–590.

Lynch, S. M., DeHart, D. D., Belknap, J. E., & Green, B. L. (2012). *Women's pathways to jail: The roles and intersections of serious mental illness and trauma*. Washington, DC: U.S. Department of Justice, Office of Justice Programs, Bureau of Justice Assistance.

Lynch, S. M., DeHart, D. D., Belknap, J. E., Green, B. L., Dass-Brailsford, P., Johnson, K. A., & Whalley, E. (2014). A multisite study of the prevalence of serious mental illness, PTSD, and substance use disorders of women in jail. *Psychiatric Services, 65*(5), 670–674.

Mahoney, A. M., & Daniel, C. A. (2006). Bridging the power gap: Narrative therapy with incarcerated women. *The Prison Journal, 86*(1), 75–88.

Marcus-Mendoza, S. (2010). Feminist therapy with incarcerated women: Practicing subversion in prison. *Women and Therapy, 34*(1–2), 77–92.

Martinson, R. (1974). What works? Questions and answers about prison reform. *The Public Interest, 35*, 22–54.

Messina, N., & Grella, C. (2006). Childhood trauma and women's health outcomes in a California prison population. *American Journal of Public Health, 96*(10), 1842–1848.

Miller, J. B.. (1986). *What do we mean by relationships?* Work in Progress No. 33. Wellesley, MA: Stone Center, Working Paper Series.

Millon, T. (1997). *Millon Clinical Multiaxial Inventory-III Manual* (2nd ed.). Minneapolis, MN: National Computer System.

Mills, J. F., & Kroner, D. G. (2004). A new instrument to screen for depression, hopelessness, and suicide in incarcerated offenders. *Psychological Services, 1*(1), 83–91.

Ministry of Justice - National Offender Management Service (NOMS). (2012). *A distinct approach: A guide to working with women offenders.* London, UK: Author. Retrieved February 26, 2018.

Møller, L., Stöver, H., Jürgens, R., Gatherer, A., & Nikogosian, H. (Eds.). (2007). *Health in prisons: A WHO guide to the essentials in prison health.* Copenhagen, Denmark: Regional Office for Europe.

Moloney, K. P., van den Bergh, B. J., & Moller, L. F. (2009). Women in prison: The central issues of gender characteristics and trauma history. *Public Health, 123*, 426–430.

Morey, L. C. (2007). *Personality Assessment Inventory Professional Manual.* Lutz, FL: Psychological Assessment Resources.

Muenzenmaier, K., Margolis, F., Langdon, G. S., Rhodes, D., Kobayashi, T., & Rifkin, L. (2015). Transcending bias in diagnosis and treatment for women with serious mental illness. *Women and Therapy, 38*(1–2), 141–155.

Munetz, M. R., Grande, T. P., & Chambers, M. R. (2001). The incarceration of individuals with severe mental disorders. *Community Mental Health Journal, 37*(4), 361–372.

National Resource Center on Justice Involved Women. (2016). *Fact Sheet on Justice Involved Women.* Retrieved February 26, 2018, from http://cjinvolvedwomen.org/wp-content/uploads/2016/06/Fact-Sheet.pdf

Nicholls, T. L., Roesch, R., Olley, M. C., Ogloff, J. R. P., & Hemphill, J. F. (2005). *Jail Screening Assessment Tool (JSAT): Guidelines for mental health screening in jails.* Burnaby, BC: Mental Health, Law, and Policy Institute, Simon Fraser University.

Nolan, A., Harris, A., & Derkzen, D. (2017). *An assessment of the Women-Centred Training Program.* Research Report #R-385, Ottawa, ON: Correctional Service of Canada.

Nowotny, K. M., Belknap, J., Lynch, S., & Dehart, D. (2014). Risk profile and treatment needs of women in jail with co-occurring serious mental illness and substance use disorders. *Women and Health, 54*(8), 781–795.

O'keefe, M. A., & Schnell, M. L. (2007). Offenders with mental illness in the correctional system. *Journal of Offender Rehabilitation, 45*(1–2), 81–104.

Office of the Correctional Investigator. (2015). *Annual report of the Office of the Correctional Investigator.* ISBN 1493-5295, Ottawa, ON: Author.

Overall, J. E., & Gorham, D. R. (1962). The Brief Psychiatric Rating Scale. *Psychological Reports, 10*, 799–812.

Padgett, D. K., Hawkins, R. L., Abrams, C., & Davis, A. (2006). In their own words: Trauma and substance abuse in the lives of formerly homeless women with serious mental illness. *American Journal of Orthopsychiatry, 76*(4), 461–467.

Pilgrim, D. (2010). Aspects of diagnosed mental illness and offending. In G. J. Towl & D. A. Crighton (Eds.), *Forensic psychology.* Chichester, UK: Wiley-Blackwell.

Pollack, J. (1986). *Sex and supervision: Guarding male and female inmates.* New York, NY: Greenwood Press.

Prins, S. J. (2014). Prevalence of mental illnesses in US State prisons: A systematic review. *Psychiatric Services, 65*(7), 862–872.

Reisig, M. D., Holtfreter, K., & Morash, M. (2006). Assessing recidivism risk across female pathways to crime. *Justice Quarterly, 23*(3), 384–405.

Rettinger, L. J., & Andrews, D. A. (2010). General risk and need, gender specificity and the recidivism of female offenders. *Criminal Justice and Behavior, 37*(1), 29–46.

Robeson Barrett, M., Allenby, K., & Taylor, K (2010). *Twenty years later: Revisiting the Task Force on Federally Sentenced Women.* Research Report #222, Ottawa, ON: Correctional Services Canada.

Robinson, D., Porporino, F., & Beal, C. (1998). *A review of the literature on personal emotional need factors.* Research Report # 76. Ottawa, ON: Correctional Services Canada.

Sacks, J. Y., McKendrick, K., & Hamilton, Z. (2012). A randomized clinical trial of a therapeutic community treatment for female inmates: Outcomes at 6 and 12 months after prison release. *Journal of Addictive Diseases, 31*(3), 258–269.

Salisbury, E. J., & Van Voorhis, P. (2009). Gendered pathways: A quantitative investigation of women probationers' paths to incarceration. *Criminal Justice and Behavior, 36*(6), 541–566.

Salisbury, E. J., Van Voorhis, P., & Spiropoulos, G. V. (2009). The predictive validity of a Gender-Responsive Needs Assessment: An exploratory study. *Crime & Delinquency, 55*, 550–585.

Salomone, J. (n.d.). *Towards best practice in women's corrections: The Western Australian low security prison for women.* Retrieved February 22, 2017, from https://www.correctiveservices. wa.gov.au/_files/about-us/statistics-publications/students-researchers/towards-best-practices. pdf

Saxena, P., Messina, N. P., & Grella, C. E. (2014). Who benefits from gender responsive treatment? Accounting for abuse history on longitudinal outcomes for women in prison. *Criminal Justice and Behaviour, 41*(4), 417–432.

Simpson, S. S., Yahner, J. L., & Dugan, L. (2008). Understanding women's pathways to jail: Analysing the lives of incarcerated women. *Australian and New Zealand Journal of Criminology, 41*(1), 84–108.

Spielberger, C. D., Gorsuch, R. L., Lushene, P. R., Vagg, P. R., & Jacobs, G. A. (1983). *Manual for the State-Trait Anxiety Inventory.* Palo Alto, CA: Consulting Psychologists Press.

Statistics Canada. n.d. *Table 109-5009—Adults and youths charged, by sex and offence category, Canada, provinces and territories, annual,* CANSIM (database). Retrieved February 23, 2018, from http://www5.statcan.gc.ca/cansim/

Staton, M., Leukefeld, C., & Logan, T. K. (2001). Health service utilization and victimization among incarcerated female substance abusers. *Substance Use and Misuse, 36*, 701–716.

Steadman, H. J., Osher, F. C., Robbins, P. C., Case, B., & Samuels, S. (2009). Prevalence of serious mental illness among jail inmates. *Psychiatric Services, 60*(6), 761–765.

Steadman, H. J., Scott, J. E., Osher, F., Agnese, T. K., & Robbins, P. C. (2005). Validation of the brief mental health screen. *Psychiatric Services, 56*(7), 816–822.

Stewart, L., Brine, K., Wilton, G., Power, J., & Hnain, C. (2015). *Resilience factors related to success on release for offenders with mental disorders.* Research Report #R-336. Ottawa, ON: Correctional Service of Canada.

Stewart, L., & Gobeil, R. (2015). Correctional interventions for women offenders: A rapid evidence assessment. *Journal of Criminology Research, Policy and Practice, 1*(3), 116–130.

Strub, D. S., Douglas, K. S., & Nicholls, T. L. (2016). Violence risk assessment of civil psychiatric patients with the HCR-20: Does gender matter? *International Journal of Forensic Mental Health, 15*(1), 81–96.

Swets, J. A., Dawes, R. M., & Monahan, J. (2000). Psychological science in the public interest: Psychological science can improve diagnostic decisions. *Journal of the American Psychological Society, 1*, 1–26.

Task Force on Federally Sentenced Women. (1990). *Creating choices: The response of the task force on federally sentenced women.* Ottawa, ON: Correctional Service of Canada.

Turcotte, M. (2011). *Women and health in women in Canada: A gender-based statistical report.* Ottawa, ON: Minister of Industry.

Tye, C. S., & Mullen, P. E. (2006). Mental disorders in female prisoners. *Australian and New Zealand Journal of Psychiatry, 40*(3), 266–271.

Van Wormer, K. (2001). *Counseling female offenders and victims: A strengths-based approach.* New York, NY: Springer.

Ward, T., & Brown, M. (2004). The Good Lives model and conceptual issues in offender rehabilitation. *Psychology, Crime & Law, 10*(3), 243–257.

Warren, J. I., Hurt, S., Loper, A. B., Bale, R., Friend, R., & Chauhan, P. (2002). Psychiatric symptoms, history of victimization, and violent behaviour among incarcerated female felons: An American perspective. *International Journal of Law and Psychiatry, 25*, 129–149.

Wechsler, D. (1997). *Wechsler Adult Intelligence Scale—Third Edition*. San Antonio, TX: The Psychological Corporation.

World Health Organization. (2002). *Gender and mental health*. Geneva: Author.

World Health Organization. (2006). *Gender disparities in mental health*. Washington, DC: Department of Mental Health and Substance Dependence.

World Health Organization. (2016). *Mental health: Strengthening our response*. Geneva: Author.

Zaplin, R. T. (2008). *Female offenders: Critical perspectives and effective interventions* (2nd ed.). Boston, MA: Jones and Bartlett.

Zlotnick, C., Johnson, J., & Najavits, L. (2009). Randomized controlled pilot study of cognitive-behavioural therapy in a sample of incarcerated women with substance use disorder and PTSD. *Behavior Therapy, 40*(40), 325–336.

Chapter 6
Assessing and Treating Youth Offenders

Robert D. Hoge

The focus of this chapter is the treatment of youth involved in the juvenile justice system. The term 'youth offender' encompasses various groups of youth: young people accused of a crime but not yet charged; those charged and processed within the police and judicial systems; and those adjudicated guilty and recipient of a correctional disposition. These groups form the focus of this chapter however some attention will also be paid to youth not involved in the system, but identified as at-risk for criminal behavior. Subsequently, various courses of action at different stages of processing, including the range of correctional dispositions, will be described and evaluated in terms of the principles of best practice and research.

Youth not yet involved in the police or justice system, but identified as at-risk for involvement in criminal activities constitute a critical group. The assumption is that intervening early in the developmental process can be effective in deferring later antisocial activities. These community-based prevention programs will not be discussed here; the reader is referred to Farrington and Welsh (2006, 2010) for information about evidence-based prevention programs.

6.1 Types of Programs and Dispositions

Pre-charge or pre-arrest programs are directed toward youth who have been apprehended for a crime, but not yet charged (Hoge, 2016a; Wilson & Hoge, 2012). These are generally community-based programs designed to address factors placing the youth at risk for continued criminal activity. They are often designated diversion programs as the goal is to avoid the youth's involvement in the police and judicial system.

R. D. Hoge (✉)
Department of Psychology, Carleton University, Ottawa, ON, Canada
e-mail: robert.hoge@carleton.ca

© Springer Nature Switzerland AG 2018
M. Ternes et al. (eds.), *The Practice of Correctional Psychology*,
https://doi.org/10.1007/978-3-030-00452-1_6

A wide range of dispositions are available for youth who have been adjudicated and found guilty of a crime (Hoge, 2001; Krisberg & Howell, 1998; Lipsey & Wilson, 1998). Lesser correctional dispositions include fines and community service orders. Judges may also order mental health treatment or referral to a restorative justice program. The most common disposition is probation where the youth remains in the community under the supervision of a probation officer. The youth's actions are monitored by the officer and services may be offered to address the needs of the youth.

6.2 Variations in the Juvenile Justice System

6.2.1 Crime, Age, and Policy

Juvenile justice systems vary in a number of respects (Corrado, 1992). First, they may vary in terms of what is considered a crime. For example, in some jurisdictions truancy may be considered a crime and in others a non-criminal status offense. Second, the age at which the youth is considered an adult within the system varies. This issue is complicated by the fact that in some circumstances youth can be transferred to the adult system.

As well, systems vary in terms of the ages at which youth can be charged with a crime. In some jurisdictions, 7 years is the minimum age of criminal responsibility (e.g. India, Malaysia, and Singapore; Crofts, 2016), in other cases it is 12 years (e.g., Canada and Uganda; Crofts, 2016), and in still other jurisdictions maintain no minimum age (e.g., for state-level offenses in the United States of America, 33 states have not set a minimum age for criminal responsibility; Cipriani, 2009). In any case, it is important to consider these variations in definitions of crime, age of criminal responsibility, and policy considerations when comparing crime rates across jurisdictions and time.

6.2.2 Judicial Procedures and Dispositions

Judicial procedures and dispositions are normally imposed in a legally constituted judicial system; the system will include a range of actions to address the criminal activity and procedures for processing the youth in the system. These systems vary widely in a number of respects. First, the context of the system may vary. In most cases, the system will form part of a formally constituted legal system, while in other cases youth committing a criminal act will be dealt with in a child and welfare system. An example of the latter is Scotland's Whole Systems Approach (WSA), where the majority of youth in conflict with the law are cared for by wide range of agencies working together to support the needs of the youth and their family.

Systems also differ in legal procedures. At one extreme are systems representing a *parens patriae* system whereby all interactions with the youth are directed by a judicial authority, usually a judge, supposedly acting in the best interest of the youth. Legal rights are normally not granted to the youth in these systems. At the other extreme are systems where the youth is granted the full range of legal rights as in the adult system. That is, they have a right to representation by counsel, access to a jury trial, etc. This issue is somewhat complicated by the fact that, within many juvenile justice systems, considerable discretion is exercised in the treatment of the youthful offender. For example, a police officer may decide to release a youth with a warning given his or her age; a prosecuting attorney may decide not to proceed with charges given the youth's age and the nature of the offense; or a judge may dismiss a case based on maturity issues.

6.2.3 Punitive and Rehabilitative Measures

Another dimension in which systems differs concerns the relative emphasis on punitive and rehabilitative measures. Youth in some systems are held accountable through punitive sanctions such as fines, close probation supervision, and custody in some form. In other systems, the emphasis is on rehabilitation through counselling and other interventions.

Most systems in Canada and the U.S. occupy mid-points on these continua. That is, they process youth in a defined legal system where due process protections will be available (although perhaps not the extent as the adult systems). These systems will depend on both punitive and rehabilitation strategies. However, there is likely considerable variation in the actual nature of dispositions, the relative emphasis on punitive and rehabilitative interventions, and the extent of dependence on the best practices discussed below.

6.3 Frequency and Prevalence

Frequency or incidence indices refer to numbers of criminal acts committed. These are often expressed in relative terms. For example, data indicate that during a certain year there were 1890 incidences of serious crime per 100,000 of population. Prevalence indices, on the other hand, indicate the numbers of youth committing certain types of crime. These are also often presented in relative terms; for example, 26% of male youth were convicted of some type of crime within a region.

Estimating the frequency of criminal activity among youth and the prevalence of youth engaging in such activity is complicated by various factors, particularly where comparisons are made across time and across jurisdictions. One complication relates to the way in which the criminal act is defined. Rates may appear higher in one area because status offenses such as truancy are considered criminal acts, while they are not included in other areas. Similarly, comparing rates between areas with different minimum ages of criminal responsibility (or ages considered adult), may causes crime rates to appear relatively higher/lower.

Information on frequency and prevalence rates comes in several forms, most of which are either some form of official statistics, or self-report data. Official statistics are based on records of arrests, convictions, and dispositions. These are collected, by police and court officials and analyzed and reported in the United States by the Uniform Crime Reports of the Federal Bureau of Investigation (2015), and by the Revised Uniform Crime Reporting Survey (UCR) of Statistics Canada (2016) in Canada.

Examples of the incidence of criminal activity on the part of Canadian youth are available from recent analyses of the UCR (Statistics Canada, 2016). In 2016, 101,000 youth ages 12–17 were accused of a Criminal Code offence. This resulted in a youth crime rate of 4322 per 100,000 youth. The rates per 100,000 were 1281 for violent crimes and 2124 for property crimes. The analyses indicate that the majority of crimes for which youth were charged were minor in nature: theft under $5000, mischief, and minor assault (i.e., not resulting in serious injury). Data from the Revised Uniform Crime Survey (2016) also show that the youth crime rate has been declining steadily over the past 10 years: a 42% decline shown between 2000 and 2014.

However, there are limitations associated with these data. First, they are only as good as the record keeping of the agencies providing the information. Second, and more important, the data reflect only crime detected by authorities and processed within the justice and court systems. This means that information from official sources underestimates actual criminal activity to one degree of another. Some crimes are not detected at all and, for one reason or another, where it is detected the action is not processed by the system.

Self-report data provide a second source of information on frequency and prevalence. In this case the youth provides direct information via a survey regarding participation in various types of criminal acts. These analyses generally indicate a higher frequency of criminal activity than the official statistics.

To conclude, while both sources of information have limits, they still provide us with useful information about the extent of criminal activity among youth. The data also allow us to state general conclusions. First, the majority of youth are essentially responsible and law abiding citizens. This does not mean that they do not engage in inappropriate and illegal behavior sometimes. This can be expected from adolescents with their immature self-control and decision abilities and a preference for risk taking. However, in the majority of these cases the transgressions are minor and do not involve the police or courts.

A small number of adolescents do engage in criminal acts that come to the attention of the police and may result in charges and processing. However, these are generally minor crimes and the youth does not persist in criminal activities. Much of this involves what we refer to as adolescent-limited delinquency. A very small number of youth do engage in more serious criminal activity, and some of this activity involves violence. Further, a small number engage in crime, whether violent or not, chronically. We use the term life-course-persistent delinquency to describe some of these cases. While all criminal activity of youth requires attention, it is the small number of violent and chronic offenders that require close attention.

6.4 Theoretical Models Relevant to Service Delivery

Developing models of the causes of youthful criminal activity has a long and varied history (Shoemaker, 1996). As well, a large body of empirical research on the correlates and causes of delinquency has emerged, some of it guided by the theoretical developments and some more atheoretical in nature (Bonta & Andrews, 2017). Contemporary theoretical efforts can be divided into four broad categories (Bonta & Andrews, 2017; Shoemaker, 1996; Thornberry et al., 2012). Biological theories implicate genetic factors potentially associated with criminal acts and/or neurological and hormonal processes underlying the acts. Psychological constructs form a second category of theories. This encompasses formulations ranging from psychoanalytic concepts to social learning constructs. The emphasis in these cases is on internal processes within the youth. Finally, social and economic theories locate the causes of youthful criminal behavior in environmental conditions. These may be based on broad political theories such as Marxism or on more specific formulations involving the family, community, or school environments.

While each of the theoretical approaches has yielded important insights into the factors and conditions contributing to youthful criminal acts, human behavior is too complex to be explained in terms of narrowly focused constructs. For this reason, more integrative theories have emerged that attempt to incorporate a range of biological, individual, and social constructs into an explanatory framework. Further, these theories have led to a large body of empirical research focusing on the causes of criminal activity and effective ways of addressing the problem.

The Risk-Need-Responsivity (RNR) model represents an attempt to incorporate the integrative theories and contemporary empirical research into a model useful in guiding assessment and treatment decisions (Bonta & Andrews, 2017; Hoge, 2016b). Subsequent discussions of assessment, diagnosis and intervention issues will be guided by this model.

Risk factors are characteristics of the youth or his or her circumstances associated with engagement in criminal acts. We can identify the major risk factors with some confidence from the theories noted above and from a large body of empirical research on risk (Farrington, 1998; Grieger & Hosser, 2014; Heilbrun, Lee, & Cottle, 2005; Hoge, 2001). The major categories of identified risk factors include history of conduct disorder/criminal activity, dysfunctional family circumstances/parenting, poor school/vocational performance, antisocial peer relations, substance abuse, poor use of leisure time, dysfunctional personality/behaviour characteristics, and antisocial attitudes/values.

Identifying risk factors is considered important because it helps to establish the level of intervention appropriate in a particular case. This relates to the risk principle of case classification: intensive interventions should be reserved for high-risk cases, while moderate and lower risk cases require less intensive services or lower levels of supervision. A youth arrested for a relatively minor crime, whom was raised in a positive home environment and doing well in school, requires fewer services than a youth with a severe drug problem, who is experiencing school failure and associating with antisocial peers.

Two considerations are relevant to the risk principle. First, agencies generally have limited resources, and there is no sense in employing them in cases that do not require services. Second, involvement of youth in the police and judicial systems may have negative consequences (McAra & McVie, 2007; Petitclerc, Gatti, Vitaro, & Treblay, 2012). Thus, youth with lower levels of risk should not be involved in the systems at all if possible. However, risk level is only one factor that might impact a decision about disposition. The nature of the crime, and the youth's criminal history may also be relevant.

Need factors are risk factors that can be changed, and, if changed, may reduce the youth's level of risk for continued criminal activity. Some risk factors are static; that is, they are not subject to change. An example is criminal history. The other risk factors are dynamic; that is, they are subject to change through interventions. Dysfunctional parenting is an example. Parents can be trained through counselling or more structured programs to adopt more effective supervision and disciplinary practices with the child. Antisocial attitudes and values have been shown to be strong predictors of criminal activity. However, these attitudes and values can be replaced with more positive attitudes and behaviors through counseling and treatment interventions. The same point can be made with respect to the other risk factors. Changes in those areas may not be easy, but the issues can be addressed and where successfully addressed the likelihood of engaging in those activities will be reduced (Vieira, Skilling, & Peterson-Badall, 2009).

Need factors are relevant to the Need Principle of Case Classification: interventions should be directed to the specific needs of the client. If, for example, the antisocial behaviors seem to relate to a lack of supervision in the home, associations with antisocial peers, and drug use, then those should be the targets of service. Youth come to crime from a variety of directions, and this should be recognized in case planning. A 'one size fits all' strategy simply does not work with youthful offenders.

Responsivity constitutes the third key concept within the RNR model. Responsivity factors are defined as characteristics of the youth or his or her circumstances that, while not directly related to criminal activity, may have an impact on the individual's responses to interventions. The responsivity factor may relate to the youth's age, gender, cultural group membership or to the cognitive or social maturity of the youth. A youth with limited intellectual capacity will likely respond differently to a cognitive behavioral intervention than one at a more normal level. Similarly, a youth with low motivation for changing his or her behavior would need to be approached differently than one with a high level of readiness for change.

Strength or protective factors are also represented as responsivity factors within the RNR model. These include characteristics of the youth (e.g., high levels of maturity, interest in sports, academic competencies) and his or her environment (e.g., cooperative parent, supportive teacher, sport facilities within the community). Responsivity factors, both negative and positive, relate to the Responsivity Principle of Case Classification; these factors should be considered in case planning.

6.5 Diagnosis and Assessment

One of the principles of best practice emphasizes the importance of conducting careful assessments of characteristics of the youth and his or her circumstances prior to developing an intervention plan. These assessments are important whether attempting to provide diagnoses of mental health conditions or evaluations of the youth's risk and need factors. Various studies from the clinical literature (Grove & Vrieze, 2013; Grove, Zald, Lebow, Snitz, & Nelson, 2000) and forensic literature (Harris, Rice, Quinsey, & Cormier, 2015) have demonstrated that structured and standardized assessment instruments yield more valid and reliable assessments than clinical assessments.

While mental health or cognitive assessments are sometimes employed in judicial and correctional contexts (Grisso, Vincent, & Seagrave, 2005), the emphasis in this section is on forensic assessments of risk and needs. In this connection we can note that several standardized assessment tools are available for guiding these assessments: Structured Assessment of Violence Risk in Youth (SAVRY; Bartel, Borum, & Forth, 2005); Estimate of Risk of Adolescent Sexual Offense Recidivism (ERASOR; Worling & Curwen, 2001); Washington State Juvenile Court Assessment (WSJCA; Barnoski & Markussen, 2005; and Youth Level of Service/Case Management Inventory 2.0 (YLS/CMI 2.0; Hoge & Andrews, 2011). Some of these assessment tools represent actuarial measures. That is, they are based on items empirically linked with criminal activity and incorporate procedures for deriving quantitative indices of risk. Other measures represent structured professional judgments. These incorporate structured procedures into clinical judgments. Discussion of these instruments is provided by Borum and Verhaagen (2006), Hoge (2012), and Hoge and Andrews (1996, 2010).

6.6 Interventions

6.6.1 Best Practices from Literature

A considerable research literature has focused on the effectiveness of various approaches to addressing the factors placing individuals at risk for initiating criminal activity or persisting in that activity (Bonta & Andrews, 2017; Lipsey, 2009; McGuire, 2004; Welsh et al., 2012). This is referred to as the "what works" literature, and conclusions from this literature are referred to as best practices in addressing risk for criminal activity.

This discussion begins with three general conclusions from this literature. First, it is clear from research that punitive sanctions, particularly those based on incarceration or intensive supervised probation, are not associated with significant reductions in recidivism rates (Bonta & Andrews, 2017). In fact, they are often associated with increases in recidivism. This is particularly true where programs based on the punitive sanctions are compared with interventions based on the principles of best practice. Any involvement in the police or judicial systems may function as a risk factor; this does not mean that the use of punitive sanctions such as incarceration is always inappropriate. There are circumstances where a youth has committed a very serious crime or has failed to respond to earlier interventions where a punitive sanction such as incarceration may be required. As well, public opinion must be taken into account in dealing with youth crime.

A second conclusion is that appropriate interventions delivered with integrity can be effective in reducing the youth's risk for criminal activity. In other words, there are services we can deliver which will have a positive effect. Two important qualifications are included in the conclusion. First, interventions must be appropriate and reflect the Principles of Best Practice (reviewed below). Second, the services must be delivered 'with integrity.' That is, they must be delivered in the way intended by qualified and trained professionals. Research has shown that program integrity is an important determination of the success of an intervention (Bonta & Andrews, 2017).

A third conclusion is that appropriate interventions delivered with integrity can show positive cost/benefit ratios. In other words, there are programs where the monetary benefits of the program (e.g., reduced arrest, charge, incarceration rates; reduced school drop-outs, reduced self-harm efforts) exceed the costs of delivering the programs (e.g., salaries, rents, cost of materials). The Welsh et al. (2012) review provides a review of results from contemporary cost-benefit studies.

6.6.2   RNR Principles of Best Practice

The RNR model identifies a number of principles of best practice defining appropriate treatments. Some of these principles are strongly supported by the evaluation research mentioned above, while in other cases the principle is based on a smaller research base combined with clinical observations. This research is discussed by Bonta and Andrews (2017), Hoge (2016b), and Koehler, Losel, Akoensi, and Humphreys (2013). The reader is referred to those reviews for more detailed discussions of the research.

The first principle reflects the importance of conducting standardized and validated assessments of the client. Research from clinical and forensic literatures demonstrates that programs employing structured and validated assessments are more effective than those not employing any formal assessment procedures or those based solely on clinical procedures.

A second set of principles emphasizes the importance of observing the risk, need, and responsivity rules of case classification. Effective programs focus intensive efforts on higher risk cases, focus interventions on the specific needs of the youth, and take account of responsivity principles in case planning. In fact, research demonstrates that observing all three is associated with more significant reductions in recidivism than the case where one, two, or none is observed (Bonta & Andrews, 2017).

Another principle states that, where feasible, services should be delivered in the community rather than an institutional setting. This principle reflects, in part, the caution regarding the use of incarceration. The principle is also based on research showing more positive outcomes for interventions delivered in the youth's community setting in comparison with outcomes associated with institutionalization. This result would seem reasonable. The problems that a youth brings to the situation exist in his or her home, community and school environment. If those problems are to be addressed, they are best addressed in the contexts in which they exist. The use of diversion and community-based wrap-around programs reflect this principle.

The importance of providing services in the institutional setting constitutes another principle. If it is necessary to institutionalize a youth to incarceration, a mental health facility or other residential setting, it is important to identify the risk and need factors of the youth and address them in that setting. It accomplishes very little to simply confine a youth to an institution without any effort to address his or her needs. In fact, it probably makes the situation even worse by exposing the youth to other antisocial youth and antisocial values.

Still another principle states that interventions should be multimodal, particularly in the case of higher risk youth. These youths normally do not enter the system with a single risk factor, rather, they often exhibit a range of related problems (e.g., poor relations with parent, school failure, negative peer associations, substance abuse). These issues cannot be address in isolation but must be addressed in a comprehensive manner. "Wrap Around" programs such as Multisystemic Therapy (Henggeler, Schoenwald, Borduin, Rowland, & Cunningham, 1998), involve a range of professionals addressing the youth's problems in the home, community, and school setting.

Effective problems also take care to utilize evidence-based programs. That is, in choosing programs directed toward behavioral and attitude change, attention is paid to research evidence for the effectiveness of the program relevant to the group under care. Information about evidence-based programs and practices are provided by Guerra, Kim, and Boxer (2008) and Lipsey and Wilson (1998). Structured cognitive modification programs directed toward dysfunctional behaviors and attitudes show the most promise of success with these youths.

Another principle states that intervention programs should be based to the extent possible on strength factors brought by the youth to the situation. If, for example, the youth exhibits an interest in sports or that he or she derives satisfaction from certain school activities, these can be utilized in the intervention program. Similarly, a parent who expresses concern for the youth and a willingness to cooperate in treatment efforts can be an important resource. Utilizing the youth's strengths can increase the likelihood that an intervention will succeed and may also assist in developing a positive relation with the youth.

Finally, a core principle within the RNR model reflects the importance of delivering services to the youthful offender in a humane manner and with the goal of addressing the full range of risk and need factors presented by the youth. As well, the principle states that intervention efforts should take account the full range of responsivity factors. These may include the youth's gender, ethnic group identity, cognitive functioning, and mental health status. Readiness or motivation for change may represent a responsivity factor.

6.7   Future Implications

Three areas meriting continuing efforts will be discussed, two involving additional research and one involving educational efforts. The first recommendation involves additional research on the factors associated with juvenile offending. We have seen that considerable progress has been made in both theory and research in the identification of critical risk factors and processes associated with antisocial behavior of youth. However, there remain some lacunae.

6.7.1   Research Needs

First, more attention has been paid to the initiation of criminal activity and less attention to why some individuals desist from these activities once initiated. Second, continuing research on a developmental perspective is needed. We have information on trajectories of offending (Farrington, 2005; Moffitt, 2003) and the risk factors associated with offending at the different developmental stages. However, much of this information is static in nature; in other words, it does not inform us about the way in which developmental processes are involved (Guerra, Williams, Tolan, & Modecki, 2008; (Vincent & Grisso, 2005).

Third, we have more information about initiation of criminal activity than desistance from those activities. Why is it that some individuals with an active criminal career during adolescence desist from those activities during the early adult years, while others continue the activities? The initiation of criminal activity and desistence from that activity during the later adolescent and early adult years is of particular concern (Loeber & Farrington, 2012).

A fourth need is for more research on individual differences in the causes of criminal activity. While some attention has been paid to risk factors operating in the case of female juvenile offenders (Hoge & Robertson, 2008; Pusch & Holtfreter, 2018), less attention has been paid to possible variations in risk factors across cultural groups. Similarly, the prediction of offending for developmentally delayed and mentally ill youth has been neglected. Advances are being made in our research methods, particularly meta-analytic techniques, and it may be expected that continuing advances will be made in these areas.

Another area of need concerns the development of more effective interventions. Previous discussions have documented that our knowledge of effective interventions has advanced considerably. We have derived important principles of best practice and identified a large number of evidence-based programs. However, work remains to be done on individual differences in responses to interventions, the critical features of interventions, and the development of effective implementation strategies (Guerra, Kim, & Boxer, 2008).

A specific responsivity factor involves readiness or motivation for change. Many of our youth are in a state of denial and either passively or actively resistant to treatment. While progress has been made in addressing this issue (Miller & Rollnick, 2002), solutions to the problem remain elusive.

Identifying critical features of intervention programs is also important (Guerra, Kim, & Boxer, 2008). Multisystemic Therapy has been identified as a successful program under some circumstances. However, this is a complicated program incorporating a number of processes, it is not always clear what the critical processes are (e.g., the intensive training of personnel, close contact with youth and family, focus on a range of risk factors). More analytic work needs to be done within program evaluation research.

Another aspect of improving service delivery involves developing better strategies for implementing effective programs. Part of the issue concerns political forces determining the selection and support of programming. Other concerns involve insuring that quality control procedures are in place. Research has clearly established that program quality or fidelity is critical to the success of program delivery (Bonta, Bourgon, Rugge, Gress, & Gutierrez, 2013; Vincent, Guy, Perrault, & Gershenson, 2016). Unfortunately, we see many programs that should be working but are not successful because of defects in service delivery. The keys here are to provide effective training for service providers and conduct careful process and impact evaluation research.

6.7.2   Educational Needs

A final set of recommendations focus on education efforts. The efforts should be directed toward politicians and other policy makers, the public, and those within juvenile justice systems responsible for service delivery. The structure of juvenile justice systems and procedures represented in those systems generally rest with politicians and other policy makers. They are usually responsible for laws establishing these systems and procedures and for decisions about the funding of services. A variety of forces may affect the decision processes, but the assumptions of policy makers play an important role. As well, politicians are generally elected by popular vote and are highly influenced by their perceptions of what the public thinks.

There is a widespread belief that a significant percentage of policy makers and the public favor a 'get tough' or punitive approach to dealing with youthful offenders. However, research suggests that the opinion may not be that widespread, and that the problem relates to the way in which surveys ask the question. When the public is given a choice about courses of action, a more positive view emerges, with rather widespread agreement that rehabilitative strategies may be more effective (Cullen, Fisher, & Applegate, 2000; Hough & Roberts, 2012). This is particularly true when the public is provided with information about the relative costs and benefits of rehabilitative versus punitive strategies. Costs associated with the punitive strategies are significant, particularly those relating to incarceration (Cohen, Piquero, & Jennings, 2010; Piquero, Jennings, & Farrington, 2013).

In any case, experts in this area and familiar with the most recent research have an obligation to educate politicians and the public in the principles of best practice. The research strongly supports the view that justice policy focusing on the needs of the youth (i.e. factors placing the youth at risk for criminal activity) and providing interventions carefully targeting those needs provides the best strategy for controlling crime and that view should be presented to these audiences.

A similar educational challenge concerns professionals involved in the juvenile justice systems and those providing services to these youths from other systems (e.g. education, mental health, and child protection). Those selected for those positions in these systems should be screened for their attitudes, values, and beliefs regarding the treatment of these youth. At a minimum, personnel should demonstrate capability of working in a positive way with very challenging youth. They should also show a willingness to adopt positive strategies in shaping the attitudes and behaviour of the youth. Continuing education efforts to familiarize staff with research developments relating to the principles of best practice should also be offered on a continuing basis.

It must be admitted that these educational recommendations reflect the child welfare and rehabilitation orientation reflected in this chapter. Systems embracing a more punitive orientation may not endorse the recommendations. However, experience suggests that many systems do reflect the more positive view and simply need encouragement and direction to follow best practices.

6.8 Technology and Innovation

Technology likely has a limited role to play in judicial processing beyond record keeping. Computer-based self-report measures of attitudes and personality are available. The client records his or her responses on a computer and the software program calculates scores and sometimes interprets those scores with reference to normative data or in some cases according to diagnostic rules.

Some of the standardized risk/need instruments noted above have software which allows recording of information provided by the clinician. The actuarial measures will then provide estimates of risk for reoffending based on certain rules. In some cases the program will provide programming recommendations. An additional advantage of these programs is that they enable agencies to accumulate data on variables of importance. These data may indicate the number of clients at various levels of risk dealt with, the frequency with which needs are identified, and the kinds of interventions being provided.

However, some caution should be observed in applying technology to the assessment, diagnosis, and programming processes. First, assessments from the standardized instruments should not be allowed to dictate decisions. For example, a high-risk score on an actuarial measure should not be the sole basis for a disposition decision. Professional overrides should always be built into the system so that final decisions rest with the responsible professional. Second, the human element should never be removed from the process. Face-to-face interactions between the client and clinician are important from the point of view of collecting observations of the client and for helping to establish a relationship with the client. That relationship is critical to the success of any therapeutic intervention.

6.9   Conclusion

The public often expresses concern about youth crime (Zimring, 1998). Some of this concern likely arises from fear of being a victim of crime along with the emotional and monetary costs associated with victimization. There is also a larger concern with the monetary and emotional costs to society of youth crime. Some of the monetary costs are associated with the loss experienced by victims but some also relates to the costs of maintaining the police, courts, probation and correctional services, and other services provided within the system. However, there is a larger fear on the part of the public that youth crime may represent a breakdown of society. That is, it may reflect that parents, schools, and other social institutions are not capable of insuring that youth develop as responsible law-abiding individuals. Some may place the blame for this situation on economic factors or on a general decline in moral standards. Whatever the analysis, this can be a major fear for members of the public.

This chapter has attempted to describe different aspects of the systems given responsibility for managing youth crime. Aspects of juvenile justice systems were identified as were major courses of action available within those systems. Those courses of action were evaluated in terms of the RNR model which proposes a set of evidence-based principles of best practice. These are presented as useful in guiding interventions with these juvenile offenders. Continuing research may require modification of these principles, but at present they represent the best guides we have for addressing the problem of youth crime.

References

Barnoski, R., & Markussen, S. (2005). Washington State Juvenile Court Assessment. In T. Grisso, T. Vincent, & D. Seagrave (Eds.), *Mental health screening and assessment in juvenile justice* (pp. 271–282). New York, NY: Guilford.

Bartel, P., Borum, R., & Forth, A. (2005). Structured Assessment of Violence Risk in Youth (SAVRY). In T. Grisso, T. Vincent, & D. Seagrave (Eds.), *Mental health screening and assessment in juvenile justice* (pp. 295–310). New York, NY: Guilford.

Bonta, J., & Andrews, D. A. (2017). *The psychology of criminal conduct* (6th ed.). New York, NY: Routledge.

Bonta, J., Bourgon, G., Rugge, T., Gress, C., & Gutierrez, L. (2013). Taking the leap from pilot project to wide-scale implementation of the Strategic Training Initiative in Community Supervision (STICS). *Justice Research and Policy, 15*, 17–45.

Borum, R., & Verhaagen, D. (2006). *Assessing and managing violence risk in juveniles.* New York, NY: Guilford.

Cipriani, D. (2009). *Children's rights and the minimum age of criminal responsibility: A global perspective.* New York, NY: Ashgate.

Cohen, M. A., Piquero, A. R., & Jennings, W. G. (2010). Estimating the costs of bad outcomes for at-risk youth and the benefits of early childhood interventions to reduce them. *Criminal Justice Policy Review, 21*, 391–434.

Corrado, R. R. (1992). Introduction. In R. R. Corrado, N. Bala, R. Linden, & M. Le Blanc (Eds.), *Juvenile justice in Canada: A theoretical and analytical assessment* (pp. 1–20). Toronto, ON: Buttersworth.

Crofts, T. (2016). Reforming the age of criminal responsibility. *South Africa Journal of Psychology, 46*(4), 436–448.

Cullen, E. T., Fisher, B. S., & Applegate, B. K. (2000). Public opinion about punishment and corrections. In M. Tonry (Ed.), *Crime and justice: A review of research* (Vol. 27, pp. 1–79). Chicago, IL: University of Chicago Press.

Farrington, D. P. (1998). Predictors, causes and correlates of male youth violence. In M. Tonry & M. H. Moore (Eds.), *Youth violence (crime and Justice)* (Vol. 24, pp. 421–475). Chicago, IL: University of Chicago Press.

Farrington, D. P. (2005). *Integrated developmental and life-course theories of offending.* New Brunswick, NJ: Transaction.

Farrington, D. P., & Welsh, B. C. (2006). *Saving children from a life of crime: Early risk factors and effective interventions.* New York, NY: Oxford.

Federal Bureau of Investigation. (2015). *Uniform crime reports.* Washington, DC: Author.

Grieger, L., & Hosser, D. (2014). Which risk factors are really predictive? An analysis of Andrews and Bonta's "Central Eight" risk factors for recidivism in German youth correctional facility inmates. *Criminal Justice and Behavior, 41*, 613–634.

Grisso, T., Vincent, G., & Seagrave, D. (Eds.). (2005). *Mental health screening and assessment in juvenile justice.* New York, NY: Guilford.

Grove, W. M., & Vrieze, S. J. (2013). The clinical versus mechanical prediction controversy. In K. F. Geisinger (Ed.), *APA handbook of testing and assessment in psychology: Volume 2. Testing and assessment in clinical and counseling psychology.* Washington, DC: American Psychological Association.

Grove, W. M., Zald, D. H., Lebow, B. S., Snitz, B. E., & Nelson, C. (2000). Clinical versus mechanical prediction: A meta-analysis. *Psychological Assessment, 12*, 19–30.

Guerra, N. G., Kim, T. E., & Boxer, P. (2008). What works: Best practices with juvenile offenders. In R. D. Hoge, N. G. Guerra, & P. Boxer (Eds.), *Treating the juvenile offender* (pp. 79–102). New York, NY: Guilford.

Guerra, N. G., Williams, K. R., Tolan, P. H., & Modecki, K. L. (2008). Theoretical and research advances in understanding the causes of juvenile offending. In R. D. Hoge, N. G. Guerra, & P. Boxer (Eds.), *Treating the juvenile offender* (pp. 33–53). New York, NY: Guilford.

Harris, G. T., Rice, M. E., Quinsey, V. L., & Cormier, C. A. (2015). *Violent offenders : Appraising and managing risk* (3rd ed.). Washington, DC: American Psychological Association.

Heilbrun, K., Lee, R., & Cottle, C. (2005). Risk factors and intervention outcomes: Meta-analyses of juvenile offending. In K. Heilbrun, N. Goldstein, & R. Redding (Eds.), *Juvenile delinquency: Prevention, assessment and interventions* (pp. 111–133). New York, NY: Oxford University Press.

Henggeler, S. W., Schoenwald, S. K., Borduin, C. M., Rowland, M. D., & Cunningham, P. B. (1998). *Multisystemic treatment of antisocial behavior in children and adolescents*. New York, NY: Guilford.

Hoge, R. D. (2001). *The juvenile offender: Theory, research, and applications*. Norwell, MA: Kluwer.

Hoge, R. D. (2012). Forensic assessments of juveniles: Practice and legal considerations. *Criminal Justice and Behavior, 39*, 1255–1270.

Hoge, R. D. (2016a). Policy essay: Juvenile court and diversion. *Criminology and Public Policy, 15*, 1–9.

Hoge, R. D. (2016b). Risk, need, and responsivity in juveniles. In K. Heilbrun (Ed.), *APA handbook of psychology and juvenile justice* (pp. 179–196). Washington, DC: American Psychological Association Press.

Hoge, R. D., & Andrews, D. A. (1996). *Assessing the youthful offender: Issues and techniques*. New York, NY: Springer.

Hoge, R. D., & Andrews, D. A. (2010). *Evaluation of risk for violence in juveniles*. New York, NY, Oxford.

Hoge, R. D., & Andrews, D. A. (2011). *Youth Level of Service/Case Management Inventory 2.0 User's manual*. North Tonawanda, NY: Multi-Health Systems.

Hoge, R. D., & Robertson, L. A. (2008). The female juvenile offender. In R. D. Hoge, N. G. Guerra, & P. Boxer (Eds.), *Treating the juvenile offender* (pp. 258–277). New York, NY: Guilford.

Hough, M., & Roberts, J. V. (2012). Public opinion, crime, and criminal justice. In M. Maguire, R. Morgan, & R. Reiner (Eds.), *The Oxford handbook of criminology* (pp. 279–299). New York, NY: Oxford University Press.

Koehler, J. A., Losel, F., Akoensi, T. D., & Humphreys, D. K. (2013). A systematic review and meta-analysis of the effects of young offender treatment programs in Europe. *Journal of Experimental Criminology, 9*, 19–43.

Krisberg, B., & Howell, J. C. (1998). The impact of the juvenile justice system and prospects for graduated sanctions in a comprehensive strategy. In R. Loeber & D. P. Farrington (Eds.), *Serious and violent juvenile offenders: Risk factors and successful interventions* (pp. 346–366). Thousand Oaks, CA: Sage.

Lipsey, M. W. (2009). The primary factors that characterize effective interventions with juvenile offenders: A meta-analytic review. *Victims and Offenders, 4*, 124–147.

Lipsey, M. W., & Wilson, D. B. (1998). Effective intervention for serious juvenile offenders: A synthesis of research. In R. Loeber & D. P. Farrington (Eds.), *Serious and violent juvenile offenders: Risk factors and successful interventions* (pp. 313–345). Thousand Oaks, CA: Sage.

Loeber, R., & Farrington, D. P. (Eds.). (2012). *From juvenile delinquency to adult crime*. New York, NY: Oxford.

McAra, L., & McVie, S. (2007). Youth justice? The impact of system contact on patterns of desistance from offending. *European Journal of Criminology, 4*, 1477–3708.

McGuire, J. (2004). *Understanding psychology and crime: Perspectives on theory and action*. Berkshire, UK: Open University Press.

Miller, W. R., & Rollnick, S. (2002). *Motivational interviewing: Preparing people for change*. New York, NY: Guilford.

Moffitt, T. E. (2003). 'Life-course-persistent' and 'adolescent-limited' antisocial behavior: A developmental taxonomy. *Psychological Review, 100*, 674–701.

Petitclerc, A., Gatti, U., Vitaro, F., & Treblay, R. E. (2012). Effects of juvenile court exposure on crime in young adulthood. *Journal of Child Psychology and Psychiatry, 54*, 291–297.

Piquero, A. R., Jennings, W. G., & Farrington, D. P. (2013). The monetary costs of crime to middle adulthood: Findings from the Cambridge study in delinquent development. *Journal of Research in Crime and Delinquency, 50*, 53–74.

Pusch, N., & Holtfreter, K. (2018). Gender and risk assessment in the juvenile offender: A meta-analysis. *Criminal Justice and Behavior, 45*, 56–81.

Shoemaker, D. J. (1996). *Theories of delinquency*. New York, NY: Oxford.

Statistics Canada. (2016). *Revised uniform crime reporting survey*. Ottawa, ON: Author.

Thornberry, T. P., Giordano, P. G., Uggen, C., Matsuda, M., Masten, A. S., Bulten, E., & Donker, A. G. (2012). Explanations for offending. In R. Loeber & D. P. Farrington (Eds.), *From juvenile delinquency to adult crime* (pp. 47–85). New York, NY: Oxford.

Vieira, T. A., Skilling, T. A., & Peterson-Badall, M. (2009). Matching court-ordered services with treatment needs: Predicting treatment success with young offenders. *Criminal Justice and Behavior, 36*, 385–401.

Vincent, G., & Grisso, T. (2005). A developmental perspective on adolescent personality, psychopathology, and delinquency. In T. Grisso, T. Vincent, & D. Seagrave (Eds.), *Mental health screening and assessment in juvenile justice* (pp. 22–43). New York, NY: Guilford.

Vincent, G. M., Guy, L. S., Perrault, R. T., & Gershenson, B. (2016). Risk assessment matters: But only when implemented well: A multisite study in juvenile probation. *Law and Human Behavior, 15*, 1–14.

Welsh, B. C., Lipsey, M. W., Rivara, F. P., Hawkins, J. D., Aos, S., & Hollis-Peel, M. E. (2012). Promoting change, changing lives: Effective prevention and intervention to reduce serious offending. In R. Loeber & D. P. Farrington (Eds.), *From juvenile delinquency to adult crime* (pp. 245–277). New York, NY: Oxford.

Wilson, H. A., & Hoge, R. D. (2012). The effect of youth diversion programs on recidivism: A meta-analytic review. *Criminal Justice and Behavior, 42*, 1–22.

Worling, J. R., & Curwen, M. A. (2001). *Estimate of risk of adolescent sexual offense recidivism (ERASOR)*. Toronto, ON: Thistletown Regional Centre.

Zimring, F. E. (1998). *American youth violence*. New York, NY: Oxford.

Chapter 7
Assessing and Treating Violent Offenders

Mark E. Olver and Keira C. Stockdale

In this chapter, we focus specifically on the assessment and treatment of adult violent offenders. The class of offending behavior is general violence, that is, crimes against the person that may involve physical, threatened, or psychological harm, excluding sexually motivated crimes or intimate partner violence; both of which have large specialized literatures outside the scope of this chapter. We also contain our focus to adult offenders, given that special developmental issues apply to youth offenders.

The chapter begins with an overview of the frequency and prevalence of violent offending. We follow with a discussion of the theoretical context guiding service delivery focusing on the General Personality and Cognitive Social Learning (GPCSL) theory of criminal behavior and Risk-Need-Responsivity (RNR) model of offender service delivery (Bonta & Andrews, 2017). We then review mental health and diagnostic considerations with violent offender populations, and follow with an overview of tools and approaches for violence risk assessment, providing guidelines for its explicit linkages with violence reduction interventions. The most substantive part of this chapter is a review of the violent offender treatment literature: we discuss *what works, what might work*, and *what doesn't work* based on a thorough review of the literature, providing a sampling of approaches from each. We conclude with suggested future directions and innovations for violent offender research and practice.

M. E. Olver (✉)
Department of Psychology, University of Saskatchewan, Saskatoon, SK, Canada
e-mail: mark.olver@usask.ca

K. C. Stockdale
Department of Psychology, University of Saskatchewan, Saskatoon, SK, Canada

Saskatoon Police Service, Saskatoon, SK, Canada
e-mail: keira.stockdale@police.saskatoon.sk.ca

© Springer Nature Switzerland AG 2018   143
M. Ternes et al. (eds.), *The Practice of Correctional Psychology*,
https://doi.org/10.1007/978-3-030-00452-1_7

7.1 Frequency and Prevalence of Violent Offending

Interpersonal violence is a significant global problem. The World Health Organization (WHO) estimates approximately 1.6 million deaths worldwide owing to violence, 86% are attributable to interpersonal violence or self-inflicted violence. In addition, the WHO estimates that each death resulting from interpersonal violence is matched by 10–40 times as many physical injuries requiring medical attention. The economic costs of violence are also substantial. In a literature review of the economic impacts of crime, the WHO estimated the total economic impact of violence in the United States (US) alone to be approximately 3.3% of its gross domestic product, or over $300 billion (i.e., taking into account impacts on employment, lost productivity, pain and suffering). Further, the total economic impact in England and Wales from violent crime (including homicide and sexual offenses) was estimated to be around $42 billion.

Correctional settings in various international jurisdictions have a high proportion of persons convicted for violent crimes. According to the 2015 Corrections and Conditional Release Statistical Overview (Public Safety Canada, 2016), 69% of men and women in federal custody in Canadian corrections were serving sentences for a violent crime. By extension, in the California Department of Corrections, 70.6% of persons in state prisons were serving sentences for violent offenses. Comparatively, in Her Majesty's Prison Service in the United Kingdom (UK), approximately 55% of adult male offenders in custody were serving sentences for violent offenses (i.e., violence against the person, sexual offenses, robbery, weapons offenses). Thus, approximately one half to two thirds of persons in correctional settings in the western world are incarcerated for a violent offense.

This naturally begs the question as to what proportion of persons convicted for violent crimes are subsequently charged or convicted for a new violent offense. Meta-analytic reviews of violent recidivism studies are particularly informative since these are aggregations of outcome studies conducted in several jurisdictions. For instance, Bonta, Blais, and Wilson (2014), in a meta-analysis of 126 recidivism prediction studies in mentally disordered offenders (MDOs) reported a mean violent recidivism base rate of 23% over an average 4.9 years follow-up. Yang, Wong, and Coid (2010), in a multilevel meta-analysis of 28 violence risk assessment studies, reported a mean base rate for violent recidivism of 24.9% over an unspecified follow-up time. Hanson and Morton-Bourgon (2009), in a meta-analysis of 118 sexual offender recidivism prediction studies, reported a mean base of general violent recidivism (i.e., sexual and nonsexual violence) of 19.5% ($k = 50$) over an average of 70 months follow-up. In all, base rates of general violent recidivism vary between 20% and 25% over an approximate 5–6 years follow-up depending on the sample and setting. It is important to bear in mind that several factors influence recidivism base rates including the definition of the criterion variable (e.g., charges vs. convictions), length of follow-up (i.e., longer follow-ups naturally yield higher base rates), the level of specificity of the criterion variable, and the risk level of the offender. In regards to the latter point, large representative samples of offenders have demonstrated high risk men to have rates of violent recidivism in excess of

50% over 4–5 years follow-up while low risk offenders will yield violent recidivism base rates below 10% over comparable follow-up times (Wong & Gordon, 2006).

7.2 Theoretical Models Relevant to Service Delivery

The guiding framework for the assessment, treatment, and management of violence risk is ultimately an integrated and multidimensional model of the origins and maintenance of violent and antisocial behavior that has direct implications for service delivery. There are several candidate models here, but we will narrow our attention to the General Personality and Cognitive Social Learning (GPCSL) theory of criminal conduct originally advanced by Andrews and Bonta (1994) and refined in the years to follow. GPCSL is a comprehensive model that recognizes the roles of biological (e.g., genetic factors, temperament, brain injury/impairment), psychological (e.g., weak attachments, abuse in the family or origin), and social-environmental-contextual (e.g., lack of opportunity, low SES, high crime neighborhood) vulnerabilities that can predispose individuals to various forms of antisocial behavior.

Building on influential work such as Sutherland's (1947) Differential Association Theory and Burgess and Akers' (1966) Differential Association Reinforcement Theory, GPCSL contends that specific forms of antisocial behavior are ultimately learned through social learning principles, via direct and vicarious exposure to anti-social role models (and lack of exposure to anti-criminal models) and maintained through ongoing analysis of the relative rewards and costs of criminal behavior. Attitudes and values that influence and sustain antisocial behavior are developed and crystalized over time, and constitute a set of cognitive processes and structures that legitimize, or even value, antisocial behavior as a way to respond to conflict, meet personal or financial needs, bolster esteem, or navigate life's issues. Antisocial or violent behavior becomes increasingly likely in response to the specific demands of a given situation whether this be assaulting one's spouse in the midst of a domestic dispute, committing an armed robbery to secure money for drugs, or conducting a targeted hit on a witness scheduled to testify in court.

The GPCSL is the guiding framework for the risk-need-responsivity (RNR; Andrews, Bonta, & Hoge, 1990; Andrews, Zinger, et al., 1990) model of service delivery. The RNR model informs the integration of offender assessment and treatment, from the point of intake, to case planning, service implementation, case monitoring, and case closure (see Andrews, Bonta, & Wormith, 2006). Briefly, the risk principle states that service intensity should be matched to the risk level of the client, such that higher risk offenders receive more services and lower risk offenders receive less intensive services. It also notes that this requires capacity to accurately appraise an individual's risk for recidivism (whether this be broad or specific outcomes) in order to identify the "right" persons for the appropriate services (i.e., "who" to treat).

The need principle states that dynamic risk variables that are involved in the origin and maintenance of criminal behavior, termed criminogenic needs, should be prioritized for risk reduction services (i.e., "what" to treat). Bonta and Andrews

(2017) place priority on the eight well established criminogenic domains that broadly predict recidivism across outcomes and offender populations. Referred to as the Central Eight, these include offense history, antisocial attitudes, antisocial peers, antisocial personality pattern, education/employment, family/marital, substance abuse, and leisure/recreation; all of which, with the exception of formal criminal history, are dynamic in nature and modifiable through correctional programming, community supervision, strengthening prosocial bonds, or other human service capacities. Applied to violent offenders, there are criminogenic needs that are both general (per the Central Eight) and specific (e.g., weapon use, anger problems, aggressive interpersonal style) that warrant targeting through services to reduce risk. Such services involve not only reducing criminogenic needs, but replacing them with prosocial competencies and new skill areas that equip offenders to think, behave, and respond to problems differently.

Finally, the responsivity principle offers guidance on the "how" of service delivery. General responsivity notes that cognitive behavioral methods of behavior change should be employed as the foundation of offender services, and that service providers need to exercise warmth, empathy, patience, respect, and compassion in service delivery. Dowden and Andrews (2004) have also termed these interpersonal elements to be core correctional practices. Specific responsivity states that services should be tailored to characteristics of the individual that impact response to, and the capacity to benefit from services such as culture, learning style, cognitive ability, literacy, motivation, and personality among other factors.

An updated meta-analysis of 374 offender service delivery outcome studies (Andrews & Bonta, 2010a) has demonstrated that programs adhering to all three RNR principles generate the largest reductions in recidivism (effect size [ES] = 0.26), compared to studies in which programs followed two (ES = 0.18), or one (ES = 0.02) principle, and with services following no principles finding a small increase in recidivism (ES = −0.02). Of note, Andrews and Bonta's (2010b) expanded risk-need-responsivity (RNR) model has several associated principles and corollaries, although RNR are the basic tenets. For instance, the model also acknowledges the importance of recognizing and building upon client strengths to assist the individual in moving on to a more rewarding and satisfying life characterized by less crime and violence. Readers are also directed to works on the Good Lives Model (GLM; see Ward, Mann, & Gannon, 2007), which has several defining features in common with the expanded RNR model, but places special emphases on the client developing a crime-free life worth living through learning to fulfill the attainment of basic human goods (e.g., friendship, community, autonomy, excellence in play and work, happiness, creativity, etc.).

7.3   Diagnosis and Assessment of Violent Offenders

The diagnosis and assessment of violent offenders is critical in the management of violence risk and the prevention of future violence. Proper diagnosis and comprehensive assessment can aid case formulation and guide treatment planning and delivery.

7.3.1 Mental Disorder and Violence

7.3.1.1 Diagnostic Issues

The association of violence with mental disorder, and the risk relevance of mental health symptoms have been fraught with some controversy. Evidence abounds from Swedish (Hodgins, 1993), Danish (Hodgins, Mednick, Brennan, Schulsinger, & Engberg, 1996), and US (Swanson, 1994) epidemiological catchment studies, that lifetime prevalence rates of violence are three to four times higher among persons with major mental health diagnoses such as major depression, mania, and schizophrenia, than among cohorts without a lifetime diagnosis. However, rates of violence were even higher among individuals with a history of substance use disorder or SUD (generally upwards of 20%), or co-occurring SUD with another mental disorder, known as dual diagnosis, or DD (Rezansoff, Moniruzzaman, Gress, & Somers, 2013). In a major meta-analysis of more than 200 studies, Douglas, Guy, and Hart (2009) examined the associations of psychosis with violence, finding broadly speaking, that the presence of psychosis increased the odds of violence by two to three times. Moderator analyses demonstrated the effect was strongest in community settings, however, it was considerably weaker in correctional and forensic mental health settings.

On the flip side, major mental health diagnoses are frequently overrepresented in North American correctional samples, who in turn, have higher rates of violent behavior than the general public. In their examination of male admissions to Correctional Service of Canada (CSC), Brink, Doherty, and Boer (2001) found that approximately 30% of custody admissions met criteria for a mood disorder, 8% psychotic disorder, 18% anxiety disorder, and about three quarters (76%) for any substance use disorder. Two further investigations on CSC samples reported bases rates for antisocial personality disorder (ASPD) of 55–60% (Hodgins & Coté, 1993; Kingston, Olver, Harris, Wong, & Bradford, 2015). In a large British Columbia Corrections sample, Rezansoff et al. (2013) reported that 61% of individuals in custody had any diagnosis in the past 5 years, 21% had a non-substance related mental disorder (NSMD), 10% had a substance use disorder (SUD), and 23% had a DD as defined above.

The source of some controversy is to what extent NSMDs, that is, major mental health conditions absent an SUD diagnosis, are inherently criminogenic and risk relevant. Rezansoff et al. (2013), in a massive Canadian epidemiological catchment study of more than 31,000 male offenders released from British Columbia Provincial Corrections and followed up 3 years post release, found that cases with no lifetime history of mental disorder vs. those with an NSMD had comparable rates of recidivism (at 31% and 34%, respectively). By contrast, approximately 56% of offenders with either an SUD diagnosis alone, or with DD, were convicted for a new offense during the release period. A follow-up meta-analysis by Bonta et al. (2014) examined the Central Eight and clinical predictors of general and violent recidivism among samples of MDOs. While each of the Central Eight evinced small to moderate and significant effect sizes in the prediction of general or violent recidivism, very few of the clinical predictors (e.g., psychosis, hospitalization) were predictive of outcome, with the exception being personality disorder in general, and antisocial personality disorder or psychopathy, in particular. In the Bonta et al. (2014) meta-analysis, SUDs were operationalized in terms of the substance abuse risk-need domain of the Central Eight. Individual studies to follow in mentally disordered general offender (Kingston et al., 2016) and sexual offender (Kingston et al., 2015) samples have similarly found PD and SUD to be predictive of outcome, while NSMD has not. Further, in these studies, the same set of static and dynamic risk factors that predict recidivism among nonmentally disordered offenders have predictive relevance for MDOs.

There are a number of important themes here. First, SUD, personality disorder (PD), and ASPD are inherently criminogenic, that is, they embody collections of criminogenic needs, or they themselves are criminogenic (e.g., a problem with drug and alcohol use, or an entrenched personality disorder marked by emotional instability and behavioral impulsivity). Research has also demonstrated that such diagnoses have a greater density of criminogenic needs (Kingston et al., 2015), in addition to higher rates of recidivism. These disorders also have high prevalence rates among offender populations, not uncommonly upwards of 50–75% depending on the sample and setting. Second, active symptoms of psychosis can also be criminogenic, such as the presence of paranoid delusions and command hallucinations which may compel the individual to perpetrate acts of serious violence. Indeed, Douglas et al. (2009) found that such symptoms were associated with a threefold increase in the odds of violence. Accordingly, most structured violence risk assessment tools include an item or two that assesses mental health concerns and its potential linkage to violence (e.g., Historical Clinical Risk-20, Versions 2 and 3; Violence Risk Scale). Third, the same general predictors of violence are found across both MDO and non-MDO samples (Bonta et al., 2014). For instance, absent a history of violence or other salient risk markers, an NSMD is not likely to have a particularly strong association with violence, which may explain why psychosis has weaker links to violence and criminal recidivism among correctional samples.

7.3.2   Violence Risk Assessment: Overview of Tools and Approaches

The assessment of violence risk is a complex and multistep process that involves collecting and aggregating multiple sources of information (e.g., interview, case file, collateral contacts), using multiple assessment methods (e.g., psychometric testing, risk assessment checklists, diagnostic approaches), across multiple domains of functioning (e.g., attitudes, family and relationships, history of violence, work/school, mental health and emotional functioning, community supports). Such assessments will usually incorporate one or more structured forensic assessment measures to inform appraisals of risk and dangerousness. Such evaluations should be comprehensive, thorough, and evaluate the credibility of information obtained from various sources. They should take into consideration cultural or contextual considerations of the individual, as well as the psychometric properties of the measures used with the population in question. Whenever possible, risk assessments should also identify strengths and resiliencies within the individual that could help mitigate risk. Douglas and Kropp (2002) remind us, however, that risk assessment should ultimately be about violence prevention as opposed to pure prediction per se. That is, risk appraisals should be linked to treatment planning, service delivery, and risk management (e.g., monitoring, supervision), to prevent a violent offense from reoccurring.

While a large number of risk assessment instruments have been developed, a smaller collection have been developed for the appraisal of violence risk, and will be briefly reviewed. Bonta (1996) developed a generational framework for classifying risk assessment tools which is instrumental here. The first generation involved the use of unstructured clinical judgment to appraise risk (e.g., gut feelings or intuitive hunches). The procedure typically involved use of a clinical interview and possibly review of case documentation and was informal, unsystematic, and ultimately demonstrated to be a weak and inaccurate means of detecting violence risk (Mossman, 1994).

Second generation approaches are static actuarial tools, that is, structured rating scales with items identified from the statistical properties of variables within the dataset, based on their association with the criterion of interest (e.g., violent recidivism). In some instances, items may be differentially weighted based on their association with the criterion with more predictive items receiving heavier weights. Item ratings are ultimately summed to generate a numeric risk score, which in turn is linked to a summary risk classification (e.g., low, medium, high), and rates of recidivism associated with that classification rating over a defined follow-up period (e.g., within 5 years of release to the community). Hanson and Morton-Bourgon (2009) term such tools as empirical actuarial, given that they involve linking risk scores to recidivism estimates associated with a particular score or group of scores. An example of a second generation empirical actuarial violence risk instrument would be the Violence Risk Appraisal Guide-Revised (VRAG-R; Rice, Harris, & Lang, 2013). The VRAG-R is composed of 12 differentially weighted predictors that encompass offense history, demographics, and relevant criminal behavior-clinical variables. The tool was developed and validated using a cumulative sample of sexual and violent offenders who were hospitalized or on remand, obtained from past validation work with earlier iterations of the tool. With possible scores ranging from −34 to +46, scores can be arranged into nine risk bands linked to 5-year and 15-year rates of violent recidivism. Rice et al. (2013) reported high predictive accuracy of VRAG-R scores (AUC = 0.75).

Bonta's (1996) third generation of risk assessment included tools with static and dynamic risk variables, generated through theory and research. Ostensibly such measures could inform treatment planning and evaluate changes in risk (i.e., on the dynamic variables) through treatment or other change agents. These could include empirical actuarial tools with dynamic items (i.e., items are summed to generate numeric scores) or structured professional judgment (SPJ) tools (i.e., item ratings are examined but not summed to yield a summary risk rating). An example of the former is the Level of Service Inventory-Revised (LSI-R; Andrews & Bonta, 1995), a 54-item dynamic empirical actuarial tool organized around ten risk-need domains that incorporate the Central Eight. Possible scores range from 0 to 54 and are organized into one of five risk bands of Low, Medium-Low, Medium, Medium-High, and High risk needs. The risk bands are linked to 1-year rates of reincarceration. The score magnitude and risk band inform service intensity (e.g., treatment and supervision) while the profile of criminogenic needs identify where to intervene to reduce and manage risk. A meta-analysis of variants of the Level of Service scales (Olver, Stockdale, & Wormith, 2011, 2014) found the LSI-R to have good predictive accuracy for violent recidivism ($r = 0.23$, equivalent AUC = 0.68, $k = 14$).

Finally, the fourth generation refers to instruments that guide service delivery from the point of intake to case closure (Andrews et al., 2006). Fourth generation instruments can also identify specific targets for treatment and evaluate rehabilitation progress (Campbell, French, & Gendreau, 2009). Validated exemplars of the fourth generation may include the Level of Service/Case Management Inventory (LS/CMI; Andrews, Bonta, & Wormith, 2004), the Historical Clinical Risk-20 Version 3 (HCR-20 V3; Douglas, Hart, Webster, & Belfrage, 2011), and the Violence Risk Scale (VRS; Wong & Gordon, 1999–2003). While the LS/CMI is a shorter (43-item) case management extension of the LSI-R, the HCR-20 V3 and VRS are both violence specific risk tools with static and dynamic items to assess risk and identify targets for risk management. The HCR-20 V3 is an SPJ tool, unique in that a distinction can be made as to whether a risk variable is present vs. relevant to violence risk. The profile of item ratings are scrutinized to generate risk estimates (low, medium, high) to inform case prioritization, imminence of possible violence, and severity of potential harm. The VRS, in turn, is a dynamic empirical actuarial tool in which static and dynamic item ratings are summed to yield risk scores linked to violent recidivism estimates. Unique to the VRS is a structured change rubric to evaluate treatment readiness and change on the dynamic items across repeated assessments. Meta-analytic evidence supports the predictive accuracy of all three tools for violent recidivism. In a multi-level modeling meta-analysis of violence risk tools, Yang et al. (2010) reported significant predictive accuracy for future violence for both the VRS (AUC = 0.65, $k = 4$) as well as an earlier variant of the HCR-20 (AUC = 0.71, $k = 16$).

In all, results from meta-analysis demonstrate that most established tools tend to have broadly equivalent predictive accuracy for their targeted outcomes. Although this may leave the clinician scratching their head about what tool or tools to use, Bonta's (1996) generational framework offers some guidance. Not all tools can inform treatment, and even those tools that can, not all of them have a structured mechanism for assessing rehabilitation progress and change. While some instruments are comparatively general in their item content, others include both general and violence specific items to guide the delivery of violence reduction services. Depending on the clinician's assessment philosophy, they may have a preference for SPJ or actuarial tools (or happily use both). As such, the instruments have overlapping but also distinct potential uses and purposes, beyond mere recidivism prediction, and into the domains of violence prevention and risk management.

7.4 Interventions with Violent Offenders: What Works, What Might Work, and What Doesn't Work

Per the RNR model, violent offender assessment identifies who to treat (risk), what to treat (need), and how to treat (responsivity). Intervention involves the task of providing rehabilitation services to reduce and manage violence risk and improve prosocial functioning. We organize this section according to, in our view based on the substantive literature, what works to reduce violent offending in adults, what might work, and what does not work. The scope of our review includes reducing and managing hostility and aggression, interpersonal violence within institutional (hospital and prison) settings, and focusing primarily on violent recidivism upon release to the community. The extant research has included a combination of: (1) pre-post evaluations on important treatment targets; (2) linkage of within-treatment change to institutional and community violence and aggression; (3) single treatment outcome studies of a violence reduction regime relative to a comparison control; and (4) meta-analyses or research syntheses of the aforementioned designs.

7.4.1 What Works for Reducing Violent Offending? An Overview

Table 7.1 lists a collection of violence reduction interventions and programs with varying degree of support for their effectiveness in reducing violence and aggression. The models are organized under two broad categories. First are comprehensive, multi-intervention, integrated violence reduction programs such as the Violence Reduction Program (Wong & Gordon, 2013) and Violence Prevention Program (Cortoni, Nunes, & Latendresse, 2006) in Canada, New Zealand's High Risk Special Treatment Units (Polaschek & Kilgour, 2013), and Violent Offender Therapeutic Programme (VOTP) from Australia (Ware, Ciepulcha, & Matsuo, 2011) and the UK (Braham, Jones, & Hollin, 2008). These comprehensive programs (or CPs) tend to target a broad array of criminogenic needs linked to violence and aggression, they utilize a combination of group and individual treatment modalities, use manualized interventions, have a coordinated referral and intake process that includes pretreatment, interim assessment, and posttreatment assessments of violence risk, employ a multidisciplinary treatment team of corrections and mental health professionals to run groups, respond to urgent situations, monitor progress, attend to medical issues, and help clients consolidate and maintain gains and ultimately transition out of custody. As these programs tend to be run in prisons or forensic hospitals, they are often complimented by adjunctive therapies and other skills based programs (e.g., educational upgrading, vocational retraining, substance abuse treatment).

Second, the other class of interventions listed are singular focused interventions (focused programs or FPs) that tend to target selected criminogenic needs (e.g., anger, criminal attitudes, aggression) or a particular domain of functioning (e.g., cognitive, affective, behavioral) linked to violence risk. While these individual interventions can be offered as standalone programs, they can often be combined together as constituent elements of the comprehensive multi-intervention violence programs referenced previously. These interventions are intended to work, in part, by helping the individual develop new cognitive, affective, or behavioral skills to remediate the domain linked to violence and aggression.

Of note, there is a distinction between an intervention technique and a formal intervention program; the latter is a systematized collection of interventions that may be used to promote cognitive, affective, and/or behavioral change. This review is intended to cover programs rather than individual interventions, although some of these might be briefly discussed or listed as they pertain to programs. For instance, motivational interviewing (Miller & Rollnick, 2002) can be a highly effective clinical technique for engaging resistant clientele and effecting positive change; it is frequently used in the CPs and FPs but on its own it would not constitute a standalone program, so we do not discuss it as such. A large number of relevant examples are listed in Table 7.1, but owing to space considerations, only a few illustrative examples will be covered here. Before delving into some of these examples, broad evidence will be reviewed from the meta-analytic literature to provide a context and evidentiary framework for what works for reducing violent offending.

Table 7.1 Efficacy of interventions in the treatment of violent offenders for the reduction of crime and general violence

What works	What might work	What does not work

Comprehensive Multi-Intervention Programs
• Violence Reduction Program
• Violence Prevention Program
• Violent Offender Treatment Program (Australia)
• High Risk Special Treatment Units (NZ)
• High intensity rehabilitative community supervision programs (e.g., STICS)
  Focused Intervention/Single Need Programs
• Cognitively based programs targeting offender thinking and/or attitudes
  – Reasoning and Rehabilitation
  – Moral Reconation Therapy
  – Thinking for a Change
  – Cognitive Self-Change
• Anger management
• Behavioral modification approaches
  – Social skills training/assertiveness
  – Contingency management (e.g., token economies)
• Problem solving skills training
• Relapse prevention
• Substance abuse treatment
• Pharmacotherapy
	• Aggression Replacement Therapy
	• Trauma focused approaches
	• Animal assisted interventions
	• Yoga and meditation programs
	• Re-entry programs
	• Third wave therapies
	• Therapeutic communities
		• Poorly coordinated milieu therapy
		• Unstructured and nondirective counselling
		• Correctional quackery
		• Other common-sense movement interventions
		• Boot camps
		• Shock incarceration
		• Shaming approaches
		• Criminal sanctions applied in isolation

7.4.1.1 What Works?

Results from Meta-analysis and Illustrative Examples

Dowden and Andrews (2000) conducted a meta-analysis of 35 violent offender treatment outcome studies, all of which were based on male offender samples, and 70% of which featured adult offenders. They examined the effectiveness of risk reduction intervention programs as a function of the RNR principles on violent recidivism post release. Using the binomial effect size display, which equates to the percent difference in rates of recidivism between the treatment and comparison groups (e.g., adheres to principle vs. does not adhere to principle), they found greater adherence to a given principle to be associated with larger reductions in violent recidivism. Adherence to the risk principle was associated with a 12% reduction in violent recidivism ($k = 36$), adherence to the need principle, a 20% reduction ($k = 19$), and adherence to general responsivity, a 19% reduction ($k = 18$). Conversely non-adherence to the principles were associated with little or no decrease in violent recidivism ($ES = 0.00$ to 0.04). Moreover, while the most promising services ($k = 13$) yielded 20% reductions in violent recidivism, inappropriate services were associated with a small increase (1%) in violent recidivism ($k = 23$); of concern, at the time, a substantially larger proportion of studies were practicing frankly inappropriate interventions. Targeting criminogenic needs was associated with reductions in violent recidivism, specifically, negative affect/anger ($ES = 0.15$, $k = 16$), antisocial attitudes ($ES = 0.14$, $k = 14$), and relapse prevention ($ES = 0.20$, $k = 12$). Not targeting these needs was associated with much more modest reductions (4–5%). However, targeting non-criminogenic needs (fear of official punishment, vague emotional problem), was associated with fewer reductions in recidivism (2–3%) than if they were not targeted (9–10%).

Jolliffe and Farrington (2007) conducted a systematic review some years later, and focused specifically on general violent offender programs, excluding programs that also extended to domestic and sexual violence (in contrast to Dowden & Andrews, 2000). Consequently, they had a smaller collection of studies ($k = 11$) which included newer investigations subsequent to Dowden and Andrews (2000); however, their findings and conclusions are very similar. In brief, Jolliffe and Farrington (2007) found violent offender programs that had the following attributes generated significant reductions in violent recidivism: targeted anger control ($d = 0.14$, $k = 6$), practiced cognitive skills ($d = 0.16$, $k = 7$), used role plays ($d = 0.19$, $k = 6$), employed relapse prevention ($d = 0.13$, $k = 5$), and assigned offender homework ($d = 0.37$, $k = 3$). Interestingly, programs that did not employ empathy training generated larger effects ($d = 0.20$, $k = 5$). Similarly, they found that programs employing very few or no effective program features (e.g., anger control, cognitive skills, roleplays) had a mean effect size of approximately $d = 0.00$, while substantially greater benefit in terms of recidivism reduction was found for programs employing two effective features ($d = 0.29$) or three such features ($d = 0.36$).

The Dowden and Andrews (2000) and Jolliffe and Farrington (2007) meta-analyses, to our knowledge, are the only formal quantitative reviews of the impact of violence reduction programs on violent outcomes in offender samples, some of which included CPs, while others included FPs to address certain core needs or domains of functioning. Several evaluations of each have since been conducted and we review some illustrative examples. We review Canada's Violence Reduction Program (VRP) and New Zealand's High Risk Special Treatment Unit (HRSTU) as two RNR-based CPs. We then turn to an examination of cognitively based programs and anger management as examples of FPs that can work to reduce violent offending.

Illustrative Examples of Comprehensive Programs

Violence Reduction Program (VRP)

The Violence Reduction Program (VRP; Wong & Gordon, 2013; Wong, Gordon, & Gu, 2007), originated as the Aggressive Behaviour Control (ABC) program, a high intensity CBT-based violence reduction program operated out of a high security correctional mental health facility in Saskatoon, Canada, the Regional Psychiatric Centre (RPC). In the years to follow, the VRP has been implemented in hospitals and prisons throughout the world. The VRP can be organized into three broad phases that link assessment and treatment, with interventions delivered based on the individual's readiness to change and progress routinely monitored throughout. Phase I ("Opening the Door to Change") involves an intake employing the VRS to assess risk for future violence, identify criminogenic needs to be prioritized for risk reduction, and evaluation of the individual's awareness of their problem areas and readiness to change. Motivation enhancement strategies (such as use of MI) are employed and work is done to strengthen engagement and the alliance. Phase II ("Skill Acquisition") entails the completion of therapy groups complemented with individual treatment sessions and homework assignments to develop cognitive, affective regulation, and behavior management skills to reduce the use of violence and aggression and increase the frequency of nonviolent and prosocial behavior. Phase III ("Relapse Prevention") involves the development of an individualized relapse prevention plan to support living in the community without violence, coordinated release planning, and helping clients consolidate, generalize, and transfer treatment gains.

Evaluations of the VRP and its variants have been positive. Wong et al. (2005) found that the VRP was effective in reducing institutional offending among super maximum security men and in helping them safely reintegrate into the general prison population posttreatment. Di Placedo, Simon, Witte, Gu, and Wong (2006) further found that among gang affiliated violent offenders, those men who had completed the VRP had lower rates of violent and general recidivism on their release to the community, compared to a matched control group of high risk gang affiliated offenders who did not receive the program. Lewis, Olver, and Wong (2013) subsequently found that men attending the VRP who lowered their risk substantially (scoring in the top quartile for VRS change score), had lower rates of violent reconviction (23.1%) than men who did not fare as well (46.4%). Relatedly, in the same treated sample of men, Olver, Lewis, and Wong (2013) found that treatment change was significantly associated with decreased violent recidivism, even after controlling for Psychopathy Checklist-Revised (PCL-R; Hare, 1991, 2003) score. Finally, Wong, Gordon, Gu, Lewis, and Olver (2012) compared two high psychopathy groups, a VRP treatment and a control, assessed on the PCL-R and matched on offense history, demographic, and risk variables, on several indices of general and violent recidivism. Although the two groups did not differ significantly on the frequency or number of new convictions, treated men had significantly shorter aggregate sentences for new convictions. As sentence length is a proxy of severity, the men in essence were committing less serious offenses consistent with a harm reduction model.

New Zealand's High Risk Specialized Treatment Units (HRSTUs)

The High Risk Specialized Treatment Units (HRSTUs) refer to a collection of four prison based high intensity violence reduction programs operated out of New Zealand Department of Corrections. Polaschek and Kilgour (2013) provide the following history and overview of the HRSTUs. Preceded by the Montgomery House Violence Prevention Project established in 1987, the HRSTU commenced in 1998 with the Rimutaka Violence Prevention Unit (VPU) and subsequent units opening in 2008 and 2009. Grounded in the RNR principles, the current HRSTU model is a high intensity comprehensive program that is a hybrid of closed group cognitive behavioral therapy (CBT) skill sessions, and a democratic therapeutic community where interpersonal processes are the primary mechanism of change. Clientele are adult male high risk high needs violent offenders. Men are assessed on the VRS at intake to assess risk, identify treatment targets, and readiness for change, and reassessed at program completion to evaluate risk reduction. The HRSTUs house approximately 150 men across the four programs, of whom approximately 2/3 successfully complete the program. Staff verbalize commitment to the program and Maori cultural values and practices are integrated into program content and modality of service delivery. The core treatment program itself is organized into 99 group sessions at 2.5 h each. Akin to the VRP, the HRSTU treatment is arranged into three phases: Phase I focuses on offender engagement, including the establishment of a prosocial identity; Phase II focuses on prosocial skills acquisition, improving coping and targeting criminogenic influences; and Phase III focuses on the future, including the development of individualized safety plans that identify potential high risk situations and developing resources and strategies to effectively cope with these.

There is a strong history of evaluation of the HRSTU programs. Polaschek, Wilson, Townsend, and Daly (2005) conducted the initial evaluation of Rimutaka VPU on a small sample of treated men (*n* = 22), and found that they had significantly lower rates of violent reconviction (32%) relative to a comparison control (63%). A subsequent evaluation on an extended sample (*n* = 56) by Polaschek (2011) still found group differences between treated men and a matched comparison condition, but this was much smaller at just 10% ($\varphi = 0.11$) and not significant. Polaschek and Kilgour (2013) note that a review in the mid-2000s identified issues with program fidelity, that may have attenuated findings in Polaschek (2011), the outcome of which was to develop a detailed program manual which as adopted by the HRSTUs. In their report, Polaschek and Kilgour (2013) note that an accumulated sample of 164 treatment completers rated on the VRS pre and posttreatment, evidenced significant change and hence risk reduction by more than half a standard deviation ($d = 0.62$) and had fewer treatment needs at discharge. Most recently, Polaschek, Yesberg, Bell, Casey, and Dickson (2016) examined a mediation model of this program and sample, finding that treatment program completion was significantly associated with decreased violent reconviction after accounting for baseline dynamic violence risk as measured by the VRS.

Illustrative Examples of Focused Programs

We narrow our attention to focused programs that have a greater evidence base, such as enough to conduct a meta-analysis, noting a few things. First, very few, if any, of these evaluations focus specifically on violent offenders or on targeting or changing violent outcomes or even aggression for that matter. Much of the extant literature focuses on reduction of general recidivism as the target. Second, quantitative reviews have not consistently differentiated whether the intervention is delivered as a standalone program (e.g., anger management) or were incorporated as one element within a broader comprehensive multi-target multi-intervention program. Third, many of these reviews (particularly for anger problems) have focused on non-offender, non-forensic samples, which limits their relevance, and we attempt to draw ties where applicable.

Cognitive Based Programs

Under this rubric we include the family of interventions that target the thinking style, criminal attitudes, irrational beliefs, and cognitive distortions that violent persons engage in that increase their risk for violent offending. This would include Reasoning and Rehabilitation (Ross & Fabiano, 1985), Cognitive Self-Change (Bush & Brian, 1993), Moral Reconation Therapy (Little & Robinson, 1986), Thinking for a Change (Bush, Glick, & Taymans, 1997) and other targeted cognitive and/or attitude programs. Such programs may teach the individual to recognize key assumptions and errors in logic and reasoning (or baldly criminal attitudes), and to teach them strategies to confront, challenge, and change criminogenic thinking. Further distinctions in program foci may be organized in terms of the content of criminal thinking (e.g., criminal attitudes such as violence is an acceptable way to vent anger or solve conflict) or the process of criminal thinking (e.g., reading hostile meanings into ambiguous situations). Falling under the rubric of cognitive programs would include cognitive problem-solving skills programs (e.g., Stop and Think), which teach the individual to evaluate the situation, generate possible alternatives, evaluate the possible consequences of a given course of action (for themselves and others), and then to select a preferably prosocial and nonviolent course of action that will help resolve the situation.

Reasoning and Rehabilitation (also known as R&R, and not to be confused with RNR) is one of the oldest and most familiar programs for targeting and correcting impulsive, egocentric thinking of offenders and to teach them to evaluate the potential consequences of their behavior and impact on others. Tong and Farrington (2008) conducted an updated meta-analysis of R&R implemented across 19 evaluations in institutional and community settings across four countries (Canada, Sweden, UK, and US). R&R demonstrated a significant effect overall, amounting to a 14% reduction in general reoffending. The authors concluded that the program was effective in both institutional and community settings, and in Canada and the UK, but not the US. The results affirmed Wilson, Bouffard, and MacKenzie's (2005) earlier review across seven R&R evaluations, which found a small effect size overall ($d = 0.16$) for the reduction of recidivism. Landenberger and Lipsey (2005) conducted a meta-analysis of CBT-based interventions with offenders across 58 studies; a large part of this evaluation was identifying moderators of treatment effectiveness, including comparative evaluations of different CBT programs and intervention components. Although there was an overall effect for CBT based programs in reducing recidivism, participation in R&R specifically was not significantly associated with any added advantage compared to other offender CBT programs in terms of recidivism reduction; that is, R&R may work, but there was little evidence to suggest that it is any better than other established CBT programs.

Moral reconation therapy (MRT) draws on Kohlberg's theory of moral reasoning, positing that offenders tend to have deficiencies in moral development, assisting them in developing skills to counter such moral and behavioral concerns. Wilson et al. (2005) also reviewed MRT in their meta-analysis across six evaluations, finding MRT participants to have significantly lower rates of recidivism than the comparison group of offenders, with an effect approaching moderate in magnitude ($d = 0.36$). Of note, even the highest quality evaluations generated similar effects ($d = 0.33$). The Landenberger and Lipsey (2005) review, as with R&R, did not find participation in MRT to be associated with substantively larger decreases in recidivism compared to other CBT programs.

At a broader level, targeting criminal cognitions in some capacity is associated with reductions in both violent and general recidivism. Dowden and Andrews (2000) as noted previously, found that violent offender programs targeting antisocial attitudes (intervention not specific, however) generated reductions in violent recidivism. Landenberger and Lipsey (2005) further found that inclusion of cognitive restructuring (i.e., recognizing and modifying criminogenic thinking) as a core intervention in CBT programs to be significantly associated ($B = 0.27$) with larger effect sizes in reducing recidivism. Inclusion of cognitive skills (i.e., general skills of thinking and decision-making), however was not associated with greater improvements in recidivism reduction ($B = 0.02$) relative to other CBT programs, even though such programs may "work" on their own strictly speaking.

Anger Management

Anger management approaches exist both as standalone programs (FPs) as well as being incorporated as part of a multi-intervention CP. They can vary considerably on the level of structure involved, whether the program is manualized, and whether offered in group or individual format. Common themes include identifying triggers and cues associated with anger, strategies to decrease physiological and emotional arousal along with their cognitive concomitants and behavioral consequences. Although several quantitative reviews have been conducted of anger management interventions, these have predominantly or exclusively included non-offender (and often included university student) samples. Importantly, some evaluations have examined important behavioral proxies, such as aggressive behavior, which may have relevance to offender samples. Broadly speaking, quantitative reviews of anger management have demonstrated reductions in self-reported anger of treated participants relative to comparison controls across a range of modalities, with CBT (ES = 0.60, k = 0.42) and relaxation based approaches (ES = 0.67, k = 37) having the largest volume of empirical support (Saini, 2009). A further quantitative review of particular interest, conducted by DiGiuseppe and Tafrate (2003) of anger management interventions across 57 studies, found participation in anger management to be associated with decreased aggression (ES = 1.16, k = 28). Applied to offenders more specifically, the Dowden and Andrews (2000) meta-analysis, as previously noted, found targeting anger/negative affect as a criminogenic need to be associated with decreased violent recidivism. Perhaps equally compelling, the Landenberger and Lipsey (2005) meta-analysis found offender CBT programs featuring anger control as a treatment intervention to be significantly associated with larger effect size magnitudes (B = 0.32) in the reduction of general recidivism.

Why Do CPs and FPs Work to Reduce Violent Offending?

In short, these programs adhere to RNR principles, broadly speaking. First, evaluations show that CPs often tend to target moderate to high risk offenders, per the risk principle. Second, effective programs also target risk relevant areas (i.e., criminogenic needs) through the assessment of dynamic risk factors at intake, targeting identified needs through treatment modules, and monitoring progress toward risk reduction. Third, these programs focus on developing prosocial cognitive, affect regulation, and behavior skills to reduce risk and develop alternatives to violence and aggression (a.k.a. general responsivity). Fourth, the programs also tend to be biopsychosocial in nature; for instance, psychotropic medication can be a prominent component in addition to CBT-based services, with cultural and/or spiritual domains often an important addition to the traditional focus on affect, behavior, and cognition. Fifth, the programs have also been established long enough to have a track record of monitoring effectiveness and what elements work and do not work. Sixth, when implemented in the spirit with which they were developed, these programs, particularly the CPs, tend to be well-staffed and supervised with trained personnel from psychology, psychiatry, social work, nursing, and corrections (security, operations, and probation/parole). Seventh, the programs are structured to incorporate responsive interventions (e.g., motivational components to prepare people for treatment or to promote engagement by less willing clients, groups, interventions, and assignments adapted to lower cognitive functioning offenders or individuals with literacy deficits). Eighth, the programs have manualized components to promote treatment integrity. Finally, effective programs also have some continuity of care, such as transition services to the community (e.g., contact with a residence, potential employer, follow-up services), to inform adherence to special conditions and promote as smooth a reintegration as possible.

A natural question to this end is, "how much treatment is enough?" There have been heuristics advanced from the treatment dosage literature on the minimum allotment of hours of intervention based on the individual's risk level. A problem, however, is that there is invariably some element of arbitrariness and dosage guidelines do not necessarily account for the content or comprehensiveness of the program or its quality of implementation (see Simourd & Olver, 2018, in press for a critical appraisal). For instance, in their meta-analysis of the risk principle, Andrews and Dowden (2006) found that programs adhering to the risk principle, but which did not target criminogenic need or follow responsivity considerations yielded no reductions in recidivism. While guidelines such as a minimum 100 h for moderate risk cases (i.e., most typical offenders) and 300 h for the highest risk cases have been advanced (Hanson et al., 2017), other programs have documented positive treatment effects with under 50 h (Kroner & Makahashi, 2012). Although higher risk cases do require more services, effective violence reduction programs need to adhere to other critical programmatic considerations as outlined above.

Finally, it is important to bear in mind that not all programs have all of the above elements. Moreover, such elements may not be implemented properly and even an extremely strong program on paper can be rendered worthless by poor implementation. A meta-analysis by Lowenkamp, Latessa, and Smith (2006) of 38 programs evaluated using a program evaluation tool, the Correctional Program Assessment Inventory (CPAI), found that programs adhering to their core treatment philosophy and the principles of effective intervention netted greater reductions in recidivism; however, poor implementation was associated with little reduction in recidivism. As a testament to this, CPAI score significantly predicted recidivism across the programs. A quality program is only as strong as its implementation.

7.4.2 What Might Work for Reducing Violent Offending?

The class of interventions that we identified as what might work are potentially helpful, yet: (1) are not sufficient as standalone interventions; (2) tend to be new and not yet evaluated; (3) have yet to develop the same evidence base as traditional therapies; and/or (4) have generated mixed results. We review five therapies under this framework: animal assisted interventions, trauma informed and trauma focused therapies, the "third wave therapies", aggression replacement training, and therapeutic communities.

7.4.2.1 Animal Assisted Interventions

Animal assisted interventions (AAI) have become popular in correctional programming in recent years (Dell & Poole, 2015). Most popular are the use of naturally affiliative animals such as dogs and cats, although horses (as in the case of equine therapy) and other animals have also been used. Kruger and Serpell (2006) define AAIs as "any intervention that intentionally includes or incorporates animals as part of a therapeutic or ameliorative process or milieu" (p. 25). AAI proponents underscore the nonjudgmental, affectionate, and accepting nature of therapy animals, who can empower and model patience, respect, trust, and acceptance to their human clients (Dell & Poole, 2015).

The formal outcome research on AAI correctional programs is admittedly sparse (Dell & Poole, 2015), and the limited research has frequently been of poor quality and yielded mixed findings (Swyers, 2014). While there may be a number of personal and emotional benefits to offenders (Dell & Poole, 2015), how AAIs directly reduce risk for future violence and promote reintegration is less clear. Cooke and Farrington (2016) conducted a meta-analysis of dog training programs (DTPs) in correctional facilities (mostly throughout the US) and found significant effects for reducing recidivism ($d = 0.78$). However, DTPs are somewhat different from AAIs in that offenders specifically learn to train dogs either to learn basic commands to increase their chances of being adopted, or for service purposes, as in the case of therapy or guide dogs, although common benefits with traditional AAI (e.g., increased patience, self-efficacy, improved relationships, improved coping) have been noted (Cooke & Farrington, 2016).

7.4.2.2 Trauma Informed and Trauma Focused Therapy

Trauma informed approaches acknowledge the impact and significance of trauma on the individual and promoting recovery and healing from the trauma (King, 2017). Their application to offenders has salience given the prominence of trauma faced in the lives of women and men in custody. Also of relevance, the prison setting itself has the potential to re-traumatize individuals such as through lockdowns, strip searches, unit frisks, exposure to institutional aggression, or authoritarian staff (Miller & Najavits, 2012). Untreated trauma and its physical, psychological, and emotional sequelae can serve as an impediment to therapeutic engagement, and thus trauma informed approaches may enable the individual to benefit more fully from other correctional programming (e.g., CBT); in this sense, trauma is treated as a responsivity issue (Miller & Najavits, 2012). It is further important to distinguish what has been termed trauma informed correctional care, as described above, vs.

trauma focused approaches which tend to prioritize the treatment of trauma as the mainstay of therapy (Miller & Najavits, 2012).

In criminal justice contexts, most of the evidence for trauma informed or trauma focused approaches appears to have been garnered with incarcerated women offenders (King, 2017), although there have also been applications with male sex offenders (Levenson & Grady, 2016). Proponents of gender informed assessment and treatment approaches contend that trauma may have special salience for female offenders (Van Voorhis, Wright, Salisbury, & Bauman, 2010). A systematic review by King (2017) found that women participating in trauma informed approaches had decreases in self-reported post-traumatic symptomatology, and that there were additional benefits beyond services as usual. Only two of the investigations examined linkages with recidivism; each found some reductions in return to custody although no association with possible reductions in violence was examined.

7.4.2.3 "New Wave" CBT Approaches

Following on the developments of behavior therapy (first wave), and cognitive and cognitive behavioral therapy (second wave), the so-called "third" or "new wave" refers to recent advances in CBT that share some common features such as mindfulness, acceptance, and metacognition (Öst, 2008). Therapeutic approaches such as Dialectical Behavior Therapy (DBT), Acceptance and Commitment Therapy (ACT), Emotion Focused Therapy (EFT), and Schema Focused Cognitive Therapy (SCFT) have frequently been grouped under the "new wave" banner. The classification of therapies as "new wave" has generated some controversy, however, as not all authorities endorse these approaches as novel or support the classification of certain approaches in this manner (Hofmann, Sawyer, & Fang, 2010). We briefly review DBT and mindfulness based approaches, which have been grouped under the "new wave", in the treatment of concerns relevant to violent offenders. Although additional "new wave" approaches (e.g., ACT, EFT) have been incorporated into offender treatment programs, the outcome literature on such approaches with this population is scant.

There is ample evidence that DBT works with severe personality pathology such as borderline personality disorder (BPD) in both women and men, which has an elevated base rate (25–30%) in correctional settings (Black et al., 2007; Conn et al., 2010). DBT is a therapeutic approach intended to treat emotional dysregulation and its concordant behavioral problems, and comprises four components: mindfulness, distress tolerance, emotional regulation, and interpersonal effectiveness (Linehan, 1993). A meta-analysis of 22 DBT studies reported positive impacts on reducing anger and aggression, both overall and in the context of BPD (Frasier & Vela, 2014). Of the $k = 4$ male and female forensic/correctional samples included in this review, each reported reductions in self-reported anger or aggression and/or reductions in aggressive and disciplinary incidents. Mindfulness, in turn, is a specific intervention component employed in DBT, although it is frequently used as an intervention in its own right or combined with other therapeutic approaches (e.g., mindfulness based cognitive therapy). Mindfulness has been defined as essentially being a state of non-judgmental awareness of the moment-to-moment present (Kabat-Zinn, 2005). A meta-analysis of eight mindfulness and related Buddhist-based intervention approaches in correctional settings found associations between use of mindfulness based interventions and improvements on indexes of depression, hostility, and substance use (Shonin, Van Gordon, Slade, & Griffiths, 2013). None of the studies however examined associations with violent, criminal, or otherwise antisocial behavior, and Shonin et al. (2013) noted that the overall quality of the studies was quite poor.

7.4.2.4 Aggression Replacement Training

Aggression Replacement Training (ART) was originally developed in the 1980s by Arnold Goldstein and Barry Glick (Goldstein & Glick, 1987) as a cognitive-behavioral program for aggressive adolescents in residential care. A multi-component program composed of affective (anger control), cognitive (moral reasoning), and behavioral (social skills training) interventions, ART has since been applied to diverse client groups and settings, including adult violent offenders (e.g., Barto Lynch, 1995). While previously included in other systematic reviews and identified as a promising program, a specific review of ART was recently conducted by Brännström, Kaunitz, Andershed, South, and Smedslund (2016). Sixteen studies met inclusion criteria for this review, only four of which included adult samples. Unfortunately, limited conclusions could be drawn regarding the impact of ART owing to methodological limitations inherent in this small group of studies (e.g., limited follow-up). In addition, the Landenberger and Lipsey (2005) review did not find participation in ART to be associated with substantively larger decreases in recidivism compared to other CBT programs.

7.4.2.5 Therapeutic Communities

The idea behind therapeutic communities (TC) is that the treatment environment, or community, serves as the rehabilitative agent, through interpersonal learning opportunities that are generated from patient interactions with staff and other co-patients. In their review of TC programs, Day and Doyle (2010) note that democratic TCs are most frequently applied to violent offenders and are characterized by the following: staff and patients are involved in decision making, free interaction among staff and patients, confronting negative behavior in the present along with its impact on others, and an expectation that community members learn to tolerate one another. Day and Doyle (2010) note mixed success of prison based democratic TCs in the treatment of violent offenders as well as lack of formal evaluations; from their review associations appear to be stronger for reducing general as opposed to violent recidivism. Taylor (2000) reported an updated evaluation of Grendon Prison's democratic TC in the UK that examined 7-year release outcomes of 400 men admitted to the TC between 1984 and 1989, relative to the general prison population and a waitlist control. Men in the TC had non-significantly lower rates of violent reconviction (30%) than waitlist controls (37%), with larger differences observed in terms of general recidivism (66% vs. 73%, respectively). There was also a modest association between length of stay within the TC and reduced violent reconviction.

7.4.2.6 Why Might These Approaches Work?

Some of these approaches do not directly target criminogenic needs per se (e.g., antisocial attitudes, aggressive behavior, delinquent peers), while others clearly do (e.g., emotional dysregulation and anger arousal). In addition, these approaches may indirectly target some criminogenic need domains that can confer skills development and are risk relevant. For instance, if an individual who resolves their prior trauma and develops effective coping strategies (e.g., mindfulness, relaxation, journaling, grounding techniques), they may be less likely to drink or use other substances as a way to cope, thereby lowering their risk. The same individual may also be in a better position to engage other programming or opportunities for reintegration and risk reduction, per the responsivity principle. And further, such skills may transfer to managing other stressors and emotional states that may previously have erupted in violence. Some of these interventions, however, may not be established to the same degree, or have the therapeutic principles as well articulated, or the treatment approaches manualized, as seen with conventional CBT-based mainstream correctional programs. In other instances where the program is clearly established (e.g., DBT), it would be important that it also be integrated with other approaches in the context of a broader violence risk reduction program.

7.4.3 What Does Not Work?

This final section concerns those approaches outlined in Table 7.1 that have been demonstrated to not work, whether this be reducing crime in general or violent offending in particular. Latessa, Cullen, and Gendreau (2002) invoke the term correctional quackery (CQ) to refer to a collection of interventions derived from the commonsense movement that are not based on existing knowledge of what causes crime or what programs have been demonstrated to change offender behavior (see also Gendreau, Smith, & Thériault, 2009). Examples include boot camps, scared straight or shock incarceration approaches, wilderness challenge approaches, other shaming approaches (e.g., sandwich board justice), poorly executed therapeutic communities, nondirective relationship-dependent counseling, unstructured milieu and group approaches, and other faddish approaches such as heart mapping, angel-in-you-therapy, finger painting, acupuncture, diets, and aura focus among others (Gendreau et al., 2009). It is important to note that also included in the list of ineffective approaches are basic criminal justice sanctions (i.e., prison or probation terms). Absent the provision of correctional programs, incarceration in and of itself tends to do little to deter future antisocial behavior. If deterrence did work with offenders, then formal criminal history should not be the robust predictor of recidivism that it is!

Andrews, Zinger, et al. (1990) examined this systematically and found that use of criminal sanctions alone was associated with a 7% increase in recidivism, while frankly inappropriate approaches, such as those characterized as CQ above, were similarly associated with a 6% increase in recidivism. Dowden and Andrews (2000) reported a slight increase in violent offending for weak or inappropriate services ($\varphi = -0.01$), while Jolliffe and Farrington (2007) similarly reported no effect ($d = 0.00$) for programs that had either very few or no evidence informed therapeutic elements. In a meta-analysis of 44 boot camp outcome studies, MacKenzie, Wilson, and Kider (2001) found these interventions to yield no reduction in recidivism relative to comparison controls ($OR = 1.02$). That is, individuals were equally likely to reoffend, whether they participated in the boot camp or not. The null effect was observed across adult and juvenile studies.

7.4.3.1   Why Don't These Approaches Work?

For one, they fly in the face of RNR, as such interventions tend not to consider risk level or dosage in assigning treatment (e.g., overtreating offenders or mixing high and low risk cases), they do not target criminogenic needs or involve the establishment of prosocial skills as alternatives to violent or otherwise criminal behavior, and they are not responsive or receptive to the unique needs of clientele. Rather, in contrast to general responsivity which advocates for warm, empathic, humane, respectful, firm but fair approaches, these approaches may involve shaming, hostile or aversive interactions (e.g., yelling, scolding, berating) or other ineffective punitive strategies, abuse of authority, targeting non-criminogenic needs, and/or failing to teach or model prosocial behavior skills. Some approaches, particularly, unstructured milieu approaches may involve limited staff-client interaction, opening up the possibility for rule violations, victimization of vulnerable clients by others, and many missed opportunities for prosocial role modeling from staff. At best such approaches are ineffective, and at worst, they can violate human rights and cause harm.

7.5   Future Implications

What work remains to be done at the level of training, practice, research and correctional administration in the assessment and treatment of violent offenders? First, in completing this review, we were surprised in a number of respects at how *little* research there appeared to be in terms of formal evaluations of violence reduction programs. While Dowden and Andrews (2000) included violent individuals of all stripes, Jolliffe and Farrington (2007) included only general violent offender treatment programs, finding only 11 studies from a search of 22 databases, that met a minimum threshold for quality. By contrast, formal evaluations of general crime reduction programs or even sex offender treatment programs are quite numerous. Further, the volume of child and youth intervention research has numbers of studies quite literally in the hundreds, for reducing delinquent, antisocial, violent, or aggressive behavior across many different contexts such as schools, juvenile justice and so forth (e.g., Lipsey, 2009). As such, there is not only a need for further evaluations of violence reduction programs, but methodologically strong evaluations of evidence informed programs, and their therapeutic components, in terms of impacts on violence reduction. Naturally, the results of investigations should be reported in ways that are amenable to meta-analytic aggregation. These do not necessarily have to be randomized controlled trials, but could also be strong quasi experimental or correlational designs, taking into account important methodological considerations such as controlling for risk (e.g., matching groups) and follow-up time, such as articulated in the Collaborative Outcome Data Committee (2007).

Second, another theme readily apparent in this review is that a quality program is only as effective as its implementation. Important research featuring the CPAI has highlighted not only that better implemented programs have better outcomes, but that most programs, unfortunately are poorly implemented Latessa et al. (2002). Use of treatment fidelity measures such as the CPAI or other validated program assessment measure can assist programs in fully adhering to RNR principles and maximizing outcomes. The multisystemic therapy (MST) literature, featuring high intensity multimodal interventions delivered to youth and families, is a good illustration of high treatment fidelity and linkages with reduced crime and violence (see Henggeler, Schoenwald, Borduin, Rowland, & Cunningham, 2009 for detailed description and review). We know treatment fidelity matters; it seems we just need to do a better job of adhering to it.

Third, the issue of staff and student training bears mentioning. Undergraduate and graduate training in correctional psychology and criminal justice provides an important foundation for further professional training (e.g., internships and practica) and entry into various frontline, academic, or administrative career roles. Clinical psychology, psychiatry, forensic nursing, law, social work, occupational and recreational therapy, addictions, and other corrections specialization programs are various examples of professional programs that can provide an entryway to the criminal justice field. But once the trainee gets there, naturally the training should not stop, although unfortunately this is not always the case. There is a need for continual and integrated training across professional lines on evidence informed practice: (1) in terms of the structure, content, and implementation of violence reduction programs; and (2) staff-offender interactions, per general responsivity and core correctional practices (Dowden & Andrews, 2004) to maximize effectiveness and gain. Treatment is not only the domain of mental health staff, but all frontline professionals who come in routine contact with offenders and have repeated opportunities to intervene in a helpful way, as well as management to support the staffing and effective delivery of such programs. Without these essential elements, programs are likely to fall substantially short intended goals or experience "drift" over time.

7.6 Technology and Innovation

How can technology and innovation be envisioned to influence the process of growth and knowledge accumulation and dissemination in the service of changing violent offender behavior? An important innovation impacting research and practice in our view is in the monitoring and evaluation of offender change. Gordon and Wong (2010) use the term offense analogue behaviors (OABs) to refer to offense linked proxy behaviors that emerge in institutional or custodial settings, where supervision is often tighter and structure is greater. Other terms such as offense paralleling behaviors have also been used (Daffern, Jones, & Shine, 2010). In short, OABs are the manifestation of criminogenic needs in a secure environment and signals to service providers that these domains remain treatment targets and merit further attention. Some examples of OABs could be adherence to the con code (as a proxy for antisocial attitudes), involvement in disciplinary incidents (as a proxy for impulsivity), or heated verbal attacks or physical altercations (as a proxy, or direct indication even, of problems with emotional regulation and interpersonal aggression). By contrast, offense replacement behaviors (ORBs) are prosocial behaviors, skills, and strategies that serve as alternatives to OABs and would indicate that risk is being reduced and the concordant criminogenic need is being addressed. Some examples could include following institutional rules and engaging in one's correctional plan (as indicators of addressing issues with impulsivity and antisocial attitudes), practicing skills of assertiveness in interpersonal interactions (as a substitute for aggression), or using positive coping (e.g., perception checks, time outs, mindfulness) to manage negative emotional arousal (as a means of addressing problems with anger).

Gordon and Wong (2010) argue that monitoring and targeting OABs and ORBs should be part of a violence reduction regime (and indeed these are elements of VRP); that is, services should target managing and reducing OABs, while teaching and modeling ORBs. To this end, an OAB/ORB guide has been developed (Gordon & Wong, 2009–2014) to monitor and evaluate OABs and ORBs in a risk reduction program. Of note, OABs and ORBs can be monitored in community contexts (e.g., violating supervision orders, associating with negative peers, demonstrating negative attitude toward community supervision). The important consideration is that reducing OABs and increasing ORBs is the responsibility of all service providers who come in contact with the offender, whether they be correctional officers, probation/parole officers, therapists and so forth. This also gets at the very heart of core correctional practices and the RNR principles in action. Not only do such processes need to be monitored, but they need to be: (1) formally evaluated, such as through pretreatment, interim, and posttreatment evaluations; and (2) linked to outcomes (e.g., decreased violent recidivism in custody and the community), through ongoing internal evaluations. Such efforts can have a positive impact informing effective correctional practice by way of strengthening formal linkages between assessment and treatment to better understand and capitalize on the process of offender change.

7.7   Conclusion

This chapter provided a review, synthesis, and discussion of assessment and treatment approaches, in research and practice, with adult violent offender populations. Given the length and depth of our review our closing message is brief. Readers are reminded that the overarching purpose of human service delivery with violent offenders is the prevention of further violence. This begins with a comprehensive assessment of violence risk, need, and responsivity issues to, respectively, inform the intensity of risk reduction services, prioritize areas to intervene, and to identify special considerations of the individual (e.g., motivation, mental health functioning, literacy) that can impact response to, and the capacity to benefit from, treatment. Programs, in turn, need to target both general and violence specific needs through the development of prosocial behavioral skills and strategies to move toward leading a more satisfying life without violence. Reassessments of possible risk reduction and identification of outstanding needs can inform how well such efforts are being achieved as well as release recommendations. In turn, for successful reintegration to occur, thoughtful release and transition planning to bolster supports, identify community resources, and aid continuity of care is paramount. Programs, be they in the institution or community, are only as good as the people who staff them, and the integrity with which they run them. Staff training, administrative and managerial support, and proper funding are all required to sustain programs that work. When this can be done, single treatment outcome studies, correlational designs, and meta-analytic reviews indicate that evidence informed programs can work to reduce violent offending. There is a need for further research—both individual studies and meta-analytic reviews and the extension of what works to male and female, youth and adult, and racially and ethnically diverse populations; however, we believe the steps taken so far give justification for cautious optimism in the assessment and treatment of violent offenders.

References

Andrews, D. A., & Bonta, J. (1994). The psychology of criminal conduct. Cincinnati, OH: Anderson.

Andrews, D. A., & Bonta, J. L. (1995). The level of service inventory—revised. Toronto, ON: Multi Health Systems.

Andrews, D. A., & Bonta, J. (2010a). The psychology of criminal conduct (5th ed.). New Providence, NJ: LexisNexis.

Andrews, D. A., & Bonta, J. (2010b). Rehabilitating criminal justice policy and practice. Psychology, Public Policy, and Law, 16, 39–55.

Andrews, D. A., Bonta, J., & Hoge, R. D. (1990). Classification for rehabilitation: Rediscovering psychology. Criminal Justice and Behavior, 17, 19–52.

Andrews, D. A., Bonta, J., & Wormith, J. S. (2004). Level of service/case management inventory (LS/CMI): An offender assessment system. User's guide. Toronto, ON: Multi-Health Systems.

Andrews, D. A., Bonta, J., & Wormith, J. S. (2006). The recent past and near future of risk and/or need assessment. Crime & Delinquency, 52, 7–27.

Andrews, D. A., & Dowden, C. (2006). Risk principle of case classification in correctional treatment. *International Journal of Offender Therapy and Comparative Criminology, 50*, 88–100.

Andrews, D. A., Zinger, I., Hoge, R. D., Bonta, J., Gendreau, P., & Cullen, F. T. (1990). Does correctional treatment work? A clinically-relevant and psychologically informed meta-analysis. *Criminology, 28*, 369–404.

Barto Lynch, J. (1995). *The use of aggression replacement training with adult offenders. A program for violent and aggressive inmates.* Louisville, KY: Spalding University.

Black, D. W., Gunter, T., Allen, J., Blum, N., Arndt, S., Wenman, G., & Sieleni, B. (2007). Borderline personality disorder in male and female offenders newly committed to prison. *Comprehensive Psychiatry, 48*, 400–405.

Bonta, J. (1996). Risk-needs assessment and treatment. In A. T. Harland (Ed.), *Choosing correctional options that work: Defining the demand and evaluating the supply* (pp. 18–32). Thousand Oaks, CA: Sage.

Bonta, J., & Andrews, D. A. (2017). *The psychology of criminal conduct* (6th ed.). New York, NY: Routledge.

Bonta, J., Blais, J., & Wilson, H. A. (2014). A theoretically informed meta-analysis of the risk for general and violent recidivism for mentally disordered offenders. *Aggression and Violent Behavior, 19*, 278–287.

Braham, L., Jones, D., & Hollin, C. R. (2008). The violent offender treatment program (VOTP): Development of a treatment program for violent patients in a high security psychiatric hospital. *International Journal of Forensic Mental Health, 7*, 157–172.

Brännström, L., Kaunitz, C., Andershed, A., South, S., & Smedslund, G. (2016). Aggression replacement training (ART) for reducing antisocial behavior in adolescents and adults: A systematic review. *Aggression and Violence Behavior, 27*, 30–41.

Brink, J., Doherty, D., & Boer, A. (2001). Mental disorder in federal offenders: A Canadian prevalence study. *International Journal of Law and Psychiatry, 24*, 339–356.

Burgess, R. L., & Akers, R. L. (1966). A differential association-reinforcement theory of criminal behavior. *Social Problems, 14*, 128–147.

Bush, J., & Brian, B. (1993). *Options: A cognitive change program.* Longmont, CO: National Institute of Corrections.

Bush, J., Glick, B., & Taymans, J. (1997). *Thinking for a change: Integrated cognitive behavior change program.* Washington, DC: National Institute of Corrections, U.S. Department of Justice.

Campbell, M. A., French, S., & Gendreau, P. (2009). The prediction of violence in adult offenders: A meta-analytic comparison of instruments and methods of assessment. *Criminal Justice and Behavior, 36*, 567–590.

Collaborative Outcome Data Committee. (2007). *Guidelines for the evaluation of sexual offender treatment outcome research (CODC Guidelines), part 2: User report 2007-03.* Ottawa, ON: Public Safety and Emergency Preparedness Canada.

Conn, C., Warden, R., Stuewig, J., Kim, E. H., Harty, L., Hastings, M., & Tangney, J. P. (2010). Borderline personality disorder among jail inmates: How common and how distinct? *Corrections Compendium, 4*, 6–13.

Cooke, B. J., & Farrington, D. P. (2016). The effectiveness of dog-training programs in prison: A systematic review and meta-analysis of the literature. *The Prison Journal, 96*, 854–876.

Cortoni, F., Nunes, K. & Latendresse, M. (2006). *An examination of the effectiveness of the violence prevention programme.* Research report R-178. Ottawa, ON: Correctional Service of Canada.

Daffern, M., Jones, L., & Shine, J. (Eds.). (2010). *Offence paralleling behaviour: An individualized approach to offender assessment and treatment.* Chichester, UK: Wiley.

Day, A., & Doyle, P. (2010). Violent offender rehabilitation and the therapeutic community model of treatment: Towards integrated service provision. *Aggression and Violent Behavior, 15*, 380–386.

Dell, C. A., & Poole, N. (2015). Taking a PAWS to reflect on how the work of a therapy dog supports a trauma-informed approach to prisoner health. *Journal of Forensic Nursing, 11*, 167–173.

Di Placedo, C., Simon, T. L., Witte, T. D., Gu, D., & Wong, S. C. P. (2006). Treatment of gang members can reduce recidivism and institutional misconduct. *Law and Human Behavior, 30*, 93–114.

DiGiuseppe, R., & Tafrate, R. C. (2003). Anger treatment for adults: A meta-analytic review. *Clinical Psychology Science and Practice, 10*, 70–84.

Douglas, K. S., Guy, L. S., & Hart, S. D. (2009). Psychosis as a risk factor for violence to others: A meta-analysis. *Psychological Bulletin, 135*, 679–706.

Douglas, K. S., Hart, S. D., Webster, C. D., & Belfrage, H. (2011). *Historical clinical risk management (version 3): Professional guidelines for evaluating risk of violence [Draft 2.1].* Vancouver, BC: Mental Health, Law, and Policy Institute, Simon Fraser University.

Douglas, K. S., & Kropp, P. R. (2002). A prevention-based paradigm for violence risk assessment: Clinical and research applications. *Criminal Justice and Behavior, 29*, 617–658.

Dowden, C., & Andrews, D. A. (2000). Effective correctional treatment and violent reoffending: A meta-analysis. *Canadian Journal of Criminology, 42*, 449–476.

Dowden, C., & Andrews, D. A. (2004). The importance of staff practice in delivering effective correctional treatment: A meta-analytic review of core correctional practice. *International Journal of Offender Therapy and Comparative Criminology, 48*, 203–214.

Frasier, S. N., & Vela, J. (2014). Dialectical behavior therapy for the treatment of anger and aggressive behavior: A review. *Aggression and Violent Behavior, 19*, 156–163.

Gendreau, P., Smith, P., & Thériault, Y. L. (2009). Chaos theory and correctional Treatment: Common sense, correctional quackery, and the law of fartcatchers. *Journal of Contemporary Criminal Justice, 25*, 384–396.

Goldstein, A. P., & Glick, B. (1987). *Aggression replacement training: A comprehensive intervention for aggressive youth.* Champaign, IL: Research.

Gordon, A., & Wong, S. (2009–2014). *Offense analogue behaviour (OAB) & offense replacement behaviour (ORB) rating guide.* Saskatoon: Psynergy Consulting and University of Saskatchewan.

Gordon, A., & Wong, S. C. P. (2010). Offense analogue behaviours as indicator of criminogenic need and treatment progress in custodial settings. In M. Daffern, L. Jones, & J. Shine (Eds.), *Offence paralleling behaviour: An individualized approach to offender assessment and treatment* (pp. 171–183). Chichester, UK: Wiley.

Hanson, R. K., Bourgon, G., McGrath, R. J., Kroner, D., D'Amora, D. A., Thomas, S. S., & Tavarez, L. P. (2017). *A five-level risk and needs system: Maximizing assessment results in corrections through the development of a common language.* Seattle, WA: Justice Center, Council of State Governments.

Hanson, R. K., & Morton-Bourgon, K. (2009). The accuracy of recidivism risk assessments for sexual offenders: A meta-analysis of 118 prediction studies. *Psychological Assessment, 21*(1), –21.

Hare, R. D. (1991). *Manual for the revised psychopathy checklist.* Toronto, ON: Multi-Health Systems.

Hare, R. D. (2003). *The Hare psychopathy checklist-revised* (2nd ed.). Toronto, ON: Multi-Health Systems.

Henggeler, S. W., Schoenwald, S. K., Borduin, C. M., Rowland, M. D., & Cunningham, P. B. (2009). *Multisystemic therapy for antisocial behavior in children and adolescents.* New York, NY: Guilford.

Hodgins, S. (1993). The criminality of mentally disordered persons. In S. Hodgins (Ed.), *Mental disorder and crime* (pp. 1–21). Newbury Park, CA: Sage.

Hodgins, S., & Coté, G. (1993). The criminality of mentally disordered offenders. *Criminal Justice and Behavior, 20*, 115–129.

Hodgins, S., Mednick, S. A., Brennan, P. A., Schulsinger, F., & Engberg, M. (1996). Mental disorder and crime: Evidence from a Danish birth cohort. *Archives of General Psychiatry, 53*, 489–496.

Hofmann, S. G., Sawyer, A. T., & Fang, A. (2010). The empirical status of the "new wave" of cognitive behavioral therapies. *Psychiatric Clinics of North America, 33*, 701–710.

Jolliffe, D., & Farrington, D. P. (2007, December). *A systematic review of the national and international evidence on the effectiveness of interventions with violent offenders, Series 16/07*. London, UK: Ministry of Justice Research.

Kabat-Zinn, J. (2005). *Coming to our sense: Healing ourselves and the world through mindfulness*. New York, NY: Hyperion.

King, E. A. (2017). Outcomes of trauma-informed interventions for incarcerated women: A review. *International Journal of Offender Therapy and Comparative Criminology, 61*, 667–688.

Kingston, D. A., Olver, M. E., Harris, M., Booth, B. D., Gulati, S., & Cameron, C. (2016). The relationship between mental illness and violence in a mentally disordered offender sample: Evaluating criminogenic and psychopathological predictors. *Psychology, Crime & Law, 22*, 678–700.

Kingston, D. A., Olver, M. E., Harris, M., Wong, S. C., & Bradford, J. M. (2015). The relationship between mental disorder and recidivism in sexual offenders. *International Journal of Forensic Mental Health, 14*, 10–22.

Kroner, D. G., & Makahashi, M. (2012). Every session counts: The differential impact of previous programmes and current programme dosage on offender recidivism. *Legal and Criminological Psychology, 17*, 136–150.

Kruger, K. A., & Serpell, J. A. (2006). Animal-assisted interventions in mental health: Definitions and theoretical foundations. In A. H. Fine (Ed.), *Handbook no animal-assisted therapy: Theoretical foundations and guidelines for practice* (2nd ed., pp. 21–38). San Diego, CA: Elsevier.

Landenberger, N. A., & Lipsey, M. W. (2005). The positive effects of cognitive-behavioral programs for offenders: A meta-analysis of factors associated with effective treatment. *Journal of Experimental Criminology, 1*, 451–476.

Latessa, E. J., Cullen, F. T., & Gendreau, P. (2002). Beyond correctional quackery: Professionalism and the possibility of effective treatment. *Federal Probation, 66*(2), 43–49.

Levenson, J., & Grady, M. (2016). Childhood adversity, substance abuse, and violence: Implications for trauma-informed social work practice. *Journal of Social Work Practice, 16*, 24–45.

Lewis, K., Olver, M. E., & Wong, S. C. P. (2013). The violence risk scale: Predictive validity and linking treatment changes with recidivism in a sample of high risk offenders with psychopathic traits. *Assessment, 20*, 150–164.

Linehan, M. (1993). *Cognitive-behavioral treatment of borderline personality disorder*. New York, NY: Guilford.

Lipsey, M. W. (2009). The primary factors that characterize effective interventions with juvenile offenders: A meta-analytic overview. *Victims and Offenders, 4*, 124–147.

Little, G. L., & Robinson, K. D. (1986). *How to escape your prison*. Memphis, TN: Eagle Wing Books.

Lowenkamp, C. T., Latessa, E. J., & Smith, P. (2006). Does correctional program quality really matter? The impact of adhering to the principles of effective intervention. *Criminology and Public Policy, 5*, 575–594.

MacKenzie, D. L., Wilson, D. B., & Kider, S. B. (2001). Effects of correctional boot camps on offending. *Annals of the American Academy of Political and Social Sciences, 578*, 126–143.

Miller, N. A., & Najavits, L. M. (2012). Creating trauma-informed correctional care: A balance of goals and environment. *European Journal of Psychotraumatology, 3*, 17246.

Miller, W. R., & Rollnick, S. (2002). *Motivational interviewing: Preparing people for change*. New York, NY: Guilford.

Mossman, D. (1994). Assessing predictions of violence: Being accurate about accuracy. *Journal of Consulting and Clinical Psychology, 62*, 783–792.

Olver, M. E., Lewis, K., & Wong, S. C. P. (2013). Risk reduction treatment of high risk psychopathic offenders: The relationship of psychopathy and treatment change to violent recidivism. *Personality Disorders: Theory, Research, and Treatment, 4*, 160–167.

Olver, M. E., Stockdale, K. C., & Wormith, J. S. (2014). Thirty years of research on the Level of Service scales: A meta-analytic examination of predictive accuracy and sources of variability. *Psychological Assessment, 26*, 156–176.

Olver, M. E., Stockdale, K. C., & Wormith, J. S. (2011). A meta-analysis of predictors of offender treatment attrition and its relationship to recidivism. *Journal of Consulting and Clinical Psychology, 79*, 6–21.

Öst, L. (2008). Efficacy of the third wave of behavioral therapies: A systematic review and meta-analysis. *Behavior Research and Therapy, 46*, 296–321.

Polaschek, D. L. L. (2011). High-intensity rehabilitation for violent offenders in New Zealand: Reconviction outcomes for high- and medium-risk prisoners. *Journal of Interpersonal Violence, 26*, 664–682.

Polaschek, D. L. L., & Kilgour, T. G. (2013). New Zealand's special treatment units: The development and implementation of intensive treatment for high risk male prisoners. *Psychology, Crime, & Law, 19*, 511–526.

Polaschek, D. L. L., Wilson, N. J., Townsend, M. R., & Daly, L. R. (2005). Cognitive-behavioral rehabilitation for high-risk violent offenders. An outcome evaluation of the violence prevention unit. *Journal of Interpersonal Violence, 20*, 1611–1627.

Polaschek, D. L. L., Yesberg, J. A., Bell, R. K., Casey, A. R., & Dickson, S. R. (2016). Intensive psychological treatment of high-risk violent offenders: Outcome and pre-release mechanisms. *Psychology, Crime, & Law, 22*, 344–365.

Public Safety Canada. (2016). *Corrections and conditional release statistical overview (2015)*. Public Safety Canada: Ottawa, ON Retrieved from http://www.publicsafety.gc.ca

Rezansoff, S. N., Moniruzzaman, A., Gress, C., & Somers, J. M. (2013). Psychiatric diagnoses and multiyear criminal recidivism in a Canadian provincial offender population. *Psychology, Public Policy, and Law, 19*, 443–453.

Rice, M. E., Harris, G. T., & Lang, C. (2013). Validation of and revision of the VRAG and SORAG: The Violence Risk Appraisal Guide—Revised (VRAG-R). *Psychological Assessment, 25*, 951–965.

Ross, R. R., & Fabiano, E. A. (1985). *Time to think: A cognitive model of delinquency prevention and offender rehabilitation*. Johnson City, TN: Institute of Social Sciences and Arts.

Saini, M. (2009). A meta-analysis of the psychological treatment of anger: Developing guidelines for evidence-based practice. *Journal of the American Academy of Psychiatry and Law, 37*, 473–488.

Simourd, D. J., & Olver, M. E. (2018, in press). Prescribed correctional treatment dosage: Cautions, commentary, and future directions. *Journal of Offender Rehabilitation*.

Shonin, E., Van Gordon, W., Slade, K., & Griffiths, M. D. (2013). Mindfulness and other Buddhist-derived interventions in correctional settings: A systematic review. *Aggression and Violent Behavior, 18*, 365–372.

Sutherland, E. H. (1947). *Principles of criminology* (4th ed.). Philadelphia, PA: Lippincott.

Swanson, J. (1994). Mental disorder, substance abuse, and community violence: An epidemiological approach. In J. Monahan & H. J. Steadman (Eds.), *Violence and mental disorder: Developments in risk assessment* (pp. 101–136). Chicago, IL: University of Chicago Press.

Swyers, K. (2014). Prison-Based Animal Programs (PAPs) and mental health outcome measures. University Honors Theses, Paper 29.

Taylor, R. (2000). A seven year reconviction study of HMP Grendon therapeutic community. Home Office Research Findings No. 115. London, UK: Home Office.

Tong, L. S., & Farrington, D. P. (2008). Effectiveness of reasoning and rehabilitation in reducing reoffending. *Psciothema, 20*(1), 20–28.

Van Voorhis, P., Wright, E. M., Salisbury, E., & Bauman, A. (2010). Women's risk factors and their contributions to existing risk/needs assessment: The current status of a gender responsive supplement. *Criminal Justice and Behavior, 37*, 261–288.

Ward, T., Mann, R. E., & Gannon, T. A. (2007). The good lives model of offender rehabilitation: Clinical implications. *Aggression and Violent Behavior, 12*, 87–107.

Ware, J., Ciepulcha, C., & Matsuo, D. (2011). The violent offenders therapeutic programme (VOTP)—Rationale and effectiveness. *Australasian Journal of Correctional Staff Development, 6*, 1–12.

Wilson, D. B., Bouffard, L. A., & MacKenzie, D. L. (2005). A quantitative review of structured, group-oriented, cognitive-behavioral programs for offenders. *Criminal Justice and Behavior, 32*, 172–204.

Wong, S., & Gordon, A. E. (1999–2003). *The violence risk scale.* Saskatoon, SK: Regional Psychiatric Centre and University of Saskatchewan.

Wong, S. C. P., & Gordon, A. (2006). The validity and reliability of the violence risk scale: A treatment-friendly violence risk assessment tool. *Psychology, Public Policy, and Law, 12*, 279–309.

Wong, S. C. P., & Gordon, A. (2013). The violence reduction programme: A treatment programme for violence-prone forensic clients. *Psychology, Crime & Law, 19*, 461–475.

Wong, S. C. P., Gordon, A., & Gu, D. (2007). Assessment and treatment of violence-prone forensic clients: An integrated approach. *British Journal of Psychiatry, 190*(Suppl), s66–s74.

Wong, S. C. P., Gordon, A., Gu, D., Lewis, K., & Olver, M. E. (2012). The effectiveness of violence reduction treatment for psychopathic offenders: Empirical evidence and a treatment model. *International Journal of Forensic Mental Health, 11*, 336–349.

Wong, S. C. P., Vander Veen, S., Leis, T. A., Parrish, H., Gu, D., Usher Liber, E., & Middleton, H. L. (2005). Reintegrating seriously violent and personality-disordered offenders from a supermaximum security institution into the general offender population. *International Journal of Offender Therapy and Comparative Criminology, 49*, 362–375.

Yang, M., Wong, S. C. P., & Coid, J. (2010). The efficacy of violence prediction: A meta-analytic comparison of nine risk assessment tools. *Psychological Bulletin, 136*, 740–767.

Chapter 8
Assessing and Treating Psychopaths

Jennifer Vitale

Estimated to comprise up to 50% of incarcerated offender populations, psychopathic individuals are recognizable to most legal and correctional professionals. Long represented in the clinical literature (e.g., Pinel, 1806) but differentiated most comprehensively from other offender types in Cleckley's (1941/1996) "The Mask of Sanity", the psychopathic personality is characterized by distinctive affective, interpersonal, and behavioral features. Central to most conceptualizations of the syndrome is a selfish, callous lack of emotional connection to others, combined with superficial charm, irresponsibility, impulsivity, and chronic antisocial behavior (Cleckley, 1941/1996; Cooke, Michie, & Hart, 2006; Hare, 1991; Lykken, 1995). This chapter will: (1) Provide background on the conceptualization of psychopathy and differentiate it from antisocial personality disorder; (2) Summarize relevant data on baserates of psychopathy across groups and cultures; (3) Review the relatively limited literature on treatment for psychopathy; and (4) Make recommendations for improving our knowledge and use of psychological interventions in this group.

8.1 Conceptualization and Assessment of Psychopathy

In the years since Cleckley highlighted the syndrome, researchers and clinicians have repeatedly affirmed the need to distinguish these individuals from other antisocial types (Hare, 2016; Lykken, 1995; Verona, Sprague, & Sadeh, 2012). In particular, the differences between psychopathy and Antisocial Personality Disorder (ASPD) as assessed by various editions of the Diagnostic and Statistical Manual (DSM) of the American Psychiatric Association (APA, 2013) have been

J. Vitale (✉)
Hampden-Sydney College, Hampden-Sydney, VA, USA
e-mail: jvitale@hsc.edu

© Springer Nature Switzerland AG 2018   173
M. Ternes et al. (eds.), *The Practice of Correctional Psychology*,
https://doi.org/10.1007/978-3-030-00452-1_8

emphasized (e.g., Crego & Widiger, 2015; Verona et al., 2012). Although the DSM has historically included criteria for sociopathy or antisocial personality disorder that overlap with characteristics of the prototypical psychopath (e.g., selfishness, guiltlessness, callousness, impulsivity), these criteria were not meant to identify this subgroup of antisocial individuals, specifically. Further, as the DSM moved towards limiting the criteria for ASPD to more specific behavioral criteria (e.g., conduct disorder present before age 15, repeatedly performing acts that are grounds for arrest), there was increasing likelihood of excluding some individuals who would be considered psychopathic using Cleckley's criteria and—even more likely—including many who would not. Because of the much higher prevalence of APSD (roughly 2–3 times greater than psychopathy) there will be many individuals who meet DSM criteria for ASPD who are not psychopathic (Hare & Neumann, 2008; Ogloff, 2006).

Given that the DSM classification of ASPD does not effectively distinguish between those antisocial individuals with and without psychopathic features, assessment tools designed to capture the psychopathy syndrome were developed. The most influential amongst these have been Hare's psychopathy Checklist and its progeny (i.e., the Psychopathy Checklist-Revised, the Psychopathy Checklist: Screening Version, and the Psychopathy Checklist: Youth Version). The Psychopathy Checklist-Revised (PCL-R; Hare, 2003), in particular, has risen to prominence as the most accepted diagnostic tool and the standard against which other psychopathy assessment instruments are typically measured (Fulero, 1995; Hare, 2016).

8.1.1 Assessing Psychopathy Using the PCL-R

Designed to identify the psychopathic individual as conceptualized by Cleckley and others in the clinical literature (see Table 8.1 for a comparison of Cleckley criteria and PCL-R items) the PCL-R is composed of 30 items which are rated as 0 "not applicable to the individual", 1 "applicable only to a certain extent", or 2 "applicable to the individual" based on information obtained from semi-structured interviews and file reviews. Items tap the interpersonal (e.g., "superficial charm"), affective (e.g., "lack of remorse or guilt"), and impulsive/antisocial lifestyle (e.g., "irresponsibility, juvenile delinquency") features of the syndrome. The measure has a four-factor structure (Hare, 2016; Neumann, Hare, & Newman, 2007), which can be used to model a higher-order two factor model (Hare & Neumann, 2008) where Factor 1 (F1) captures the interpersonal/affective features of the syndrome, and Factor 2 (F2) captures the lifestyle/antisocial features. Despite the existence of unique correlates of Factors 1 and 2 (Dolan & Anderson, 2003; Salekin, Neumann, Leistico, & Zalot, 2004), Hare and colleagues (e.g., Hare, 2003, 2016; Neumann et al., 2007) have argued that there is not good evidence to suggest that any one component of psychopathy is primary over any other and that psychopathy is best conceptualized as a unidimensional construct. Further, although there is some taxonomic evidence suggesting the scale reflects a continuous construct (e.g., Guay,

Table 8.1 Cleckley criteria (Cleckley, 1941/1996) and PCL-R items (Hare, 1991, 2003)

Cleckley criteria	PCL-R items
Superficial charm and good "intelligence"	Glibness/superficial charm
Pathologic egocentricity and incapacity for love	Grandiose sense of self-worth
Untruthfulness and insincerity	Need for stimulation/Proneness to boredom
General poverty in major affective reactions	Conning/manipulative
Unresponsiveness in general interpersonal relations	Pathological lying
Lack of remorse or shame	Shallow affect
Inadequately motivated antisocial behavior	Lack of remorse or guilt
Poor judgement and failure to learn by experience	Callous/lack of empathy
Unreliability	Poor behavioral controls
Specific loss of insight	Parasitic lifestyle
Fantastic and uninviting behavior with (or without) drink	Promiscuous sexual behavior
Failure to follow any life plan	Lack of realistic, long-term goals
Sex life impersonal, trivial, and poorly integrated	Early behavior problems
Absence of delusions and other signs of irrational thinking	Irresponsibility
Absence of nervousness or psychoneurotic manifestations	Impulsivity
Suicide rarely carried out	Failure to accept responsibility
	Many short-term marital relationships
	Juvenile delinquency
	Revocation of conditional release
	Criminal versatility

Ruscio, Knight, & Hare, 2007; Walters, Ermer, Knight, & Kiehl, 2015), a total score of 30 or higher has typically been used in the United States and Canada as a threshold for classifying individuals as psychopathic; In European samples, a slightly lower cut-score of 25 or 26 has been recommended (Cooke & Michie, 1999).

With its inclusion of items directly assessing criminality (e.g., "revocation of conditional release", "criminal versatility") as well as the reliance on extensive collateral information, the PCL-R is well-suited for use in correctional or other forensic settings. It has also proven to be a powerful predictor of general, violent, and sexual reoffending (Hare, 1996; Hemphill, Templeman, Wong, & Hare, 1998). As a result, the instrument is commonly used for risk assessment, management, and monitoring (Hurducas, Singh, de Ruiter, & Petrila, 2014; Neal & Grisso, 2014).

The reliance on the PCL-R for assessing psychopathy has been criticized by those researchers and practitioners concerned that the criminality and/or violence captured by the PCL-R items may not be a "core" feature of the psychopathy syndrome (e.g., Bishopp & Hare, 2008; Cooke et al., 2006; Lilienfeld, 1994). These critics note that although Cleckley (1941/1996) included "inadequately motivated antisocial behavior" among his original 16 criteria, criminal behavior (and specifically violent criminal behavior) was not viewed as a necessary component of the syndrome.

As a result of these concerns, alternative measures of the psychopathy construct have been developed that place significantly less emphasis on the overtly criminal behavior of these individuals and focus instead on other behavioral and personality features of the disorder. These instruments typically involve self-reports of behavior and personality traits, and include the Psychopathic Personality Inventory (PPI; Lilienfeld & Andrews, 1996) and the Triarchic Psychopathy Measure (TriPM; Brislin, Drislane, Smith, Edens, & Patrick, 2015; Patrick, Fowles, & Krueger, 2009). However, although there has been an increase in the use of these instruments to assess psychopathy, particularly in community samples and for research purposes, the PCL-R continues to dominate research and practice within institutional settings.

8.1.1.1 Use of the PCL-R Across Populations

Of direct interest to those using the PCL-R in applied settings is the generalizability of the instrument to alternative samples (e.g., Cooke & Michie, 1999; Kosson, Smith, & Newman, 1990; Sullivan, Abramowitz, Lopez, & Kosson, 2006; Sullivan & Kosson, 2006; Verona & Vitale, 2006). Because much of the early research using the PCL-R was limited to samples of incarcerated, European American males in the US and Canada, there was for many years little evidence to support the generalizability of the measure and associated construct across other populations. Such work is crucial, as differences in the expression of psychopathy across cultural groups, race, or gender would have important implications for the use of the PCL-R in applied settings. Moreover, while there has been an increase in research focused on the correlation and expression of psychopathy in other groups, particularly female offenders and minority (i.e., African-American and Latino) offenders (see Beryl, Chou, & Völlm, 2014; Verona & Vitale, 2006; Sullivan & Kosson, 2006 for reviews), the results of these investigations have not always been clear-cut. For example, although there is good evidence for the reliability of psychopathy assessments among female populations (see Beryl et al., 2014; Verona & Vitale, 2006) and across racial and cultural groups (see Sullivan & Kosson, 2006) the evidence for the generalizability of behavioral and etiology-relevant correlates of psychopathy across gender and race is less consistent.

Among samples of African American offenders, key deficits in emotion-related responding and attention processing, well-documented among European American male offenders, have not been reliably demonstrated (e.g., Baskin-Sommers, Newman, Sathasivam, & Curtin, 2011; Lorenz & Newman, 2002; Newman, Schmitt, & Voss, 1997). Further, research with female offenders has found only limited evidence for the presence of expected deficits in emotion-related responding and passive avoidance learning (e.g., Anton, Baskin-Sommers, Vitale, Curtin, & Newman, 2012; Vitale, MacCoon, & Newman, 2011; Vitale & Newman, 2001).

There may also be gender and race differences in the relationship between PCL-R assessed psychopathy and violence, a possibility with clear implications for use of the instrument in applied settings. Walsh (2013) showed that in a sample of

424 adult male jail inmates, PCL-R scores were a better predictor of violence among European American offenders than among either African American or Latino offenders. Similarly, Edens, Campbell, and Weir (2007) reported meta-analytic results suggesting that within ethnically diverse juvenile samples, psychopathy was a weaker correlate of violent recidivism than within primarily European American samples. These differences may also be observed across gender, as research provides some evidence that psychopathy may be a less powerful predictor of recidivism in incarcerated female samples (Weizmann-Henelius, Virkkunen, Gammelgard, Eronen, & Putkonen, 2015).

Some of these observed differences across race and gender may be associated with macro-level variables that differ across populations. For example, in a large-scale (n = 33,016; 58% female/42% male) study that examined Self-Report Psychopathy Scale (SRP) scores across gender and world regions, Neumann, Schmitt, Carter, Embley, and Hare (2012) found that in their female sample, Gross Domestic Product per capita (GDPpc) was negatively correlated with the expression of the interpersonal/affective traits associated with psychopathy, suggesting an association between GDPpc and the expression of core psychopathy features. Because the authors did not provide data for males on this correlate, it is not possible to determine if this finding is specific to females. Nevertheless, it emphasizes the possibility that the expression of psychopathy may be influenced by environmental factors. Consistent with this possibility, at least one study has shown that Socioeconomic Status (SES) moderates the relationship between psychopathy and crime differently across race, as Walsh and Kosson (2007) found a significant SES × psychopathy interaction on recidivism among European American but not African American participants.

In summary:

- PCL-R assessed psychopathy has emerged as a crucial construct within forensic and correctional settings (DeMatteo et al., 2014).
- The PCL-R is generally correlated with criminal recidivism, although the predictive power of the instrument may be somewhat weaker in female and minority offender samples.
- The PCL-R can be used reliably across diverse populations, but there may be some group differences in the expression of the syndrome and in the deficits associated with the syndrome.

8.2 Prevalence of Psychopathy

Overall, the baserate of PCL-R assessed psychopathy in offender populations has been reported between 10% and 15% in forensic psychiatric settings, and 15–50% in non-psychiatric prison populations (Hare, 1991, 2003; Herve, Mitchell, & Cooper, 2004; Salekin, Rogers, Ustad, & Sewell, 1998). Rates appear to differ, however, across gender and racial and cultural groups.

8.2.1   North American Samples Versus European Samples

In keeping with the recommendation for a lower cut-score when working with European populations, there is a significant difference between the mean PCL-R scores of incarcerated North American offenders ($M = 22.1$; $SD = 7.9$) and those of incarcerated European offenders ($M = 17.5$; $SD = 7.3$) (Sullivan & Kosson, 2006). However, the difference in mean scores between psychiatric samples (i.e., patients or inmates in psychiatric or secure hospitals) across North America and Europe are considerably smaller, with a mean of 21.5 (6.9) in North American samples and 22.5 (8.0) in European samples. Taken together, these data may not reflect differences in overall levels of the syndrome across nations, but instead may be due to differences in how mentally disordered offenders are classified and placed within different nations' legal systems (Hobson & Shine, 1998), as well as differences in overall baserates of incarceration across countries (Rasmussen, Storsæter, & Levander, 1999). The baserates of psychopathy across nations also vary widely, with North American populations typically showing higher percentages of those meeting a threshold for psychopathy (i.e., PCL-R $\geq$ 30) than European nations. Interestingly, this difference maintains even when lower cut-scores are employed in the European samples.

8.2.2   Male Samples Versus Female Samples

There are well-documented differences in the mean scores and baserates of psychopathy between male and female offender populations (see Verona & Vitale, 2006 for a review). Although there are a small number of studies that show base rates of psychopathy in women similar to those in men when using the PCL-R and the traditional cut-score for psychopathy, the majority of studies using PCL measures (i.e., PCL-R, PCL-YV, PCL-SV) with female offenders have found lower rates of psychopathy, with reported prevalence rates for female offender samples as low as 6% (Jackson, Rogers, Neumann, & Lambert, 2002), and several falling between 11% and 17% (e.g., O'Connor, 2001; Salekin, Rogers, & Sewell, 1997; Strand & Belfrage, 2005; Warren et al., 2003).

Similarly, in their self-report psychopathy study within community samples across nations, Neumann et al. (2012) found that levels of SRP-assessed psychopathy were generally lower for females than for males across world regions. This finding is consistent with studies that have found differences in the mean scores for males and females in institutionalized samples using the PCL-R and the PCL: SV, as well as in undergraduate, noninstitutionalized, and adolescent samples (see Verona & Vitale, 2006).

8.2.3   African American Samples Versus European American Samples

There has been an important shift in interpretation of mean scores and baserates of psychopathy among African American offender populations. Early reviews, based on a relatively limited number of samples, highlighted differences in mean PCL-R scores across racial groups, with African American offenders attaining higher scores than European American offenders (e.g., Cooke, Kosson, & Michie, 2001; Kosson et al., 1990). These data lead some to conclude that psychopathy rates were elevated in this group (Lynn, 2002). However, as research has accumulated, this conclusion has been challenged. In a meta-analysis of 21 studies (n = 8890), only a small (i.e., an average of less than 1 point)—albeit statistically significant—difference in PCL-R total scores across race was found (Skeem, Edens, Camp, & Colwell, 2004), disputing the argument that levels of psychopathy differ in any clinically meaningful way between African American and European American samples.

In summary:

- Overall rates of psychopathy are elevated in offender populations relative to community samples.
- Baserates for psychopathy are higher in North American prison samples than in European prison samples.
- Baserates for psychopathy are lower in female samples, relative to male samples.
- Baserates for psychopathy are similar across Blacks and Whites in North American samples.

8.3   Intervention: What Works, What Might Work, What Doesn't Work

Despite the prominence pf psychopathic individuals within the criminal justice system, there is an unfortunate paucity of research on the effectiveness of treatment for the syndrome. As a result of the absence of controlled studies of treatment for psychopathic individuals, it is difficult—if not impossible—to differentiate clearly those techniques or programs that might have some benefit for these individuals from those that do not (D'Silva, Duggan, & McCarthy, 2004; Reidy, Kearns, & DeGue, 2013). Interventions tailored specifically to this group are rare, and when psychopathic individuals are included in treatments with other offenders, the impact of these treatments on this key subgroup are not always explored. Further, when the response of these individuals to these treatments is examined, the interpretation of these results can be difficult. In a striking example of this challenge, D'Silva et al. (2004) were forced to abandon a planned meta-analysis when it was discovered that there was an insufficient number of appropriate studies (i.e., controlled treatment studies involving PCL-assessed psychopathy) to conduct the analysis. Further, studies often do not provide sufficient detail regarding the specific therapeutic techniques/programs utilized, and do not employ the same treatments more than once, thereby limited the evidence for any particular approach. As a result, it is difficult to draw firm conclusions.

These limitations of the literature are due at least in part to the prevailing belief that psychopathic individuals are not only resistant to treatment, but that treatment could have an adverse effect on them (D'Silva et al., 2004; Polaschek, 2014). For a number of years, most professionals' answer to the question of "what works" for treating psychopathic individuals was "nothing". Discussions were dominated by this argument, which was based primarily on a limited set of studies in combination with theoretical models that conceptualized the psychopathic individual as untreatable (e.g., Cleckley, 1941/1996; Lykken, 1995).

In recent years, however, there has been an increase in researchers' willingness to consider that this position may not be well-substantiated by the existing literature. As a result, there is more interest in examining the impact of existing treatment on psychopathy and in pioneering new approaches to treating this challenging group. Although there is still significant ground to be gained, research is beginning to suggest that the answer to the question "what works" might be a somewhat more optimistic—if still relatively cautious—"some things, for some psychopathic individuals, under some conditions".

Two issues should be separated in discussions of the treatment of psychopathic offenders. The first is the question of whether existing treatments used within offender populations are more, less, or equally effective for psychopathic offenders as for nonpsychopathic offenders. If existing treatments are effective for most offenders, regardless of their psychopathy designation, then there would be less need to devise psychopathy-specific treatment programs. The second issue follows directly from this proposal, and involves the potential benefits of tailoring treatments to psychopathy based on existing causal models of the syndrome. Given these issues, in the next section, the literature on the treatability of psychopathic individuals will be reviewed, and a description of one psychopathy-specific treatment approach that has been tested and presented in the literature will be provided.

8.3.1 Are Psychopathic Individuals Less Responsive to Treatment Than Nonpsychopathic Offenders?

There is evidence that community and correctional interventions can be effective in reducing criminal behavior, particularly when these treatments are structured, behavior-oriented, targeted towards those with greatest need (i.e., high-risk offenders), and focused on relevant areas (e.g., procriminal attitudes) (Bonta & Andrews, 2015). Given that psychopathic individuals commit a disproportionate amount of violent and nonviolent crime, it would be useful to determine if psychopathy status impacts the effectiveness of these treatments.

The question of effectiveness of treatment for psychopathy can be addressed multiple ways: First, researchers can work to determine if treatment positively impacts psychopathic individuals' criminal behaviors and attitudes and if the magnitude of these individuals' treatment gains are similar to those of nonpsychopathic individuals. Second, clinical researchers can test for changes in the affective and interpersonal features of psychopathy as a result of treatment. Third, the in-treatment behaviors of psychopathic individuals can be compared to those of nonpsychopathic participants. Even if research was to demonstrate clearly that psychopathic individuals who complete treatment can benefit from these programs, if they are as less likely than other offenders to comply with or complete treatment, then this would suggest a need for treatment innovation. Currently, most research has focused on the first and third approaches, although there is increasing interest in understanding treatment impact beyond effects on violent and/or criminal behavior.

Richards, Casey, and Lucente (2003) examined the impact of three different treatment settings on substance use/abuse and criminal behavior within a sample of 404 women incarcerated in a maximum security setting. The treatment approach in each setting emphasized either a cognitive–behavioral orientation with focus on skill building and attitude change or a Heuristic System orientation, which focused on treatment tailored to the individual within the context of their addiction history. Regardless of the treatment orientation, results at follow-up showed that psychopathy predicted violence during treatment (although not at release) and also nonviolent recidivism. Women scoring 30 or higher on the PCL-R were excluded from the study, however, which limits the interpretation of these data. While it is possible that these high-scoring individuals would have shown even greater levels of violent behavior and recidivism, there may also be differences in the treatment responses of high PCL-R scorers (i.e., $\geq$30) that cannot be observed in these data.

Olver and Wong (2009) reported on recidivism within a sample of incarcerated sex offenders who received treatment as part of a 6–8 month cognitive-behaviorally oriented treatment that emphasized relapse prevention. Results showed that treated psychopathic individuals recidivated at a faster rate and showed a smaller decline in their risk for violence than treated nonpsychopathic individuals. A similar pattern was observed by Looman, Abracen, Serin, and Marquis (2005), who found that psychopathic individuals treated in a residential program emphasizing a cognitive-behavioral approach showed higher recidivism than nonpsychopathic individuals treated in the program.

Taken together, these studies suggest that treatment will be ineffective for most psychopathic individuals. However, this conclusion is hindered by the absence of untreated psychopathy comparison groups. Given that psychopathy is closely associated with violence and recidivism, even psychopathic individuals who have benefited from therapeutic intervention would likely continue to exhibit higher rates of antisocial behavior than nonpsychopathic individuals. A more useful comparison would be between those psychopathic individuals who have received treatment and those who have not.

Abracen, Looman, Ferguson, Harkins, and Mailoux (2011) conducted such a study, comparing the recidivism of a sample of sex offenders (including psychopathic individuals) participating in an inpatient, cognitive-behavioral relapse prevention treatment with a matched sample of untreated offenders. Unfortunately, no differences between the treated and untreated groups were observed for violent, sexual reconvictions, psychopathy classification notwithstanding. In the absence of a treatment effect for nonpsychopathic offenders, it is difficult to conclude that the psychopathic individuals were resistant to treatment, specifically.

Two additional studies that have examined reoffending and have played an especially influential role in shaping perceptions of psychopathic individuals' amenability to treatment were conducted by Harris, Rice, and Cormier (1994) and Seto and Barbaree (1999). Further, these studies are most often among those cited when referencing the intractability of the syndrome or the possibility that treatment will exacerbate psychopathic individuals' violent and criminal behavior.

In the study by Harris et al. (1994), the authors retrospectively assigned psychopathy scores to a group of incarcerated offenders who had participated in an intensive therapeutic community from 1968 to 1978. In their analysis, the authors compared the treatment group of 176 patients with a matched group of untreated offenders at an average 10-year follow-up. Using a cut score of 25 on the PCL-R, the authors found that treatment did not have a beneficial effect on the recidivism rates of the psychopathic offenders. The results of this study have been particularly impactful on the basis of the additional finding that the 10.5 year violent recidivism rate for treated psychopathic offenders was *higher* than that of the untreated psychopathic comparison group (77% versus 55%, respectively). As a result, this study has been used to support the proposal that psychopathic individuals actually deteriorate as a result of their participation in treatment.

In recent years, the Harris et al. (1994) study and the conclusions drawn from it have faced criticism. Primary among these critiques has been the nature of the treatment program itself, which was geared towards breaking down unconscious defense mechanisms, was non-voluntary, primarily peer-led, and included nontraditional and potentially ethically questionable practices such as isolation, nudity, and administration of hallucinogenic drugs (e.g., LSD) (D'Silva et al., 2004; de Ruiter, Chakhssi, & Bernstein, 2016; Polaschek, 2015). Given that by the time of the Harris et al. study's publication such treatment practices would have been considered outdated—if not actively harmful—the results of the program seem, at best, irrelevant to the question of psychopathy treatment today.

Whereas critiques of Harris et al. (1994) emphasize primarily the failure to consider the quality of the treatment provided, other issues have arisen regarding the review of Seto and Barbaree (1999). In this study, the authors examined rates of reoffending among participants in a sex offender treatment program at a 23-month follow-up. Not only did psychopathic individuals fail to benefit from treatment, the results showed that it was the psychopathic sex offenders who exhibited the most positive in-session behavior who were the ones most likely to seriously reoffend at follow-up—a troubling finding, to say the least. There are two important caveats, however. First, Barbaree (2005) has since highlighted the importance of examining treatment outcomes over time, rather than drawing strong conclusions from immediate results. In a follow-up study of these same participants that included data from 3, 5, and 6 years post-treatment, no significant association between psychopathic in-patient behavior and likelihood of reoffending was found (Barbaree, 2005), suggesting that the earlier result was not stable. Second, psychopathy in the original study was defined by a median split on the PCL-R, resulting in a cut-score of 15. The authors also noted that the observed effect maintained even when a lower cut-score of 10 was utilized. Given that it would be unlikely that most clinicians and researchers would conceptualize an individual with a score of 11 on the PCL-R (on which scores range from 0 to 40) as "psychopathic", these results may be illuminating less the impact of treatment on those with high-scores on the PCL-R and, instead, be providing some important information specific to the recidivism and treatment response of particularly low-scoring individuals (i.e., offenders with scores less than 10).

Results from Draycott, Short, and Kirkpatrick (2015) also affirm that initial outcomes should be accepted cautiously and that follow-up data is necessary to demonstrate the stability of change (positive *or* negative). In their earlier study, which examined the responses of individuals at different levels of psychopathy to a treatment that utilized a primarily cognitive-behavioral approach in a small group setting, the authors found that at a 9-month follow-up, psychopathic offenders exhibited significantly higher levels of interpersonal dominance than the non-psychopathic participants, suggesting that the treatment might have had an adverse rather than beneficial effect on their interpersonal functioning (Draycott, Askari, & Kirkpatrick, 2011). However, in a follow-up study Draycott et al. (2015) showed that at 33 months post-treatment, the levels of interpersonal dominance amongst these individuals had returned to baseline levels. While it is unclear what accounted for this pattern of change, the result shows that apparently negative changes in psychopathic functioning exhibited during and immediately after treatment may not reflect lasting negative change.

Positive therapeutic changes may be also unstable. Skeem, Monahan, and Mulvey (2002) examined high psychopathy patients receiving outpatient treatments (primarily therapy, or therapy + medication) and found that at initial follow-up, psychopathic individuals who had received "intensive" outpatient treatment (i.e., seven or more sessions) showed reduced violence compared to those psychopathic individuals who had received fewer than seven sessions. Unfortunately, this difference was not significant at the later follow-ups periods.

More promising data come from Chakhssi, deRuiter, and Berstein (2010), who examined the treatment outcomes of 74 personality-disordered male offenders in in-patient forensic hospitals in the Netherlands. These programs typically emphasize a cognitive-behavioral approach with an emphasis on relapse prevention (de Ruiter et al., 2016). Psychopathy classification was based on PCL-R scores determined by file reviews, and a cut-score of 26 was used to designate patients as psychopathic (n = 27). Consistent with their in-patient placement, offenders in the sample had been convicted of violent crimes, including homicide, sexual assault, and violent robbery, and the mean time in treatment was approximately 4 years.

Outcome measurements included assessment of risk-relevant institutional behaviors using the Behavioral Status Index (BEST-Index), which includes four categories: social skills, insight, interpersonal hostility, and physical violence, capturing adaptive social behavior, communication skills, level of insight, and attribution of responsibility, among other specific behaviors/attitudes.

Patients were assessed 6 months following admission and then at 6 month intervals after that. When psychopathic and non-psychopathic offenders were compared on the BSI, the results showed no significant differences between groups on total score, nor in the areas of social skills, insight, or interpersonal hostility; both groups showed some improvement in these areas over the course of treatment (Chakhssi et al., 2010). However, there was a significant time by group interaction for violent behavior, which was associated with a small improvement for non-psychopathic offenders and a slight deterioration for psychopathic individuals. Additional analyses showed that this deterioration was attributable to a small subgroup (22%) of the psychopathic offenders. Similar findings are reported by Hildebrand and de Ruiter (2012), who found little difference in the treatment outcomes in a group of inpatient offenders classified using a PCL-R median split (PCL-R = 22) on risk factors for violence including egocentrism, hostility, impulsivity, lack of insight, and negative and distrustful attitudes.

Wong, Gordon, Gu, Lewis, and Olver (2012) also provide evidence for a positive impact of treatment, with a focus on reductions in psychopathic violence. Their study assessed violent and sexual reoffending amongst offenders who participated in the Clearwater Program, a high-intensity (i.e., 15–20 contact hours per week), residential, cognitive-behaviorally oriented program meant for moderate- to high-risk offenders. The authors showed that psychopathic offenders were more likely to fail in treatment than nonpsychopathic offenders, although the overall completion rate by psychopathic participants was still high (73%). However, post-release follow-up revealed that psychopathic individuals who had completed the program showed significantly reduced rates of violent recidivism relative to those who did not complete treatment (60.6% vs. 91.7%), as well as nonsignificant reductions in sexual reoffending (42.2% vs. 50%). Although the study is limited as a result of the absence of a true matched comparison group, it does provide some preliminary evidence that psychopathic violence can be reduced through the implementation of intensive treatment.

8.3.2 Psychopathic Individuals' In-Treatment Behavior

The poor prognosis for psychopathic individuals may have been exaggerated historically, and claims of psychopathic intractability overstated. However, there is substantial evidence to indicate that this group is particularly challenging to treat. Although the conclusions drawn from early studies may have been too absolute, there is consistent evidence that, compared to nonpsychopathic offenders, psychopathic individuals show poorer program adjustment and higher attrition (e.g., Berger, Rotermund, Vieth, & Hohnhorst, 2012; Hobson, Shine, & Roberts, 2000; Hornsveld, Kraaimaat, Muris, Zwets, & Kanters, 2015; Olver & Wong, 2009; Richards et al., 2003), as well as more disruptive and noncompliant behavior in treatment (Hare, Clark, Grann, & Thornton, 2000; Hildebrand & de Ruiter, 2012; Hildebrand, de Ruiter, & Nijman, 2004).

Based on the review of the treatment literature, several points emerge:

- The historical view that psychopathic individuals are "untreatable" reflects an overreliance on particular findings and a focus on potentially unreliable outcomes.
- Some evidence suggests that adult offenders with psychopathy who complete intensive CBT and risk-reduction oriented treatment programs respond similarly to these interventions as nonpsychopathic offenders.
- There is ample evidence that psychopathic individuals are more likely to be disruptive in treatment and do not retain in treatment at the same rates as non-psychopathic individuals.
- The treatment literature has been limited by a prevailing, pessimistic prognosis, potentially resulting in the exclusion of these individuals from treatment research and undermining interest in developing novel treatments for this group.
- Despite renewed interest in the treatment possibilities surrounding the psychopathy syndrome, the literature remains inadequate for determining "best practice" in the area.

The next sections address two areas of potential growth: The first of these areas involves treatment for adolescents with psychopathic traits. The second involves treatments designed specifically to address the etiological processes theorized to underlie the psychopathy syndrome.

8.3.3   Treatment for Adolescents with Psychopathic Traits

As for adults, evidence for the effectiveness of specific treatments with adolescents with psychopathic features is limited, although some data are accumulating to suggest that treatment may make a positive impact in this group. For example, Gretton, McBride, Hare, and O'Shaughnessy (2000) compared the long-term (~10 year) outcomes of adolescent sex offenders categorized as psychopathic using the PCL:YV (cutscore of 30) who had either completed or failed to complete an outpatient, sexual offender treatment program. Although there were no differences between the two groups for rates of nonviolent reoffending or sexual reoffending, high scorers who completed treatment showed significantly lower rates of violent reoffending (33% versus 88%). Although improvement appeared to be limited only to outcomes involving violent reoffending, this finding does suggest some impact of treatment on these individuals.

Caldwell (2011) reported on a sample of male juvenile delinquents participating in an intensive treatment for highly aggressive delinquent boys. The program was housed in a secure juvenile detention facility on the grounds of a state psychiatric and forensic hospital. The program emphasized high levels of contact, with one social worker, one psychologist, and a half psychiatry position for every 20 juveniles. The day-to-day running of the program was overseen by a psychiatric nurse manager (versus security staff), and on-unit programming was controlled on a daily basis by mental health staff (Caldwell & Van Rybroek, 2005).

The treatment model used was based on Monroe, Van Rybroek, and Maier's (1988) concept of "decompression", which is geared towards reducing antagonism between juveniles and service providers, and decreasing withdrawal from treatment. Rather than removing juveniles from treatment, this approach moves towards individualized treatment when increased security precautions are needed.

Psychopathy was assessed using the PCL: Youth Version and data was collected on institutional behavior, as well as reoffending at a mean follow-up of 54 months. Results showed that treatment overall was related to significant improvement in behavioral outcomes. Juveniles who participated in the treatment were charged with significantly fewer re-offenses than a comparison group.

Importantly, scores for the affective, behavioral, and antisocial facets of the PCL:YV, were *not* associated with behavioral outcomes at the conclusion of treatment, providing evidence that these features did not moderate the impact of treatment (Caldwell, 2011). Further, although scores on the interpersonal facet were associated with behavior scores at admission, there was no difference in behavioral outcomes for high versus low scorers on this facet at the final time point. In other words, those with high interpersonal facet scores showed the greatest improvement in behavioral outcomes, in part because there was a significant amount of ground to gain.

Similarly, Salekin, Tippey, and Allen (2012) showed that a secure facility treatment program meant to increase motivation and positive emotion, and decrease callousness in youth with conduct problems was associated with a significant decrease in psychopathy scores. Further, this reduction occurred across the callous/interpersonal, affective, and impulsivity trait domains of psychopathy.

While others have examined the results of interventions targeted directly to adolescents with significant behavioral problems, McDonald, Dodson, Rosenfield, and Jouriles (2011) examined the impact of an intervention geared towards mothers of individuals with conduct issues. Project Support (Jouriles et al., 2010) is an intervention program geared towards teaching child behavior management skills and providing instrumental and emotional support to mothers. The intervention is administered through 1–1.5 h in-home sessions provided roughly once a week for an extended period by master's level providers. It utilizes instruction, practice, and feedback to enhance the mother's skills, including: attentive and nondirective play, listening, contingent praise and positive attention, and appropriate instructions and commands. In addition, the therapist works with the mothers to improve their decision making skills in applied contexts (i.e., setting realistic household budget priorities, selecting child-care providers, etc.) and also works to connect mothers with material and social support.

Participants in the study by McDonald et al. (2011) were 66 mothers and their children (ages 4–9), at least one of whom was exhibiting high levels of conduct problems. Families were randomly assigned to a control condition or to Project Support. The results showed a decrease in psychopathic features in the children in Project Support, and further showed that this decrease was mediated by positive changes in mother's parenting behavior.

In summary:

- Data suggest that adolescents with psychopathic traits may benefit from treatment at the same rates as comparison groups.
- Intensive in-patient treatments utilizing cognitive behavioral and behavior management approaches, and indirect interventions focused on parent training have both resulted in improvement in this group.
- Additional research is needed to compare the effectiveness of approaches and to determine what factors may hinder participation in or completion of treatment.

8.3.4 Developing Novel, Etiology-Based Treatments for Psychopathy

Newman and colleagues (e.g., Newman, 1998; Wallace, Schmitt, Vitale, & Newman, 2000) have proposed that psychopaths are characterized by a deficit in response modulation. According to this model, psychopathic individuals are deficient in their ability to redirect attention automatically from the primary focus of their goal directed behavior to the evaluation of secondary stimuli. For example, when focused on the goal of winning money on a computerized gambling task, these individuals fail to attend to contextual cues signaling changes in the likelihood of reward (e.g., Newman, Patterson, & Kosson, 1987). Given such a deficit, Wallace et al. (2000) have argued that simply changing the content of psychopathic thought (e.g., teaching social skills and anger management, as in traditional cognitive therapy) will result in only limited treatment gains. According to the model, psychopathic individuals will be unable to access these changes in their thinking as easily as nonpsychopathic individuals, and so they will be less likely to use these more adaptive, prosocial cognitions to regulate their behavior. Thus, the authors argue that treatment for psychopathic individuals should focus initially on the development of strategies that will allow these individuals to compensate for their basic information processing deficit (Wallace et al., 2000). In theory, such an approach would provide a means for psychopathic individuals to benefit more fully from other interventions they receive, thereby helping to boost the effects of cognitive behavioral or other therapies.

In a test of this proposal, Baskin-Sommers, Curtin, and Newman (2015) examined the impact of a cognitive remediation intervention in a sample of psychopathic offenders. In a cognitive remediation intervention, the emphasis is on training individuals in the particular cognitive skills—such as paying attention to contextual cues, sustained attention, and working memory—that underlie behavior (Klingberg, 2010; Wykes & van der Gaag, 2001). Such approaches have been shown to be promising in the treatment of both attention deficit-hyperactivity disorder and schizophrenia (Stevenson, Whitmont, Bornholt, Livesey, & Stevenson, 2002).

In order to apply cognitive remediation to psychopathy, Baskin-Sommers et al. (2015) targeted the response modulation deficit associated with psychopathy and examined the efficacy of this intervention in a sample of 124 incarcerated, substance dependent adult male offenders who were classified as psychopathic or nonpsychopathic. The study had several stages:

1. Offenders were pretested on a set of tasks that assessed both response modulation-related and unrelated skills.
2. Offenders were randomly assigned to one of two treatment conditions:

    In the psychopathy-specific "attention to context" condition, inmates participated in a 1-h, computer based training session once a week for 6 weeks that used three tasks targeting the RM deficit. Each task required individuals to practice attending to peripheral or nonsalient cues and noticing changes in contextual information (e.g., rule changes).

    In the non-psychopathy specific control condition, participants also completed a 1-h computer-based training session once a week. However, in this condition the tasks were not selected to address specifically the RM deficit but focused instead on providing practice inhibiting behavior and regulating emotion reactions more generally.
3. At the conclusion of the 6 week treatment period, offenders were reassessed on the three training tasks as well as the tasks used at pre-testing.

    The results of the post-treatment assessment were promising. Consistent with the possibilities of cognitive remediation, psychopathic individuals in the "attention to context" (i.e., the psychopathy specific) training group demonstrated significant improvement not only on the three training tasks, but also on the RM-related tasks that had been used at pre-testing. Conversely, psychopathic participants in the control condition showed no significant improvement over the course of training on the non-psychopathy-specific training tasks and showed significantly less improvement on the post-training RM tasks than those in the "attention to context" group. However, because this this treatment approach has not yet been associated with changes in overt antisocial behavior or psychopathic attitudes, it is not clear the extent to which these changes impacted positively the overall functioning of these individuals.

8.4   Summary and Future Directions

1. Despite clinical lore, there is only limited and inconclusive evidence that psychopathic individuals are untreatable. However, there are also too few systematic studies of the effects of treatment on psychopathy to provide clear guidance

regarding best practice in this area. Generally, treatments provided to psychopathic individuals have been the same as those provided for other aggressive, persistently antisocial offenders. Further, although it may not be the case that psychopathic individuals respond less well to these interventions if they complete them, there is evidence that these individuals are more likely to drop-out of these programs. On this basis, the following recommendations are made:

- Psychopathic individuals should continue to be provided with those treatments that meet best-practices standards for the majority of violent offenders. Until it can be shown that certain modes of treatment work particularly well for this group, their response to existing treatments should be clearly documented and made available.
- The impact of treatment on psychopathic individuals should be systematically researched and published. Immediate outcomes, as well as repeated follow-up assessments (preferably over years) should be conducted to demonstrate the stability of treatment gains or deteriorations. Outcome data should include specific behavioral variables, such as institutional behavioral assessments and violent and nonviolent re-offending, but also measures of attitudes, emotional responsiveness, and interpersonal beliefs.
- Whenever possible, studies should compare treated psychopathic individuals and untreated psychopathic individuals. Because psychopathy is associated with elevated levels of recidivism (as well as negative attitudes such as hostility and callousness), comparisons between these individuals and nonpsychopathic individuals will likely obscure gains within the psychopathic groups (i.e., they may have improved in treatment, but still reoffend at a higher rate than nonpsychopathic individuals).

2. Research with adolescent samples suggests that adolescents with psychopathic features may benefit from treatment. Further, evidence is accumulating that intervention may reduce psychopathic features among adolescents with significant behavior problems. On this basis, the following recommendations are made:

- Interventions targeted towards children and adolescents with psychopathic traits should be further developed and expanded. In addition, the effectiveness of treatments within this group should be compared to the effectiveness of interventions for psychopathic adults. If adolescents are more likely to exhibit treatment gains, increasing accessibility to treatment within this population would be a strategic use of resources.
- Research studies should be conducted to determine what modes of intervention are most effective within this group. Previous research has shown some success for programs focusing on both the juveniles themselves and on parents. Additional research is necessary to replicate these successes and to determine what treatments work most effectively in this population.

3. Preliminary evidence exists to show that treatment can be targeted specifically to the processes theorized to underlie the psychopathy syndrome. For example, it has been argued that by addressing core deficits associated with information

processing among psychopathic individuals, approaches such as cognitive remediation could serve to enhance the impact of other therapies in these offenders. However, the research is extremely limited at this time, which gives rise to the following recommendations:

- Researchers and clinicians should consider how research on the etiology of psychopathy could be used to inform the development of novel treatment strategies better suited to the particular deficits demonstrated by this group (Wallace et al., 2000).
- Researchers should develop controlled protocols for the administration of cognitive remediation in this group and show both that psychopathic offenders can reliably improve their functioning as a result of this intervention and that this improvement in processing is associated with positive behavioral and attitudinal outcomes.
- Other models of psychopathy should be considered as sources for the development of syndrome-specific treatments. For example, negative childhood events and trauma have been associated with psychopathy (Christian, Meltzer, Thede, & Kosson, 2017; Hawes, Dadds, Frost, & Hasking, 2011; Mills-Koonce et al., 2014). According to de Ruiter et al. (2016), Schema Therapy (ST; Young, Klosko, & Weishaar, 2003), which was developed for patients who may not benefit from traditional cognitive-behavioral approaches, and which emphasizes exploration of negative childhood experiences, building of a connection between therapist and client, and identification and addressing of maladaptive coping styles, may be well-suited to this group.

Alternatively, based on research identifying different correlates of the two PCL-R factors, Wong and Olver (2016) recommend a two-component risk reduction approach designed to address separately the two factors of psychopathy. Because the antisocial/lifestyle factor (F2) has been shown to be the better predictor of violence, and because many of the components of this factor are static (e.g., juvenile delinquency) the authors argue that treatment for psychopathic individuals should instead target the dynamic risk factors associated violence. Conversely, because the affective/interpersonal factors (F1) are not reliably associated with prediction of violence, it would be expected that treatments targeted to these features will be unlikely to impact significantly the likelihood of future violence. However, these features do predict treatment noncompliance, disruption, and attrition, highlighting the need to address these characteristics in order to improve treatment success.

Olver, Lewis, and Wong (2013) studied a sample of incarcerated, violent male offenders enrolled in a cognitive-behaviorally oriented "ABC" treatment program that targeted high-risk offenders and focused on those characteristics linked strongly to crime and violence (e.g., anger problems, antisocial attitudes). Importantly, although psychopathy was associated with decreased positive change in Violence Risk Scale scores, regression analysis revealed that this reduction was associated only with the Affective component of psychopathy, a finding which affirms the argument that considering the psychopathy factors separately when investigating treatment compliance and response may be especially important.

8.5 Conclusion

Psychopathic individuals are present in significant numbers within the criminal justice system, where their persistent antisocial behavior strains both human and financial resources. Upon release they are more likely to reoffend than nonpsychopathic offenders, resulting in greater cost to their communities and—typically—return to the system.

Despite the seriousness of this syndrome, little systematic research has been conducted examining treatment within this population. Early negative conceptualizations, strengthened by a small number of documented treatment failures, led to the conclusion that these individuals were "untreatable", and potentially discouraging innovative treatments and research in this area.

Although it now appears that there may be some treatments that impact positively the functioning of psychopathic individuals, it is not clear yet the extent or duration of these benefits. Further, because psychopathic individuals are more likely to drop out of treatment, any benefits are limited to those potentially unusual individuals who complete treatment.

Moving forward, information regarding the responses of psychopathic individuals to existing treatments must be collected, and interventions targeted to this resistant group must be developed and systematically tested. Despite some advances, the field as a whole is still in the early stages of development and growth is urgently needed.

References

Abracen, J., Looman, J., Ferguson, M., Harkins, L., & Mailoux, D. (2011). Recidivism among treated sexual offenders and comparison subjects: Recent outcome data from the Regional Treatment Centre (Ontario) high-intensity Sex Offender Treatment Programme. *Journal of Sexual Aggression, 17*, 142–152.

American Psychiatric Association. (2013). *Diagnostic and statistical manual of mental disorders* (54th ed.). Washington, DC: Author.

Anton, M., Baskin-Sommers, A. R., Vitale, J., Curtin, J. J., & Newman, J. P. (2012). Differential effects of psychopathy and antisocial personality disorder symptoms on cognitive and fear processing in female offenders. *Cognitive, Affective, & Behavioral Neuroscience, 12*, 761–776.

Barbaree, H. E. (2005). Psychopathy, treatment behavior, and recidivism: An extended follow-up of Seto and Barbaree. *Journal of Interpersonal Violence, 20*, 1115–1131.

Baskin-Sommers, A. R., Curtin, J. J., & Newman, J. P. (2015). Altering the cognitive-affective dysfunctions of psychopathic and externalizing offender subtypes with cognitive remediation. *Clinical Psychological Science, 3*, 45–57.

Baskin-Sommers, A. R., Newman, J. P., Sathasivam, N., & Curtin, J. J. (2011). Evaluating the generalizability of a fear deficit in psychopathic African American offenders. *Journal of Abnormal Psychology, 120*, 71–78.

Berger, K., Rotermund, P., Vieth, E. R., & Hohnhorst, A. (2012). The prognostic value of the PCL-R in relation to the SUD treatment ending. *International Journal of Law and Psychiatry, 35*, 198–201.

Beryl, R., Chou, S., & Völlm, B. (2014). A systematic review of psychopathy in women within secure settings. *Personality and Individual Differences, 71*, 185–195.

Bishopp, D., & Hare, R. D. (2008). A multidimensional scaling analysis of the PCL-R: Unfolding the structure of psychopathy. *Psychology, Crime, & Law, 14*, 117–132.

Bonta, J., & Andrews, D. A. (2015). *The psychology of criminal conduct* (6th ed.). London, UK: Routledge.

Brislin, S. J., Drislane, L. E., Smith, S. T., Edens, J. F., & Patrick, C. J. (2015). Development and validation of triarchic psychopathy scales from the Multidimensional Personality Questionnaire. *Psychological Assessment, 27*, 838–851.

Caldwell, M. F. (2011). Treatment-related changes in behavioral outcomes of psychopathy facets in adolescent offenders. *Law and Human Behavior, 35*, 275–287.

Caldwell, M. F., & Van Rybroek, G. J. (2005). Reducing violence in serious juvenile offenders using intensive treatment. *International Journal of Law & Psychiatry, 28*, 622–636.

Chakhssi, F., deRuiter, C., & Berstein, D. (2010). Change during forensic treatment in psychopathic versus nonpsychopathic offenders. *Journal of Forensic Psychiatry & Psychology, 21*, 660–682.

Christian, E. J., Meltzer, C. L., Thede, L. L., & Kosson, D. S. (2017). The relationship between early life events, parental attachment, and psychopathic tendencies in adolescent detainees. *Child Psychiatry and Human Development, 48*, 260–269.

Cleckley, H. (1941/1996). *The mask of sanity*. St. Louis, MO: Mosby.

Cooke, D. J., Kosson, D. S., & Michie, C. (2001). Psychopathy and ethnicity: Structural, item, and test generalizability of the Psychopathy Checklist—Revised (PCL-R) in Caucasian and African American participants. *Psychological Assessment, 13*, 531–542.

Cooke, D., & Michie, C. (1999). Psychopathy across cultures: North America and Scotland compared. *Journal of Abnormal Psychology, 108*, 58–68.

Cooke, D. J., Michie, C., & Hart, S. D. (2006). Facets of clinical psychopathy: Towards clearer measurement. In C. Patrick (Ed.), *Handbook of psychopathy* (pp. 91–106). New York, NY: Guilford Press.

Crego, C., & Widiger, T. A. (2015). Psychopathy, DSM-5, and a caution. *Personality Disorders: Theory, Research, and Treatment, 5*, 335–347.

DeMatteo, D., Edens, J. F., Galloway, M., Cox, J., Smith, S. T., Koller, J. P., & Bersoff, B. (2014). Investigating the role of the Psychopathy Checklist-Revised in United States case law. *Psychology, Public Policy, and Law, 20*, 96–107.

De Ruiter, C., Chakhssi, F., & Bernstein, D. P. (2016). Treating the untreatable psychopath. In C. Gacono (Ed.), *The clinical and forensic assessment of psychopathy: A practitioner's guide* (pp. 388–402). New York, NY: Routledge.

Dolan, M. C., & Anderson, I. M. (2003). The relationship between serotonergic function and the Psychopathy Checklist: Screening version. *Journal of Psychopharmacology, 17*, 216–222.

Draycott, S., Askari, R., & Kirkpatrick, K. (2011). Patterns and change in psychopathic interpersonal behavior in forensic inpatient treatment. *Personality and Mental Health, 5*, 200–208.

Draycott, S., Short, R., & Kirkpatrick, K. (2015). Long-term patterns in interpersonal behavior amongst psychopathic patients in secure inpatient treatment: A follow-up study. *Personality and Mental Health, 9*, 124–132.

D'Silva, K., Duggan, C., & McCarthy, L. (2004). Does treatment really make psychopaths worse? A review of the evidence. *Journal of Personality Disorders, 18*, 163–177.

Edens, J. F., Campbell, J. S., & Weir, J. M. (2007). Youth psychopathy and criminal recidivism: A meta-analysis of the psychopathy checklist measures. *Law and Human Behavior, 31*, 53–75.

Fulero, S. M. (1995). Review of the Hare Psychopathy Checklist–Revised. In J. C. Conoley & J. C. Impara (Eds.), *Twelfth mental measurements yearbook* (pp. 453–454). Lincoln, NE: Buros Institute.

Gretton, H. M., McBride, M., Hare, R. D., & O'Shaughnessy, R. (2000). *Psychopathy and recidivism in adolescent offenders: A ten-year follow-up*. Paper presented at the 19th Annual Conference of the Association for the Treatment of Sexual Abusers (ATSA), San Diego, CA.

Guay, J. P., Ruscio, J., Knight, R. A., & Hare, R. D. (2007). A taxometric analysis of the latent structure of psychopathy: Evidence for dimensionality. *Journal of Abnormal Psychology, 116*, 101–116.

Hare, R. D. (1991). *Manual for the Hare Psychopathy Checklist—Revised* (1st ed.). Toronto, ON: Multi-Health Systems.

Hare, R. D. (2003). *Manual for the Hare Psychopathy Checklist—Revised* (2nd ed.). Toronto, ON: Multi-Health Systems.

Hare, R. D. (1996). Psychopathy: A clinical construct whose time has come. *Criminal Justice and Behavior, 23*, 25–54.

Hare, R. D. (2016). Psychopathy, the PCL-R, and criminal justice: Some new findings and current issues. *Canadian Psychology, 57*, 21–34.

Hare, R. D., Clark, D., Grann, M., & Thornton, D. (2000). Psychopathy and the predictive validity of the PCL-R: An international perspective. *Behavioral Sciences and the Law, 18*, 623–645.

Hare, R. D., & Neumann, C. S. (2008). Psychopathy as a clinical and empirical construct. *Annual Review of Clinical Psychology, 4*, 217–246.

Harris, G. T., Rice, M. E., & Cormier, C. A. (1994). Psychopaths: Is a therapeutic community therapeutic? *Therapeutic Communities, 15*, 283–299.

Hawes, D. J., Dadds, M. R., Frost, A. D. J., & Hasking, P. A. (2011). Do childhood callous-unemotional traits drive change in parenting practices? *Journal of Clinical and Child & Adolescent Psychology, 40*, 507–518.

Hemphill, J. F., Templeman, R., Wong, S., & Hare, R. D. (1998). Psychopathy and crime: Recidivism and criminal careers. In D. J. Cooke, R. D. Hare, & A. Forth (Eds.), *Psychopathy: Theory, research and implications for society* (pp. 375–399). Dordrecht, The Netherlands: Kluwer Academic Publishers.

Herve, H., Mitchell, D., & Cooper, B. S. (2004). Psychopathy and unlawful confinement: An examination of perpetrator and event characteristics. *Canadian Journal of Behavioural Science, 36*, 137–145.

Hildebrand, M., & de Ruiter, C. (2012). Psychopathic traits and change on indicators of dynamic risk factors during inpatient forensic psychiatric treatment. *International Journal of Law & Psychiatry, 35*, 276–288.

Hildebrand, M., de Ruiter, C., & Nijman, H. (2004). PCL-R psychopathy predicts disruptive behavior among male offenders in a Dutch forensic psychiatric hospital. *Journal of Interpersonal Violence, 19*, 13–29.

Hobson, J., & Shine, J. (1998). Measurement of psychopathy in a UK prison population referred for long-term psychotherapy. *British Journal of Criminology, 38*, 504–515.

Hobson, J., Shine, J., & Roberts, R. (2000). How do psychopaths behave in a prison therapeutic community? *Psychology, Crime and Law, 6*, 139–154.

Hornsveld, R. H., Kraaimaat, F. W., Muris, P., Zwets, A. J., & Kanters, T. (2015). Aggression replacement training for violent young men in a forensic psychiatric outpatient clinic. *Journal of Interpersonal Violence, 30*, 3174–3191.

Hurducas, C. C., Singh, J. P., de Ruiter, C., & Petrila, J. (2014). Violence risk assessment tools: A systematic review of surveys. *The International Journal of Forensic Mental Health, 13*, 181–192.

Jackson, R. L., Rogers, R., Neumann, C. S., & Lambert, P. L. (2002). Psychopathy in female offenders: An investigation of its underlying dimensions. *Criminal Justice and Behavior, 29*, 692–704.

Jouriles, E. N., McDonald, R., Rosenfield, D., Norwood, W. D., Spiller, L., Stephens, N., … Ehrensaft, M. (2010). Improving parenting in families referred for child maltreatment: A randomized controlled trial examining effects of Project Support. *Journal of Family Psychology, 24*, 328–338.

Klingberg, T. (2010). Training and plasticity of working memory. *Trends in Cognitive Sciences, 14*, 317–324.

Kosson, D. S., Smith, S. S., & Newman, J. P. (1990). Evaluating the construct validity of psychopathy in Black and White male inmates: Three preliminary studies. *Journal of Abnormal Psychology, 99*, 250–259.

Lilienfeld, S. O. (1994). Conceptual problems in the assessment of psychopathy. *Clinical Psychology Review, 14*, 17–38.

Lilienfeld, S. O., & Andrews, B. P. (1996). Development and preliminary validation of a self-report measure of psychopathic personality traits in noncriminal populations. *Journal of Personality Assessment, 66*, 488–524.

Looman, J., Abracen, J., Serin, R., & Marquis, P. (2005). Psychopathy, treatment change, and recidivism in high-risk, high-need sexual offenders. *Journal of Interpersonal Violence, 20*, 549–568.

Lorenz, A. R., & Newman, J. P. (2002). Do emotion and information processing deficiencies found in Caucasian psychopaths generalize to African-American psychopaths? *Personality and Individual Differences, 32*, 1077–1086.

Lykken, D. T. (1995). *The antisocial personalities*. Hillsdale, NJ: Erlbaum.

Lynn, R. (2002). Racial and ethnic differences in psychopathic personality. *Personality and Individual Differences, 32*, 273–316.

McDonald, R., Dodson, M. C., Rosenfield, D., & Jouriles, E. N. (2011). Effects of a parenting intervention on features of psychopathy in children. *Journal of Abnormal Child Psychology, 39*, 1013–1023.

Mills-Koonce, W. R., Wagner, N. J., Willoughby, M. T., Stifter, C., Blair, C., & Granger, D. A. (2014). Greater fear reactivity and psychophysiological hyperactivity among infants with later conduct problems and callous-unemotional traits. *Journal of Child Psychology and Psychiatry, 56*, 147–154.

Monroe, C. M., Van Rybroek, G. J., & Maier, G. J. (1988). Decompressing aggressive inpatients: Breaking the aggression cycle to enhance positive outcome. *Behavioral Sciences and the Law, 6*, 543–557.

Neal, T. M. S., & Grisso, T. (2014). Assessment practices and expert judgment methods in forensic psychology and psychiatry: An international snapshot. *Criminal Justice and Behavior, 41*, 1406–1421.

Neumann, C. S., Hare, R. D., & Newman, J. P. (2007). The super-ordinate nature of psychopathy. *Journal of Personality Disorders, 21*, 102–117.

Neumann, C. S., Schmitt, D. S., Carter, R., Embley, I., & Hare, R. D. (2012). Psychopathic traits in females and males across the globe. *Behavioral Sciences & the Law, 30*, 557–574.

Newman, J. P. (1998). Psychopathic behavior: An information processing perspective. In D. J. Cooke, A. E. Forth, & R. D. Hare (Eds.), *Psychopathy: Theory, research and implications for society* (pp. 81–104). Boston, MA: Kluwer Academic.

Newman, J. P., Patterson, C. M., & Kosson, D. S. (1987). Response perseveration in psychopaths. *Journal of Abnormal Psychology, 96*, 145–148.

Newman, J. P., Schmitt, W. A., & Voss, W. (1997). Processing of contextual cues in psychopathic and nonpsychopathic offenders. *Journal of Abnormal Psychology, 106*, 563–575.

O'Connor, D. A. (2001). *The female psychopath: Validity and factor structure of the revised Psychopathy Checklist (PCL-R) in women inmates*. Unpublished doctoral dissertation, Florida State University, Tallahassee.

Ogloff, J. R. (2006). Psychopathy/antisocial personality disorder conundrum. *Australian and New Zealand Journal of Psychiatry, 40*, 519–528.

Olver, M. E., Lewis, K., & Wong, S. C. P. (2013). Risk reduction treatment of high-risk psychopathic offenders: The relationship of psychopathy and treatment change to violent recidivism. *Personality Disorders: Theory, Research, and Treatment, 4*, 160–167.

Olver, M. E., & Wong, S. C. P. (2009). Therapeutic responses of psychopathic sexual offenders: Treatment attrition, therapeutic change, and long-term recidivism. *Journal of Consulting and Clinical Psychology, 77*, 328–336.

Patrick, C. J., Fowles, D. C., & Krueger, R. F. (2009). Triarchic conceptualization of psychopathy: Developmental origins of disinhibition, boldness, and meanness. *Development and Psychopathology, 21*, 913–938.

Pinel, P. (1806). *A treatise on insanity* (Translated by D. Davis). New York, NY: Hafner

Polaschek, D. L. (2014). Adult criminals with psychopathy: Common beliefs about treatability and change have little empirical support. *Current Directions in Psychological Science, 23,* 296–301.

Polaschek, D. L. (2015). (Mis)understanding psychopathy: Consequences for policy and practice with offenders. *Psychiatry, Psychology and Law, 22,* 500–519.

Rasmussen, K., Storsæter, O., & Levander, S. (1999). Personality disorders, psychopathy, and crime in a Norwegian prison population. *International Journal of Law and Psychiatry, 22,* 91–97.

Reidy, D. E., Kearns, M. C., & DeGue, S. (2013). Reducing psychopathic violence: A review of the treatment literature. *Aggression and Violent Behavior, 8,* 527–538.

Richards, H. J., Casey, J. O., & Lucente, S. W. (2003). Psychopathy and treatment response in incarcerated female substance abusers. *Criminal Justice and Behavior, 30,* 251–276.

Salekin, R. T., Neumann, C. S., Leistico, A.-M. R., & Zalot, A. A. (2004). Psychopathy in youth and intelligence: An investigation of Cleckley's hypothesis. *Journal of Clinical Child and Adolescent Psychology, 33,* 731–742.

Salekin, R. T., Rogers, R., & Sewell, K. W. (1997). Construct validity of psychopathy in a female offender sample: A multitrait–multimethod evaluation. *Journal of Abnormal Psychology, 106,* 576–585.

Salekin, R. T., Rogers, R., Ustad, K. L., & Sewell, K. W. (1998). Psychopathy and recidivism among female inmates. *Law and Human Behavior, 22,* 109–128.

Salekin, R. T., Tippey, J. G., & Allen, A. D. (2012). Treatment of conduct problem youth with interpersonal callous traits using mental models: Measurement of risk and change. *Behavioral Sciences & the Law, 30,* 470–486.

Seto, M. C., & Barbaree, H. E. (1999). Psychopathy, treatment behavior and sex offender recidivism. *Journal of Interpersonal Violence, 14,* 1235–1248.

Skeem, J. L., Edens, J. F., Camp, J., & Colwell, L. H. (2004). Are there ethnic differences in levels of psychopathy? A meta-analysis. *Law and Human Behavior, 28,* 505–527.

Skeem, J. L., Monahan, J., & Mulvey, E. P. (2002). Psychopathy, treatment involvement, and subsequent violence among civil psychiatric patients. *Law and Human Behavior, 26,* 577–603.

Stevenson, C. S., Whitmont, S., Bornholt, L., Livesey, D., & Stevenson, R. J. (2002). A cognitive remediation programme for adults with Attention Deficit Hyperactivity Disorder. *Australian and New Zealand Journal of Psychiatry, 36,* 610–616.

Strand, S., & Belfrage, H. (2005). Gender differences in psychopathy in a Swedish offender sample. *Behavioral Sciences & the Law, 23,* 837–850.

Sullivan, E. A., Abramowitz, C. S., Lopez, M., & Kosson, D. S. (2006). Reliability and construct validity of the psychopathy checklist-revised for Latino, European American, and African American male inmates. *Psychological Assessment, 18,* 382–392.

Sullivan, E. A., & Kosson, D. S. (2006). Ethnic and cultural variations in psychopathy. In C. J. Patrick (Ed.), *Handbook of psychopathy* (pp. 437–458). New York, NY: Guilford Press.

Verona, E., Sprague, J., & Sadeh, N. (2012). Inhibitory control and negative emotion processing psychopathy and antisocial personality disorder. *Journal of Abnormal Psychology, 121,* 498–510.

Verona, E., & Vitale, J. E. (2006). Psychopathy in women: Assessment, manifestations, and etiology. In C. Patrick (Ed.), *Handbook of psychopathy* (pp. 415–436). New York, NY: Guilford Press.

Vitale, J. E., & Newman, J. P. (2001). Response perseveration in psychopathic women. *Journal of Abnormal Psychology, 110,* 644–647.

Vitale, J. E., MacCoon, D. G., & Newman, J. P. (2011). Emotion facilitation and passive avoidance learning in psychopathic female offenders. *Criminal Justice and Behavior, 38,* 641–658.

Wallace, J. F., Schmitt, W. A., Vitale, J. E., & Newman, J. P. (2000). Experimental investigations of information processing deficiencies and psychopathy: Implications for diagnosis and treatment. In C. Gacono (Ed.), *Clinical and forensic assessment of psychopathy* (pp. 87–110). Hillsdale, NJ: Erlbaum.

Walsh, Z. (2013). Psychopathy and criminal violence: The moderating effect of ethnicity. *Law and Human Behavior, 37*, 303–311.

Walsh, Z., & Kosson, D. S. (2007). Psychopathy and violent crime: A prospective study of the influence of socioeconomic status and ethnicity. *Law and Human Behavior, 31*, 209–229.

Walters, G. D., Ermer, E., Knight, R. A., & Kiehl, K. A. (2015). Paralimbic biomarkers in taxometric analyses of psychopathy: Does changing the indicators change the conclusion? *Personality Disorders: Theory, Research, and Treatment, 6*, 41–52.

Warren, J. I., Burnette, M. L., South, S. C., Preeti, C., Bale, R., Friend, R., & Van Patten, I. (2003). Psychopathy in women: Structural modeling and comorbidity. *International Journal of Law and Psychiatry, 26*, 223–242.

Weizmann-Henelius, G., Virkkunen, M., Gammelgard, M., Eronen, M., & Putkonen, H. (2015). The PCL-R and violent recidivism in a prospective follow-up of a nationwide sample of female offenders. *Journal of Forensic Psychiatry and Psychology, 26*, 667–685.

Wong, S. C. P., Gordon, A., Gu, D., Lewis, K., & Olver, M. E. (2012). The effectiveness of violence reduction treatment for psychopathic offenders: Empirical evidence and a treatment model. *International Journal of Forensic Mental Health, 11*, 336–349.

Wong, S. C. P., & Olver, M. E. (2016). Risk reduction treatment of psychopathy and applications to mentally disordered offenders. In K. Warburton & S. Stahl (Eds.), *Violence in psychiatry* (pp. 323–331). Cambridge, UK: Cambridge University Press.

Wykes, T., & van der Gaag, M. (2001). Is it time to develop a new cognitive therapy for psychosis—Cognitive remediation therapy (CRT)? *Clinical Psychology Review, 21*, 1227–1256.

Young, J. E., Klosko, J. S., & Weishaar, M. E. (2003). *Schema therapy: A practitioner's guide.* New York, NY: Guildford.

Chapter 9
Assessing and Treating Men Who Have Committed Sexual Offenses

Sarah Moss, Maria Simmons, Sydney Trendell, and Skye Stephens

Sexual offending encompasses a wide range of illegal sexual behaviors, including, but not limited to contact offenses (direct contact with a victim, such as sexual assault), non-contact offenses (no direct contact with the victim, such as exhibitionism) and offenses facilitated by technology (e.g., viewing child sexual exploitation images). There are also various grey zones, such as revenge pornography (posting sexually explicit images of others without their consent), that our legal system is evolving to address. Those who commit sexual offenses are a heterogeneous population and vary in their motivations to offend, risk level, and response to intervention.

The chapter reviews the extant literature on sexual offending, with an explicit focus on adult males who have committed sexual offenses. We do not cover the literature on adolescents who have committed sexual offenses (see Seto & Lalumière, 2010), females who have committed sexual offenses (see Cortoni, 2018), or those who have committed internet offenses (see Seto, 2013). In this chapter, we briefly review the frequency and prevalence of sexual offending with a focus on victimization and review major theoretical models that guide our discussion of assessment and treatment. We conclude our review with a discussion of important areas of further inquiry and the use of technology in assessment and treatment.

S. Moss (✉) · S. Trendell · S. Stephens
Psychology Department, Saint Mary's University, Halifax, NS, Canada
e-mail: Sarah.moss@smu.ca; Sydney.trendell@smu.ca; Skye.stephens@smu.ca

M. Simmons
Department of Psychiatry, Dalhousie University, Halifax, NS, Canada
e-mail: maria.simmons@dal.ca

© Springer Nature Switzerland AG 2018
M. Ternes et al. (eds.), *The Practice of Correctional Psychology*,
https://doi.org/10.1007/978-3-030-00452-1_9

9.1   Frequency and Prevalence

Data from the United States, suggests that 18% of women are sexually assaulted during their lifetime (Kilpatrick, Resnick, Ruggiero, Conoscenti, & McCauley, 2007). Despite these rates, as few as 5% of sexual assaults are reported to the police (Johnson, 2012; Perreault, 2015). As such, quantifying the frequency of sexual offenses is difficult because these offenses are rarely reported to authorities (Brennan & Taylor-Butts, 2008; Sinha, 2013). Although reporting rates are low, many victims disclose their victimization to unofficial sources (e.g., family members or friends; Brennan & Taylor-Butts, 2008).

Several trends have been identified in crime-based data on sexual assault. First, young men are disproportionately perpetrators and women are disproportionately victims (e.g., Brennan & Taylor-Butts, 2008; Vaillancourt, 2010). In understanding these differences, age is an important consideration. Rates of victimization for males are highest for those between the ages of 3 and 14, as males represented 29% of victims under the age of 12, 12% of those aged 12–18, and 8% of adult victims (Kong, Johnson, Beattie, & Cardillo, 2003). These rates likely underestimate prevalence, as males are less likely to report their victimization (e.g., Kubiak et al., 2017). Overall, young victims are overrepresented in rates of sexual assault, as more than half of victims of sexual offending were under the age of 18 in 2007 (Brennan & Taylor-Butts, 2008). Additionally, victims are most often known to the perpetrator of the offense (e.g., Fisher, Cullen, & Turner, 2000; Statistics Canada, 2011).

9.1.1   Special Populations

The assessment and treatment of those who have committed sexual offenses occurs across many different contexts, such as community outpatient clinics, correctional facilities, forensic mental health settings (i.e., forensic hospitals), and civil commitment centres. These different contexts influence how men who have committed sexual offenses are assessed, managed, and treated. We briefly highlight two special contexts, forensic mental health settings and civil commitment, both of which have been the focus of empirical research.

The forensic mental health system is predominately focused on those who are being assessed or treated for: (1) incompetency or (2) not guilty by reason of insanity (NGRI). The terminology for these concepts varies depending on the country (e.g., incompetency and NGRI are terms used in the United States, and unfit to stand trial and not criminally responsible on account of mental disorder are used in Canada), but the principles behind them are largely similar. In the United States, it is estimated that 5–15% of defense attorneys raise concerns about a defendant's competency, though fewer receive a formal competence evaluation (Hoge, Bonnie, Poythress, & Monahan, 1992; Poythress, Bonnie, Hoge, Monahan, & Oberlander, 1994). Similarly, insanity defenses are not commonly used with those who have committed sexual offenses (Weiss & Watson, 2008). For example, in a Canadian study 2% of individuals found not criminally responsible on account of a mental disorder had committed an index sexual offense (Crocker et al., 2015).

Another context that is important to consider is civil commitment, which is present in 20 states (ATSA, 2010). To be civilly committed the person must have committed a sexual offense and have a diagnosed mental disorder that puts them at increased risk for committing a future sexual offense. Those who are civilly committed are detained in treatment facilities until their mental health condition improves (see Doren, 2002 for more information). In Canada, the closest equivalent to civil commitment is a Dangerous Offender designation, which if successful could result in an indeterminate sentence. The majority of those designated dangerous offenders have committed a sexual offense (Trevethan, Crutcher, & Moore, 2002). One of the key differences between dangerous offender designations and civil commitment is that a dangerous offender designation occurs during the sentencing phase of criminal proceedings, whereas civil commitment occurs after the individual has completed their judicial sentence. Evaluation of the effectiveness of these policies are difficult to establish, as very few committed individuals are released and there is a debate on the ethics of civil commitment (readers are directed to Yung, 2013 and Elwood, 2009 for discussion).

9.2 Diagnosis and Assessment

9.2.1 Empirically Supported Risk Factors

Clinicians have an important role in the assessment and management of those who have committed sexual offenses. Briefly, assessment should be multidimensional and include self-report, collateral sources, a review of official documentation, and standardized psychological instruments. In these assessments, several domains should be covered, such as offense details, psychosocial history, mental and physical health, psychosexual functioning, and cognition. The focus in the present section is on the assessment of empirically supported risk factors (e.g., Hanson & Morton-Bourgon, 2005; Mann, Hanson, & Thornton, 2010) and different approaches to risk assessment.

In a comprehensive review, Mann et al. (2010) identified the following as empirically supported risk factors: paraphilic sexual interests, sexual preoccupation, offense supportive attitudes, emotional congruence with children, lack of emotionally intimate relationships, impulsivity, poor problem solving, self-regulation problems, difficulties following rules, hostility, and negative social influences. Given the importance of these factors in predicting sexual recidivism, any comprehensive assessment should include an assessment of these factors using assessment tools and procedures that have strong empirical support.

In the present section, we focus on paraphilic interests, sexual preoccupation, and antisociality as they have been identified as the strongest predictors of recidivism (e.g., Hanson & Morton-Bourgon, 2005). More specifically, paraphilic interests and sexual preoccupation are the strongest predictors of sexual recidivism (Hanson & Morton-Bourgon, 2005). Antisociality is a significant predictor of nonsexual offending in those who have committed sexual offenses and includes several of the empirically supported risk factors listed above, such as impulsivity, self-regulation problems, hostility, and poor problem solving (Hanson & Morton-Bourgon, 2005; Mann et al., 2010).

9.2.2   Paraphilias and Sexual Preoccupation

9.2.2.1   Paraphilias

Paraphilias represent atypical sexual interests for persons, objects, or activities that are considered to fall outside the realm of normative sexual interests. Paraphilias are only diagnosed as mental disorders if they result in distress and/or functional impairment (American Psychiatric Association, 2013). The *Diagnostic and Statistical Manual of Mental Disorders—Fifth Edition* (*DSM-5*) defines eight paraphilias (see Table 9.1; American Psychiatric Association, 2013); however, it is notable that there are other paraphilic interests not explicitly included in the *DSM-5*. Paraphilias are more common in men than women, which may be partially explained by higher sexual drive (e.g., Dawson, Bannerman, & Lalumière, 2016). There is considerable

Table 9.1 Paraphilias in the *Diagnostic and Statistical Manual of Mental Disorders—Fifth Edition*

Paraphilia	Definition
Voyeuristic Disorder	Sexual interest in viewing unsuspecting people engaged in sexual activity, naked, or undressing.
Exhibitionistic Disorder	Sexual interest in indecent exposure to unsuspecting persons.
Frotteuristic Disorder	Sexual interest in touching or rubbing against someone who does not consent to these activities.
Sexual Masochism Disorder	Sexual interest in experiencing physical or psychological suffering.
Sexual Sadism Disorder	Sexual interest in inflicting physical or psychological suffering on others.
Pedophilic Disorder	Sexual interest towards prepubescent children without secondary sex characteristics.
Fetishistic Disorder	Sexual interest towards non-living objects or non-genital parts of the body.
Transvestic Disorder	Sexual interest in cross-dressing.

Note. Definitions taken from the *DSM-5* (American Psychiatric Association, 2013). Interested readers are directed to Seto, Kingston, and Bourget (2014) for a comprehensive review and discussion of paraphilic interests comorbidity amongst paraphilias. For example, in clinical and forensic samples there is a high rate of comorbidity between voyeurism and other paraphilic disorders, such as exhibitionism and frotteurism (e.g. Freund, 1990; Krueger & Kaplan, 2016). The presence of multiple paraphilias is important to document during an assessment as it is associated with higher rates of sexual recidivism (e.g., Hanson & Morton-Bourgon, 2005).

The following paraphilias have been identified as important motivators of sexual offending: pedophilia, hebephilia, sadism, voyeurism, exhibitionism, frotteurism, and paraphilic coercive disorder, which would likely be seen in a higher number of those who have committed sexual offenses (Pullman, Stephens, & Seto, 2016). Two of the abovementioned paraphilias are not explicitly mentioned in *DSM-5* but are sometimes present in those who have committed sexual offenses. Hebephilia refers to a sexual interest in pubescent children, which has a high degree of overlap with pedophilia and similar sexual offending correlates (Stephens, Seto, Goodwill, & Cantor, 2017, 2018). Paraphilic coercive disorder refers to the preference for coercive sexual interactions. Some men who have committed sexual offenses display an arousal pattern suggestive of a greater response to cues of coercion than consent (Harris, Lalumière, Seto, Rice, & Chaplin, 2012).

Despite these findings, it is important to note that the relationship between sexual offending and paraphilias is not synonymous. For example, pedophilia has been estimated to be present in 50–60% of those who offend against children, whereas 40–50% offend against children for other reasons (Seto, 2008). This suggests that not all those convicted of a sexual offense have been diagnosed with paraphilic disorders and not all individuals who have paraphilias engage in illegal sexual behavior (Cantor & McPhail, 2015; Seto, 2018).

9.2.2.2   Sexual Preoccupation

Sexual preoccupation refers to a significant interest in sex that dominates one's functioning (Mann et al., 2010). Sexual preoccupation is a term that has strong conceptual overlap with hypersexuality. Hypersexuality refers to diminished control over sexual fantasies, sexual urges, or sexual behaviors that can manifest in two ways; (1) acts done onto oneself such as frequent masturbation and excessive pornography use, or (2) relational sexual acts, such as frequent sex with multiple partners (Kafka, 2010; Kingston & Bradford, 2013; Långström & Hanson, 2006). There has been some research on the prevalence of hypersexuality among those who have committed sexual offenses. For example, Kingston and Bradford (2013) found 12% of individuals who committed sexual offenses had hypersexuality. Moreover, certain components of hypersexuality were strongly correlated with sexual aggression (Malamuth, 2003; Ward, Polaschek, & Beech, 2006). For example, college men who are sexually aggressive were more likely to engage in higher levels of sexual fantasies and urges and to have a greater number of sexual partners, in comparison to non-coercive men (Malamuth, 2003).

9.2.3 Assessment of Paraphilic Interests and Sexual Preoccupation

Seto et al. (2014) have provided a comprehensive overview of the assessment of paraphilic sexual interests highlighting the importance of a multimodal examination that includes a mental status exam to identify co-occurring mental disorders, a psychosexual history, a sex hormone profile, and psychophysiological testing to identify sexual arousal patterns (Seto et al., 2014). In the present section we review some of the more commonly used assessment measures that are used to assess paraphilic interests and sexual preoccupation.

A frequently used psychophysiological measure in the assessment of paraphilias is phallometric assessment. Phallometry measures change in penile circumference or volume in response to sexual stimuli that differ by age and gender, as well as the presence or the absence of violence (Laws, 2009; Seto et al., 2014). In a recent meta-analysis, phallometric testing was predictive of sexual recidivism and discriminated between those who offended against children in comparison to those who offended against adults, those who committed non-sexual offenses, and community controls (McPhail et al., 2017).

Efforts have been dedicated to developing alternative measures to the phallometric assessment because of limitations related to cost, participant resistance due to discomfort, and accessibility (Seto et al., 2014). Viewing time is one such alternative that involves people rating their sexual interest in images while time spent viewing is unobtrusively recorded. A meta-analysis by Schmidt, Babchishin, and Lehmann (2017) suggested that viewing time discriminated between those who offended against children and control groups. To our knowledge, the ability of viewing time to predict sexual recidivism has not been examined.

Additionally, assessors often utilize self-report to examine sexual thoughts, fantasies, and urges, which has utility in the assessment of paraphilias and sexual preoccupation. Many of these measures have embedded validity indices that allow for an examination of response style, which is particularly useful given that those who are being assessed may be motivated to mislead the assessor. One example of a self-report inventory is the *Multiphasic Sex Inventory II* (MSI-II; Nichols & Molinder, 2000), which assesses sexual characteristics of adult males who have committed a sexual offense. The MSI-II can contribute to the assessment of psychosexual history and paraphilic interests and be used to measure treatment progress (Hoberman & Riedel, 2016). The original version of the MSI has shown to be effective in various areas including, differentiating offender subtypes based on victim type and aiding in the assessment of paraphilic interests (Angioli, 2016; Simkins, Ward, Bowman, & Rinck, 1989).

There are also examples of measures designed to assess paraphilias that can be scored using victim information. These measures are based on research that has examined the behavioral correlates of paraphilic interests (e.g., there exist several indicators that would increase the likelihood of pedophilia, such as child pornography use; Seto, Cantor, & Blanchard, 2006). For example, the *Revised Screening Scale for Pedophilic Interests* (or SSPI-2) is a useful tool for the assessment of pedophilia in those who offend against child victims. The SSPI-2 is composed of five items: boy victim, multiple child victims, extrafamilial victims, young child victims under the age of 12, and child pornography; all of which have been found to be correlated with pedophilia (Seto, Stephens, Lalumière, & Cantor, 2017b). The SSPI-2 has been shown to have convergent and divergent validity and is predictive of sexual recidivism (Seto, Sandler, & Freeman, 2017a).

9.2.4   Antisocial Orientation

Antisocial orientation is another important construct to assess, given the significant role it plays in understanding criminal offending (e.g., Andrews & Bonta, 2010). Antisocial orientation describes an individual who is impulsive, aggressive, and engages in general criminal behavior (e.g., Andrews & Bonta, 2010). It is a broad term that encompasses several related consturcts. Antisocial Personality Disorder (ASPD) is a personality disorder in the *DSM-5* that reflects a longstanding pattern of disregard for the rights of others and societal norms (American Psychiatric Association, 2013). Psychopathy refers to a personality constellation that encompasses a socially deviant lifestyle that most closely maps onto the criteria for ASPD; however, it also includes interpersonal and affective deficits (e.g., lack of remorse, callousness, and a grandiose sense of self). In the *DSM-5*, ASPD is recognized as a mental health disorder, whereas psychopathy is not. Psychopathy has been found to be more prevalent in those who sexually offend against adults and those who are polymorphic (offend against both children and adults), compared to those who sexually offend against children or who commit incest (e.g., Olver & Wong, 2006; Porter et al., 2000).

A frequently used assessment tool is the *Psychopathy Checklist-Revised* (PCL-R), a 20-item checklist that assesses psychopathy (Hare, 2003). Meta-analyses suggest that the PCL-R is a significant predictor of recidivism in those who have committed sexual offenses; however, the social deviance factor is a stronger predictor than the interpersonal-affective deficits factor (Hawes, Boccaccini, & Murrie, 2013). This has led to significant debate, as some have argued that this factor is redundant with risk assessment tools that already capture criminal history (see Skeem & Cooke, 2010 for discussion and Hare & Neumann, 2010 for a response). It is notable that psychopathic traits can interact with other risk factors, such as paraphilic sexual interests and the presence of both may confer an even higher risk for sexual recidivism than when either is present alone (Hawes et al., 2013).

9.2.5   Risk Assessment

A central feature of assessment of men who have committed sexual offenses involves risk assessment. Despite public perception of high rates of sexual recidivism (e.g., Katz-Schiavone, Levenson, & Ackerman, 2008), meta-analyses have reported 10–15% of those with a sexual offense reoffend (e.g., Hanson & Morton-Bourgon, 2005; Helmus, Hanson, Thornton, Babchishin, & Harris, 2012). Nevertheless, addressing future sexual offending is of high importance. Two types of risk factors are commonly included in risk assessment: (1) static risk factors that are typically historical and cannot change, such as age at first offense, and (2) dynamic (criminogenic) risk factors that can change, such as substance use. Dynamic factors are often the focus of treatment interventions as they are changable and add incrementally to static risk factors in the prediction of recidivism (e.g., Hanson, Harris, Scott, & Helmus, 2007).

There are many risk assessment tools that are used and it is beyond the scope of the chapter to review them all. Risk assessments generally rely on either an actuarial or a structured professional judgment (SPJ) approach. Actuarial risk measures involve assessing risk factors that have been statistically found to be associated with recidivism. Actuarial measures include specific instructions on how to combine items into a final score, which is associated with a recidivism estimate. Conversely, SPJ tools utilize risk factors that have been identified in the literature as significant predictors of recidivism; however, there are no instructions on how to combine the items into a final score, as the final risk determination is achieved through structured clinical judgement (see Hart & Logan, 2011 for full explanation of the SPJ approach). A meta-analysis conducted by Hanson and Morton-Bourgon (2009) examined the accuracy of risk assessments by comparing actuarial and SPJ measures. They found that actuarial approaches had the highest predictive accuracy, followed by SPJ tools, and lastly unstructured professional judgement. We briefly review a few of the more frequently used risk assessment measures in both domains.

9.2.5.1 Actuarial Risk Assessments

Actuarial risk scales are among the most commonly used risk assessment tools for sexual recidivism and the most frequently used tools are the *STATIC* family of measures (Archer, Buffington-Vollum, Stredny, & Handel, 2006; Jackson & Hess, 2007). For example, the *STATIC-99R* contains 10 historical risk factors (e.g., history of sexual offending) associated with sexual recidivism (e.g., Hanson & Morton-Bourgon, 2009). Although it is easy to score, the *STATIC-99R* is criticized for being entirely composed of static risk factors, thereby ignoring dynamic risk factors, which are important in risk management (e.g., Hanson & Harris, 2000). To assess dynamic risk factors, the *STABLE-2007* (Hanson et al., 2007) was developed to be used in conjunction with the *STATIC-99R*. In contrast to the *STATIC-99R*, the *STABLE-2007* includes risk factors that are changeable through intervention, such as hostility towards women. Eher, Matthes, Schilling, Haubner-MacLean, and Rettenberger (2012) reported that the *STABLE-2007* significantly predicted sexual recidivism (see Eher et al., 2012 for a full history of the *STABLE* tools) and the *STABLE-2007* adds to the predictive validity of the *STATIC-99* (Hanson et al., 2007).

Another actuarial tool is the *Violence Risk Scale—Sexual Offender version* (VRS-SO; Wong, Olver, Nicholaichuk, & Gordon, 2003), which measures static and dynamic risk factors, as well as stages of change. The VRS-SO measures seven static factors regarding legal history and victim characteristics and 17 dynamic factors across atypical sexual interests, criminality, and treatment responsivity categories. The VRS-SO has demonstrated good psychometric properties (Canales, Olver, & Wong, 2009; Olver, Wong, Nicholaichuk, & Gordon, 2007) and is predictive of sexual recidivism (Beggs & Grace, 2010; Olver et al., 2007).

9.2.5.2 Structured Professional Judgement

There are several SPJ tools for sexual offending that include a significant number of dynamic risk factors allowing the assessor to provide a comprehensive risk formulation and recommendations for risk management (e.g., Logan, 2016). One example of a SPJ tool is the *Sexual Violence Risk—20* (SVR-20; Boer, Hart, Kropp, & Webster, 1997). This tool includes static and dynamic risk factors across 20 items, covering the domains of psychosocial adjustment, sexual offenses, and future plans. The SVR-20 has been found to be associated with recidivism (de Vogel, de Ruiter, van Beek, & Mead, 2004; Hanson & Morton-Bourgon, 2009). Another SPJ measures is the *Risk of Sexual Violence Protocol* (RSVP), which can be used to better guide risk formulation and management (Laws, n.d.; Hart et al., 2003).

9.2.5.3 Assessment of Protective Factors

An advancement in the risk assessment field is the more explicit consideration of protective factors. Protective factors are characteristics that decrease risk for recidivism and include factors such as social support, healthy sexual interests, and problem solving skills (see de Vries Robbé, Mann, Maruna, & Thornton, 2015b for full explanation of protective factors). One recently developed measure that examines protective factors is the *Structured Assessment of Protective Factors* for violence risk (SAPROF; de Vogel, de Ruiter, Bouman, & de Vries Robbe, 2009) and its authors suggest using the SAPROF in conjunction with dynamic actuarial risk assessments (de Vries Robbé, de Vogel, Koster, & Bogaerts, 2015a). The inclusion of protective factors in risk assessment adds incremental validity to static and dynamic risk factors (de Vries Robbé, de Vogel, et al., 2015a); however, some have argued that protective factors are the inverse of risk factors and that their inclusion in risk assessment is redundant (see Harris & Rice, 2015 for a discussion).

9.3   Theoretical Models Relevant to Service Delivery

9.3.1   Risk Needs Responsivity Model

The risk-need-responsivity (RNR) model is the gold standard for the management of those who have committed offenses (Fortune & Ward, 2014). The three main principles of the RNR model are the *risk principle*, which states that risk level should guide service delivery (e.g., higher risk cases should receive more services than lower risk cases); the *needs principle* that risk management must target dynamic risk factors directly linked to criminal behavior; and the *responsivity principle* that interventions should be tailored to individual learning styles, abilities and motivational factors (Andrews, Bonta, & Hoge, 1990; Stinson & Becker, 2013). This model has been applied successfully to those who have sexually offended and have a mental health disorder (e.g., Bonta, Law, & Hanson, 1998; Gannon, King, Miles, Lockerbie, & Willis, 2011) and those who have sexually offended who have not been diagnosed with a mental health disorder (e.g., Bonta & Andrews, 2007; Hanson, Bourgon, Helmus, & Hodgson, 2009). While there have been critiques of the RNR model, specifically in its preoccupation with risk management (Ward & Maruna, 2007; Ward, Yates, & Willis, 2012), meta-analyses have suggested that RNR is an effective approach to the management of those who have committed sexual offenses (Hanson et al., 2009; Lösel & Schmucker, 2005).

9.3.2   Good Lives Model

The Good Lives Model (GLM; Ward & Brown, 2004; Ward & Gannon, 2006; Ward & Stewart, 2003) was developed to address some of the limitations of the RNR model. Proponents of the GLM model argue that mitigating and managing the risk of reoffending is not sufficient for rehabilitation. As a result, treatment programs must provide individuals with skills to develop fulfilling lives and therefore address criminogenic and non-criminogenic needs (Ward & Brown, 2004; Willis, Yates, Gannon, & Ward, 2012). The GLM focuses on encouraging individuals to develop positive psychological wellbeing through the acquisition of human goods. The GLM relies on the underlying assumption that all humans have the same basic needs and aspirations in life and criminal behavior results from an inability to attain these desired values in a prosocial way (i.e., because of inadequate access to sufficient resources; Fortune & Ward, 2014). Alternatively, the pursuit of primary goals can cause a ripple effect in the individual's life and the unexpected outcomes contribute to offending behavior (Lindsay, Ward, Morgan, & Wilson, 2007; Ward & Gannon, 2006; Willis et al., 2012). Within this model, criminal activity is not seen as an end goal, rather a means to an end (Yates, 2016).

The GLM targets approach goals, meaning that the treatment looks for ways to achieve the goals in place of a prosocial life (which does not include offending) rather than focusing on avoiding offending as an end goal. There are two suggested ways to reduce risk, the first is to attain primary goods through external and internal resources in a way that is conducive to a crime-free life. The second is through indirect motivation to participate in treatment by planning to attain involvement in a project the individual cares deeply about (Dumas & Ward, 2016). This model suggests that rehabilitation should provide those who have committed sexual offenses with necessary resources to attain their goals in a prosocial manner, while recognizing that those who have committed offenses may need different levels of support to develop the skills required to implement and develop a prosocial life plan.

Despite addressing the limitations of the RNR model, there has been discussion about the added contribution of GLM to programs (Ward, Collie, & Bourke, 2009). Ward and Stewart (2003) have suggested that sexual offending treatment programs adapt a hybrid approach by incorporating principles of both RNR and the GLM. Although the GLM has been established as a theoretical treatment model for those who have committed sexual offenses, there is a need for additional research (Stinson & Becker, 2013). For example, there is a limited knowledge regarding the efficacy of the GLM in treatment (Willis, Ward, & Levenson, 2014).

9.4 Interventions

Overall, there is debate about the effectiveness of interventions for individuals who have committed sexual offenses and significant disagreement on best practices for conducting treatment studies. This debate is in part fuelled by the absence of high quality treatment studies that use a Randomized-Controlled Trial design (RCT; randomizing those who commit offenses to treatment conditions, including a control group), which is a significant limitation, as RCTs are the strongest methodological design to establish treatment effectiveness. RCTs are challenging to conduct in forensic settings for numerous reasons. For example, there are ethical concerns about withholding treatment from individuals who have committed sexual offenses. As a result, some have argued for alternatives to RCTs, such as comparing rates of recidivism for treated individuals compared to the expected recidivism rates published with actuarial tools (Marshall & Marshall, 2007). Despite the possibility of such alternatives, many have argued that the evidence base for treatment is weak due to the absence of RCTs (Dennis et al., 2012; Seto et al., 2008).

Given the significant debate, meta-analyses are important in clarifying the effectiveness of treatment. Several meta-analyses have been conducted (see Dennis et al., 2012; Hanson et al., 2002; Lösel & Schmucker, 2005; Schmucker & Lösel, 2008, 2015), despite the lack of high quality empirical studies. The most recent meta-analysis included 29 studies of 4939 treated compared to 5448 untreated individuals who committed sexual offenses. They found a small effect for treatment with those who had completed treatment having a 10.1% recidivism rate compared to a 13.7% recidivism rate in the untreated group (Schmucker & Lösel, 2015). One significant moderator was the type of treatment offered to participants. Multisystemic therapy (intensive treatment program offered to youth that targets multiple domains, such as individual characteristics, family, peer, and community contexts) had the largest effects, which likely contributed to the finding that there is a larger effect size for adolescents receiving treatment compared with adults. Cognitive-Behavioral Therapy (CBT) was the only other treatment that had a significant effect on recidivism and will be the focus here when discussing psychological interventions.

9.4.1 Psychological Interventions

CBT is a comprehensive treatment that involves teaching clients skills, such as cognitive restructuring, understanding the cycle of sexual abuse, anger management, social skills, and understanding the perspective of victims (e.g., Geer, Estupinan, & Manguno-Mire, 2000; Marshall, 1999). A crucial focus in CBT treatment is the focus on cognitions, which is of great importance because they can lead to offense supportive attitudes that minimize or justify sexual offending (e.g., Blumenthal, Gudjonsson, & Burns, 1999), or lead the individual to misinterpret social cues leading to offending behavior (e.g., Blake & Gannon, 2008). Offense supportive attitudes are an important dynamic risk factor and recent longitudinal research has suggested that they likely play a contributing role in sexual aggression in men living in the community (Hermann & Nunes, 2016).

Another focus in CBT is working to promote behavioral change, which can be achieved using numerous methods; however we will briefly highlight behavioral reconditioning and relapse prevention. All behavioral reconditioning approaches have the same goal of decreasing sexual arousal to paraphilic stimuli or increasing arousal to appropriate stimuli. For example, satiation therapy involves masturbation to an appropriate fantasy until ejaculation followed by continued masturbation to an inappropriate fantasy. This contrasts with arousal reconditioning, which involves an individual masturbating to an appropriate sex stimuli or appropriate fantasies (Freund & Dougher, 2011). Although some studies have cited the effectiveness of behavioral reconditioning (Hunter, Ram, & Ryback, 2008; Marshall, 1979), others have found that there is a lack of ecological validity (Rea et al., 2003). This suggests that while this treatment may have positive effects in a laboratory, it is not likely to be effective in promoting persistent change in a natural setting. Further, the use of behavioral reconditioning is based on the premise that paraphilic interests are malleable and although there is some debate, many researchers argue that such interests are imutable (e.g., Seto, 2012).

Another major component of CBT programs is relapse prevention (RP), which has remained a dominant treatment framework with over 50% of treatment providers endorsing this model (McGrath, Cumming, Burchard, Zeoli, & Ellerby, 2010). RP treatment programs focus on the potential cognitive, affective, and behavioral factors (e.g., thoughts, feelings, places, people, and situations) that could lead to recidivism and how decisions can impact one's ability to avoid or manage high-risk situations (e.g., Laws & Ward, 2011). One of the few RCTs on the treatment of adult males who had committed sexual offenses relied heavily on the RP model, but found negligible results. Marques, Wiederanders, Day, Nelson, and van Ommeren (2005) randomized 704 individuals to RP treatment (including CBT skills delivered in the context of this model) or no treatment. Results suggest that reoffense rates were similar across groups; however, the treatment group committed less sexually intrusive reoffenses than the control group. Aside from the interpretation that treatment is ineffective for those who have committed sexual offenses, several possibilities were raised that could potentially explain these results. For example, the study was limited due to unequal treatment and non-treatment groups, as the treatment group was hospitalized whereas the control group was not.

9.4.2 Biological Interventions

A variety of biological interventions have been utilized, particularly when there are concerns regarding paraphilic sexual interests or sexual preoccupation. Pharmacological approaches are most commonly utilized, which involve the use of medications to reduce male testosterone (Kutcher, 2010). There are a variety of medications that may be used, including androgen deprivation therapies (including medroxyprogesterone acetate and cyproterone acetate; Kutcher, 2010) and gonadotropin releasing hormones (Amelung, Kuhle, Konrad, Pauls, & Beier, 2012). The effectiveness of pharmacological treatment in the reduction of sex drive is controversial and there are many issues when examining treatment efficacy, such as small sample sizes and treatment dropout (Amelung et al., 2012; Hucker, Langevin, & Bain, 1988). Further, there may be a selection bias, as individuals who consent to this form of treatment are more likely to be aware of their risk (Amelung et al., 2012). Meta-analyses suggest that hormonal medications show the highest mean effect on recidivism rates (Schmucker & Lösel, 2008); however, the benefits are also to be considered in light of significant side effects of these medications leading to high dropout rates and non-compliance.

9.5 Future Directions

Research on those who have committed sexual offenses has grown exponentially and there have been significant advancements in our understanding of assessment and management. Perhaps one of the most significant advancements is research on early intervention and prevention of sexual crimes against children. The Prevention Project Dunkelfeld is a program developed to provide services to individuals with pedophilia who are help-seeking and not currently involved in the legal system (Beier et al., 2009). This program is an example of a primary prevention program that targets at-risk individuals for treatment services. Initial pilot results show a significant reduction in dynamic risk factors in the treatment group

(Beier et al., 2015). Future research is needed to aid in the development of this type of programming in North America, as there are significant barriers in this region (e.g., mandatory reporting; Lasher & Stinson, 2016). Additionally, many individuals offend aginast children for reasons other than a sexual interest in children and prevention initiatives should be broadened to reach these individuals for primary prevention programming.

Recent research has also examined the effects of adversarial allegiance in forensic psychology, including in high stakes evaluation of those who have committed sexual offenses (e.g., Fabian, 2011; Murrie, Boccaccini, Guanera, & Rufino, 2013; Neal, 2016). Despite adequate reliability, the scoring of risk assessment tools suggests partisan allegiance in civil commitment evaluations. Risk estimates assigned by experts are often in favour of the side that retained the expert, beyond what would be expected by standard error (Murrie, Boccaccini, Johnson, & Janke, 2008; Murrie et al., 2009). Additional research on clinician bias and its impact on decision-making is needed as well as innovative methods to reduce clinician bias in decision-making.

9.6 Technology and Innovation

As technology has become ubiquitous in our world, it can only be assumed that efforts would be dedicated to integrating technology in both the identification and treatment of those who have committed sexual offenses. One way of utilizing technology would involve reaching individuals who have sexual interest in children and may be at risk of committing a sexual offense. These individuals may face many issues when disclosing their sexual interest to mental health professionals (see Glaser, 2010 for further explanation of this dilemma as well as the discussion of prevention strategies discussed above). The use of technology can provide opportunities for confidential and accessible outreach initiatives and treatment that is likely more appealing. For example, technology allows individuals to potentially access anonymous online support who may be struggling not to offend due to sexual interest in children (e.g. Troubled Desire, https://www.troubled-desire.com/en/about.html).

Further, online educational opportunities are available for professionals who may work with those who have committed sexual offenses. Some examples of these training programs include the Sex Offender Awareness Program at the Justice Institute of British Columbia, the Forensic Training Institute, and the Global Institute of Forensic Research. These programs offer opportunities to learn specific skills, such as how to assess individuals who have committed sexual offenses or apply a type of treatment modality, as well as opportunities to learn about sub-populations of those who commit offenses, such as those with an intellectual disability. The online training movement increases the accessibility of high quality training.

9.7   Conclusion

Men who have committed sexual offenses are a heterogeneous population. Statistics on the frequency of sexual violence suggest that it is a widespread, but an underreported issue. When assessing and managing those who commit sexual offenses it is important to conduct a comprehensive multimodal assessment. The assessment should involve the examination of empirically supported risk factors and incorporate risk assessment tools. Risk assessments should be used to guide the management of those who have committed sexual offenses. Research has suggested that treatment has a small effect on reducing recidivism, particularly when the RNR model is followed and CBT is utilized. Although the field has grown exponentially, there remains important future research directions, such as continuing early intervention and prevention efforts and addressing adversarial allegiance. There is also a need for future research on the role of technology in making assessment, treatment, and training more accessible.

References

Amelung, T., Kuhle, L., Konrad, A., Pauls, A., & Beier, K. (2012). Androgen deprivation therapy of self-identifying, help seeking pedophiles in Dunkelfeld. *International Journal of Law and Psychiatry, 35*, 176–184. https://doi.org/10.1016/j.ijlp.2012.02.005

American Psychiatric Association. (2013). *Diagnostic and statistical manual of mental disorders* (5th ed.). Washington, DC: Author.

Andrews, D. R., & Bonta, J. (2010). *The psychology of criminal conduct* (5th ed.). New Providence, NJ: Matthew Bender & Company.

Andrews, D. A., Bonta, J., & Hoge, R. D. (1990). Classification for effective rehabilitation: Rediscovering psychology. *Criminal Justice and Behavior, 17*, 19–52. https://doi.org/10.1177/0093854890017001004

Angioli, S. (2016). A comparison of the Affinity 2.5's viewing time measure and The Multiphasic Sex Inventory II's (MSI II) Molester Comparison scale. *Dissertation Abstracts International, 77*.

Archer, R. P., Buffington-Vollum, J. K., Stredny, R. V., & Handel, R. W. (2006). A survey of psychological test use patterns among forensic psychologists. *Journal of Personality Assessment, 87*, 84–94. https://doi.org/10.1207/s15327752jpa8701_07

ATSA (2010). *Civil commitment of sexually violent predators*. Retrieved from http://www.atsa.com/civil-commitment-sexually-violent-predators

Beggs, S. M., & Grace, R. C. (2010). Assessment of dynamic risk factors: An independent validation study of the Violence Risk Scale: Sexual Offender Version. *Sexual Abuse: A Journal of Research and Treatment, 22*, 234–251. https://doi.org/10.1177/1079063210369014

Beier, K. M., Grundmann, D., Kuhle, L. F., Scherner, G., Konrad, A., & Amelung, T. (2015). The German Dunkelfeld project: A pilot study to prevent child sexual abuse and the use of child abusive images. *Journal of Sexual Medicine, 12*, 529–542. https://doi.org/10.1111/jsm.1278

Beier, K. M., Neutze, J., Mundt, I. A., Ahlers, C. J., Goecker, D., Konrad, A., … Schaefer, G. A. (2009). Encouraging self-identified pedophiles and hebephiles to seek professional help: First results of the Prevention Project Dunkelfield (PPD). *Child Abuse & Neglect, 33*, 543–549. https://doi.org/10.1016/j.chiabu.2009.04.002

Blake, E., & Gannon, T. (2008). Social perception deficits, cognitive distortions, and empathy deficits in sex offenders. *Trauma, Violence, & Abuse, 9*, 34–55. https://doi.org/10.1177/1524838007311104

Blumenthal, S., Gudjonsson, G., & Burns, J. (1999). Cognitive distortions and blame attribution in sex offenders against adults and children. *Child Abuse & Neglect, 23*, 129–143. https://doi.org/10.1016/S0145-2134(98)00117-3

Boer, D. P., Hart, S. D., Kropp, P. R., & Webster, C. D. (1997). *Manual for the Sexual Violence Risk—20: Professional guidelines for assessing risk of sexual violence*. Vancouver, BC: The Mental Health, Law, and Policy Institute.

Bonta, J. & Andrews, D. A. (2007). *Risk-need-responsivity model for offender assessment and treatment*. (User Report No. 2007-06). Ottawa, ON: Public Safety Canada.

Bonta, J., Law, M., & Hanson, K. (1998). The prediction of criminal and violent recidivism among mentally disordered offenders: A meta-analysis. *Psychological Bulletin, 123*, 123–142. https://doi.org/10.1037/0033-2909.123.2.123

Brennan, S., & Taylor-Butts, A. (2008). Sexual assault in Canada 2004 and 2007. *Canadian Centre for Justice Statistics Profile Series, 19*, 1–20.

Canales, D. D., Olver, M. E., & Wong, S. C. (2009). Construct validity of the Violence Risk Scale—Sexual Offender version for measuring sexual deviance. *Sexual Abuse, 21*, 474–492. https://doi.org/10.1177/1079063209344990

Cantor, J. M., & McPhail, I. V. (2015). Sensitivity and specifity of the phallometric test for hebephilia. *The Journal of Sexual Medicine, 12*, 1940–1950. https://doi.org/10.1111/jsm.12970

Cortoni, F. (2018). *Women who sexually abuse: Assessment, treatment, and management*. Brandon, VT: Safer Society Press.

Crocker, A. G., Nicholls, T. L., Seto, M. C., Charette, Y., Cote, G., & Caulet, M. (2015). The national trajectory project of individuals found not criminally responsible on account of a mental disorder in Canada. Part 2: The people behind the label. *Canadian Journal of Psychiatry, 60*, 106–116.

Dawson, S. J., Bannerman, B. A., & Lalumière, M. (2016). Paraphilic interests: An examination of sex differences in a nonclinical sample. *Sexual Abuse: A Journal of Treatment and Research, 28*, 20–45. https://doi.org/10.1177/1079063214525645

de Vogel, V., de Ruiter, C., Bouman, Y., & de Vries Robbe, M. (2009). *Guidelines for the assessment of protective factors for violence risk. English version*. Utrecht, The Netherlands: Forum Educatief.

de Vogel, V., de Ruiter, C., van Beek, D., & Mead, G. (2004). Predictive validity of the SVR-20 and Static-99 in a Dutch sample of treated sex offenders. *Law and Human Behavior, 28*, 235–251. https://doi.org/10.1023/B:LAHU.0000029137.41974.eb

de Vries Robbé, M., de Vogel, V., Koster, K., & Bogaerts, S. (2015a). Assessing protective factors for sexually violent offending with the SAPROF. *Sexual Abuse: A Journal of Research and Treatment, 27*, 51–70. https://doi.org/10.1177/1079063214550168

de Vries Robbé, M., Mann, R. E., Maruna, S., & Thornton, D. (2015b). An exploration of protective factors supporting desistance from sexual offending. *Sexual Abuse: A Journal of Research and Treatment, 27*, 16–33. https://doi.org/10.1177/1079063214547852

Dennis, J. A., Khan, O., Ferriter, M., Huband, N., Powney, M. J., & Duggan, C. (2012). Psychological interventions for adults who have sexually offended or are at risk of offending. *Cochrane Database of Systematic Reviews*. https://doi.org/10.1002/14651858.CD007507.pub2

Doren, D. M. (2002). *Evaluating sex offenders: A manual for civil commitments and beyond*. Thousand Oaks, CA: Sage Publications.

Dumas, L., & Ward, T. (2016). The good lives model of offender rehabilitation. *The Behavior Therapist, 39*, 175–177.

Eher, R., Matthes, A., Schilling, F., Haubner-MacLean, T., & Rettenberger, M. (2012). Dynamic risk assessment in sexual offenders using STABLE-2000 and the STABLE-2007: An investigation of predictive and incremental validity. *Sexual Abuse: A Joruanl of Research and Treatment, 24*, 5–28. https://doi.org/10.1177/1079063211403164

Elwood, R. W. (2009). Mental disorder, predisposition, prediction, and ability to control: Evaluating sex offenders for civil commitment. *Sexual Abuse: A Journal of Research and Treatment, 21*, 395–411. https://doi.org/10.1177/1079063209347723

Fabian, J. M. (2011). Paraphilias and predators: The ethical application of psychiatric diagnoses in partisan sexually violent predator civil commitment proceedings. *Journal of Forensic Psychology Practice, 11*, 82–98. https://doi.org/10.1080/15228932.2011.521723

Fisher, B. S., Cullen, F. T., & Turner, M. G. (2000). *The sexual victimization of college women*. Research Report. Washington, DC: U.S. Department of Justice, Bureau of Justice Statistics and National Institute of Justice.

Fortune, C., & Ward, T. (2014). Integrating strength-based practice with forensic CBT: Good lives model of offender rehabilitation. In R. C. Tafrate & D. Mitchell (Eds.), *Forensic CBT: A handbook for clinical practice* (pp. 436–452). Chichester, UK: John Wiley & Sons.

Freund, K. (1990). Courtship disorder. In W. L. Marshall, D. L. Laws, & H. E. Barbaree (Eds.), *Handbook of sexual assault: Issues, theories, and treatment of the offendes* (pp. 195–207). New York, NY: Springer.

Freund, R., & Dougher, M. (2011). Behavioral techniques to alter sexual arousal. In B. Schwartz (Ed.), *Handbook of sex offender treatment* (pp. 25-1–25-10). Kingston, NJ: Civic Research Institute.

Gannon, T., King, T., Miles, H., Lockerbie, L., & Willis, G. (2011). Good lives sexual offender treatment for mentally disordered offenders. *The British Journal of Forensic Practice, 13*, 153–168. https://doi.org/10.1108/14636641111157805

Geer, J. H., Estupinan, L. A., & Manguno-Mire, G. M. (2000). Empathy, social skills, and other relevant cognitive processes in rapists and child molesters. *Aggression and Violent Behavior, 5*, 99–126. https://doi.org/10.1016/S1359-1789(98)00011-1

Glaser, B. (2010). Sex offender programmes: New technology coping with old ethics. *Journal of Sexual Aggression, 16*, 261–274. https://doi.org/10.1080/13552600.2010.483139

Hanson, R. K., Bourgon, G., Helmus, L., & Hodgson, S. (2009). The principles of effective correctional treatment also apply to sexual offenders: A meta-analysis. *Criminal Justice and Behavior, 36*, 865–891. https://doi.org/10.1177/0093854809338545

Hanson, R. K., Gordon, A., Harris, A. J. R., Marques, J. K., Murphy, W., Quinsey, V. L., & Seto, M. C. (2002). First report of the Collaborative Outcome Data Project on the effectiveness of treatment for sexual offenders. *Sexual Abuse: A Journal of Research and Treatment, 14*, 169–194. https://doi.org/10.1177/107906320201400207

Hanson, R. K., & Harris, A. J. R. (2000). Where should we intervene: Dynamic predictors of sexual offense recidivism. *Criminal Justice and Behavior, 27*, 6–35. https://doi.org/10.1177/0093854800027001002

Hanson, R. K., Harris, A. J. R., Scott, T. L., & Helmus, L. (2007). *Assessing the risk of sexual offenders on community supervision: The Dynamic Supervision Project* (Corrections Research User Report No. 2007-05). Ottawa, ON: Public Safety Canada.

Hanson, R. K., & Morton-Bourgon, K. E. (2005). The characteristics of persistent sexual offenders: A meta-analysis of recidivism studies. *Journal of Consulting and Clinical Psychology, 73*, 1154–1163. https://doi.org/10.1037/0022-006X.73.6.1154

Hanson, R. K., & Morton-Bourgon, K. E. (2009). The accuracy of recidivism risk assessments for sexual offenders: A meta-analysis of 118 prediction studies. *Psychological Assessment, 21*, 1–21. https://doi.org/10.1037/a0014421

Hare, R. D. (2003). *The Hare Psychopathy Checklist-Revised (PCL-R)* (2nd ed.). Toronto, ON: Multi-Health Systems.

Hare, R. D., & Neumann, C. S. (2010). The role of antisociality in the psychopathy construct: Comment on Skeem and Cooke (2010). *Psychological Assessment, 22*, 446–454. https://doi.org/10.1037/a0013635

Harris, G. T., Lalumière, M. L., Seto, M. C., Rice, M. E., & Chaplin, T. C. (2012). Explaining the erectile responses of rapists to rape stories: The contributions of sexual activity, non-consent, and violence with injury. *Archives of Sexual Behavior, 41*, 221–229. https://doi.org/10.1007/s10508-012-9940-8

Harris, G. T., & Rice, M. E. (2015). Progress in violence risk assessment and communication: Hypothesis versus evidence. *Behavioral Sciences and the Law, 33*, 128–145. https://doi.org/10.1002/bsi.2157

Hart, S. D., Kropp, R., Laws, D. R., Klaver, J., Logan, C., & Watt, K. A (2003). *The Risk for Sexual Violence Protocol (RSVP)—Structured professional guideline for assessing risk of sexual violence*. Vancouver, BC: Simon Fraser University, Mental Health, Law and Policy Institute. Retrieved from: http://pacific-assmt.com/wp-content/uploads/2010/04/RSVP-JSA-review.pdf

Hart, S. D., & Logan, C. (2011). Formulation of violence risk using evidence-based assessments: The structured professional judgment approach. In P. Sturmey & M. McMurran (Eds.), *Forensic case formulation* (pp. 83–106). Wiley-Blackwell: Chichester, UK.

Hawes, S. W., Boccaccini, M. T., & Murrie, D. C. (2013). Psychopathy and the combination of psychopathy and sexual deviance as predictors of sexual recidivism: Meta-analytic findings using the Psychopathy Checklist-Revised. *Psychological Assessment, 25*, 233–243. https://doi.org/10.1037/a0030391

Helmus, L., Hanson, R. K., Thornton, D., Babchishin, K. M., & Harris, A. J. (2012). Absolute recidivism rates predicted by Static-99R and Static-2002R sex offender risk assessment tools vary across samples: A meta-analysis. *Criminal Justice and Behavior, 39*, 1148–1171. https://doi.org/10.1177/0093854812443648

Hermann, C. A., & Nunes, K. L. (2016). Implicit and explicit evaluations of sexual aggression predict subsequent sexually aggressive behavior in a sample of community men. *Sexual Abuse: A Journal of Research and Treatment*. https://doi.org/10.1177/1079063216682952

Hoberman, H. M., & Riedel, R. G. (2016). Structured psychological assessment in evaluations of sexual offenders: Nature and applications. In A. Phenix, H. M. Hoberman, A. Phenix, & H. M. Hoberman (Eds.), *Sexual offending: Predisposing antecedents, assessments and management* (pp. 279–329). New York, NY: Springer.

Hoge, S. K., Bonnie, R. J., Poythress, N., & Monahan, J. (1992). Attorney-client decision-making in criminal cases: Client competence and participation as perceived by their attorneys. *Behavioral Sciences and the Law, 10*, 385–394. https://doi.org/10.1002/bsl.2370100308

Hucker, S., Langevin, R., & Bain, J. (1988). A double blind trial of sex drive reducing medication in pedophiles. *Annals of Sex Research, 1*, 227–242.

Hunter, J. A., Ram, N., & Ryback, R. (2008). Use of satiation therapy in the treatment of adolescent-manifest sexual interest in male children: A single-case, repeated measures design. *Clinical Case Studies, 7*, 54–74. https://doi.org/10.1177/1534650107304773

Jackson, R., & Hess, D. (2007). Evaluation for civil commitment of sex offenders: A survey of experts. *Sexual Abuse: A Journal of Research and Treatment, 19*, 425–448. https://doi.org/10.1177/107906320701900407

Johnson, H. (2012). Limits of criminal justice response: Trends in police and court processing of sexual assault. In E. A. Sheehy (Ed.), *Sexual assault in Canada: Law, legal practice and women's activism* (pp. 613–634). Ottawa, ON: University of Ottawa Press.

Kafka, M. P. (2010). Hypersexual disorder: A proposed diagnosis for DSM-V. *Archives of Sexual Behavior, 39*, 377–400. https://doi.org/10.1007/s10508-009-9574-7

Katz-Schiavone, S., Levenson, J. S., & Ackerman, A. R. (2008). Myths and facts about sexual violence: Public perceptions and implications for prevention. *Journal of Criminal Justice and Popular Culture, 15*, 291–311.

Kilpatrick, D. G., Resnick, H. S., Ruggiero, K. J., Conoscenti, L. M., & McCauley, J. (2007) *Drug-facilitated, incapacitated, and forcible rape: A national study*. National Crime Victims Research & Treatment Center. Retrieved from http://www.antoniocasella.eu/archila/Kilpatrick_drug_forcible_rape_2007.pdf

Kingston, D., & Bradford, J. (2013). Hypersexuality and recidivism among sexual offenders. *Sexual Addiction & Compulsivity, 20*, 91–105. https://doi.org/10.1080/10720162.2013.768131

Kong, R., Johnson, H., Beattie, S., & Cardillo, A. (2003). Sexual offences in Canada. Juristat. *23;6*. Catalogue no. 85-002-XIE.

Krueger, R. B., & Kaplan, M. S. (2016). Non-contact paraphilic sexual offenses. In A. Phenix & H. M. Hoberman (Eds.), *Sexual offending: Predisposing anetecedents, assessments and management* (pp. 79–102). New York, NY: Springer.

Kubiak, S., Brenner, H., Bybee, D., Campbell, R., Cummings, C., Darcy, K., … Kovera, M. B. (2017). Sexual misconduct in prison: What factors affect whether incarcerated women will report abuses committed by prison staff? *Law and Human Behavior, 41*(4), 361–374.

Kutcher, M. R. (2010). The chemical castration of recidivist sex offenders in Canada: A matter of faith. *Dalhousie Law Journal, 33*, 193–216.

Långström, N., & Hanson, R. K. (2006). High rates of sexual behavior in the general population: Correlates and predictors. *Archives of Sexual Behavior, 35*, 37–52.

Lasher, M. P., & Stinson, J. D. (2016). Adults with pedophilic interests in the United States: Current practices and suggestions for future policy and research. *Archives of Sexual Behavior.* https://doi.org/10.1007/s10508-016-0822-3

Laws, D. R. (2009). Penile phelthysmography: Strengths, limitation, innovations. In D. Thornton & R. D. Laws (Eds.), *Cognitive approaches to the assessment of sexual interest in sexual offenders* (pp. 7–29). Malden, MA: John Wiley & Sons.

Laws, D. R. (n.d.). *The risk for sexual violence protocol* .[PDF document]. Retrieved from https://pdfs.semanticscholar.org/79f5/6a5dc43f6ea5979ff847f0716412bf8046d2.pdf

Laws, D. R., & Ward, T. (2011). *Desistance and sexual offending: Alternatives to throwing away the keys.* New York, NY: Guilford Press.

Lindsay, W. R., Ward, T., Morgan, T., & Wilson, I. (2007). Self-regulation of sex offending, future pathways and the good lives model: Applications and problems. *Journal of Sexual Aggression, 13*, 37–50. https://doi.org/10.1080/13552600701365613

Logan, C. (2016). Structured professional judgement: Applications of sexual offender risk assessment and management. In A. Phenix & H. Hoberman (Eds.), *Sexual offending* (pp. 571–588). New York, NY: Springer.

Lösel, F., & Schmucker, M. (2005). The effectiveness of treatment for sexual offenders: A comprehensive meta-analysis. *Journal of Experimental Psychology, 1*, 117–146. https://doi.org/10.1007/s11292-004-6466-7

Malamuth, N. M. (2003). Criminal and noncriminal sexual aggressors. *Annals of the New York Academy of Sciences, 989*, 33–58. https://doi.org/10.1111/j.1749-6632.2003.tb07292.x

Mann, R. E., Hanson, R. K., & Thornton, D. (2010). Assessing risk for sexual recidivism: Some proposals on the nature of psychologically meaningful risk factors. *Sexual Abuse: A Journal of Research and Treatment, 22*, 191–217. https://doi.org/10.1177/1079063210366039

Marques, J. K., Wiederanders, M., Day, D. M., Nelson, C., & van Ommeren, A. (2005). Effects of a relapse prevention program on sexual recidivism: First results from California's Sex Offender Treatment and Evaluation Project (SOTEP). *Sexual Abuse: A Journal of Research and Treatment, 17*, 79–107. https://doi.org/10.1177/107906320501700108

Marshall, W. L. (1979). Satiation therapy: A procedure for reducing deviant sexual arousal. *Journal of Applied Behavior Analysis, 12*, 377–389. https://doi.org/10.1901/jaba.1979.12-377

Marshall, W. L. (1999). Current status of North American assessment and treatment programs for sexual offenders. *Journal of Interpersonal Violence, 14*(3), 221–239. https://doi.org/10.1177/088626099014003002

Marshall, W. L., & Marshall, L. E. (2007). The utility of the random controlled trial for evaluating sexual offender treatment: The gold standard or an inappropriate strategy? *Sexual Abuse: A Journal of Research and Treatment, 19*, 175–191. https://doi.org/10.1177/1079063207001900207

McGrath, R. J., Cumming, G. F., Burchard, B. L., Zeoli, S., & Ellerby, L. (2010). *Current practices and trends in sexual abuser management: The Safer Society 2009 North American Survey.* Brandon, VT: Safer Society Press.

McPhail, I. V., Hermann, C. A., Fernane, S., Fernandez, Y. M., Nunes, K. L., & Cantor, J. M. (2017). Validity in phallometric testing for sexual interests in children: A meta-analytic review. *Assessment.* https://doi.org/10.1177/1074191117706139

Murrie, D. C., Boccaccini, M. T., Guanera, L. A., & Rufino, K. A. (2013). Are forensic experts biased by the side that retained them? *Psychological Science, 24*, 1889. https://doi.org/10.1177/0956797613481812

Murrie, D. C., Boccaccini, M. T., Johnson, J. T., & Janke, C. (2008). Does interrater (dis)agreement on Psychopathy Checklist scores in sexually violent predator trials suggest partisan allegiance in forensic evaluation? *Law and Human Behavior, 32*, 352–362.

Murrie, D. C., Boccaccini, M. T., Turner, D. B., Meeks, M., Woods, C., & Tussey, C. (2009). Rater (dis)agreement on risk assessment measures in sexually violent predator proceedings: Evidence of adversarial allegiance in forensic evaluation? *Psychology, Public Policy, and Law, 15*, 19–53. https://doi.org/10.1037/a0014897

Neal, T. M. S. (2016). Are forensic experts already biased before adversarial legal parties hire them? *PLoS One.* https://doi.org/10.1371/journal.pone.0154434

Nichols, H., & Molinder, I. (2000). *Multiphasic Sex Inventory II.* Fircrest, WA: Nichols & Molinder Assessments.

Olver, M. E., & Wong, S. C. P. (2006). Psychopathy, sexual deviance, and recidivism among sex offenders. *Sexual Abuse: A Journal of Research and Treatment, 18*, 65–82. https://doi.org/10.10007/s11194-006-9006-3

Olver, M. E., Wong, S. C. P., Nicholaichuk, T., & Gordon, A. (2007). The validity and reliability of the Violence Risk Scale—Sexual Offender Version: Assessing sex offender risk and evaluating therapeutic change. *Psychological Assessment, 19*, 318–329. https://doi.org/10.1037/1040-3590.19.3.318

Perreault, S. (2015). *Criminal victimization in Canada, 2014.* Ottawa, ON: Statistics Canada.

Porter, S., Fairweather, D., Drugge, J., Herve, H., Brit, A., & Boer, D. (2000). Profiles of psychopathy in incarcerated sexual offenders. *Criminal Justice and Behavior, 27*, 216–233. https://doi.org/10.1177/0093854800027002005

Poythress, N. G., Bonnie, R. J., Hoge, S. K., Monahan, J., & Oberlander, L. B. (1994). Client abilities to assist counsel and make decisions in criminal cases. *Law and Human Behavior, 18*, 437–452. https://doi.org/10.1007/BF01499049

Pullman, L., Stephens, S., & Seto, M. C. (2016). A motivation-facilitation model of adult male sexual offending. In C. A. Cuevas & C. M. Rennison (Eds.), *The handbook on the psychology of violence* (pp. 482–500). New York, NY: John Wiley and Sons.

Rea, J. A., Williams, D., Saunders, K. J., Dixon, M., Wright, K., & Spradlin, J. E. (2003). Covert sensitization: A generalization analysis in the laboratory and natural environment through the use of a portable-penile plethysmograph. *The Behavior Analyst Today, 4*, 192.

Schmidt, A., Babchishin, K., & Lehmann, R. (2017). A meta-analysis of viewing time measures of sexual interest in children. *Archives of Sexual Behavior, 46*, 287–300. https://doi.org/10.1007/s10508-016-0806-3

Schmucker, M., & Lösel, F. (2008). Does sexual offender treatment work? A systematic review of outcome evaluations. *Psicotherma, 20*, 10–19.

Schmucker, M., & Lösel, F. (2015). The effects of sexual offender treatment on recidivism: An international meta-analysis of sound quality evaluations. *Journal of Experimental Criminology, 11*, 597–630. https://doi.org/10.1007/s11292-015-9241-z

Seto, M. C. (2008). *Understanding pedophilia and sexual offending against children: Theory, assessment, and intervention.* Washington, DC: American Psychological Association.

Seto, M. C. (2012). Is pedophilia a sexual orientation. *Archives of Sexual Behavior, 41*, 231–236. https://doi.org/10.1007/s10508-011-9882-6

Seto, M. C. (2013). *Internet sex offenders.* Washington, DC: American Psychological Association.

Seto (2018). Pedophilia and sexual offending against children: Theory, assessment, and intervention (Second Edition). Washington, DC: American Psychological Association.

Seto, M. C., Cantor, J. M., & Blanchard, R. (2006). Child pornography offenses are a valid diagnostic indicator of pedophilia. *Journal of Abnormal Psychology, 115*, 610–615.

Seto, M. C., Kingston, D. A., & Bourget, D. (2014). Assessment of the paraphilias. *Psychiatric Clinics of North America, 37*, 149–256. https://doi.org/10.1016/j.psc.2014.03.001

Seto, M. C., & Lalumière, M. L. (2010). What is so special about male adolescent sexual offending? A review and test of explanations through meta-analysis. *Psychological Bulletin, 136*, 525–575. https://doi.org/10.1037/a0019700

Seto, M. C., Marques, J. K., Harris, G. T., Chafflin, M., Lalumiere, M. L., Miner, M. H., … Quinsey, V. L. (2008). Good science and progress in sexual offender treatment are intertwined: A response to Marshall and Marshall (2007). *Sexual Abuse: A Journal of Research and Treatment, 20*, 247–255. https://doi.org/10.1177/107906320831733

Seto, M. C., Sandler, J. C., & Freeman, N. J. (2017a). The revised screening scale for pedophilic interests: Predictive and concurrent validity. *Sexual Abuse, 29*, 636–657. https://doi.org/10.1079063215618375

Seto, M. C., Stephens, S., Lalumière, M. L., & Cantor, J. M. (2017b). The revised screening scale for pedophilic interests (SSPI-2): Development and criterion-related validation. *Sexual Abuse, 29*, 619–635. https://doi.org/10.1177/1079063215612444

Simkins, L., Ward, W., Bowman, S., & Rinck, C. M. (1989). The Multiphasic Sex Inventory: Diagnosis and prediction of treatment response in child sexual abusers. *Annals of Sex Research, 2*, 205–226. https://doi.org/10.1007/BF00849716

Sinha, M. (2013). Measuring violence against women: Statistical trends. *Juristat: Canadian Centre for Justice Statistics, 1.*

Skeem, J. L., & Cooke, D. J. (2010). Is criminal behavior a central component of psychopathy? Conceptual directions for resolving the debate. *Psychological Assessment, 22*, 433–445. https://doi.org/10.1037/a00008512

Statistics Canada. (2011). *Family violence in Canada, a statistical profile.* Retrieved from http://www.statcan.gc.ca/pub/85-224-x/85-224-x2010000-eng.pdf

Stephens, S., Seto, M. C., Goodwill, A. M., & Cantor, J. M. (2017). Evidence of construct validity in the assessment of hebephilia. *Archives of Sexual Behavior, 47*, 301–309. https://doi.org/10.1007/s10508-016-0907-z

Stephens, S., Seto, M. C., Goodwill, A. M., & Cantor, J. M. (2018). Age diversity among victims of hebephilic sexual offenders. *Sexual Abuse, 30*, 322–339. https://doi.org/10.1177/1079063216666837

Stinson, J. D., & Becker, J. V. (2013). *Treating sex offenders: An evidence-based manual.* New York, NY: The Guildford Press.

Trevethan, S., Crutcher, N., & Moore, J-P. (2002). *A profile of federal offenders designated as dangerous offenders or serving long-term supervision orders* (Research Report R-125). Retrieved from http://publications.gc.ca/collections/collection_2010/scc-csc/PS83-3-125-eng.pdf

Vaillancourt, R. (2010). *Gender differences in police-reported violent crime in Canada, 2008.* Ottawa, ON: Statistics Canada.

Ward, T., & Brown, M. (2004). The good lives model and conceptual issues in offender rehabilitation. *Psychology, Crime & Law, 10*, 243–257. https://doi.org/10.1080/10683160410001662744

Ward, T., Collie, R. M., & Bourke, P. (2009). Models of offender rehabilitation: The good lives model and the risk-need-responsivity model. In A. R. Anthony, L. A. Craig, & K. D. Browne (Eds.), *Assessment and treatment of sex offenders* (pp. 293–310). West Sussex, UK: Wiley-Blackwell.

Ward, T., & Gannon, T. A. (2006). Rehabilitation, etiology, and self-regulation: The comprehensive good lives model of treatment for sexual offenders. *Aggression and Violent Behavior, 11*, 77–94. https://doi.org/10.1016/j.avb.2005.06.001

Ward, T., & Maruna, S. (2007). *Rehabilitation: Beyond the risk paradigm.* New York, NY: Routledge.

Ward, T., Polaschek, D. L. L., & Beech, A. R. (2006). *Theories of sexual offending.* West Sussex, UK: John Wiley & Sons.

Ward, T., & Stewart, C. (2003). The treatment of sex offenders: Risk management and good lives. *Professional Psychology: Research and Practice, 34*(4), 353–360. https://doi.org/10.1037/0735-7028.34.4.353

Ward, T., Yates, P. M., & Willis, G. M. (2012). The good lives model and the risk need responsivity model: A critical response to Andrews, Bonta, and Wormith (2011). *Criminal Justice and Behavior, 39*, 94–110. https://doi.org/10.1177/0093854811426085

Weiss, K. J., & Watson, C. (2008). NGRI and Megan's Law: No exit? *Journal of the American Academy of Psychiatry and the Law, 36*, 117–122.

Willis, G. M., Ward, T., & Levenson, J. S. (2014). The Good Lives Model (GLM): An evaluation of GLM operationalization in North American treatment programs. *Sexual Abuse: A Journal of Research and Treatment, 26*, 58–81. https://doi.org/10.1177/1079063213478202

Willis, G. M., Yates, P. M., Gannon, T. A., & Ward, T. (2012). How to integrate the good lives model into treatment programs for sexual offending: An introduction and overview. *Sexual Abuse: A Journal of Research and Treatment, 25*, 123–142. https://doi.org/10.1177/1079063212452618

Wong, S., Olver, M. E., Nicholaichuk, T. P., & Gordon, A. (2003). *The Violence Risk Scale—Sexual Offender version (VRS–SO)*. Saskatoon, SK: Regional Psychiatric Centre and University of Saskatchewan.

Yates, P. M. (2016). Models of sexual offender treatment. In A. Phenix, H. M. Hoberman, A. Phenix, & H. M. Hoberman (Eds.), *Sexual offending: Predisposing antecedents, assessments and management* (pp. 591–604). New York, NY: Springer Science + Business Media. https://doi.org/10.1007/978-1-4939-2416-5_27

Yung, C. R. (2013). Civil commitment for sexual offenders. *American Medical Association Journal of Ethics, 15*, 873–877.

Chapter 10
Assessing and Treating Radicalized Offenders

Yvonne Stys

Despite the historic prevalence of radical ideological thought, there is a relative dearth of research, examination, and exploration regarding this type of offender in a correctional setting. Indeed, it was not until after the events of September 11th that a more intensive examination of radicalization generally, as well as radicalization in a correctional context, was brought to bear. Consequently, the quantity (and arguably quality) of information that is available regarding radicalized offender populations, their characteristics, effective assessment and appropriate intervention is much less rich than would be for a carceral population such as women offenders, sex offenders, or the general offender population, although the field is steadily gaining ground.

This chapter will review the current state of affairs in regard to radicalized offenders, with a view to informing correctional practitioners of issues, challenges, and considerations when developing management plans for ideologically-motivated individuals which may include assessments of risk and options for intervention. Summaries of assessment and intervention considerations will be contextualized in theoretical frameworks which offer potential avenues for psychological approaches while highlighting the requirement for a more comprehensive understanding of radicalization in order to address the unique needs and motivations of these particular offenders.

10.1 Frequency and Prevalence

The frequency of radicalization in institutional settings varies considerably from jurisdiction to jurisdiction for many reasons, including but not limited to how radicalization is defined and measured, the religious and geopolitical realities in a

Y. Stys (✉)
Research Branch Correctional Service Canada, Ottawa, ON, Canada

© Springer Nature Switzerland AG 2018
M. Ternes et al. (eds.), *The Practice of Correctional Psychology*,
https://doi.org/10.1007/978-3-030-00452-1_10

particular region, and/or the potential for incarceration of these types of offenders (considering the often lethal nature of these types of offences). The terms *radicalized offender, violent extremist prisoner, extremist offender,* and *terrorist* (among others) are often used interchangeably among prison jurisdictions and academics alike. Regardless of the terminology, the common thread that differentiates these offenders from others is the underlying motivation—the use of violence for ideological purposes, rather than traditional criminal ones (Silke, 2014; Stys & Michel, 2014). For clarity and consistency, this chapter will use the term *radicalized offender* to refer to this specific sub-type of offender.

While crime rates regarding particular offence types often serve as a clue to determining the prevalence of a particular offender in an institutional setting, such a connection is generally not feasible when speaking to the radicalized offender population. These offenders may or may not be convicted under terrorism-related legislation; depending on the prosecution of their particular case, the time of their offence, or their individual ideology, they may be convicted of other (often lesser) crimes or they may have been convicted of an offence that existed prior to the implementation of terrorism legislation. Alternatively, their radical views may have had nothing to do with their crimes of conviction, their extreme ideologies only being discovered (or developed) post-incarceration.

These are among the reasons why a simple count of the number of terrorist-convicted offenders in a carceral setting is an underestimate of the true number of radicalized offenders in a prison. Indeed, without conducting a systematic review to identify radicalized offenders in the prison population, guided by distinct and clear definitions of radicalization, a true prevalence will remain elusive. It is due to these and many other challenges in determining prevalence that, in the *Handbook on The Management of Violent Extremist Prisoners and the Prevention of Radicalization to Violence in Prisons,* the United Nations Office on Drugs and Crime (UNODC, 2016) states that it is "impossible to give a figure for the number of violent extremist prisoners that are currently held around the world" (p. 5). In support of the UNODC conclusion regarding prevalence, statistics surrounding the incarceration rates of radicalized individuals are not included the systematic reporting produced by most correctional jurisdictions. Nevertheless, some select penal systems have attempted to provide transparency around its radicalized offender population, with proportions of the total offender population reported to be terrorist convicted, radicalized, or of national security interest ranging from less than 0.01% of the total offender population for many countries (such as the United Kingdom, the United States, Canada, and Indonesia, to name a few; Federal Bureau of Prisons, 2017; Home Office, 2017; Jones, 2014; Stys & McEachran, 2016) to approximately 10% of the offender population in Saudi Arabia (Hubbard, 2016), and 25% in Israel (Yehoshua, 2014).

Some look to figures surrounding conversions to a particular religion in a prison setting as an indicator for the prevalence of radicalization. However, it should be noted that there is a significant difference between converting to or taking up a more fundamentalist form of a religion and being a violent extremist. Research has illustrated that religious conversion in a prison setting most often benefits offender reintegration and rehabilitation efforts (Hamm, 2009; Johnson, 2004; Schaefer, Sams,

& Lux, 2016), and should therefore not be viewed as an indicator of increased risk of reoffending or risk of violence. Indeed, even among those who take up more radical belief systems, it is highly unlikely that the belief system will materialize into a violent act within the prison or upon release (Hamm, 2013). One should therefore not infer that the number of conversions to Islam or any other type of belief system in a prison setting is equivalent to an indicator of a rate of radicalization in said prison system. Similarly, it is important to appreciate that the prevalence of radicalized offenders in a prison setting is not synonymous with an elevated level of risk.

10.2 Theoretical Model(s) Relevant to Service Delivery

In order to explore and understand effective service delivery for radicalized offenders, it is important to first understand the underpinnings of radicalization and the various pathways that may lead individuals to become radicalized toward violence. There are numerous theories in this regard (see Young, Zwenk, & Rooze, 2013 for a comprehensive review), but many if not most scholars have moved away from the idea that violent radicalism is based in personality, finite traits, or psychopathy[1] (Monahan, 2012; Silke, 1998). Instead, evidence points toward an understanding that, like other types of criminality, radicalization is a dynamic process in which there are both static and dynamic factors at play. What is clear from the existing empirical research is that there is not one singular profile or pathway to radicalization (Gill & Young, 2011; Gurski, 2016; Horgan, 2008), instead the process is individual to each person and cannot be generalized to a particular group of people or ideological belief. This section will review three prominent theories that are relevant to psychological service delivery for radicalized offenders and offer theoretically-based opportunities for effective intervention: Staircase theory, the Significance Quest model, and the Individual Vulnerability, Exposure, Emergence (IVEE) theory of radicalization.

Moghaddam's Staircase theory (2005) offers an individual-focused perspective on the development of radical extremist behaviour, outlining several psychological process stages (floors) through which an individual may progress and which may lead, ultimately, to participation in a violent act. Society at large is believed to exist on the ground floor, and it is a perceived injustice that leads individuals to consider options for improvement on the first floor. The development of prosocial solutions to injustice leads back to the ground floor, while an inability to reconcile the injustice leads to feelings of anger and frustration on the second floor. Here, the individual seeks to blame a target for the injustice, and their willingness to act violently toward

---

[1] The exception to the findings regarding psychopathy are lone-actors, who have been found to have a significantly higher rate of mental illness as compared to group-based radicals or the general population at large (Corner & Gill, 2015; Horgan, 2008). Lone actors, or "lone wolves" are single actors who use violence linked to a formulated ideology, whether their own or that of a larger organization, and who do not receive orders, direction, or material support from outside sources (UNODC, 2016).

this target propels them to the third floor, where they are waiting to be engaged by a sympathetic violent organization. The willing acceptance of this group and its social identity moves the individual to the fourth floor, where they are isolated from their friends and family, and an "us versus them" philosophy is indoctrinated. If an opportunity for violence is presented, and inhibitions have been satisfactorily overcome, the fifth floor, the violent act, will be reached (Fig. 10.1).

The Significance Quest Model of Radicalization, posited by Kruglanski, Chen, Dechesne, Fishman, and Orehek (2009), builds on established psychological theories regarding the human need for esteem, achievement, meaning, and competence, among others, and posits that the terrorist goals which have been outlined in the literature (such as honor, vengeance, religion, loyalty, etc.) are actually driven by one motivating force—the quest for significance. The authors propose that the radicalization process unfolds over time and requires the presence of three components: (1) an arousal of the goal of significance, (2) the identification of terrorism/violence as the appropriate means to significance, and (3) a commitment shift resulting in a dominance of the goal of significance and a devaluation of other goals and concerns that are incompatible with terrorism. This theory emphasizes that the ideology which is selected is simply a means to obtaining the ultimate goal of significance (a justification for terrorism-related violence), however it is precisely the ideology that provides the social network support system that facilitates the progression towards violence (Kruglanski et al., 2014).

Bouhana and Wikström's IVEE (2011) model of radicalization contributes an ecological perspective to the radicalization discourse, taking into specific consideration the impact of an individual's environment on their propensity to radicalize. IVEE shifts the focus from the individual pathway approach to examine, from a situational action theory perspective, the development of radicalization in a more holistic manner. The authors argue that the development of attitudes supportive of

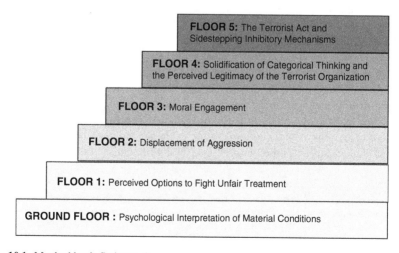

Fig. 10.1 Moghaddam's Staircase theory

violent extremism are rooted in factors that impact on an individual's vulnerability to a number of radicalizing moral contexts, their exposure to radicalizing ecological settings, and the degree to which radicalizing environments are permitted to emerge in society due to systemic factors. By understanding the complex reciprocity between the individual, ecological, and systemic factors involved in the radicalization process, one can work to influence each factor in turn in order to affect, protect against, and prevent radicalization.

The propensity for violent radicalization to be viewed as a dynamic process with multiple mediating factors existing at various time points provides the practitioner with an optimistic array of opportunities for intervention. As the radicalization process and influencing factors are different for each individual, the comprehensive understanding of the specific contexts and circumstances for each offender in order to target interventions rests upon reliable tools and assessments developed specifically for radicalized persons.

10.3   Diagnosis and Assessment

The state of assessment for the radicalized offender population is in its relative infancy as compared to assessments that have been developed for other types of offender subtypes (such as violent or sex offenders), having been hampered by several methodological, ideological, and logistical challenges (Horgan, 2008; Sarma, 2017). As previously noted, the pathway to radicalization is individual and dynamic in nature, and a terrorist "profile" with fixed, measurable traits does not exist—attributes which do not lend themselves well to the use of actuarial tools. Coupled with low base rates, a lack of comparison groups, and challenges related to specificity, it is no wonder that most correctional systems worldwide do not use specialized risk assessments for their radicalized offenders, despite a desire to do so (Axford, Stys, & McEachran, 2015; Correctional Service Canada, 2015).

Nevertheless, the utility of developing, validating, and implementing risk assessments specific to this population cannot be overstated. Research has illustrated that radicalized offenders have needs and motivations that are unique from the general offender population, and that the intake assessments designed to measure criminogenic needs (and subsequently influence correctional plans for intervention, rehabilitation, and reintegration into society) may be mis-assessing, and consequently under or over-programming, for those offenders who are ideologically, rather than criminally, motivated (Pressman & Flockton, 2012; Stys & McEachran, 2016). Further, while the application of tools developed for forensic assessment (such as the HCR20 or the PCL-R) have been proposed for use with the radicalized offender population, their validity for these offenders has been vehemently questioned, even by the authors themselves (Monahan, 2012).

Considering the complexity of the construct, structured professional judgement (SPJ) tools, which allow for a more prescriptive or guided examination of risk indicators while being flexible enough to consider individual context (Guy, Packer, & Warnken, 2012) have been favoured in this field. One such tool, developed by the United Kingdom's National Offender Management Service (NOMS) specifically for criminally convicted populations in a western correctional context, is the Extremism Risk Guidelines (ERG22+; Lloyd & Dean, 2015). Using a case formulation approach, the ERG22+ seeks to assess risk and needs in convicted extremist offenders (and those offenders for whom there are credible concerns about their potential to commit such offences in the future) against 22 factors which map on to three dimensions: engagement, intent, and capability. Built with the risk-need-responsivity (RNR) principle in mind (Andrews & Bonta, 2010), the dynamic assessment allows for effective case management and targeted intervention, the effects of which can be measured by subsequent reassessment.

Another frequently cited assessment tool is the Violent Extremism Risk Assessment (VERA-2; Pressman & Flockton, 2012, 2014). Similar to the ERG22+, the VERA-2 consists of 31 indicators which are dispersed across five categories: beliefs and attitudes, context and intent, history and capability, commitment and motivation, and protective' indicators. The tool has been applied to incarcerated individuals in the Australian correctional system, and has been informed both by evidence and expert feedback. Pressman and Flockton (2012) note that the VERA 2 should be considered a complementary component to comprehensive risk assessment, and unlike the ERG22+, is intended for use with individuals who have already been convicted of a violent extremist or terrorist-designated offence.

The relative strength of the ERG22+ and the VERA-2 is that they can be applied to all radicalized offender types—they are not specific to any one ideology and therefore do not suffer from limitations in practical utility or discriminatory prejudgement in their application. Several other assessments have been developed for specialized groups of radicals, including the Terrorist Radicalization Assessment Protocol (TRAP-18), which is specific to lone-wolf terrorists (Meloy, Hoffmann, Guldimann, & James, 2012), as well as the Assessment and Treatment of Radicalization Scale (ARTS), for the assessment of extreme religious beliefs originating from the Middle-East (Loza, 2007; Loza, Bhawanie, Nussbaum, & Maximenco, 2013).

Regardless of the assessment, considerable work remains to be conducted in the validation of these tools in order that they meet the standards set forth for robust, reliable, and valid risk assessments. In an examination of the available tools against established standards, Scarcella, Page, and Furtado (2016) found that just over half of the methodological quality markers required for a transparent methodological description of the instruments were reported in publicly-available documentation, and that the amount of reported psychological properties was even fewer, with only a third available across the various studies. Nevertheless, as noted by Silke (2014), the use of tools such as the ERG22+ and the VERA-2 is more useful in assessing terrorist risk than the application of pre-existing tests which were not designed for radicalized offenders.

10.4   Intervention(s)

As outlined earlier in the chapter, radicalization to violence has come to be viewed as a dynamic process of change towards the use of violence to achieve ideological goals. As the individual has proceeded through a variety of personal, interpersonal, social, and/or ecological developments in order to become comfortable with the idea of acting violently on behalf of their ideology, it is logical to conclude that this process can be reversed, or that there is a process by which the violent act can come to be viewed as unfathomable. Prison settings have been proposed to be ideal locations in which to disengage individuals from their violent extremist pathways, as they provide an environment where offenders are effectively cut off from their negative networks, influences, and psychological pressures (Global Counterterrorism Forum, 2012a; Horgan, 2014) while providing opportunities to engage with individuals and groups which offenders normally do not have the opportunity to communicate with in the community (Yehoshua, 2014).

To date, approaches to intervention with radicalized offenders have taken two forms:

1. De-radicalization: an attempt to change the ideological views, attitudes, and beliefs of radicalized individuals to conform to a more moderate, less extreme interpretation (Morris, Eberhard, Rivera, & Watsula, 2010; Speckhard, 2011); and
2. Disengagement: an attempt to change an individual's commitment to, and involvement in, violent activity in support of their radical ideology (Bjørgo & Horgan, 2009; UNODC, 2016).

Utilized in countries such as Saudi Arabia, Egypt, Singapore, and Indonesia, de-radicalization programs typically involve Muslim clerics or "reformed" extremists counselling radicalized offenders to understand the "true meaning" behind religious scriptures and compelling them to view violence towards others as a misunderstanding of religious text. Unfortunately, a growing body of evidence suggests that de-radicalization programs focusing solely on changing belief systems are not effective in curbing the desire to act violently in support of an ideology. Rather, the psychological readiness required to alter beliefs coupled with the context of the prison environment can result in extreme ideologies becoming, in fact, further entrenched as a result of these types of interventions (Horgan & Altier, 2012; Kruglanski, Gelfand, & Gunaratna, 2010; Leuprecht, Hataley, Moskalenko, & McCauley, 2010).

In addition to issues regarding the lack of applicability of these approaches to other types of extremism (i.e., right wing radicals; Bjørgo & Horgan, 2009), there exists a fundamental ethical dilemma regarding de-radicalization. For most (if not all) Western countries, freedoms of religion and expression ensure that holding radical views is not a criminal offence, and therefore changing radical views is not within the purview of correctional interventions. To illustrate, a 2003 decision by the United Nations Human Rights Committee held that a domestic "ideology conversion system", which aimed to alter the political opinion of an inmate, had violated the offender's freedom of expression and had amounted to discrimination on the basis of political opinion.

A view to interventions which focus on disengagement, or moving the offender away from the use of violent behaviour as a means of ideological expression, has been offered as the preferential intervention approach (UNODC, 2016). In this approach to intervention, physical or psychological processes contribute to an individual distancing themselves from extremist behaviours (Horgan, 2014). In some cases, the process of disengagement (changing behaviour) ultimately results in de-radicalization (changing beliefs), although de-radicalization is not a necessary result of disengagement (Bjørgo & Horgan, 2009). Many radicals continue to adhere to their extreme belief systems while participating in society as law-abiding, non-violent citizens.

In the prison context, disengagement interventions can include psychological services, cognitive-behavioural programmes, social interventions, faith-based guidance, mentoring initiatives, education, vocational training, and social, cultural and recreation programs (Danish Department of Prisons, 2014; Michel & Stys, 2014; UNODC, 2016). While a greater number of correctional jurisdictions are implementing programming for their radicalized offender populations, international surveys have demonstrated that specialized programs for these offenders are not yet the norm, and many of these disengagement efforts are the same programs that are being offered to other, non-radicalized offenders (Axford et al., 2015).

Given previously-noted complexities in the assessment of radicalization coupled with the individual nature of the radicalization process, it is unsurprising that a universal model of disengagement does not exist. A number of guiding principles for effective interventions have, however, been circumscribed. In 2012, The Global Counterterrorism Forum (GCTF) produced the *Rome Memorandum on Good Practices for Rehabilitation and Reintegration of Violent Extremist Offenders*, with the challenges related to implementing these programs being laid out in the Sydney Memorandum shortly after (2012b). Additional documents were subsequently published aiming to provide more comprehensive guidance regarding the role of psychologists and religious scholars/ideological experts in rehabilitation and reintegration programs (Hedayah & ICCT, 2013; United Nations Interregional Crime and Justice Research Institute & Government of Spain, 2013), and the recent UNODC Handbook (2016) includes a section on the effective implementation of programs and interventions for violent extremist offenders. Recommendations tend to be detailed and wide-ranging, reiterating basic standards for the management of incarcerated persons, but coupled with academic literature, the following principles summarize the most important considerations:

1. Radicalized offenders have unique needs and motivations which require the development of specialized interventions, or at a minimum the adaptation of evidence-based programs to suit the specific needs and motivations of ideologically-motivated offenders (GCTF, 2012a; Michel & Stys, 2014; UNODC, 2016).

2. Empirical validation of interventions should be a primary consideration. It is essential that interventions are clearly scoped to include appropriate short and long-term goals and priorities, and that repeated measurement is used to determine effectiveness (Hamm, 2013; Hedayah & ICCT, 2013; Silke, 2014; Veldhuis, 2015; Veldhuis & Kessells, 2013).
3. The most effective interventions adhere to the RNR principle (Andrews & Bonta, 2010), targeting those who are deemed to be a higher risk of reoffending and of committing serious harm (risk principle), address factors that directly contribute to offending (need principle), and be delivered in a way and style that maximizes learning for individuals (responsivity principle; Dean, 2016; Mullins, 2010).
4. Interventions should be culturally, regionally, and contextually sensitive while considering the nature of the violent extremist group and the individual circumstances of the offender (Gunaratna, Jerard, & Rubin, 2011; Neumann, 2010; UNODC, 2016).
5. Interventions should focus on the social and psychological process whereby an individual is motivated to engage, as well as those attitudes, beliefs and perceptions that enable them to violently offend. Domains which have been identified as particularly impactful for clinical focus include social relations, coping, identity, ideology, action orientation, disillusionment, and personal significance (Barrellea, 2015; UNODC, 2016; Webber et al., 2017).
6. Linking prison interventions with reintegration support systems, specifically local community players, support organizations, and family members, should be a core consideration and component of successful interventions (Axford et al., 2015; Parker, 2013; Veldhuis, 2015).

Despite the confident guidelines and recommendations, it is important to note that most radicalized offender interventions have not been empirically studied, or if they have been studied, results are often not publically available (El-Said, 2015)—a significant detriment to the field. Those de-radicalization or disengagement programs that have been evaluated often suffer from limitations in outcome measurement (depending mostly on short-term recidivism rate data) and low participation rates (Mastroe & Szmania, 2016).

The Healthy Identity Intervention (HII), a psychologically informed program which strives to meet the prescribed recommendations and which has seen some empirical validation, was developed by NOMS and seeks to reduce or manage the risk of committing extremist offenses (including extremist violence) in custody and in the community (Dean, 2016; Lloyd & Dean, 2015). The intervention focuses on mitigating the individual's relationship with, and preparedness to offend on behalf of, the extremist group, cause, or ideology by addressing personal identity issues, facilitating disillusionment with involvement, managing feelings associated with identification and group conflict, and challenging the legitimacy of violence to achieve political and social change. The structured program is delivered by psychologists and probation officers who tailor the intervention's content to the specific assessed risks, needs, strengths, and circumstances of each participant, with progress being measured through changes in assessed risk (Dean, 2014, 2016).

The previously reviewed theories of radicalization emphasize the role of society—peer groups, family, and the surrounding ecology—in the radicalization to violence process. It stands to reason, therefore, that recommended interventions would take into account mechanisms for effective reintegration through release into a supportive, understanding, and equipped society in order to prevent the offender from returning to an un-protective social environment and being drawn back into the extremist environment (Veldhuis, 2015). Unfortunately, most correctional jurisdictions do not report providing community transitioning programming that have been specifically designed for their radicalized offenders (Axford et al., 2015). Encouragingly, the number of countering violent extremism (CVE) community programs are steadily growing, and offer potential avenues for partnership to allow for the successful release and reintegration of these individuals (Ellis & Abdi, 2017; Radicalization Awareness Network, 2014). Another promising avenue for partnership rests in community-based situation tables (i.e., hub models), which bring together representatives from various social service providers in order to triage and manage high-risk community cases (Nilson, 2015). Situation tables offer a capable, multi-systemic option for linking institutional and community service providers to establish a continuum of care, and consequently a greater potential for community success, for radicalized offenders (Stys, 2017).

It should be noted that while current research suggests that group-based violent extremism is not caused by a distinct personality trait, disorder or profile, understanding that mental illnesses may be a factor for those radicalized offenders who are not part of a radical group (i.e., lone actors or lone wolves) is an important consideration for effective interventions with these offenders. Treating mental illness or supporting emotional or psychological disturbance may be an appropriate strategy for the effective rehabilitation and reintegration of these particular individuals.

10.5   Future Implications

Fundamentally, there is much to be learned about radicalization, its assessment, and effective intervention in order to bring correctional administration for radicalized offenders to a level that is currently enjoyed by other subtypes of offenders. At the ground level, all institutional staff, from security to psychology to programming, must be trained on what radicalization is (a dynamic process involving varied ideologies), what it is not (simply "Islamic terrorism"), when it is cause for concern (when the ideology is instrumentalized through violence), and what their specific roles and responsibilities are when it comes to reporting, assessing, and intervening.

Understanding and intervening with a radicalized individual can only be successful if the means of understanding (i.e., risk assessments) are reliable and valid for the population. In light of the fact that many validation efforts have depended on the same commonly-available open source or third party information, efforts should be made to validate and revalidate tools such as the ERG22+ and the VERA-2 within a wider sample base. Small sample sizes may require the collective pooling of data across correctional jurisdictions and countries—no insignificant administrative feat to be sure, but worth the effort in evidentiary robustness. While it may be tempting to simply use the indicators and factors outlined in developed tools as "checklists" for radical behaviour, only through training in the tools, and learning about the theory and evidence behind them, will the assessor truly be able to understand and reliably apply the SPJ approach. This training is a critical investment for correctional jurisdictions.

Prior to embarking on a best fit assessment for a particular correctional environment, the question of "what are we looking to measure" must be posed. For security personnel, this is often a question of threat risk assessment—what level of threat does this individual pose to themselves, to other offenders, and to the staff at this institution? This is a distinctly different question than those often posed by psychologists—what are the needs that need to be addressed and what is the risk of reoffending once released if these needs are not met? Risk assessment means different things to different people in a correctional setting, and clear communication regarding final goals is required.

Ultimately, the goal of effective corrections is to rehabilitate offenders so that, upon their release, they can reintegrate into society as law-abiding, contributing members of the community. Programs and interventions, both during incarceration and in the community, should continue to focus on disengagement rather than de-radicalization, and the strength and effectiveness of various interventions should continue to be assessed empirically and applied in a culturally sensitive manner.

10.6 Technology and Innovation

Opportunities for exploiting technological tools for the benefit of radicalized offenders are currently limited. While incarcerated, access to the internet, on-line applications, or virtual communities is tightly restricted and/or completely unfeasible. In addition, conditions associated with release often stipulate that radicalized offenders cannot associate with those who are or who have been connected with radical groups, or they completely prohibit access to the internet altogether. With disengagement as a primary focus of a reintegration plan, it may be possible, where parole conditions allow, for parole officers to assist radicalized offenders to harness the power of on-line communities which offer education and pro-social support to those looking to disengage from ideologically-motivated violent behaviour. However, as engagement with these communities (and the effectiveness of such interventions) have yet to be evaluated, such assistance is limited to ideation rather than recommendation.

10.7   Conclusion

The management approaches chosen for radicalized offender populations should provide for the overall safety and security of everyone in the institution (staff and offenders alike), in part by accurately identifying and addressing individual offender's risks, needs, and motivations through effective, evidence-based programs and interventions. Coupled with community-oriented disengagement and pro-social re-engagement measures, there is no reason to doubt that radicalized offenders can become non-violent, contributing members of society. The ability of psychological service providers to learn from existing theories and evidence, apply best practices, and effect behavioural change among the radicalized offender population will only improve as the evidence-base in the field matures.

References

Andrews, D. A., & Bonta, J. (2010). *The psychology of criminal conduct* (5th ed.). New Providence, NJ: LexisNexis.

Axford, M., Stys, Y., & McEachran, R. (2015). *International consultation: Best practices in the management of radicalized offenders* (Research Report R-361). Ottawa, ON: Correctional Service of Canada.

Barrellea, K. (2015). Pro-integration: Disengagement from and life after extremism. *Behavioral Sciences of Terrorism and Political Aggression, 7*(2), 129–142.

Bjørgo, T., & Horgan, J. (2009). *Leaving terrorism behind: Individual and collective disengagement.* Abington, PA: Routledge.

Bouhana, N., & Wikström, P. O. (2011). *Al Qa'ida-influenced radicalisation: A rapid evidence assessment guided by situational action theory* (Occasional Paper 97). London, UK: Home Office.

Corner, E., & Gill, P. (2015). A false dichotomy? Mental illness and lone-actor terrorism. *Law and Human Behavior, 39*(1), 23–34.

Correctional Service of Canada. (2015). *Best practices in the assessment, intervention and management of radicalized offenders: Proceedings from the International Roundtable and Mini-Symposium on Radicalized Offenders.* Ottawa, ON: Author.

Danish Department of Prisons and Probation & the Danish Ministry of Children, Gender Equality, Integration and Social Affairs. (2014). *Back on track: A pilot project on the prevention of radicalisation among inmates.* Copenhagen, Denmark: Authors.

Dean, C. (2014). The healthy identity intervention: The UK's development of a psychologically informed intervention to address extremist offending. In A. Silke (Ed.), *Prisons, terrorism and extremism: Critical issues in management, radicalisation and reform* (pp. 89–107). London, UK: Routledge.

Dean, C. (2016, September). *Addressing violent extremism in prisons and probation: Principles for effective programs and interventions.* Policy Brief, Global Center on Cooperative Security.

Ellis, B. H., & Abdi, S. (2017). Building community resilience to violent extremism through genuine partnerships. *American Psychologist, 72*(3), 289–300.

El-Said, H. (2015). *New approaches to countering terrorism: Designing and evaluating counter radicalization and deradicalization programs.* Hampshire, UK: Palgrave Macmillan.

Federal Bureau of Prisons. (2017). *Statistics: Inmate offences.* Retrieved from https://www.bop.gov/about/statistics/statistics_inmate_offenses.jsp

Gill, P., & Young, J. K. (2011). *Comparing role-specific terrorist profiles*. Available at SSRN https://ssrn.com/abstract=1782008 or https://doi.org/10.2139/ssrn.1782008

Global Counterterrorism Forum. (2012a). *Rome Memorandum on good practices for rehabilitation and reintegration of violent extremist offenders*. Retrieved from https://www.thegctf.org/documents/.../Rome+Memorandum-English.pdf

Global Counterterrorism Forum. (2012b). *Sydney Memorandum: Challenges and strategies on the management of violent extremist detainees*. Retrieved from https://www.thegctf.org/documents/10307/27624/Sydney+Memorandum

Gunaratna, R., Jerard, J. A. R., & Rubin, L. (Eds.). (2011). *Terrorist rehabilitation and counter-radicalisation: New approaches to counter-terrorism*. New York, NY: Routledge.

Gurski, P. (2016). *The threat from within: Recognizing Al Qaeda-inspired radicalization and terrorism in the west*. Lanham, MD: Rowman & Littlefield.

Guy, L. S., Packer, I. K., & Warnken, W. (2012). Assessing risk of violence using structured professional judgment guidelines. *Journal of Forensic Psychology Practice, 12*(3), 270–283.

Hamm, M. (2009). Prison Islam in the age of sacred terror. *British Journal of Criminology, 49*(5), 667–685.

Hamm, M. (2013). *The spectacular few: Prisoner radicalization and the evolving terrorist threat*. New York, NY: NYU Press.

Hedayah & ICCT. (2013). *Building on the GCTF's Rome Memorandum: Additional guidance on the role of psychologists/psychology in rehabilitation and reintegration programs*. Retrieved from http://www.icct.nl/download/file/Hedayah-ICCT%20Psychology%20Good%20Practices.Pdf

Home Office. (2017). *Operation of police powers under the Terrorism Act 2000 and subsequent legislation* (Statistical Bulletin 08/17). London, UK: Home Office.

Horgan, J. (2008). From profiles to pathways and roots to routes: Perspectives from psychology on radicalization into terrorism. *The Annals of the American Academy of Political and Social Science, 618*(1), 80–94.

Horgan, J. (2014). *The psychology of terrorism* (2nd ed.). Oxford, UK: Routledge.

Horgan, J., & Altier, M. B. (2012). The future of terrorist de-radicalization programs. *Georgetown Journal of International Affairs*, 83–90.

Hubbard, B. (2016, April 9). Inside Saudi Arabia's re-education prison for jihadists. *The New York Times*. Retrieved from https://www.nytimes.com/2016/04/10/world/middleeast/inside-saudi-arabias-re-education-prison-for-jihadists.html?mcubz=0

Johnson, B. (2004). Religious programs and recidivism among former inmates: A long-term follow-up study. *Justice Quarterly, 21*, 329–354.

Jones, C. R. (2014). Are prisons really schools for terrorism? Challenging the rhetoric on prison radicalization. *Punishment & Society, 16*(1), 74–103.

Kruglanski, A. W., Chen, X., Dechesne, M., Fishman, S., & Orehek, E. (2009). Fully committed: Suicide bombers' motivation and the quest for personal significance. *Political Psychology, 30*, 331–557.

Kruglanski, A. W., Gelfand, M. J., Bélanger, J. J., Sheveland, A., Hetiarachchi, M., & Gunaratna, R. (2014). The psychology of radicalization and deradicalization: How significance quest impacts violent extremism. *Advances in Political Psychology, 35*(1), 69–93.

Kruglanski, A. W., Gelfand, M. J., & Gunaratna, R. (2010). Detainee deradicalization: A challenge for psychological science. *APS Observer, 23*(1), 1–3.

Leuprecht, C., Hataley, T., Moskalenko, S., & McCauley, C. (2010). Containing the narrative: Strategy and tactics in countering the storyline of global Jihad. *Journal of Policing, Intelligence and Counter Terrorism, 5*(1), 42–57.

Lloyd, M., & Dean, C. (2015). The development of structured guidelines for assessing risk in extremist offenders. *Journal of Threat Assessment and Management, 2*(1), 40–52.

Loza, W. (2007). *The assessment and treatment of radicalization scale: A measure of Middle-Eastern extremism*. Unpublished Manuscript.

Loza, W., Bhawanie, S., Nussbaum, D., & Maximenco, A. (2013). Assessing the prevalence of extreme Middle-Eastern ideologies among some new immigrants to Canada. *International Journal of Social Science Studies, 1*(2), 154–160.

Mastroe, C. & Szmania, S. (2016). *Surveying CVE metrics in prevention, disengagement and deradicalization programs.* Report to the Office of University Programs, Science and Technology Directorate, Department of Homeland Security. College Park, MD: START.

Meloy, J. R., Hoffmann, J., Guldimann, A., & James, D. (2012). The role of warning behaviors in threat assessment: An exploration and suggested typology. *Behavioral Sciences & the Law, 30,* 256–279.

Michel, S., & Stys, Y. (2014). *Use of programs and interventions with Canada's federally sentenced radicalized offenders* (Research Report R-345). Ottawa, ON: Correctional Service of Canada.

Moghaddam, F. M. (2005). The staircase to terrorism, a psychological exploration. *American Psychologist, 60*(2), 161–169.

Monahan, J. (2012). The individual risk assessment of terrorism. *Psychology, Public Policy, and Law, 18,* 167–205.

Morris, M., Eberhard, F., Rivera, J., & Watsula, M. (2010). *Deradicalization: A review of the literature with comparison to findings in the literatures on deganging and deprogramming.* Duke University, Institute for Homeland Security Solutions. Retrieved from https://sites.duke.edu/ihss/files/2011/12/Morris_Research_Brief_Final.pdf

Mullins, S. (2010). Rehabilitation of extremist terrorists: Learning from criminology. *Dynamics of Asymmetric Conflict, 3,* 162–193.

Neumann, B. (2010). *Prisons and terrorism: Radicalisation and de-radicalisation in 15 Countries.* ICSR, Kings College London. Retrieved from http://icsr.info/2010/08/prisons-andterrorism-radicalisation-and-de-radicalisation-in-15-countries/

Nilson, C. (2015). *The original game changers: An evaluative report on Prince Albert's Centre of Responsibility and its Role in the Advancement of Community Mobilization.* Saskatoon, SK: Centre for Forensic Behavioural Science and Justice Studies, University of Saskatchewan.

Parker, T. (2013). *Establishing a deradicalization/disengagement model for America's correctional facilities: Recommendations for countering prison radicalization.* Master's thesis, Naval Postgraduate School, Monterey, California. Retrieved from https://www.hsdl.org/?view&did=736334

Pressman, D. E., & Flockton, J. (2012). Calibrating risk for violent political extremists and terrorists: The VERA 2 structured assessment. *British Journal of Forensic Practice, 14,* 237–251.

Pressman, D. E., & Flockton, J. (2014). Violent extremist risk assessment: Issues and applications of the VERA-2 in a high-security correctional setting. In A. Silke (Ed.), *Prisons, terrorism and extremism: Critical issues in management, radicalisation and reform* (pp. 122–143). London, UK: Routledge.

Radicalization Awareness Network. (2014). *Preventing radicalisation to terrorism and violent extremism: Strengthening the EU's response.* RAN Collection, 1, 2–112.

Sarma, K. M. (2017). Risk assessment and the prevention of radicalization from nonviolence into terrorism. *American Psychologist, 72*(3), 278–288.

Scarcella, A., Page, R., & Furtado, V. (2016). Terrorism, radicalisation, extremism, authoritarianism and fundamentalism: A systematic review of the quality and psychometric properties of assessments. *PLoS One, 11*(12), e0166947. https://doi.org/10.1371/journal.pone.0166947

Schaefer, L., Sams, T., & Lux, J. (2016). Saved, salvaged, or sunk: A meta-analysis of the effects of faith-based interventions on inmate adjustment. *The Prison Journal, 96*(4), 600–622.

Silke, A. (1998). Cheshire-cat logic: The recurring theme of terrorist abnormality in psychological research. *Psychology, Crime and Law, 4*(1), 51–69.

Silke, A. (Ed.). (2014). *Prisons, terrorism and extremism: Critical issues in management, radicalisation and reform.* New York, NY: Routledge.

Speckhard, A. (2011). *Prison and community-based disengagement and de-radicalization programs for extremist involved in militant jihadi terrorism ideologies and activities* (RTO-TR-HFM-140). Neuilly-sur-Seine: NATO-Research and Technology Organisation.

Stys, Y. (2017). *Success in reintegration: The potential application of situation tables to community corrections* (RR 17-02). Ottawa, ON: Correctional Service of Canada.

Stys, Y. & McEachran, R. (2016, May). *Radicalized offenders & CSC: Evidence-based correctional management*. Paper presented at the Violence and Aggression Symposium, Saskatoon, Canada. Retrieved from https://www.usask.ca/cfbsjs/va_symposia/VA2016/Presentations/Stys%20McEachran%20presentation.pdf

Stys, Y., & Michel, S. (2014). *Examining the needs and motivations of Canada's federally incarcerated radicalized offenders* (Research Report R-344). Ottawa, ON: Correctional Service of Canada.

United Nations Interregional Crime and Justice Research Institute & the Government of Spain. (2013). *Building on the GCTF's Rome Memorandum: Additional guidance on the role of religious scholars and other ideological experts in rehabilitation and reintegration programmes*. Retrieved from http://www.unicri.it/topics/counter_terrorism/UNICRI_SPAIN_Religious_Scholars_in_Rehab.pdf

UNODC. (2016). *Handbook on the management of violent extremist prisoners and the prevention of radicalization to violence in prisons*. Retrieved from http://www.unodc.org/pdf/criminal_justice/Handbook-on-VEPs.pdf

Veldhuis, T. (2015). *Reintegrating violent extremist offenders: Policy questions and lessons learned*. Retrieved from https://cchs.gwu.edu/sites/cchs.gwu.edu/files/downloads/VeldhuisPaperFinal%20%282%29.pdf

Veldhuis, T. M., & Kessells, E. J. A. M. (2013). *Thinking before leaping: The need for more structural data analysis in detention and rehabilitation of extremist offenders* (ICCT Research Paper). Retrieved from http://www.icct.nl

Webber, D., Chernikova, M., Kruglanski, A. W., Gelfand, M. J., Hettiarachchi, M., Gunaratna, R., … Belanger, J. J. (2017). Deradicalizing detained terrorists. *Political Psychology*. https://doi.org/10.1111/pops.12428

Yehoshua, S. (2014). The Isreali experience of terrorist leaders in prison. In A. Silke (Ed.), *Prisons, terrorism and extremism: Critical issues in management, radicalisation and reform* (pp. 122–143). London, UK: Routledge.

Young, H., Zwenk, R., & Rooze, M. (2013). *A review of the literature on radicalisation and what it means for TERRA*. Retrieved from http://www.terra-net.eu/

Chapter 11
Self-Harm/Suicidality in Corrections

Matthew R. Labrecque and Marc W. Patry

Internationally, reducing prison suicide is a top priority for correctional institutions, staff, and researchers (World Health Organization, 2007). Suicide is one of the most common causes of death in prisons worldwide, with reports consistently finding higher suicide rates in inmate populations compared to the general population (Fazel, Grann, Kling, & Hawton, 2011). Inmate suicide rates have been decreasing over the past six decades; this trend is largely due to the efforts of practitioners and researchers (van Ginneken, Sutherland, & Molleman, 2017). Evidence-based approaches have shown great promise for addressing prisoner suicide and many countries have national standards and guidelines for suicide prevention in custodial settings (Daigle et al., 2007).

This chapter presents an up-to-date, clinically practical review of literature on inmate suicide and self-harm. First, we summarize prevalence of suicide within prisons. Second, we review theories about inmate suicidality. Third, we summarize diagnostic and assessment approaches relevant to suicidality within prisons, including a review of measures and tools. The fourth section summarizes treatment approaches used within prisons to address inmate suicidality. Lastly, this chapter will look at the future of prison suicide research, including the potential impact of technological advances.

There are a variety of operational definitions for constructs in this area of research and practice. One of the broadest is suicidal thoughts and behaviors (STBs), a term that encompasses a spectrum of thoughts and behaviors relating to suicide or self-injury, ranging from self-harm to completed suicide (Franklin et al., 2017). Self-injurious behavior (SIB), a construct within the broader area of STB, includes any type of direct bodily harm or disfigurement that is purposely inflicted on oneself that is not considered to be socially acceptable (Usher, Power, & Wilton, 2010). Researchers have identified a number of behaviors within SIB, including self-harm,

M. R. Labrecque · M. W. Patry (✉)
Psychology Department, Saint Mary's University, Halifax, NS, Canada
e-mail: marc.patry@smu.ca

© Springer Nature Switzerland AG 2018
M. Ternes et al. (eds.), *The Practice of Correctional Psychology*,
https://doi.org/10.1007/978-3-030-00452-1_11

parasuicide, self-injurious behavior, non-suicidal self-injury, self-mutilation, and cutting, among others (Usher et al., 2010). In this chapter, we will focus mainly on STB and SIB, though we will discuss more specific variables when it is appropriate, such as self-harm, suicidal intent, suicide attempt, and death by suicide (De Leo, Burgis, Bertolote, Kerkhof, & Bille-Brahe, 2006; Hasley et al., 2008).

11.1 Frequency and Prevalence

Suicide and self-harm rates are consistently higher in prison populations than in the general population (Fazel & Benning, 2009; Fazel et al., 2011; Hawton, Linsell, Adeniji, Sariaslan, & Fazel, 2014; Konrad et al., 2007; van Ginneken et al., 2017). Similarly, elevated rates are reliably shown in prisons internationally (Fazel et al., 2011).

A large-scale study looking at the prevalence of prison suicide in 12 countries from 2003 to 2007 found that male prisoner suicide rates varied from 58 to 150 per 100,000 prisoners and were at least three times higher than general male population suicide rates, 16 to 31 per 100,000 people (Fazel et al., 2011). While the issue of suicide in prisons is prevalent worldwide, the frequencies of inmate suicide vary between different local, state, and federal jurisdictions (Ax et al., 2007; Hayes & Rowan, 1988; Lester, 1987). For example, Australia (58 per 100,000 prisoners), Canada (70 per 100,000), Ireland (64 per 100,000), and New Zealand (67 per 100,000) appear to have lower rates of male prisoner suicide than countries like Denmark (147 per 100,000), Sweden (128 per 100,000), Norway (127 per 100,000), and Germany (105.8 per 100,000) (Fazel et al., 2011; Noonan, Rohloff, & Ginder, 2015; Opitz-Welke, Bennefeld-Kersten, Konrad, & Welke, 2013). For male inmates, suicide is the leading cause of death in American jails and the second leading cause of death in American prisons (Noonan et al., 2015), with some American jails reporting suicide rates eight times higher than the general population over a 25-year span (DuRand, Burtka, Federman, Haycox, & Smith, 1995).

Relatedly, another large-scale study considering 139,195 self-harm incidents in 26,510 prisoners in England and Wales from 2004 to 2009 found that 5–6% of male prisoners self-harmed annually, as did 20–24% of female prisoners (Hawton et al., 2014). Comparable findings have been found in places like Greece, Canada, Australia, and the United States, reporting self-harm rates between 1–5% in males and 23% in females (Fotiadou, Livaditis, Manou, Kaniotou, & Xenitidis, 2006; Howard League for Penal Reform, 1999; Maden, Chamberlain, & Gunns, 2000; Maden, Swinton, & Gunn, 1994; Smith & Kaminski, 2010; Western Australia Department of Justice, 2002; Wichmann, Serin, & Abracen, 2002; Wichmann, Serin, & Motiuk, 2002).

To an even larger extent than males, female prisoner suicide rates are higher than rates found in the general (female) population (Daigle, Labelle, & Côté, 2006; Dye, 2011; Leigey & Reed, 2010). For example, in England and Wales, from 2004 to 2009, the rates of suicide in male prisoners were on average five times that of the relevant general population—whereas female prisoner rates were 20 times higher (Hawton et al., 2014). Comparatively higher rates of suicide are also found for female prisoners in various North American and European countries (Fazel et al., 2011; Noonan et al., 2015; Opitz-Welke et al., 2013; Webb et al., 2011). Furthermore, suicide is the second leading cause of death for women in both American jails and prisons (Noonan et al., 2015). Despite findings of an elevated risk of suicide in female prisoners, there is less research available on female prisoner suicide rates than male prisoners—with suicide being seen as a 'male problem' (Dye & Aday, 2013). This has led to inadequate services being offered, even though women are more likely than men to seek treatment while in jail (Drapalski, Youman, Stuewig, & Tangney, 2009).

Suicide is generally accepted as the leading cause of death in jails and prisons and has been for many years (Hayes & Rowan, 1988; Lester, 1987), but some scholars have questioned if inmate populations are actually as high-risk as they are typically reported (Ax et al., 2007; Mumola, 2005; White, Schimmel, & Frickey, 2002). A large number of studies looking at inmate suicide simply compare the prison suicide rates to the general population rate of suicide (Hoyert, Heron, Murphy, & Kung, 2006; Mumola, 2005). This leads to a false inflation of the risk of inmates, as suicide rates vary widely between gender and age—with males in the general population having higher suicide rates (18 per 100,000) than females (4 per 100,000) (Ax et al., 2007). Furthermore, in the general population, male suicide rates increase with age while female rates do not (Ax et al., 2007). Given that the majority of imprisoned individuals are male, comparisons with general population rates that include much lower female rates make it appear as though prisoners are at a higher risk than they truly are. Mumola (2005) also argues that calculations based on the average daily population (ADP) of inmates also artificially inflate prisoner suicide rates. For instance, local jails have much higher turnover rates than state or federal prisons; therefore, the ADP may not accurately capture a larger number of inmates coming in and out a given jail throughout each year.

Regardless of the debate about inmate suicide rates as they compare to general population rates, it is clear that prison suicide has been declining for the last few decades (Ax et al., 2007; Noonan et al., 2015; Opitz-Welke et al., 2013; van Ginneken et al., 2017); inmate suicide rates declined from 24 per 100,000 prisoners in the 1980s (White & Schimmel, 1995) to 18 per 100,000 prisoners in the 1990s (Hayes, 1995), to 14 per 100,000 prisoners in the 2000s (Mumola, 2005).

11.2 Theoretical Model(s) Relevant to Service Delivery

Theories about self-injurious behavior (SIB) and suicidal thoughts and behavior (STB) have existed for over a century (Durkheim, 1897) and include biological, sociological, and psychological explanations of suicide (Franklin et al., 2017; Oquendo et al., 2014). Especially over the past 50 years, a large body of research on suicide and self-harm has focused mainly on general community samples, with a growing number of studies examining special populations such as inmates (Franklin et al., 2017; Patry & Magaletta, 2015).

This section will review the major approaches that researchers have taken to explicate and predict inmate SIB and STB. This includes a brief overview of theories and models looking to synthesize these risk factors in a way that is accurately predictive of STBs and used to inform clinical practice. The section concludes with general comments and critiques of the current state of research on suicidal thoughts and behaviors in prison.

Risk factors most commonly recognized as correlates of suicidality in community samples include preadolescent social problems (Rojas & Stenberg, 2010), breakdown of social bonds (Shiner, Scourfield, Fincham, & Langer, 2009), and family history of completed suicide (Patry & Magaletta, 2015; Qin, Agerbo, & Mortensen, 2002). In addition, the following factors have also been identified as correlates to STBs: complications from mental illness (Mann, 2003); depression and substance abuse (Douglas et al., 2004); traumatic brain injury (Decou & Lynch, 2018); Lesbian, Gay, Bisexual, and/or Queer orientation; hopelessness, social desirability (Holden, Mendoca, & Serin, 2009); violent behavior within the past year (Conner et al., 2001); history of a serious prior suicide attempt (e.g., Rosen, 1976); escape from aversive self-awareness (Baumeister, 1990); emotion dysregulation (Linehan, 1993); and perceived burdensomeness, thwarted belongingness, and capability for suicide (Van Orden et al., 2010).

A number of variables identified as correlates of STBs in the general population are also relevant in inmate populations, such as depression, childhood trauma, and substance abuse (Fagan, Cox, Helfand, & Aufderheide, 2010; Shelton, Bailey, & Banfi, 2017; Webb et al., 2011). Despite an overlap of multiple risk factors, prisoners and prison environments present many risk factors for suicidality that are not found in the community, such as reduced contact with family and stress resulting from confinement to the prison environment, which led to heightened rates of suicide in inmate populations (Barker, Kõlves, & De Leo, 2014; Fazel et al., 2011). Recent meta-analyses highlight the importance of combining environmental and individual risk factors, which a majority of studies have not done (Franklin et al., 2017; Shelton et al., 2017). Reviews of STBs in prisons have found that suicidal ideation, and behaviors, are associated with a complex mix of factors, which include both individual factors, as well as environmental factors (Jenkins et al., 2005; Marzano et al., 2016). Predictive power for any single risk factor is only slightly better than chance (Franklin et al., 2017). Though there is much room for improvement, there is still value in established risk guidelines for explaining and preventing STBs guided by a number of theoretical models of inmate suicide and/or suicidal behavior, such as the interpersonal theory of suicide (Mandracchia & Smith, 2015) and diathesis-stress models (O'Connor, 2011; Wenzel & Beck, 2008). In addition, the importation, deportation, and integrated models present differing descriptions of prison suicide (Dye & Aday, 2013).

The *stress-diathesis theory* of suicide proposes that suicidal behaviors are brought on through a combination of clinical and neurobiological factors (Mann, 2003). Complications between one or more psychiatric disorders and a psychosocial crisis leads to suicidal ideation, which in turn may result in a suicide attempt, particularly when low levels of serotonin and noradrenaline are present. This then contributes to feelings of hopelessness and impulsivity (Mann, 2003). The model posits that a psychiatric disorder is typically worsening before suicide ideation or attempt, but it is the presence of a psychosocial crisis that acts as the most proximal stressor leading to suicidal behavior (Mann, 2003; Sarchiapone, Carli, Di Giannantonio, & Roy, 2009). A review by Marzano et al. (2016) supported the stress-diathesis model of suicide; the authors found that serious suicide attempts in prison result from an interaction of individual and environmental factors. International findings from Belgium have also cited the diathesis-stress model as accurately explaining the dynamic interaction between multiple factors leading to suicide, with specific vulnerability for suicidality stemming from psychosocial crises (Hawton & Van Heeringen, 2009; Wittouck et al., 2016).

The *interpersonal theory of suicide* holds that an individual is at risk of attempting suicide when s/he has both the *capability* and the *desire* for suicide (Joiner, Brown, & Wingate, 2005; Van Orden et al., 2010). If suicidal desire (ideation) is present, capability for suicide arises from the combination of a fearlessness of death and a capacity to tolerate physical pain, leading to self-preservation mechanisms being unable to stop an individual from attempting suicide (Ribeiro et al., 2014; Smith & Cukrowicz, 2010). This theory aligns with the finding that far fewer people attempt suicide compared to those who experience suicidal thoughts and desire (Kessler, Borges, & Walters, 1999; Van Orden et al., 2010). The interpersonal theory of suicide suggests that suicidal desire is caused by the interaction of experiencing *perceived burdensomeness* and *thwarted belongingness* (Van Orden et al., 2010). A number of studies have supported this theory in that perceived burdensomeness and thwarted belongingness have been found to be individually associated with suicidal ideation in a variety of populations, including male prisoners (Mandracchia & Smith, 2015).

In general, theories of suicide in prison typically take either an importation or a deprivation approach (Dye & Aday, 2013). The *importation* model focuses on individual characteristics of prisoners, while the *deprivation* approach looks at characteristics of the prison environment (Goffman, 1961). The importation model, which is the most prevalent approach in research on prison suicide (Dye & Aday, 2013), suggests that self-harm and STBs are most accurately predicted by individual inmate characteristics that are imported into prison. Studies looking at STBs through the importation lens typically report prior suicide attempts (Magaletta, Wheat, Patry, & Bates, 2008); traumatic life experiences, such as childhood and adult physical, sexual, and emotional abuse (Clements-Nolle, Wolden, & Bargmann-Losche, 2009; Verona, Hicks, & Patrick, 2005); and demographics (Blaauw, Kerkhof, & Hayes, 2005) as predictive of suicide attempts.

In contrast, the *deprivation* model argues that high rates of STBs in prisons are due to deprivation characteristics of the prison environment (Dye & Aday, 2013). Typical deprivation risk factors include security level, isolation within the institution, lack of contact with others outside the institution, overcrowding, program availability, and levels of violence and safety (Bonner, 2006; Dye, 2011; Dye &

Aday, 2013; Huey & McNulty, 2005). Furthermore, rates of suicide within prisons do not appear to reflect rates of suicide in the general population, suggesting that variations in inmate suicide rates are caused by differences across criminal justice systems and their distinctive delivery of psychiatric care in prison (Fazel et al., 2011):

While the importation and deprivation models both highlight relevant factors relating to suicidal thoughts and behaviors of inmates, most contemporary researchers acknowledge that considering the interactions between individual inmate characteristics and prison environments leads to the fullest explanation of inmate suicide—this is recognized as the *combined* model. (Dear, 2006; Liebling, 1999, 2006; Marzano, Hawton, Rivlin, & Fazel, 2011; Towl, Snow, & McHugh, 2001). The combined model holds that each inmate reacts differently to the characteristics of prison life, and that these responses are the result of an inmate's pre-prison characteristics and levels of vulnerability, such as sociodemographic variables, psychiatric history, abuse history, and values (Liebling, 1992; Medlicott, 2001; Zamble & Porporino, 1988). The combined approach recognizes that highly vulnerable inmates may successfully cope with life in prison when conditions are less depriving. This also means that in the most depriving prison environments, inmate vulnerabilities are more likely to be exposed and may lead to maladaptive coping, even for individuals who do not present obvious risk factors (Liebling, 2006).

Each of the aforementioned theories highlight a unique set of risk factors or relation between factors that is believed to be predictive of STBs. In so doing, each approach enables practitioners to comprehend and contextualize the interaction of dynamic risk factors and protective factors in order to accurately assess the level of risk for suicide and to effectively map out important points for intervention (Mandracchia & Smith, 2015). Recent meta-analyses suggest that, while STB risk factors and the guidelines derived from these factors have been arrived at in a rational way (through expert consensus), these guidelines have not yet been appropriately evaluated (Franklin et al., 2017). According to Franklin et al. (2017), theories and guidelines must be studied longitudinally within prison populations in order to improve upon weak predictive validity. To date, most studies on inmate suicidality have used a cross-sectional approach to draw conclusions about which variables are most relevant.

Theories of suicide are also starting to acknowledge that specific STBs, such as suicidal ideation and suicidal action, possess their own unique risk factors (e.g., the interpersonal theory of suicide) (Mandracchia & Smith, 2015; May & Klonsky, 2016). To illustrate, one study found that while 13.5% of people report suicidal thoughts in their lifetime, only 4.6% reported an actual suicide attempt (Kessler et al., 1999). In order to accurately predict these two separate, albeit related, outcomes, an "ideation-to-action" framework has been recommended as a guiding approach to all suicide research in order to highlight differentiating risk factors for suicidal ideation and suicidal action research (Klonsky & May, 2014, 2015). One meta-analysis found that, in community samples, anxiety disorders, PTSD, drug use disorders, and sexual abuse history were moderately elevated in attempters compared to ideators (May & Klonsky, 2016).

Researchers investigating inmate suicide attempt lethality found that higher lethality was associated with Axis II disorders, favorable staff interactions, and the lower usage levels of drugs other than marijuana, alcohol, cocaine, or depressants (Magaletta et al., 2008). The finding that favorable staff interactions and suicide attempt lethality were associated may be explained by the opportunity for less supervision (and a subsequent suicide attempt) that having a good relationship with staff affords an inmate (Dumond & Dumond, 2005; Magaletta et al., 2008).

A meta-analysis looking at 50 years of community research from 1965 to 2015 found that there is not yet a single theory that can significantly predict STBs more accurately than others (Franklin et al., 2017), albeit some theories have more evidence supporting them. This is worth noting for practitioners, as each case requires the incorporation of multiple theories and factors in order to adequately encompass all of the variables that are present and relevant to explaining suicide in prisons. While diversity in theories and models is common for a young field, it is less than preferable from a practical and research standpoint. In many areas of research, a wide range of early theories are typically narrowed down through the accumulation of valid and reliable findings, leading to a paradigmatic shift toward a dominant theory or set of theories. Given the present state of theoretical diversity, Franklin et al. (2017) point out that the suicide research field is still in a pre-paradigmatic phase.

11.3 Diagnosis and Assessment

This section begins by examining diagnostic risk factors for self-harm and suicidal ideation and behaviors in the general community and in inmate populations. Diagnostic criteria are organized into demographic, clinical, and criminological/ institutional factors (Barker et al., 2014). Risk factors for self-injurious behavior (SIB) and suicidal thoughts and behavior (STB) are mainly derived from research considering the differences between inmates who have reported or exhibited SIB or STB with inmates who have not reported such behaviors (Smith & Kaminski, 2010).

Demographic factors associated with suicide in prisoners are being young, white, and possessing a low education level (Hawton et al., 2014). Inmate marital status has brought forth contrasting results, with some findings indicating a positive association between being married and inmate suicide (Fazel, Cartwright, Norman-Nott, & Hawton, 2008) and others finding a negative relationship (Daniel & Fleming, 2006). Regardless of sex, younger age and white ethnicity are for the most part generally and consistently associated with higher rates of self-harm in inmates (Hawton et al., 2014; Smith & Kaminski, 2010). However, these findings may be misleading due to the overrepresentation of younger individuals within prisons (Livingston, 1997). There is also some uncertainty regarding the predictive validity of inmate age, as some studies have found negative correlations between age and SIBs (CSC, 1981; Wilkins & Coid, 1991). Inmates who identify as lesbian, gay, bisexual, or transgender (LGBT) are more likely to self-harm than inmates who identify as heterosexual (Skegg, 2005). Higher self-harm rates are found in both male and female inmates with same-sex attraction (Skegg, Nada-Raja, Dickson, Paul, & Williams, 2003).

Clinical factors correlated with inmate suicide include recent suicidal ideation, history of attempted suicide, personal and family history of psychiatric problems, dysfunctional family lives including parental substance abuse and violence, currently receiving psychotropic medication, and a current diagnosis of a psychiatric disorder—most commonly: borderline personality disorder (BPD), post-traumatic stress disorder (PTSD), depression, anxiety, and substance abuse disorders, specifically alcohol abuse (Daniel & Fleming, 2006; Fazel et al., 2008; Hawton et al., 2014; Laishes, 1997; Salina, Lesondak, Razzano, & Weilbaecher, 2007; Shelton et al., 2017). Internationally, studies of inmates have found history of mental illness and psychiatric treatment to be correlated with self-injurious behavior (Dear, Thomson, Howells, & Hall, 2001; Ivanoff, 1992). For both female and male inmates, those with previous psychiatric treatment are ten times more likely to self-injure than inmates who have not had psychiatric treatment (Smith & Kaminski, 2010; Wichmann, Serin, & Abracen, 2002). Presence of secondary (but not primary) psychopathic traits also increases risk of STBs in prison inmates (Smith, Selwyn, Wolford-Clevenger, & Mandracchia, 2014).

Institutional factors are those uniquely present in those who are incarcerated. Institutional factors related to suicide include being in a single cell, being incarcerated in jail (compared to prison), lack of sufficient mental health programming and staff, being on remand, first incarceration, long prison sentence, overcrowded prison conditions, poor coping methods upon entry, bullying and harassment, recent disciplinary action, positive interactions with correctional staff, receiving a new charge or conviction, and having a life sentence or being unsentenced (Cramer, Wechsler, Miller, & Yenne, 2017; Fazel et al., 2008; Hawton et al., 2014; Kovasznay, Miraglia, Beer, & Way, 2004; Laishes, 1997; Magaletta et al., 2008). Being convicted of a violent offense, isolation, sensory deprivation, access to lethal means (e.g., a bedsheet for hanging), and lack of staff supervision and funding of suicidal inmates have also been associated with SIB in both females and males (Cookson, 1977; Daniel, 2006; Ireland, 2000).

In a large sample of English and Welsh prisoners, risk factors for completed suicide among inmates who previously self-harmed included older age and a previous self-harm incident of high or moderate lethality; for women, the most predictive risk factor was a history of more than five self-harm incidents within a year (Hawton et al., 2014). Furthermore, a meta-analysis of 34 studies reported the strongest associated factors of inmate suicide to be single occupancy cell assignment, recent suicidal ideation, history of attempted suicide, and psychiatric diagnosis or history of alcohol abuse (Fazel et al., 2008).

Also, of importance are *protective factors*, which, when present, reduce the likelihood of inmate suicidality. Some examples include removal of lethal means, consistent 24-h monitoring, social connectedness (e.g., pseudo-families), communication with family, participation in support groups, education concerning medication use, cell placement with social support, and use of religious or spiritual service (Cramer et al., 2017). Incorporation of protective factors into assessment and management planning for inmates is currently an underutilized tool. Research on protective factors is limited but growing (e.g., Wang et al., 1997; World Health Organization, 2007).

The most common self-injurious behavior in both female and male inmates is cutting or scratching (Barker et al., 2014; Hawton et al., 2014). The second most common SIB differs between sexes, with females being more likely to engage in self-strangulation and males more likely to poison themselves, overdose, or swallow an indigestible object (Hawton et al., 2014). The lethality of SIB is typically lower in female prisoners than male prisoners (Hawton et al., 2014). Lethality of suicide attempts have been found to be associated with positive staff interactions, previous LSD/PCP use, and diagnosis of an Axis II disorder (Magaletta et al., 2008).

In both males and females, hanging is the most common method of death by suicide, followed by cutting (Hawton et al., 2014; Magaletta et al., 2008). Cutting as a method of previous self-harm has been identified as predictive of future death by suicide (Cooper et al., 2005), with a study of English and Welsh prisoners finding over half of reported suicides occurred within 1 month of a self-harm incident (typically cutting) (Hawton et al., 2014).

Risk of suicide for prisoners is highest in the early period of incarceration (Forrester & Slade, 2014); in one study 32% of suicides occurred within the first week of incarceration (Shaw, Baker, Hunt, Moloney, & Appleby, 2004). Furthermore, male prisoners die most often after being brought directly to jail from the courts (Forrester & Slade, 2014). Early screening provides a window of opportunity for practitioners to identify at risk individuals and reduce the likelihood of inmate suicide attempts (Patry & Magaletta, 2015).

Early, quick and accurate diagnosis and assessment are crucial; this is best achieved through proper planning and training combined with use of valid and reliable assessment tools. Although screening instruments for suicide risk in forensic settings are not widely standardized (Perry, Marandos, Coulton, & Johnson, 2010), there are a number of tools available, some of which were originally developed for community or clinical use, while others have been created specifically for use within prisons (Gould, McGeorge, & Slade, 2017). When selecting assessment tools, practitioners must carefully consider the prison environment as well as the demographic being assessed in order to bring about the most accurate results (Gould et al., 2017). Assessment of STBs may be done via an embedded suicidality scale within a personality measure (e.g., PAI) or by a standalone measure specifically made for assessing STBs (e.g., SRAS).

The *Personality Assessment Inventory* (PAI), while originally developed for the general population, has become popular for forensic practitioners due to its strong psychometric properties, brevity, low cost, and well-established comparative community, clinical, and forensic norms (Morey, 2007). This instrument provides a wide-range of information for correctional practitioners, yielding high utility as a general screening tool (Morey, 2007). More specifically, the PAI suicidal ideation scale (suicidal ideation scale—SUI) has shown predictive potential for identifying suicidality in inmates (Patry & Magaletta, 2015). The SUI considers the severity of suicidal ideation and serves as an important initial assessment during inmate intake (Morey, 2003).

The Suicide Potential Index (SPI) is an aggregate index, consisting of risk factors assessed in the PAI, that has been found to be related to a history of a suicide attempt and other factors relevant to suicide (Hopwood, Baker, & Morey, 2008; Patry & Magaletta, 2015). Patry and Magaletta (2015) found that the SUI and the Suicide Potential Index (SPI) demonstrated convergent validity when used with a large sample ($n = 1120$) of both male and female U.S. inmates, while still capturing different sets of information; the SPI demonstrated incremental validity for differentiating an ideator from someone at risk for an attempt. These two indices, the SUI and the SPI, are best used in combination as an intake screening tool.

The *Depression, Hopelessness, and Suicide Scale* (DHS; Mills & Kroner, 2005) was designed for use with Canadian inmates, based on the theory that depression and hopelessness are related to risk for self-harm and suicide. High-risk DHS scores have been correlated with suicide attempts in prisoners (Mills & Kroner, 2005). The DHS is a brief, 39-item option for assessing risk for STB in inmates. Critics have suggested that use of the DHS be combined with consideration of environmental characteristics relating to prison life, as there are no items in the DHS pertaining to this category of risk factors (Marzano et al., 2011).

The *Suicide Risk Assessment Scale* (SRAS) is a 9-item scale developed as a supplement for use with clinical assessment of suicide risk (Cohen, Motto, & Seiden, 1966). However, the SRAS has been shown to be more effective at predicting suicide risk than individual psychiatric assessment (Wichmann, Serin, & Motiuk, 2002). The SRAS has also been shown to be more effective than other commonly used scales at predicting STB in inmates and is included in Correctional Service Canada's Offender Intake Assessment (Daigle et al., 2006).

The *Suicide Probability Scale* (SPS) was not initially intended for use in inmate populations, but the SPS was found to have good predictive validity in a study looking at a 10-year follow-up of STB rates in a large group of prisoners (Cull & Gill, 1982; Naud & Daigle, 2010). The 36-item SPS focuses on hopelessness, hostility, negative self-evaluation, and suicidal ideation (Cull & Gill, 1982). The SPS totals these ratings and classifies inmates into four categories: Sub-clinical, Mild, Moderate, Severe (Cull & Gill, 1982). Some argue that the 20-min-long administration time is too long for the SPS to be a feasible initial intake-screening tool and use ought to be reserved for cases requiring secondary screening assessment (Gould et al., 2017).

Daigle et al. (2006) investigated the effectiveness of the SRAS and the SPS. They found that both scales were effective at screening inmates for suicide risk, especially in the long-term (Daigle et al., 2006). They considered the SRAS to be the superior measure, based on its brevity and its positive psychometric characteristics.

The *Minnesota Multiphasic Personality Inventory* (MMPI-II-RF; Glassmire, Tarescavage, Burchett, Martinez, & Gomez, 2016), is a popular multiscale measure used within forensic settings (Archer, Buffington-Vollum, Stredny, & Handel, 2006). Specifically, five items that represent the construct of Suicidal/Death Ideation (SUI) are used within the MMPI-II-RF to assess suicidality (Tellegen & Ben-Porath,

2008/2011). The MMPI-II-RF Technical Manual reports correlations between the SUI items and conceptually related factors such as history of suicide attempts and suicidal ideation (Tellegen & Ben-Porath, 2008/2011). Glassmire and colleagues (2016) reported incremental value from SUI data after accounting for information from clinical interviews, making a strong argument for the validity of the MMPI-II-RF's SUI items.

Given that actuarial assessments, such as the SRAS, help to minimize the subjectivity of clinical judgement, actuarial instruments may be well suited for initial screening for at-risk inmates, while individual clinical assessments are especially appropriate in cases requiring follow-up assessment planning over the long-term (Gould et al., 2017). Combining assessment tools with clinical interviewing and judgement also brings about more accurate results in community samples, especially in suicide prevention (Brown, Jones, Betts, & Wu, 2003; Eyman & Eyman, 1992; Rogers & Oney, 2005; Yufit, 1991). Despite the large number of actuarial assessments for suicidality, the literature is lacking in structured professional judgement (SPJ) tools for clinical assessment (Cramer et al., 2017).

The Suicide Assessment Manual for Inmates (SAMI) consists of 20 risk factors derived from the literature and is one of the few SPJs that aims to address suicidality (Zapf, 2006). During administration, the assessor rates each risk factor on a 3-point scale with the aid of sample questions to assess suicidality-related constructs. Despite these promising characteristics, the SAMI has not been adequately validated; previous findings showed poor factor structure, and predictive validity is a concern as well (Cramer et al., 2017).

A second SPJ tool is the Short-Term Assessment of Risk and Treatability (START), a one-page semi-structured interview that attempts to facilitate decision-making over a 1-month period of risk assessment (Webster, Martin, Brink, Nicholls, & Desmarais, 2009). START focuses on seven domains: substance use, self-neglect, absenteeism, self-harm, suicide, victimization likelihood, and externalized violence (Webster et al., 2009). Critics argue that the START is too heavily focused on violence risk factors to be a useful suicidality-specific risk tool (Cramer et al., 2017).

11.4   Intervention(s): What Works, What Might Work, and What Doesn't Work

Interventions for inmate SIB and STB are crucial aspects of a prison's mental health system. If an inmate is at risk of suicide the correctional staff must deliver a relevant intervention aimed at managing the current behaviors and reducing the likelihood of their reoccurrence.

A large majority of treatment interventions for SIB and STB used in prison settings are based on intervention approaches first found to be effective in general and clinical populations (Shelton et al., 2017). There is still a good deal of uncertainty about which interventions are most effective and feasible for dealing with inmate STBs (Marzano et al., 2016). However, there are a number of interventions which have been evaluated and found to possess robust, positive findings including: cognitive behavioral therapy (CBT), dialectical behavior therapy (DBT), and staff training (Barker et al., 2014; Shelton et al., 2017). Interventions found to have mixed efficacy include: assessment, care in custody and teamwork (ACCT) systems, and acceptance and commitment therapy (ACT). Lastly, we briefly present manual assisted cognitive behavior therapy (MACT), an emerging approach showing some promise, but which does not yet have support for use in correctional settings.

Cognitive behavioral therapy (CBT) involves various sets of psychosocial approaches to intervening and correcting a problem behavior (Freeman, Pretzer, Fleming, & Simon, 2004). CBT approaches aim to target maladaptive cognitions and make a positive change in psychological symptoms such as self-harm or suicidal behaviors (Pratt, Gooding, Awenat, Eccles, & Tarrier, 2016). CBT's overarching framework focusses on cognitive restructuring—which involves acknowledging and challenging dysfunctional beliefs and cognitions related to the target problem behaviors, such as self-harming or suicidal ideation, in order for the individual to learn productive coping mechanisms (Brown et al., 2005). CBT can be delivered individually or in a group setting (Freeman et al., 2004).

CBT approaches aimed at reducing STBs have recently been developed for use with prisoners, such as the cognitive behavioral suicide prevention (CBSP) treatment (Pratt et al., 2016; Tarrier et al., 2013). The available research looking at CBSP, although limited, has shown promise for the efficacy of the treatment in reducing STBs in prisoner populations (Franklin et al., 2017; Pratt et al., 2016). Pratt et al. (2016), using a randomized controlled trial, found that a CBSP intervention gave rise to clinically relevant improvements in the number of suicidal behaviors in a group of prisoners. Additionally, a study considering a group CBT intervention, found that participation was related to lower rates of suicidal behavior in youth offenders (Rohde, Jorgensen, Seeley, & Mace, 2004). CBT is considered a feasible option for a self-harm and suicide crisis intervention within a prison setting (Franklin et al., 2017; Pratt et al., 2016).

Dialectical behavior therapy (DBT) is a form of CBT that was initially devised as a treatment program for individuals with borderline personality disorder (BPD) (Linehan, 1993). Justification for DBT as a treatment for reducing suicidal behaviors lies within the overlap between individuals with BPD and individuals who are at risk of self-harming or suicidal behavior (Usher et al., 2010). For instance, traits of BPD include extreme emotional dysregulation resulting from an interaction of an individual's biological tendencies and environmental factors—similar to symptoms of an inmate at risk for self-harming or suicidal behavior (McCann, Ball, & Ivanoff, 2000).

The main theoretical objective of DBT is for the individual to address their cognitive and emotional deficits and learn skills to overcome them (Linehan, 1993). This biosocial intervention has been found to be effective at reducing self-harm and suicidal behavior in both community, psychiatric, and most recently, forensic samples (Bohus et al., 2000; Franklin et al., 2017; Hayes, Masuda, Bissett, Luoma, & Guerrero, 2004; Low, Jones, Duggan, Power, & MacLeod, 2001; Stanley, Ivanoff, Brodsky, Oppenheim, & Mann, 1998).

The evaluation of DBT in forensic settings is limited but has put forth encouraging results, so far (Franklin et al., 2017). A review of 17 studies reported DBT as an effective intervention for self-harming and suicidal behaviors in prisoners (Dixon-Gordon, Harrison, & Roesch, 2012). Furthermore, research on female prisoners from the United Kingdom showed that DBT reduced the lethality and frequency of self-harming incidents (Nee & Farman, 2005).

Just like CBT, DBT interventions have been adopted internationally; such as by the RUSH (Real Understanding of Self-Help) program in Australia (Eccleston & Sorbello, 2002), the federal government's Correctional Services department in Canada (Usher et al., 2010), as well as in the United States and the United Kingdom (Berzins & Trestman, 2004). Although listed as an effective treatment intervention for self-harm and suicidal behaviors, Canadian correctional guidelines note that DBT is most effective in inmates with Borderline Personality Disorder and that depending on each case, practitioners may have to consider other intervention options (Usher et al., 2010).

Staff training—The specific approach an institution or a practitioner chooses when intervening in self-harming or suicidal behaviors will depend on various biological, social, and environmental factors related to each individual case—relatedly, research has also shown that adequate training for correctional staff is one of the most important characteristics of a suicide intervention or prevention plan and ought to be present regardless of the theoretical approach (Konrad et al., 2007). It is recommended that correctional staff receive suicide prevention training, along with a yearly refresher training course. Having "mock drills" prepares staff for real-life scenarios and should be included in suicide prevention training practices for all correctional staff (Hayes, 2006). Shelton et al. (2017) reviewed efficacious self-harm interventions in prisons and found that staff training was as important as the presence of either CBT or DBT in reducing problem behaviors. This was in part due to staff training leading to other positive outcomes occurring such as proper intake assessments, proper observation inmates, and appropriate referrals of problem behavior to the relevant mental health staff member (Barker et al., 2014).

Acceptance and commitment therapy (ACT) has increasingly been used to treat depression, anxiety, and other conditions related to self-harm and suicidal behaviors (Hayes et al., 2004; Usher et al., 2010). ACT's guiding theory postulates that cognitions, emotions, and behaviors are primarily related to the context in which they exist, and an individual must learn to control and explain subjective cognitions, emotions, and behaviors within these problematic contexts in order to cope effectively (Hayes et al., 2004). The ACT approach is relatively new compared to CBT and DBT approaches, and has been tested less rigorously (Usher et al., 2010). Evidence for the effectiveness of ACT for treating self-harming and suicidal behavior is mixed and limited (Hayes et al., 2004; Ruiz, 2010). Two studies looking at treatment effectiveness of ACT for depression found moderately effective results in community samples (Zettle & Hayes, 1986; Zettle & Rains, 1989). One of the only studies looking at a form of ACT and reducing self-injury found promising results, with psychiatric outpatients showing positive improvements in BPD symptoms, self-harm, and emotional regulation (Gratz & Gunderson, 2006). However, given that this is only one study and that the form of therapy was not a pure ACT therapy, ACT is not (yet) as commonly recommended for use in correctional settings.

Assessment, care in custody and teamwork (ACCT) systems interventions are currently in place in prisons in England and Wales (HM Prison Service, 2005). These systems aim to provide individualized care for inmates at risk of self-harming or suicidal behavior (HM Prison Service, 2005). ACCT provides crisis interventions as well as multidisciplinary care and follow up to inmates with conditions that affect them in the long-term, such as self-harming and suicidal behavior (Pratt et al., 2016). When an inmate is deemed to be at-risk, the ACCT is "opened" and reviews are completed every 2 weeks until the inmate's risk level has lowered, after which the ACCT is "closed" (Pratt et al., 2016). Researchers have found that ACCT shows sufficient sensitivity at recognizing inmates who are at-risk and success in subsequently providing them with treatment (Humber, Hayes, Senior, Fahy, & Shaw, 2011; Senior et al., 2007). However, more experimental research is necessary in order to determine the effectiveness of ACCT and find out in what circumstances can ACCT be used to the fullest potential (Pratt et al., 2016).

Manual assisted cognitive therapy (MACT) is an approach that combines aspects of both CBT and DBT by focusing on cognition and problem solving (Boyce, Oakley-Browne, & Hatcher, 2001; Weinberg, Gunderson, Hennen, & Cutter, 2006). To reduce self-harm and suicidal behavior, MACT combines five brief, individual sessions with a 70-page treatment manual (Evans et al., 1999). This multidimensional therapy aims to build problem solving skills, basic cognitive techniques for managing emotions and negative thinking patterns, as well as relapse prevention strategies (Evans et al., 1999). Evaluations of MACT effectiveness at reducing self-harming and suicidal behaviors is very limited for use in prisons (Weinberg et al., 2006), although research on its use in psychiatric outpatient groups and community samples have found MACT to be more effective at reducing self-harm incidents than groups receiving treatment as usual (Evans et al., 1999; Tyrer et al., 2003; Weinberg et al., 2006). These preliminary findings highlighting the brevity and cost-effectiveness of MACT are positive signs for the future of MACT, although further research is needed.

11.5 Future Implications

More research is needed in all areas related to inmate STB, including, but not limited to: training, practice, research, and correctional administration.

Proper *training* in suicide prevention for correctional workers, including correctional psychologists, is of critical importance when dealing with inmate suicide (Konrad et al., 2007; Magaletta et al., 2013; Magaletta, Patry, Cermak, & McLearen, 2017; Magaletta, Patry, Dietz, & Ax, 2007). A review of U.S. graduate training programs in school psychology advised that programs are lacking in their training for dealing with youth suicide, and school directors ought to ensure that adequate class and workshop time is being given to the subject (Liebling-Boccio & Jennings, 2013). Additionally, opportunities to work with potentially suicidal individuals during a practicum or internship is beneficial to graduate students.

It is important to quickly and accurately identify STBs among inmates, and to implement best supported practices. As noted by Franklin and colleagues (2017) in their 50-year analyses of suicide research, there is not yet a dominant approach or set of approaches to explain suicide. Research has shown that in order to be most effective, correctional practitioners must design programs that address suicide at various points in time (Konrad et al., 2007). Researchers must be guided by the gaps in literature (see: Cha et al., 2017; Franklin et al., 2017): many important questions still do not have answers. Future research will help to determine how best to diagnose, assess, prevent, and treat STBs (Franklin et al., 2017).

11.6   Technology and Innovation

Numerous innovative technologies are revolutionizing multidisciplinary treatment and research, and the field of suicide research is no different. Many researchers and practitioners have praised developments in machine learning algorithms that attempt to predict suicide using complex statistical techniques to identify factors or variables that influence suicide (Rakesh, 2017). Machine learning has become an established part of medical practice and shows great promise for the treatment of suicidal prisoners (Adams & Leveson, 2012). Suicide prediction is a good candidate for machine learning approaches due to the inherent complex nature between the many variables related to suicidality (Franklin et al., 2017).

Various studies have successfully used machine learning algorithms to retrospectively predict suicide (Delgado-Gomez, Blasco-Fontecilla, Sukno, Romas-Plascenia, & Baca-Garcia, 2012; Lopez-Castroman et al., 2011), as well as predict suicide in a sample of soldiers in psychiatric treatment (Kessler et al., 2015). Machine learning algorithms combined with simulated-patient approaches also hold potential as a training method for practitioners looking to accurately predict suicide. Simulated-patient approaches have been recommended as a useful training method for students who will be working in forensic settings (Díaz, Panosky, & Shelton, 2014).

Innovative researchers are also currently looking to identify biomarkers for suicidality. Biomarkers, as noted above, include neurotransmitter systems such as dopamine, norepinephrine, serotonin, and GABA as biomarkers, as well as imaging biomarkers such as PET scans and diffusion sensors, and cortisol systems (Olvet et al., 2014; Oquendo et al., 2014). While there is currently no single biomarker that can identify suicidality, there is likely great potential for strengthening predictive capabilities by combining biological information with machine learning, as well as with clinical and assessment data (Rakesh, 2017).

11.7 Conclusion

This chapter examined the literature on inmate suicidality and self-harm. The frequency and prevalence of inmate suicide, though slowing down, is still alarmingly high in prisons across the world. Theoretical models show some promise for explaining these occurrences, such as diathesis-stress models and the interpersonal theory of suicide, but there are significant gaps in research as to the causes of inmate STBs and SIBs. Practitioners have a variety of clinical and actuarial tools to aid them in identifying and treating at-risk inmates; current research suggests that the best screening strategies should include an actuarial tool such as the SPS, combined with clinical judgment for assessment of inmates who may have an acute risk of suicidal behavior. CBT-based models show the most promise for effective treatment. More longitudinal research with inmates is needed in order for practitioners to more effectively screen for, and treat, inmates at risk of suicide.

References

Adams, S. T., & Leveson, S. H. (2012). Clinical prediction rules. *BMJ, 344*, d8312.

Archer, R. P., Buffington-Vollum, J. K., Stredny, R. V., & Handel, R. W. (2006). A survey of psychological test use patterns among forensic psychologists. *Journal of Personality Assessment, 87*(1), 84–94.

Ax, R. K., Fagan, T. J., Magaletta, P. R., Morgan, R. D., Nussbaum, D., & White, T. W. (2007). Innovations in correctional assessment and treatment. *Criminal Justice and Behavior, 34*(7), 893–905.

Barker, E., Kõlves, K., & De Leo, D. (2014). Management of suicidal and self-harming behaviors in prisons: Systematic literature review of evidence-based activities. *Archives of Suicide Research, 18*(3), 227–240.

Baumeister, R. F. (1990). Suicide as escape from self. *Psychological Review, 97*, 90–113. https://doi.org/10.1037/0033-295X.97.1.90

Berzins, L. G., & Trestman, R. L. (2004). The development and implementation of dialectical behavior therapy in forensic settings. *International Journal of Forensic Mental Health, 3*(1), 93–103.

Blaauw, E., Kerkhof, J. F. M., & Hayes, L. (2005). Demographic, criminal, and psychiatric factors related to inmate suicide. *Suicide and Life-threatening Behavior, 35*, 63–75.

Bohus, M., Haaf, B., Stiglmayr, C., Pohl, U., Böhme, R., & Linehan, M. (2000). Evaluation of inpatient dialectical-behavioral therapy for borderline personality disorder—A prospective study. *Behaviour Research and Therapy, 38*(9), 875–887.

Bonner, R. (2006). Stressful segregation housing and psychosocial vulnerability in prison suicide ideators. *Suicide and Life-threatening Behavior, 36*, 250–254.

Boyce, P., Oakley-Browne, M. A., & Hatcher, S. (2001). The problem of deliberate self-harm. *Current Opinion in Psychiatry, 14*, 107–111.

Brown, G. K., Have, T. T., Henriques, G. R., Xie, S. X., Hollander, J. E., & Beck, A. T. (2005). Cognitive therapy for the prevention of suicide attempts: A randomized control trial. *Journal of the American Medical Association, 294*(5), 563–570.

Brown, G. S., Jones, E. R., Betts, E., & Wu, J. (2003). Improving suicide risk assessment in a managed-care environment. *CRISIS-TORONTO, 24*(2), 49–55.

Cha, C. B., Tezanos, K. M., Peros, O. M., Ng, M. Y., Ribeiro, J. D., Nock, M. K., & Franklin, J. C. (2017). Accounting for diversity in suicide research: Sampling and sample reporting practices in the United States. *Suicide and Life-Threatening Behavior, 48*(2), 131–139.

Clements-Nolle, K., Wolden, M., & Bargmann-Losche, J. (2009). Childhood trauma and risk for past and future suicide attempts among women in prison. *Women's Health Issues, 19*, 185–192.

Cohen, E., Motto, J. A., & Seiden, R. H. (1966). An instrument for evaluating suicide potential: A preliminary study. *American Journal of Psychiatry, 122*, 886–891.

Conner, K. R., Cox, C., Duberstein, P. R., Tian, L., Nisbet, P. A., & Conwell, Y. (2001). Violence, alcohol, and completed suicide: A case-control study. *American Journal of Psychiatry, 158*, 1701–1705. https://doi.org/10.1176/appi.ajp.158.10.1701

Cookson, H. M. (1977). A survey of self-injury in a closed prison for women. *British Journal of Criminology, 17*(4), 332–347.

Cooper, J., Kapur, N., Webb, R., Lawlor, M., Guthrie, E., Mackway-Jones, K., et al. (2005). Suicide after deliberate self-harm: A four-year cohort study. *American Journal of Psychiatry, 162*, 297–303.

Correctional Service of Canada. (1981). *Self-inflicted injuries and suicides*. Ottawa, ON: Correctional Service of Canada.

Cramer, R. J., Wechsler, H. J., Miller, S. L., & Yenne, E. (2017). Suicide prevention in correctional settings: Current standards and recommendations for research, prevention, and training. *Journal of Correctional Health Care, 23*(3), 313–328.

Cull, J. G., & Gill, W. S. (1982). *Manual for the suicide probability scale*. Los Angeles, CA: Western Psychological Services.

Daigle, M. S., Daniel, A. E., Dear, G. E., Frottier, P., Hayes, L. M., Kerkhof, A., … Sarchiapone, M. (2007). Preventing suicide in prisons, Part 2: International comparisons of suicide prevention services in correctional facilities. *Crisis: The Journal of Crisis Intervention and Suicide Prevention, 28*, 122–130. https://doi.org/10.1027/0227-5910.28.3.122

Daigle, M. S., Labelle, R., & Côté, G. (2006). Further evidence of the validity of the suicide risk assessment scale for prisoners. *International Journal of Law and Psychiatry, 29*(5), 343–354.

Daigle, M. S., & Côté, G. (2006). Nonfatal suicide-related behavior among inmates: Testing for gender and type differences. *Suicide and Life-Threatening Behavior, 36*(6), 670–681.

Daniel, A. (2006). Preventing suicide in prison: A collaborative responsibility of administrative, custodial and clinical staff. *Journal of the American Academy of Psychiatry and the Law, 34*, 165–175.

Daniel, A., & Fleming, J. (2006). Suicides in a state correctional system, 1992–2002: A review. *Journal of Correctional Health Care, 12*, 24–35.

De Leo, D., Burgis, S., Bertolote, J. M., Kerkhof, A. J. F. M., & Bille-Brahe, U. (2006). Definitions of suicidal behavior. *Crisis, 27*(1), 4–15.

Dear, G. (2006). *Preventing suicide and other self-harm in prison*. Houndmills, UK: Palgrave Macmillan.

Dear, G. E., Thomson, D. M., Howells, K., & Hall, G. J. (2001). Self-harm in Western Australian prisons: Differences between prisoners who have self-harmed and those who have not. *Australian and New Zealand Journal of Criminology, 34*, 277–292.

DeCou, C. R., & Lynch, S. M. (2018). Sexual orientation, gender, and attempted suicide among adolescent psychiatric inpatients. *Psychological services, 15*(3), 363.

Delgado-Gomez, D., Blasco-Fontecilla, H., Sukno, F., Romas-Plascenia, M. S., & Baca-Garcia, E. (2012). Suicide attempters classification: Toward predictive models of suicidal behavior. *Neurocomputing, 92*, 3–8. https://doi.org/10.1016/j.neucom.2011.08.033

Díaz, D. A., Panosky, D. M., & Shelton, D. (2014). Simulation: Introduction to correctional nursing in a prison setting. *Journal of Correctional Health Care, 20*(3), 240–248.

Dixon-Gordon, K., Harrison, N., & Roesch, N. H. (2012). Non-suicidal self-injury within offender populations: A integrative review. *International Journal of Forensic Mental Health, 11*(1), 33–50. https://doi.org/10.1080/14999013.2012.667513

Douglas, J., Cooper, J., Amos, T., Webb, R., Guthrie, E., & Appleby, L. (2004). "Near-fatal" deliberate self-harm: Characteristics, prevention and implications for the prevention of suicide. *Journal of Affective Disorders, 79*(1), 263–268.

Drapalski, A. L., Youman, K., Stuewig, J., & Tangney, J. (2009). Gender differences in jail inmates' symptoms of mental illness, treatment history and treatment seeking. *Criminal Behaviour and Mental Health, 19*(3), 193–206.

Dumond, R., & Dumond, D. (2005). Depression: The prisoner's plight. In S. Stojkovic (Ed.), *Managing special populations in jails and prisons* (pp. 8.1–8.51). Kingston, NJ: Civic Research Institute.

DuRand, C., Burtka, G., Federman, E., Haycox, J., & Smith, J. (1995). A quarter century of suicide in a major urban jail: Implications for community psychiatry. *American Journal of Psychiatry, 152*, 1077–1080.

Durkheim, E. (1897). *[Suicide: A study in sociology]. Le suicide: étude de sociologie*. Paris, France: F. Alcan.

Dye, M. H. (2011). The gender paradox in prison suicide rates. *Women and Criminal Justice, 21*, 290–307.

Dye, M. H., & Aday, R. H. (2013). "I just wanted to die" preprison and current suicide ideation among women serving life sentences. *Criminal Justice and Behavior, 40*(8), 832–849.

Eccleston, L., & Sorbello, L. (2002). The rush program—Real understanding of self-help: A suicide and self-harm prevention initiative within a prison setting. *Australian Psychologist, 37*(3), 237–244.

Evans, K., Tyrer, P., Catalan, J., Schmidt, U., Davidson, K., Dent, J., ... Thompson, S. (1999). Manual-assisted cognitive-behaviour therapy (mact): A randomized controlled trial of a brief intervention with bibliotherapy in the treatment of recurrent deliberate self-harm. *Psychological Medicine, 29*(1), 19–25.

Eyman, J. R., & Eyman, S. K. (1992). Psychological testing for potentially suicidal individuals. In B. Bonger (Ed.), *Suicide: Guidelines for assessment, management, and treatment* (pp. 127–143). New York, NY: Oxford University Press.

Fagan, T. J., Cox, J., Helfand, S. J., & Aufderheide, D. (2010). Self-injurious behavior in correctional settings. *Journal of Correctional Health Care, 16*, 48–66. https://doi.org/10.1177/1078345809348212

Fazel, S., & Benning, R. (2009). Suicides in female prisoners in England and Wales, 1978–2004. *The British Journal of Psychiatry, 194*(2), 183–184.

Fazel, S., Cartwright, J., Norman-Nott, A., & Hawton, K. (2008). Suicide in prisoners: A systematic review of risk factors. *Journal of Clinical Psychiatry, 69*, 1721.

Fazel, S., Grann, M., Kling, B., & Hawton, K. (2011). Prison suicide in 12 countries: An ecological study of 861 suicides during 2003–2007. *Social Psychiatry and Psychiatric Epidemiology, 46*(3), 191–195.

Forrester, A., & Slade, K. (2014). Preventing self-harm and suicide in prisoners: Job half done. *The Lancet, 383*(9923), 1109–1111.

Fotiadou, M., Livaditis, M., Manou, I., Kaniotou, E., & Xenitidis, K. (2006). Prevalence of mental disorders and deliberate self-harm in Greek male prisoners. *International Journal of Law and Psychiatry, 29*, 68–73.

Franklin, J. C., Ribeiro, J. D., Fox, K. R., Bentley, K. H., Kleiman, E. M., Huang, X., ... Nock, M. K. (2017). Risk factors for suicidal thoughts and behaviors: A meta-analysis of 50 years of research. *Psychological Bulletin, 143*, 187–232. https://doi.org/10.1037/bul0000084

Freeman, A., Pretzer, J., Fleming, B., & Simon, K. M. (2004). *Clinical applications of cognitive therapy* (2nd ed.). New York, NY: Kluwer Academic.

Glassmire, D. M., Tarescavage, A. M., Burchett, D., Martinez, J., & Gomez, A. (2016). Clinical utility of the MMPI-II-RF SUI items and scale in a forensic inpatient setting: Association with interview self-report and future suicidal behaviors. *Psychological Assessment, 28*(11), 1502.

Goffman, E. (1961). On the characteristics of total institutions. In D. Cressey (Ed.), *The prison*. New York, NY: Holt, Rinehart and Winston.

Gould, C., McGeorge, T., & Slade, K. (2017). Suicide screening tools for use in incarcerated offenders: A systematic review. *Archives of Suicide Research, 1*, 20.

Gratz, K. L., & Gunderson, J. G. (2006). Preliminary data on an acceptance-based emotion regulation group intervention for deliberate self-harm among women with borderline personality disorder. *Behaviour Therapy, 37*, 25–35.

Hasley, J. P., Ghosh, B., Huggins, J., Bell, M. R., Adler, L. E., & Shroyer, A. L. W. (2008). A review of "suicidal intent" within the existing suicide literature. *Suicide and Life-Threatening Behaviour, 38*(5), 576–591.

Hawton, K., Linsell, L., Adeniji, T., Sariaslan, A., & Fazel, S. (2014). Self-harm in prisons in England and Wales: An epidemiological study of prevalence, risk factors, clustering, and subsequent suicide. *Lancet, 383*, 1147–1154. https://doi.org/10.1016/S0140-6736(13)62118-2

Hawton, K., & Van Heeringen, K. (2009). Suicide. *Lancet, 373*, 1372–1381.

Hayes, L. M. (1995). *Prison suicide: An overview and guide to prevention*. Washington, DC: DOJ, National Institute of Corrections.

Hayes, L. M. (2006). Suicide prevention on correctional facilities: An overview. In M. Puisis (Ed.), *Clinical practice in correctional medicine* (pp. 317–328). Philadelphia, PA: Mosby-Elsevier.

Hayes, S. C., Masuda, A., Bissett, R., Luoma, J., & Guerrero, L. F. (2004). DBT, FAP, and ACT: How empirically oriented are the new behavior therapy technologies? *Behavior Therapy, 35*, 35–54.

Hayes, L. M., & Rowan, J. R. (1988). *National study of jail suicides: Seven years later*. Alexandria, VA: National Center for Institutions and Alternatives.

HM Prison Service. (2005). *Safer custody group. The ACCT approach. Caring for people at risk in prison*. London, UK: Author.

Holden, R. R., Mendoca, J. D., & Serin, R. C. (2009). Suicide, hopelessness, and social desirability: A test of an interactive model. *Journal of Consulting and Clinical Psychology, 57*, 500–504. https://doi.org/10.1037/0022-006X.57.4.500

Hopwood, C. J., Baker, K. L., & Morey, L. C. (2008). Extratest validity of selected Personality Assessment Inventory scales and indicators in an inpatient substance abuse setting. *Journal of Personality Assessment, 90*, 574–577. https://doi.org/10.1080/00223890802388533

Howard League for Penal Reform. (1999). *Scratching the surface: The hidden problem of self-harm in prisons*, Briefing Paper. London: Howard League for Penal Reform.

Hoyert, D. L., Heron, M. P., Murphy, S. L., & Kung, H. C. (2006). *Deaths: Final data for 2003*. A National Vital Statistics Report. Washington, DC: DOJ.

Huey, M., & McNulty, T. (2005). Institutional conditions and prison suicide: Conditional effects of deprivation and overcrowding. *Prison Journal, 85*, 477–491.

Humber, N., Hayes, A., Senior, J., Fahy, T., & Shaw, J. (2011). Identifying, monitoring and managing prisoners at risk of self-harm/suicide in England and Wales. *The Journal of Forensic Psychiatry & Psychology, 22*(1), 22–51.

Ireland, J. L. (2000). A descriptive analysis of self-harm reports among a sample of incarcerated adolescent males. *Journal of Adolescence, 23*(5), 605–613.

Ivanoff, A. (1992). Background risk factors associated with parasuicide among male prison inmates. *Criminal Justice and Behavior, 19*, 426–436.

Jenkins, R., Bhugra, D., Meltzer, H., Singleton, N., Bebbington, P., Brugha, T., … Paton, J. (2005). Psychiatric and social aspects of suicidal behaviour in prisons. *Psychological Medicine, 35*(2), 257–269.

Joiner, T. E., Jr., Brown, J. S., & Wingate, L. R. (2005). The psychology and neurobiology of suicidal behavior. *Annual Review in Psychology, 56*, 287–314.

Kessler, R. C., Borges, G., & Walters, E. E. (1999). Prevalence of and risk factors for lifetime suicide attempts in the national comorbidity survey. *Archives of General Psychiatry, 56*, 617–626. https://doi.org/10.1001/archpsyc.56.7.617

Kessler, R. C., Warner, C. H., Ivany, C., Petukhova, M. V., Rose, S., Bromet, E. J., … Fullerton, C. S. (2015). Predicting suicides after psychiatric hospitalization in US army soldiers: The army study to assess risk and resilience in service members (Army STARRS). *JAMA Psychiatry, 72*(1), 49–57.

Klonsky, E. D., & May, A. M. (2014). Differentiating suicide attempters from suicide ideators: A critical frontier for suicidology research. *Suicide and Life-threatening Behavior, 44*, 1–5. https://doi.org/10.1111/sltb.12068

Klonsky, E. D., & May, A. M. (2015). The three-step theory (3st): A new theory of suicide rooted in the "ideation-to-action" framework. *International Journal of Cognitive Therapy, 8*, 114–129.

Konrad, N., Daigle, M. S., Daniel, A. E., Dear, G. E., Frottier, P., Hayes, L. M., … Sarchiapone, M. (2007). Preventing suicide in prisons, Part 1: Recommendations from the International Association for Suicide Prevention Task Force on Suicide in Prisons. *Crisis: The Journal of Crisis Intervention and Suicide Prevention, 28*, 113–121. https://doi.org/10.1027/0227-5910.28.3.113

Kovasznay, B., Miraglia, R., Beer, R., & Way, B. (2004). Reducing suicides in New York state correctional facilities. *Psychiatric Quarterly, 75*, 61–70.

Laishes, J. (1997). Inmate suicides in the correctional service of Canada. *Crisis, 18*, 157–162.

Leigey, M. E., & Reed, K. L. (2010). A woman's life before serving life: Examining the negative pre-incarceration life events of female life-sentenced inmates. *Women and Criminal Justice, 20*, 302–322.

Lester, D. (1987). Suicide and homicide in USA prisons. *Psychological Reports, 61*, 126.

Liebling, A. (1992). *Suicides in prison*. London, UK: Routledge.

Liebling, A. (1999). Prison suicide and prisoner coping. In M. Tonry & J. Petersillia (Eds.), *Prison* (pp. 283–359). Chicago, IL: University of Chicago Press.

Liebling, A. (2006). The role of the prison environment in prison suicide and prisoner distress. In G. Dear (Ed.), *Preventing suicide and other self-harm in prison* (pp. 16–28). Houndmills, UK: Palgrave Macmillan.

Liebling-Boccio, D. E., & Jennings, H. R. (2013). The current status of graduate training in suicide risk assessment. *Psychology in the Schools, 50*(1), 72–86.

Linehan, M. (1993). *Cognitive-behavioral treatment of borderline personality disorder*. New York, NY: Guilford Press.

Livingston, M. (1997). A review of the literature on self-injurious behavior amongst prisoners. In G. J. Towl (Ed.), *Suicide and self-injury in prisons: Research directions in the 1990s* (pp. 21–35). Leicester, UK: British Psychological Society.

Lopez-Castroman, J., Perez-Rodriguez, M. L., Jaussent, I., Alegria, A. A., Artes-Rodriguez, A., Freed, P., … the European Research Consortium for Suicide (EURECA). (2011). Distinguishing the relevant features of frequent suicide attempters. Journal of Psychiatric Research, 45, 619–625. https://doi.org/10.1016/j.jpsychires.2010.09.017

Low, G., Jones, D., Duggan, C., Power, M., & MacLeod, A. (2001). The treatment of deliberate self-harm in borderline personality disorder using dialectical behaviour therapy: A pilot study in a high security hospital. *Behavioural and Cognitive Psychotherapy, 29*, 85–92.

Maden, A., Chamberlain, S., & Gunns, J. (2000). Deliberate self-harm in sentenced male prisoners in England and Wales: Some ethnic factors. *Criminal Behaviour and Mental Health, 10*, 199–204.

Maden, A., Swinton, M., & Gunn, J. (1994). A criminological and psychiatric survey of women serving a prison sentence. *British Journal of Criminology, 34*(2), 172–191.

Magaletta, P. R., Patry, M. W., Cermak, J., & McLearen, A. M. (2017). Inside the world of corrections practica: Findings from a national survey. *Training and Education in Professional Psychology, 11*, 10–17.

Magaletta, P. R., Patry, M. W., Dietz, E. F., & Ax, R. (2007). What is correctional about clinical practice in corrections? *Criminal Justice and Behavior, 34*, 7–21.

Magaletta, P. R., Patry, M. W., Patterson, K. L., Gross, N. R., Morgan, R. D., & Norcross, J. C. (2013). Training opportunities for corrections practice: A national survey of doctoral psychology programs. *Training and Education in Professional Psychology, 7*, 291–299.

Magaletta, P. R., Wheat, B., Patry, M., & Bates, J. (2008). Prison inmate characteristics and suicide attempt lethality: An exploratory study. *Psychological Services, 5*, 351–361.

Mandracchia, J. T., & Smith, P. N. (2015). The interpersonal theory of suicide applied to male prisoners. *Suicide and Life-threatening Behavior, 45*(3), 293–301.

Mann, J. J. (2003). Neurobiology of suicidal behaviour. *Nature Reviews. Neuroscience, 4*(10), 819.

Marzano, L., Hawton, K., Rivlin, A., & Fazel, S. (2011). Psychosocial influences on prisoner suicide: A case-control study of near-lethal self-harm in women prisoners. *Social Science and Medicine, 72*, 874–883.

Marzano, L., Hawton, K., Rivlin, A., Smith, E. N., Piper, M., & Fazel, S. (2016). Prevention of suicidal behaviour in prisons: An overview of initiatives based on a systematic review of research on near-lethal suicide attempts. *Crisis-The Journal of Crisis Intervention and Suicide Prevention, 37*(5), 323–334.

May, A. M., & Klonsky, E. D. (2016). What distinguishes suicide attempters from suicide ideators? A meta-analysis of potential factors. *Clinical Psychology: Science and Practice, 23*(1), 5–20.

McCann, R. A., Ball, E. M., & Ivanoff, A. (2000). DBT with an inpatient forensic population: The CMHIP forensic model. *Cognitive and Behavioral Practice, 7*, 447–456.

Medlicott, D. (2001). *Surviving the prison place: Narratives of suicidal prisoners*. Aldershot, UK: Ashgate.

Mills, J. F., & Kroner, D. G. (2005). Screening for suicide risk factors in prison inmates: Evaluating the efficiency of the Depression, Hopelessness and Suicide Screening Form (DHS). *Legal and Criminological Psychology, 10*, 1–12. https://doi.org/10.1348/135532504X15295

Morey, L. C. (2003). *Essentials of PAI Assessment*. Hoboken, NJ: John Wiley.

Morey, L. C. (2007). *Personality Assessment Inventory: Professional manual* (2nd ed.). Lutz, FL: Psychological Assessment Resources.

Mumola, C. (2005). *Suicide and homicide in state prisons and local jails* (BJS Special Report No. NCJ 210036). Washington, DC: DOJ, Office of Justice Programs.

Naud, H., & Daigle, M. S. (2010). Predictive validity of the suicide probability scale in a male inmate population. *Journal of Psychopathology and Behavioral Assessment, 32*, 333–342.

Nee, C., & Farman, S. (2005). Female prisoners with borderline personality disorder: Some promising treatment developments. *Criminal Behaviour and Mental Health, 15*(1), 2–16.

Noonan, M., Rohloff, H., & Ginder, S. (2015). *Mortality in local jails and state prisons, 2000–2013* (NCJ 248756). U.S. Department of Justice, Office of Justice Programs, Bureau of Justice Statistics. Retrieved from http://www.bjs.gov/content/pub/pdf/mljsp0013st.pdf

O'Connor, R. C. (2011). Towards an integrated motivational–volitional model of suicidal behaviour. In R. C. O'Connor, S. Platt, & J. Gordon (Eds.), *International handbook of suicide prevention: Research, policy and practice* (pp. 181–198). Chichester, UK: Wiley-Blackwell.

Olvet, D. M., Peruzzo, D., Thapa-Chhetry, B., Sublette, M. E., Sullivan, G. M., Oquendo, M. A., ... Parsey, R. V. (2014). A diffusion tensor imaging study of suicide attempters. *Journal of Psychiatric Research, 51*, 60–67.

Opitz-Welke, A., Bennefeld-Kersten, K., Konrad, N., & Welke, J. (2013). Prison suicides in Germany from 2000 to 2011. *International Journal of Law and Psychiatry, 36*(5), 386–389.

Oquendo, M. A., Sullivan, G. M., Sudol, K., Baca-Garcia, E., Stanley, B. H., Sublette, M. E., & Mann, J. J. (2014). Toward a biosignature for suicide. *American Journal of Psychiatry, 171*(12), 1259–1277.

Patry, M. W., & Magaletta, P. R. (2015). Measuring suicidality using the personality assessment inventory: A convergent validity study with federal inmates. *Assessment, 22*(1), 36–45.

Perry, A. E., Marandos, R., Coulton, S., & Johnson, M. (2010). Screening tools assessing risk of suicide and self-harm in adult offenders: A systematic review. *International Journal of Offender Therapy and Comparative Criminology, 54*, 803–828.

Pratt, D., Gooding, P., Awenat, Y., Eccles, S., & Tarrier, N. (2016). Cognitive behavioral suicide prevention for male prisoners: Case examples. *Cognitive and Behavioral Practice, 23*(4), 485–501.

Qin, P., Agerbo, E., & Mortensen, P. B. (2002). Suicide risk in relation to family history of completed suicide and psychiatric disorders: A nested case-control study based on longitudinal registers. *Lancet, 360*, 1126–1130. https://doi.org/10.1016/S0140-6736(02)11197-4

Rakesh, G. (2017). Suicide prediction with machine learning. *American Journal of Psychiatry Residents' Journal, 12*(1), 15–17.

Ribeiro, J. D., Witte, T. K., Van Orden, K. A., Selby, E. A., Gordon, K. H., Bender, T. W., & Joiner, T. E., Jr. (2014). Fearlessness about death: The psychometric properties and construct validity of the revision to the acquired capability for suicide scale. Psychological Assessment, 26(1), 115–126. doi:https://doi.org/10.1037/a003485.

Rogers, J. R., & Oney, K. M. (2005). Clinical use of suicide assessment scales: Enhancing reliability and validity through the therapeutic relationship. In R. I. Yufit & D. Lester (Eds.), *Assessment, treatment, and prevention of suicidal behavior* (pp. 7–27). Chichester, UK: Wiley.

Rohde, P., Jorgensen, J. S., Seeley, J. R., & Mace, D. E. (2004). Pilot evaluation of the coping course: A cognitive-behavioral intervention to enhance coping skills in incarcerated youth. *Journal of American Academy of Child and Adolescent Psychiatry, 43*(6), 669–678. https://doi.org/10.1097/01.chi.0000121068.29744.a5

Rojas, Y., & Stenberg, S. (2010). Early life circumstances and male suicide—A 30-year follow-up of a Stockholm cohort born in 1953. *Social Science & Medicine, 70*, 420–427. https://doi.org/10.1016/j.ocscimed.2009.10.026

Rosen, D. H. (1976). The serious suicide attempt: Five-year follow-up study of 886 patients. *Journal of the American Medical Association, 235*, 2105–2109. https://doi.org/10.1001/jama.235.19.2105

Ruiz, F. J. (2010). A review of acceptance and commitment therapy (ACT) empirical evidence: Correlational, experimental psychopathology, component and outcome studies. *International Journal of Psychology and Psychological Therapy, 10*(1), 125–162.

Salina, D. D., Lesondak, L. M., Razzano, L. A., & Weilbaecher, A. (2007). Co-occurring mental disorders among incarcerated women: Preliminary findings from an integrated health treatment study. *Mental Health Issues in the Criminal Justice System, 45*, 207–225.

Sarchiapone, M., Carli, V., Di Giannantonio, M., & Roy, A. (2009). Risk factors for attempting suicide in prisoners. *Suicide and Life-threatening Behavior, 39*(3), 343–350.

Senior, J., Hayes, A. J., Pratt, D., Thomas, S. D., Fahy, T., Leese, M., & Shaw, J. J. (2007). The identification and management of suicide risk in local prisons. *The Journal of Forensic Psychiatry & Psychology, 18*(3), 368–380.

Shaw, J., Baker, D., Hunt, I. M., Moloney, A., & Appleby, L. (2004). Suicide by prisoners: National clinical survey. *The British Journal of Psychiatry, 184*, 263–267.

Shelton, D., Bailey, C., & Banfi, V. (2017). Effective interventions for self-harming behaviors and suicide within the detained offender population: A systematic review. *Journal for Evidence-Based Practice in Correctional Health, 1*(2), 3.

Shiner, M., Scourfield, J., Fincham, B., & Langer, S. (2009). When things fall apart: Gender and suicide across the life-course. *Social Science & Medicine, 69*, 738–746. https://doi.org/10.1016/j.socscimed.2009.06.014

Skegg, K. (2005). Self-harm. *The Lancet, 366*, 1471–1483.

Skegg, K., Nada-Raja, S., Dickson, N., Paul, C., & Williams, S. (2003). Sexual orientation and self-harm in men and women. *American Journal of Psychiatry, 160*(3), 514–546.

Smith, P. N., & Cukrowicz, K. C. (2010). Capable of suicide: A functional model of the acquired capability component of the interpersonal-psychological theory of suicide. *Suicide and Life-threatening Behavior, 40*(3), 266–274.

Smith, H. P., & Kaminski, R. J. (2010). Inmate self-injurious behaviors: Distinguishing characteristics within a retrospective study. *Criminal Justice and Behavior, 37*(1), 81–96.

Smith, P. N., Selwyn, C. N., Wolford-Clevenger, C., & Mandracchia, J. T. (2014). Psychopathic personality traits, suicide ideation, and suicide attempts in male prison inmates. *Criminal Justice and Behavior, 41*(3), 364–379.

Stanley, B., Ivanoff, A., Brodsky, B., Oppenheim, S., & Mann, J. (1998, November). *Comparison of DBT and "treatment as usual" in suicidal and self-mutilating behavior.* 32nd Annual Convention of the Association for the Advancement of Behavior Therapy, Washington, DC.

Tarrier, N., Gooding, P., Pratt, D., Kelly, J., Awenat, Y., & Maxwell, J. (2013). *Cognitive behavioral prevention of suicide in psychosis: A treatment manual.* London, UK: Routledge.

Tellegen, A., & Ben-Porath, Y. S. (2008/2011). *Minnesota multiphasic personality inventory–2–Restructured form: Technical manual.* Minneapolis, MN: University of Minnesota Press.

Towl, G., Snow, L., & McHugh, M. (2001). *Suicide in prisons.* Oxford, UK: Blackwell.

Tyrer, P., Thompson, S., Schmidt, U., Jones, V., Knapp, M., Davidson, K., … Wessely, S. (2003). Randomized controlled trial of brief cognitive behaviour therapy versus treatment as usual in recurrent deliberate self-harm: The POPMACT study. *Psychological Medicine, 33*, 969–976.

Usher, A., Power, J., & Wilton, G. (2010). *Assessment, intervention and prevention of self-injurious behaviour in correctional environments.* Ottawa, ON: Research Branch, Correctional Service of Canada.

van Ginneken, E. F., Sutherland, A., & Molleman, T. (2017). An ecological analysis of prison overcrowding and suicide rates in England and Wales, 2000–2014. *International Journal of Law and Psychiatry, 50*, 76–82.

Van Orden, K. A., Witte, T. K., Cukrowicz, K. C., Braithwaite, S. R., Selby, E. A., & Joiner, T. E., Jr. (2010). The interpersonal theory of suicide. *Psychological Review, 117*, 575–600. https://doi.org/10.1037/a0018697

Verona, E., Hicks, B. M., & Patrick, C. J. (2005). Psychopathy and suicidality in female offenders: Mediating influences of personality and abuse. *Journal of Counseling and Clinical Psychology, 73*, 1065–1073.

Wang, E. W., Rogers, R., Giles, C. L., Diamond, P. M., Herrington-Wang, L. E., & Taylor, E. R. (1997). A pilot study of the personality assessment inventory (PAI) in corrections: Assessment of malingering, suicide risk, and aggression in inmates. *Behavioral Sciences and the Law, 15*, 469–482.

Webb, R. T., Qin, P., Stevens, H., Mortensen, P. B., Appleby, L., & Shaw, J. (2011). National study of suicide in all people with a criminal justice history. *Archives of General Psychiatry, 68*(6), 591–599.

Webster, C. D., Martin, M. L., Brink, J., Nicholls, T. L., & Desmarais, S. L. (2009). *Manual for the short-term assessment of risk and treatability (start) (version 1.1)*. Coquitlam, BC: British Columbia Mental Health & Addiction Services.

Weinberg, I., Gunderson, J. G., Hennen, J., & Cutter, C. J., Jr. (2006). Manual assisted cognitive treatment for deliberate self-harm in borderline personality disorder patients. *Journal of Personality Disorders, 20*(5), 482–492.

Wenzel, A., & Beck, A. T. (2008). A cognitive model of suicidal behavior: Theory and treatment. *Applied and Preventive Psychology, 12*(4), 189–201.

Western Australia Department of Justice. (2002). *Report of performance*. Perth, WA: Author.

White, T. W., & Schimmel, D. J. (1995). Suicide prevention: A successful five step program. In L. M. Hayes (Ed.), *Prison suicide: An overview and guide to prevention* (pp. 46–57). Washington, DC: DOJ, National Institute of Corrections.

White, T. W., Schimmel, D. J., & Frickey, R. (2002). A comprehensive analysis of suicide in federal prisons: A fifteen-year review. *Journal of Correctional Health Care, 9*(3), 321–343.

Wichmann, C., Serin, R., & Abracen, J. (2002). *Women offenders who engage in self-harm: A comparative investigation*. Ottawa, ON: Correctional Service of Canada.

Wichmann, C., Serin, R., & Motiuk, L. (2002). *Predicting suicide attempts among male offenders in federal penitentiaries*. Ottawa, ON: Correctional Service of Canada.

Wilkins, J., & Coid, J. (1991). Self-mutilation in female remanded prisoners: I. An indicator of severe psychopathology. *Criminal Behaviour and Mental Health, 1*, 247–267.

Wittouck, C., Favril, L., Portzky, G., Laenen, F. V., Declercq, F., & Audenaert, K. (2016). Correlates of suicidal ideation in incarcerated offenders: A pilot study in three Belgian prisons. *Journal of Criminal Psychology, 6*(4), 187–201.

World Health Organization. (2007). *Preventing suicide in jails and prisons*. Geneva, Switzerland: WHO Document Production Services.

Yufit, R. I. (1991). American Association of Suicidology Presidential address: Suicide assessment in the 1990's. *Suicide and Life-Threatening Behavior, 21*, 152–163.

Zamble, E., & Porporino, F. J. (1988). *Coping, behavior, and adaption in prison inmates*. New York, NY: Springer.

Zapf, P. A. (2006). *Suicide assessment manual for inmates (SAMI)*. Burnaby, Canada: Mental Health, Law and Policy Institute, Simon Fraser University.

Zettle, R. D., & Hayes, S. C. (1986). Dysfunctional control by verbal behavior. The context of reason-giving. *The Analysis of Verbal Behavior, 4*, 30–38.

Zettle, R. D., & Rains, J. C. (1989). Group cognitive and contextual therapies in treatment of depression. *Journal of Clinical Psychology, 45*, 438–445.

Chapter 12
Correctional Staff: The Issue of Job Stress

Eric G. Lambert and Nancy L. Hogan

The United States of America (henceforth, the U.S.) has one of the highest incarceration rates in the world. An estimated 1.5 million adults are incarcerated in U.S. prisons, translating to an imprisonment rate of 612 inmates per 100,000 U.S. adults (Carson, 2015; World Prison Brief, 2017). Caring for all those prisoners makes corrections a major enterprise, employing an estimated 431,000 individuals in more than 4500 jails and prisons in the U.S. (Bureau of Labor Statistics, 2017; World Prison Brief, 2017). Correctional staff are critical elements in this enterprise, as they are responsible for ensuring that correctional facilities are safely, securely, and humanely operated. Correctional staff are not only an important resource for a correctional institution, they are also an expensive one. An estimated 70–80% of the operating budget for a typical correctional organization is for staff (Camp & Gaes, 2002; Tewksbury & Higgins, 2006). More than $70 billion is spent annually on correctional facilities in the U.S., an amount larger than the gross national product of most nations (Kincade, 2016).

In order to understand how often individuals in correctional environments experience job stress, it is necessary to discuss the concept of job stress and provide a working definition of job stress. Work is a major cause of stress for many working adults (American Psychological Association, 2017; Neel, 2016). Stress from work can be referred to as job stress, work stress, or occupational stress in the literature. Additionally, different definitions have been used for job stress. Matteson and Ivancevich (1987) remarked that "stress" may be the Scientific Dictionary's most imprecise word, with literally hundreds of definitions; however, virtually all definitions categorize stress as a stimulus or a response. Kahn (1987) also noted that the

E. G. Lambert (✉)
Department of Criminal Justice, The University of Nevada, Reno, Reno, NV, USA
e-mail: ericlambert@unr.edu

N. L. Hogan
School of Criminal Justice, Ferris State University, Big Rapids, MI, USA
e-mail: Hogann@ferris.edu

© Springer Nature Switzerland AG 2018
M. Ternes et al. (eds.), *The Practice of Correctional Psychology*,
https://doi.org/10.1007/978-3-030-00452-1_12

word stress is used to refer to both damaging environment stimuli and the results of said negative stimuli. Stress, therefore, can refer to the negative stimuli itself or a person's response to the negative stimuli (Lambert, Cluse-Tolar, & Hogan, 2007). Cullen, Link, Wolfe, and Frank (1985) and Hobfoll (1989) later clarified the scientific definition of stress by referring stressful stimuli as stressors rather than stress. As such, stressors tend to result in stress over the long run. The most common usage of the term job stress in the correctional staff empirical literature is that it refers to the result of long-term exposure to workplace stressors.

In terms of the consequences of job stress, there are many negative outcomes. Negative stimuli can have different effects on staff. In 1936, Selye is generally given credit for coining the term stress from his study of exposing lab rats to what he called nocuous agents (e.g., cold, extreme noise, etc.). In 1950, he applied the term stress to human beings when he argued that protracted exposure to negative stimuli resulted in adverse physiological responses. Selye's definition of stress grew to include not only physiological reactions, but also psychological ones (Garland, Hogan, & Lambert, 2013; Matteson & Ivancevich, 1987). The most common term in the correctional literature for the psychological reaction to stressors from work is job stress, and the most common definition of job stress is the one provided by Cullen et al. (1985) of feeling job related tension, anxiety, frustration, and worry (Tewksbury & Higgins, 2006).

Staff affect the correctional work environment, and the work environment also affects staff. Poole and Pogrebin (1991) contended that "we should be asking what the organization means to the worker instead of what the worker means to the organization" (p. 170). In light of the importance and cost of staff, it is not surprising that there has been an increase in research focusing on correctional staff. How workplace factors affect the job stress of correctional staff is one significant area of research focus in the past several decades.

12.1 Frequency and Prevalence

Job stress is a problem in corrections (Anson, Johnson, & Anson, 1997; Senol-Durak, Durak, & Gençöz, 2006). Although no occupation is immune from the effects of job stress, working in corrections presents demands not found in most other occupations. Armstrong and Griffin (2004) noted that correctional workers deal with potentially violent offenders who are being supervised against their will. Correctional staff have been found to have much higher levels of job stress than workers in many other occupational fields (Johnson et al., 2005). Highly stressed staff can be a recipe for disaster for both the individual staff member and the employing organization. Relatively unstressed staff can help create a professional, productive, safe, and humane correctional facility.

There is a small, but growing body of research that has focused on the consequences of correctional staff job stress. None of the reported consequences are positive outcomes. Among correctional staff, being stressed due to work has been linked to lower support of treatment of inmates, in spite of the fact that rehabilitation is a major goal in corrections and correctional staff members have an impact on inmate behavior (Dowden & Tellier, 2004; Robinson, Porporino, & Simourd, 1997).

Stress from the job has been reported to lead to lower levels of job satisfaction (i.e., degree of enjoyment from the job) and organizational commitment (i.e., bond between the employee and the employing organization) (Byrd, Cochran, Silverman, & Blount, 2000; Hogan, Lambert, & Griffin, 2013; Hogan, Lambert, Jenkins, & Hall, 2009). Empirical research indicates that job satisfaction and organizational commitment are associated with greater support for treatment of offenders, higher levels of work performance, elevated levels of organizational citizenship behaviors (i.e., the prosocial behavior of going beyond what is expected at work), higher life satisfaction, lower job absenteeism, reduced chances of job burnout, and reduced turnover intent/turnover (Byrd et al., 2000; Lambert, Edwards, Camp, & Saylor, 2005; Lambert, Hogan, Paoline, & Baker, 2005). As such, low job satisfaction and/or organizational commitment resulting from job stress is a detrimental outcome for correctional staff and their correctional organizations.

As has long been theorized, long-term exposure to job stress has been found to result in burnout from work among correctional staff (Garner, Knight, & Simpson, 2007; Keinan & Malach-Pines, 2007; Whitehead, 1989). Burnout is a major problem in institutional corrections (Griffin, Hogan, & Lambert, 2012; Lambert, Hogan, & Altheimer, 2010; Whitehead, 1989). Keinan and Malach-Pines (2007) reported that correctional staff had higher levels of burnout compared to the general population, even higher than found for police officers. Work burnout for staff is associated with increased absenteeism, substance abuse, and turnover/turnover intent, and other related problems (Cheek & Miller, 1983; Johnson et al., 2005; Lambert, Hogan, & Altheimer, 2010).

Furthermore, high levels of work stress can result in lower job performance, more frequent absences from work, greater turnover/turnover intent, increased use of alcohol and drugs, more frequent social conflicts with coworkers and family members, decreased life satisfaction, and increased mental and physical health problems (Cheek & Miller, 1983; Finn, 1998; Lambert & Hogan, 2009b). In fact, prolonged work stress may result in the premature death by either suicide or natural causes for correctional staff (Cheek & Howard, 1984; Woodruff, 1993). Stack and Tsoudis (1997) reported that correctional staff had a 39% higher risk for suicide compared to people in other occupations. Correctional staff have an average life expectancy of 59 years, which is 16 years shorter than the U.S. average of 75 years, and prolonged job stress is considered to be one of the major reasons for their shorter life span (Tracy, 2004; Woodruff, 1993).

In light of the damage done over time by high job stress, studies have been undertaken to identify factors that either increase or decrease stress for staff. This research indicates that work environment factors are far more likely to be the cause of job stress than demographic characteristics, such as age, gender, or race (Griffin, 2006; Lambert & Hogan, 2009a; Lambert & Paoline, 2005).

12.2 Theoretical Model Relevant to Service Delivery

The job demands-resources model provides a theoretical framework for why work environment factors would be associated with work stress and for how to design interventions to reduce job stress for correctional staff (Bakker & Demerouti, 2007; Demerouti & Bakker, 2011). This model divides workplace variables into job demands and job resources. The job-demand model was developed from two previous theoretical models of job demands and conservation of resources. Karasek (1979) proposed the job demands model, which later evolved into the job demands-control model. Karasek (1979) postulated that stress would be felt by employees who had jobs with great demands and who had little control in dealing with the demands. These demands caused employees to feel psychological strain, resulting in job stress and, ultimately, burnout (Wall, Jackson, Mullarkey, & Parker, 1996). Institutional corrections is an occupation with high demands and little job control. The conservation model holds that (1) individuals seek resources to help them be successful and (2) lacking resources results in stress (Lee & Ashforth, 1996). Hobfoll (2001) maintained that the essence of conservation of resources theory is people try to acquire, preserve, safeguard, and/or nurture the things they value. Demerouti, Bakker, Nachreiner, and Schaufeli (2001) proposed the job demands-resources model, where both job demands and job resources were incorporated into the same model. This model basically divides workplace variables into demands and resources.

Job demands place a strain on workers, and, over time, strain can wear on the worker, resulting in negative outcomes, such as job stress (Hall, Dollard, Tuckey, Winefield, & Thompson, 2010; Schaufeli & Taris, 2014). Demerouti et al. (2001) contended that job demands were aspects of the job associated with psychological (or physiological) costs. Demerouti and Bakker (2011) pointed out that job demands involve unnecessary or unwanted restrictions resulting in interference with employees achieving their work goals. Basically, job demands place a strain on employees, and ultimately result in negative work outcomes like job stress (Hall et al., 2010; Schaufeli & Taris, 2014).

Job resources are work environment factors that not only help employees to do their jobs, but make work more interesting and enjoyable (Demerouti & Bakker, 2011; Hu, Schaufeli, & Taris, 2011). Demerouti et al. (2001) defined job resources as aspects of the job, whether physical, social, or organizational, that function in achieving work goals, reducing demands, or stimulating personal growth. Job resources not only aid people in being effective at work, they also can help buffer the adverse effects of job demands (Bakker & Demerouti, 2007; Mauno, Kinnunen, & Ruokolainen, 2006). Job resources can be used to either stop job demands, minimize their effects, or provide a means to deal more effectively with them. Additionally, the positive psychological feelings from having job resources and being more successful at work results in greater work participation, which, in turn, can result in employees being less focused on the negative work situations and demands (Bakker & Demerouti, 2007; Bakker, Demerouti, & Euwema, 2005).

Furthermore, missing or inadequate job resources can become a job demand, placing greater strain on the employee (Demerouti & Bakker, 2011; Schaufeli & Taris, 2014). Hobfoll (2002) indicated that the loss of valued job resources often has a greater negative impact on employees than they may have had in terms of their positive effects when they were present.

As noted by Schaufeli and Taris (2014), the job demands-resources model does not specify any particular variable as a job demand or a job resource. Likewise, Demerouti and Bakker (2011) asserted that different factors (i.e., job demands and job resources) are associated with job stress in different occupations. As such, the job demands-resources model forms an overarching theory that can be applied to many different settings. In other words, the job demands-resources model does not specify a single set of job resources and another set of job demands that result in specific positive or negative outcomes, such as job stress, across occupational fields. While there are many job demands and job resources that affect staff and are likely to either result in or reduce job stress, we focus on the major correctional job demands (i.e., fear of victimization, work-family conflict, and role stressors) and the major correctional job resources (i.e., supervision, input into decision-making, and instrumental communication). These job demands and resources are the workplace variables that are directly influenced by service delivery from a psychological interventions perspective.

12.3   Diagnosis and Assessment

12.3.1   Job Demands

12.3.1.1   Fear of Victimization

Fear of victimization refers to a concern about on-the-job safety and concern about being hurt. The correctional literature also labels it perceived dangerousness of the job (Gordon & Baker, 2017; Lambert & Hogan, 2010). Working in corrections does pose risks to staff. Staff are in charge of offenders who are being held against their will, and some inmates are violent (Armstrong & Griffin, 2004). Correctional staff have a high rate of injury compared to other occupational fields (Bureau of Labor Statistics, 2012). Konda, Tiesman, Reichard, and Hartley (2013) reported that from 1999 to 2008, there were 113 U.S. correctional staff workplace fatalities (65% committed by inmates and the remainder were accidents, suicides, or committed by a coworker), and correctional workplace violence leads to 254 injuries per 100,000 full-time employees (i.e., a total of approximately 10,000 injuries). Individuals who perceive their job as dangerous are more likely to be on edge and apprehensive at work, which can detract from the job (Lambert, Gordon, Paoline, & Hogan, 2018). Not only is actual victimization a stressful stimulus for staff, but the concern of being harmed is a job demand that wears on a staff member over time (Higgins,

Tewksbury, & Denney, 2013). Past studies have found that fear of victimization increases correctional staff job stress (Armstrong & Griffin, 2004; Lambert & Hogan, 2010; Triplett, Mullings, & Scarborough, 1996).

12.3.1.2 Work-Family Conflict

For most adults, work and home are the two main life domains (Triplett et al., 1996). In an ideal world, the home and work domains would coexist in harmony. This is not always the case (Liu, Lambert, Jiang, & Zhang, 2017). The home and work domains can and do spillover for correctional staff. This spillover is referred to as work-family conflict in the literature (O'Driscoll, Brough, & Kalliath, 2006). Greenhaus and Beutell (1985) defined work-family conflict as a form of stress that happens when work and family domains are incompatible in some way (i.e., the family role makes the work role more difficult or vice versa). Work-family conflict is bidirectional in that problems at work can cause problems at home and problems at home can cause conflict at work (Brough & O'Driscoll, 2005; Netemeyer, Boles, & McMurrian, 1996). When problems at home, such as family arguments, marital discord, children's behavioral or school problems, divorce, death of a loved one, illness of a close friend or family member, financial problems or a major financial loss, affect a staff member at work, this leads to family on work conflict (Lambert, Hogan, Camp, & Ventura, 2006; Netemeyer et al., 1996).

When problems at work affect family life, work on family conflict results, which has been grouped into three areas: time-based conflict, behavior-based conflict, and strain-based conflict (Lambert, Hogan, Camp, & Ventura, 2006; Netemeyer et al., 1996). Time-based conflict occurs when work schedules cause problems at home (Armstrong, Atkin-Plunk, & Wells, 2015; Netemeyer et al., 1996). Correctional facilities are open 24 h a day, 365 days a year, including all holidays. Rotating shift work is common. Additionally, there is always the chance of unexpected mandatory overtime. Because many posts cannot be vacated and time off often must be requested far in advance, taking time off from work for unplanned events, such as a child being part of an unexpected semi-final championship game, may not be possible. The rigidity of the correctional work schedule is not found in many other types of organizations.

Strain-based conflict occurs when staff member experiences conflict at work that causes the staff member to become upset, such as being in a physical altercation with an inmate or a verbal argument with a fellow staff member, and this tension from work follows the staff member home and causes conflict with family and/or friends (Lambert, Hogan, & Altheimer, 2010; Netemeyer et al., 1996). The very nature of holding individuals against their will increases the chances of this form of conflict.

Behavior-based conflict occurs when work roles are incompatible with roles expected at home. For example, the behaviors of being distant and emotionally detached from inmates and being suspicious of inmates' intentions and actions are not appropriate behavioral roles for interacting with family and friends at home

(Lambert, Hogan, & Altheimer, 2010; Lambert, Hogan, Camp, & Ventura, 2006; Liu et al., 2017). Lambert, Hogan, Camp, and Ventura (2006) noted that family members may become resentful of having orders barked at them or having their activities questioned.

Research supports the contention that work-family conflict is directly related to job stress among correctional staff (Armstrong et al., 2015; Lambert, Hogan, Camp, & Ventura, 2006; Triplett et al., 1996).

12.3.1.3   Role Stressors

Role stressors are work environment factors that cause strain for employees because of job characteristics, roles, or expectations. The major role stressors for correctional staff are role conflict, role ambiguity, and role overload (Triplett et al., 1996). Role conflict occurs when role behaviors conflict (i.e., balancing competing roles of enforcer and rehabilitator) or the directions for the position are inconsistent (e.g., given conflicting orders by two different supervisors) (Lambert, Hogan, Paoline, & Clarke, 2005). Basically, role conflict occurs where compliance with one role (e.g., enforcer) makes compliance with a second role (e.g., rehabilitator) more difficult, if not impossible (Ivancevich & Matteson, 1980). Role ambiguity occurs when the job itself is not clearly defined (Berkman & Neider, 1987). In other words, it refers to a lack of information about the job's responsibilities or how to perform job duties (Lambert, Hogan, Paoline, & Clarke, 2005). Role overload refers to being required to handle too many job duties and/or not being provided the necessary equipment to handle the assigned tasks (Lambert, Hogan, Paoline, & Clarke, 2005; Triplett et al., 1996). Role conflict, role ambiguity, and role overload are real possibilities in many correctional institutions. These role stressors are likely to result in job demands and strain for correctional staff, ultimately increasing job stress experienced by staff. The research to date supports the contention that the above three role stressors are positively linked to higher stress from the job (Dowden & Tellier, 2004; Lambert, Hogan, Paoline, & Clarke, 2005; Triplett et al., 1996). Conversely, job resources should result in lower job stress among correctional staff.

12.3.2   Job Resources

12.3.2.1   Supervision

Quality, supportive, and considerate supervision is a job resource. Quality supervision provides direction, guidance, and control for correctional staff to do their jobs effectively and successfully (Brough & Williams, 2007; Griffin, 2006). Quality supervision can help ensure that staff are successful, which removes the job strain of failing at work (Lambert et al., 2009). Quality supervision can also aid staff in dealing with other job demands in a more productive manner (Griffin, 2006; Grossi,

Keil, & Vito, 1996; Lambert, 2004). Moreover, a lack of quality supervision can become a job demand, increasing job stress for staff (Lambert, Hogan, Altheimer, & Wareham, 2010). In studies, quality supervision was observed to have a negative relationship with correctional staff job stress (i.e., increases in quality supervision tend to result in lower stress) (Griffin, 2006; Lambert, Hogan, Altheimer, & Wareham, 2010; Liou, 1995).

12.3.2.2 Input into Decision-Making

Input into decision-making, a job resource, deals with the perceived degree of staff involvement in organizational and job decision-making (Lambert, Paoline, & Hogan, 2006; Slate & Vogel, 1997). It reflects how power is distributed within the correctional organization, ranging from a top down decision-making process with little or no staff input to a more staff-focused one allowing for input (Lambert, Paoline, & Hogan, 2006; Stohr, Lovrich, & Wilson, 1994). Having a voice in the correctional organization sends a message to staff that they are valued, respected, and trusted, which, in turn, makes work more enjoyable. The resulting positive psychological feelings allow staff to focus on the positive aspects of working in corrections rather than the trying and demanding parts (Slate & Vogel, 1997). Furthermore, input provides an avenue for staff to affect changes in areas that result in job demands (Lambert, Hogan, & Jiang, 2010; Lambert, Paoline, & Hogan, 2006). Simply put, input into decision-making can be a buffer to stress at work. Conversely, a lack of input can be a job demand, resulting in frustration, which, in turn, increases the chances of job stress (Lambert, Minor, Wells, & Hogan, 2016). Past research has shown that input into decision-making has a negative effect (i.e., reduces) on stress from the job (Dowden & Tellier, 2004; Lambert & Paoline, 2008; Slate & Vogel, 1997).

12.3.2.3 Instrumental Communication

Instrumental communication refers to the degree that the organization formally transmits information about the job to its employees (Agho, Mueller, & Price, 1993). Lambert, Hogan, Barton, and Clarke (2002) expanded on that definition to include not only information about the job, but also information regarding general organizational processes, organizational issues, and other organizational concerns. Instrumental communication basically refers to keeping staff informed of organizational policies, requirements, expectations, and changes, and it is considered a job resource. Instrumental communication allows staff to do their jobs in a more effective and efficient manner, as well as sending a message that the organization appreciates and values staff by keeping them well informed (Lambert, Hogan, Paoline, & Stevenson, 2008). In the end, instrumental communication can result in staff feeling better about themselves, their jobs, and the organization. The resulting positive psychological feelings can help shield staff from some of the job demands of working in corrections, as well as providing them with information on how to deal with possible job demands (Lambert, Hogan, & Allen, 2006). On the other hand, a lack of instrumental communication can become a trying job demand. Being in the dark and feeling frustrated is likely to raise job stress (Cheek & Miller, 1983; Lambert, Minor, Wells, & Hogan, 2016). Cheek and Miller (1983) noted that a lack of communication can be a salient stressor for many prison staff. Among U.S. correctional staff, instrumental communication has been found to result in lower job stress (Dowden & Tellier, 2004; Lambert et al., 2008; Lambert & Paoline, 2008).

The relationships between the previously discussed job demand and resource variables with correctional staff job stress are presented in Table 12.1. In addition, possible measures for the job stress, job demand, and job resources variables are shown in Table 12.1. In order to determine the level of each of these variables, it may be necessary to measure them.

12.4 Interventions

The unique job of working in corrections probably leads to some unavoidable job stress, regardless of how well run the correctional organization is, while other factors are likely the result of work environment factors and practices that could be changed (Finn, 1998, 2000). It is important to note that there has been far more research on the causes of job stress than there has been on possible interventions to deal with job stress among correctional staff. Nevertheless, the limited research to date provides some direction on how to respond to the pressing problem of correctional staff job stress. One possible course of action is to reduce the job demands of fear of victimization, work-family conflict, and role stressors, and increase the job resources of quality supervision, input into decision-making, and instrumental communication.

Efforts should be undertaken to reduce the fear of victimization at work. Open and meaningful discussions between administrators and staff need to take place concerning what issues are heightening concerns for their safety. Some physical plant concerns, such as poor lighting or a lack of mirrors for blind areas, can easily be corrected. Enhancing both introductory and annual refresher training to increase staff's skills for dealing with conflicts and raising their confidence level may reduce their concern of being harmed on the job (Lambert, Gordon, et al., 2018). Another factor increasing fear of victimization could be understaffing (Finn, 2000). If this is a cause, then efforts should be undertaken to ensure the placement of staff is optimal to ensure a safe and secure correctional facility, as well as advocating for additional staff with the central office and the funding source. While there have only been a few empirical studies on the predictors of fear of victimization, this research indicates the work environment variables of instrumental communication, procedural justice (i.e., perceived fairness in the process for making salient organizational outcomes), and input into decision-making were related to lower levels of fear of being hurt on the job and role stressors were related to higher levels (Gordon & Baker, 2017;

Table 12.1 Effects of various job demand and resource variables on job stress and possible items to measure the latent concepts of job stress, job demands, and job resource variables

Work environment factors	Effect on job stress	Possible items to measure the latent concept
Fear of victimization	Job demand	1. Most of the time when I'm at work I don't feel that I have much to worry about (reverse coded) 2. In my job, a person stands a good chance of getting hurt 3. I work at a dangerous job 4. My job is a lot more dangerous than most other jobs 5. A lot of people I work with have been physically injured on the job
Input into decision-making	Job resource	1. When there is a problem, management frequently consults with employees on possible solutions 2. Management routinely puts employee suggestions into practice 3. Management around here allows little employee input into decision-making (reverse coded) 4. Management often asks employees their suggestions on how to carry out job related tasks and assignments
Instrumental communication	Job resource	How well informed are you by prison management about the following aspects of your job: 1. What is to be done? 2. What is most important about the job? 3. How the equipment is used? 4. Rules and regulations? 5. What you need to know to do the job correctly, including computer software?
Quality supervision	Job resource	1. I often receive feedback on my performance from my supervisor 2. On my job, I know what my supervisor expects of me 3. My supervisor asks my opinion when a work-related problem arises 4. I am free to disagree with my supervisor 5. I can tell my supervisor when things are wrong 6. My supervisor respects my work 7. My supervisor is knowledgeable and competent
Role stressor—Role ambiguity	Job demand	1. I clearly know what my work responsibilities are (reverse coded) 2. The rules that we're supposed to follow seem to be very clear (reverse coded) 3. I am unclear to whom I report and/or who reports to me 4. I do not always understand what is expected of me at work

(continued)

Table 12.1 (continued)

Work environment factors	Effect on job stress	Possible items to measure the latent concept
Role stressor—Role conflict	Job demand	1. I regularly receive conflicting requests at work from two or more people 2. When a problem comes up here, people seldom agree on how it should be handled 3. Sometimes I am criticized by one supervisor for doing something ordered by another supervisor 4. I sometimes have to bend a rule or policy to get an assignment done 5. I often receive an assignment without adequate resources and materials to get it done
Role stressor—Role overload	Job demand	1. I am responsible for almost an unmanageable number of assignments and/or inmates 2. The amount of work required in my job is unreasonable 3. The amount of work I am required to do seems to be increasing all the time
Work-family conflict—Behavior-based conflict	Job demand	1. The roles I have at home (parent, spouse/partner, care-giver, etc.) conflict with the roles that I have at this prison 2. The behaviors I learned at work do not help me to be a better parent, spouse, friend and so forth 3. Sometimes I find the behavior that I use at home is ineffective here at work
Work-Family Conflict—Strain-based conflict	Job demand	1. Work makes me too tired or irritable to fully enjoy my family social life 2. I frequently argue with my spouse/family members about my job 3. When I get home from work, I am often too frazzled to participate with family or friends 4. I find that I frequently bring home problems from work 5. Due to all the work demands, sometimes when I come home, I am too stressed to do the things I enjoy 6. Because of this job, I am often irritable at home 7. I find that my job has negatively affected my home life 8. My job makes it difficult for me to relax when I'm away from work 9. I often feel strain attempting to balance my work and home lives 10. My family/friends express unhappiness about the time I spend at work 11. My family/friends dislike how often I am preoccupied with work

(continued)

Table 12.1 (continued)

Work environment factors	Effect on job stress	Possible items to measure the latent concept
Work-family conflict—Time-based conflict	Job demand	1. My job keeps me away from my family too much 2. My time off from work does not really match other family members' schedules and/or my social needs 3. I am frequently required to work overtime when I don't want to 4. I feel that I need to work less and spend more time at home 5. I wish that I had more time to do things in my personal life 6. The uncertainty of my work schedule interferes with my family and/or social life 7. I often have to miss important family or social activities/events because of my job

Note: Theoretically and empirically, job demands are associated with higher job stress while job resources are associated with lower stress. Measures are from Appendixes from the following sources:

Lambert, E., & Hogan, N. (2009). The importance of job satisfaction and organizational commitment in shaping turnover intent: A test of a causal model. *Criminal Justice Review, 34*, 96–118

Lambert, E. G., Hogan, N. L., Camp, S. D., & Ventura, L. A. (2006). The impact of work–family conflict on correctional staff: A preliminary study. *Criminology & Criminal Justice, 6*, 371–387

Lambert, E. G., Hogan, N. L., & Allen, R. I. (2006). Correlates of correctional officer job stress: The impact of organizational structure. *American Journal of Criminal Justice, 30*, 227–246

Griffin, M. L., Hogan, N. L., & Lambert, E. G. (2014). Career stage theory and turnover intent among correctional officers. *Criminal Justice and Behavior, 41*, 4–19

Lambert, Gordon, et al., 2018; Lambert, Minor, Gordon, Wells, & Hogan, 2016). Improving perceptions of procedural justice means ensuring the process for salient organizational decisions is transparent and that honest answers are provided when questions about the process arise (Lambert, Hogan, & Griffin, 2007). As indicated shortly, both input into decision-making and instrumental communication can be improved.

The job demand of work-family conflict needs to be addressed. New hires need to be made aware that work-family conflict may arise. Correctional staff are sometimes told to leave family problems at the front door when they arrive at work and to leave work problems at the front entrance when they finish their work shift. This simplistic suggestion is not likely to deal with work-family conflict and its negative effects for correctional staff (Lambert, 2001). New hire and annual refresher training offered by psychological services needs to include how to deal with work-family conflict in a positive manner. Part of this training is to provide skills for staff not only to be aware of family on work conflict, time-based conflict, behavior-based conflict, and strain-based conflict, but how to address them. Lambert, Hogan, and Altheimer (2010) suggested that strain-based conflict may be minimized by providing interventions and coping strategies, such as employee assistance programs, peer support groups, access to the staff psychologist, coping workshops, social activities outside of work, and mediation and relaxation training. Employee psychological services need to be not only offered, but strongly encouraged at no cost to staff. Supervisors need to be trained on how to identify work-family conflict among staff and how to encourage staff to use the support services offered by the correctional organization. Finn (2000) indicated that, in order to deal with this job demand successfully, support services must include family members and not just the staff member. There needs to be some flexibility in scheduling time off from work for unexpected important family events or to deal with family crises. For example, rather than require all vacation leave to be scheduled months in advance, 2 personal days could be granted yearly in which a staff member could take with only 24 or 48 h advance notice. In addition, time management programs could be provided for staff to either avoid or deal with time-based conflict in a more positive manner (Lambert, Hogan, Camp, & Ventura, 2006).

Efforts need to be undertaken to avoid the stressors of role conflict, role ambiguity, and role overload. There needs to be a dialogue with staff for when and how these role stressors occur. Past studies have found that workplace integration, formalization, quality supervision, instrumental communication, and input into decision-making help reduce the occurrence of role conflict and role ambiguity (Lambert, Hogan, & Tucker, 2009; Liou, 1995). Proper workplace integration ensures that staff work as teams rather than compete against one another and staff are not socially isolated from one another. With different groups and units, there is a possibility that there will be competition for organizational attention and resources, resulting in an "Us versus Them" mentality. For example, in some correctional institutions, custody and treatment are seen at odds with one another, even though they are both engaged in different efforts to meet the goals of a safe, secure, and humane facility. Efforts need be undertaken to create a team-focused work environment where units cooperate rather than compete and no staff members are socially isolated or ostracized (Lambert, Hogan, & Tucker, 2009). In addition, integration can be used to have teams work together to identify and solve the factors which result in role stressors occurring.

Formalization refers to the use rules and regulations to standardize employee behavior within the organization (Taggart & Mays, 1987). Formalization is putting in place clear rules, regulations, and policies, and ensuring all employees are aware of and correctly follow them (Lambert, Paoline, & Hogan, 2006). Pandey and Scott (2002) pointed out that widely distributed written training manuals, employee handbooks, and operating documents are good ways to ensure formalization. Efforts must be undertaken that formalization is done correctly to aid staff. Excessive or irrational formalization results in bureaucratic red tape, which, in the end, hampers and irritates staff (Bozeman, Reed, & Scott, 1992). Formalization needs to be linked with the objectives and goals of the organization and done in a way to ensure it helps and does not hinder staff in completing work in a safe and effective manner (Lambert, Paoline, & Hogan, 2006).

Part of new hire and annual refresher training should cover the issue of role stressors both in how to avoid them and, if unavoidable, how to deal with them.

Supervisors and managers need to be made aware of role stressors, how to minimize their occurrence, and how to guide and support staff in dealing with them when they do arise. Additionally, staff must not be given conflicting orders or directions. To deal with role overload (and underload, the opposite of role overload), positions should be designed to have a reasonable workload, and, if not, they should be redesigned (Lambert, Hogan, Paoline, & Clarke, 2005). For example, in one correctional organization, armed patrol officers were required to drive around the perimeter fence at 10 miles an hour for their entire shift with nothing else to do, resulting in role underload. On the other hand, the yard patrol position involved constantly walking at a brisk pace all the grounds, checking all windows and doors, as well as helping with control of inmate movement, resulting in role overload. After a position analysis and redesign, the two positions switched with one another every few hours to deal with the role underload and overload issues.

Quality supervisors are critical to correctional organizations. Not only can supervisors guide, direct, and control staff so they are effective at their jobs, supervisors can help staff avoid job stress or deal with stress in a productive manner. Lambert (2004) noted that considerate, supportive, and quality supervision can also make the job more enjoyable and help staff to avoid straining work experiences. Supervisors need to be trained regarding the job demands of fear of victimization, work-family conflict, and role stressors and how to aid staff in either preventing these job demands from arising or dealing with them well. Furthermore, there needs to be open and honest communication with staff on what constitutes quality supervision and poor supervision. Once aspects that make good supervision have been identified, the organization must undertake efforts to train new and current supervisors on how to engage in quality supervision. Supervision must not only involve control of staff, but include listening to and supporting staff. In other words, quality supervision means being focused on both the technical/performance and human relations aspects of work. Supervisors need to include being people-oriented as well as task-oriented. Supervisors need to be trained in how to engage in interpersonal communication properly and effectively. Listening to staff concerns and making efforts to address these concerns is crucial. Furthermore, supervisors must be willing to answer staff questions and truthfully answer these questions (Lambert & Hogan, 2009a).

Supervisors (and managers) must engage in transactional justice. Transactional justice means being honest and forthcoming to employees and treating them with respect and dignity (Lambert, 2003). Staff must be able make suggestions and voice concerns without a fear of retaliation from supervisors or management (Lambert & Hogan, 2009a). Supervisors should recognize staff for following organizational policy and doing good work and provide meaningful and sincere praise for such. Eisenberger, Huntington, Hutchison, and Sowa (1986) theorized that employees would see though an organizational façade of indiscriminate or disingenuous praise, a strategy likely to *reduce* employee support of the organization. When staff have done something incorrect or wrong, supervisors must quickly deal with the matter. The interaction with staff in these situations should be done in private, away from inmates and other staff. In addition, the incorrect behavior rather than the staff member should be at focus. Finally, rewards and recognition for quality supervision should be instituted. Moreover, part of the regular evaluation of supervisors should include if they are perceived by staff as providing quality supervision.

Increasing staff input into job and organizational issues should be undertaken. Allowing staff input is an inexpensive approach to dealing with job stress. Correctional organizations need to engage in participatory management (Lambert, Paoline, & Hogan, 2006). Staff need to have a real voice in the organization (Thibaut & Walker, 1975). While there are different ways to gain staff input, more than just a suggestion box is needed. Correctional administrators need to institute a cultural change in the organization so staff understand that their input is being sought and is valued. Effective input into decision-making requires providing staff with salient information so they understand what is being asked, the available resources, and the boundaries. Participation in decision-making requires good and honest communication between management and staff. There are different approaches for seeking input, ranging from asking staff for their ideas, to having staff or their representative attend meetings of administrators, to holding regular participatory meetings, such as employee town hall meetings. Furthermore, administrators need to engage in walk-about management rather than waiting for staff to come to them with their ideas and suggestions (Lambert & Hogan, 2009a). Waiting in an office will not likely work to increase staff input into decision-making in a correctional organization. Administrators also need to make managers and supervisors aware of the importance of input from staff and have them encourage it.

While some think that increasing formalization and input do not go hand in hand and are contrary to one another, this is not the case. A correctional organization can increase both functional formalization and meaningful participatory management. Daft (1986) pointed out that organizations have rules and regulations in order to define boundaries for employees; in other words, they are ways for the organization to maintain control without involving upper management in every decision. Moreover, it is critical to note that input into decision-making does not mean correctional administrators are bound by staff suggestions and ideas. There are likely to be ideas that cannot be implemented for a variety of reasons. In the end, correctional managers and administrators will need to make salient organizational decisions after receiving input from staff. Input into decision-making does require allowing staff a fair opportunity for input and explaining why decisions were made (Lambert, Hogan, & Griffin, 2007). Participatory management requires practice of transactional justice, as described previously.

Instrumental communication must be improved. The flow of salient organizational information needs to be both vertical (i.e., between supervisors and subordinates) and horizontal (i.e., between employees at the same level) (Lambert et al., 2008). Staff need to be contacted to learn what barriers are impeding instrumental communication, and, once confirmed, these barriers need to be removed. Instrumental communication is not only one way, such as giving orders, but refers to two-way communication. In addition to obtaining staff feedback, this ensures the message was understood and that there are no further questions. The communication process needs to be open and honest (Lambert et al., 2002). Managers and supervisors need to be trained on the importance of instrumental communication and how it can be improved. Important organizational information is not a tool of power but a resource to help staff and the organization be successful. In some correctional institutions, some staff are provided information and other staff are kept in the dark. Integration should help ensure increased instrumental communication (Lambert & Hogan, 2009a). Work teams will be charged with making sure all team members receive and understand key information being provided. In addition, integration will lead to increased interactions between staff, which, in turn, will result in increased communication (Lambert & Hogan, 2009b). Finally, the job duties and evaluation of supervisors need to include the flow of information to all the staff they supervise.

12.5 Future Implications

Past research has also pointed to other methods to deal with correctional staff job stress. Stress reduction and coping programs need to be instituted (Finn, 2000; Keinan & Malach-Pines, 2007). Rather than merely encouraging staff to attend a stress reduction and coping program, incentives, such as being paid to attend or organized to occur during a regularly scheduled work shift should be undertaken. In addition, all correctional employees, including line staff, supervisors, managers, and administrators should be required to take the stress reduction and coping workshop. There is a need for future research on how psychological stress coping and reduction programs should be structured and instituted. In addition, studies are needed to evaluate the effectiveness of these programs.

Physical activity classes could be offered to provide a productive outlet for "blowing off steam" from job stress and to improve physical health (Keinan & Malach-Pines, 2007; Kiely & Hodgson, 1990). Incentives, such as a small cash reward or a reduction in employee pay for health insurance could be offered. Additionally, a free health club membership could be given to all staff or an exercise facility with no fees could be opened and operated on the grounds of the correctional facility. There is a need for research on what type of physical activity would be most effect in reducing stress of correctional officers (Kiely & Hodgson, 1990).

The literature also indicates that proper social support can be an effective factor in dealing with job stress (Brough & Williams, 2007; Finn, 2000; Senol-Durak et al., 2006). Staff can receive social support from coworkers, supervisors, administration, family and friends, and the community (Lambert, Minor, Wells, & Hogan, 2016). Empirical research indicates that supervisor and administration support have the strongest relationship with job stress among correctional staff (Armstrong & Griffin, 2004; Griffin, 2006; Lambert, Minor, Wells, & Hogan, 2016). Studies are needed to determine what type of social support, such as coworker, supervisory, administrative, and/or community would have the greatest impact on either avoiding or coping with stress from the job. Furthermore, the psychological services should become involved and offer assistance and treatment for correctional staff suffering from job stress (Finn, 2000).

Finally, there is pressing need to research what interventions can be done to reduce work stress effectively and efficiently and to help correctional staff deal with it in a positive manner, such as seeking help from a professional rather than bottling it up or turning to negative solutions, such as alcohol or drugs. Staff who have witnessed a traumatic event need to be required to visit with mental health professionals and cleared to come back to work. These are areas have seen little research to date (Finn, 1998, 2000).

12.6 Technology and Innovation

As previously indicated, the primary efforts to reduce correctional staff job stress are redesigning workplace structures and practices so it becomes a more psychologically positive work environment. Secondary efforts, discussed above, should provide the skills and resources through psychological services and interventions. As previously indicated, there is a significant need for psychological services interventions to address correctional staff job stress (McCraty, Atkinson, Lipsenthal, & Arguelles, 2009). New approaches are needed. Not all possible psychological interventions have been used and tested in the field of institutional corrections. For example, one intervention used in society to improve the quality of life for people and to deal with stress in a positive manner is mindfulness training (Center for Promotion of Health in the New England Workplace, 2015; McCraty, Atkinson, & Tomasino, 2003). While used at a few correctional facilities, mindfulness and other positive psychological interventions are not widespread at most correctional institutions at this time. Constructive psychological interventions not only aids staff in acting in positive coping ways to the demanding nature of working in corrections, but also aids in developing a healthy overall lifestyle (McCraty et al., 2009; Segal, Smith, Robinson, & Segal, 2017).

Technology is rapidly changing and offers a new approach to helping staff deal with stress (Berrouiguet, Baca-García, Brandt, Walter, & Courtet, 2016; Carissoli, Villani, & Riva, 2015). For example, there are new smart phone apps or computer applications/programs which can aid staff in how to deal with stress in a positive manner, such as eating healthy, dealing with stress with positive psychological states, providing time management, and help to ensure sufficient time to sleep (McCraty et al., 2009; Morris et al., 2010). There are also mindfulness and mediation smart phone apps, as well as numerous internet websites dealing with individual stress coping strategies (McCraty et al., 2003). Secure online interventions, such as chat rooms or texting, could be developed and overseen by psychology professionals for correctional staff to turn to for advice, guidance, and to vent (Berrouiguet et al., 2016). There are also technology devices which can alert staff when they are highly stressed (e.g., raised heart beat) so they can take positive action (Carissoli et al., 2015; Levinson, 2011). There is a need for new and innovative psychological interventions to be offered, including the need to incorporate new technology. These new interventions will need to be evaluated.

12.7 Conclusion

In the end, job stress is a salient issue for many correctional staff. Prolonged job stress is a losing situation not only for staff, but for correctional facilities, inmates, family and friends, and society overall. While there has been research to date, there is a need for far more research. There are many areas which may affect job stress or be affected by job stress which have not been either fully explored or even identified. For example, there is a need to examine the effects of vicarious victimization or trauma (e.g., having a fellow staff member injured, killed, or commit suicide on the job) on staff's psychological well-being, as well as their interactions with others (e.g., compassion fatigue). Likewise, more research on posttraumatic stress disorder, compassion fatigue, and mental health among correctional staff and their relationship with job stress is needed. In light of the fact that staff are a highly important and expensive resource for correctional organizations, the need to address job stress is paramount, and correctional psychological services will play a vital role in helping correctional staff deal with stress from work.

References

Agho, A. O., Mueller, C. W., & Price, J. L. (1993). Determinants of employee job satisfaction: An empirical test of a causal model. *Human Relations, 46*, 1007–1027.

American Psychological Association. (2017). *Stress in America: Coping with change*. Retrieved from https://www.apa.org/news/press/releases/stress/2016/coping-with-change.pdf

Anson, R. H., Johnson, B., & Anson, N. W. (1997). Magnitude and source of general and occupation-specific stress among police and correctional officers. *Journal of Offender Rehabilitation, 25*, 103–113.

Armstrong, G. S., Atkin-Plunk, C. A., & Wells, J. (2015). The relationship between work-family conflict, correctional officer job stress, and job satisfaction. *Criminal Justice and Behavior, 42*, 1066–1082.

Armstrong, G. S., & Griffin, M. L. (2004). Does the job matter? Comparing correlates of stress among treatment and correctional staff in prisons. *Journal of Criminal Justice, 32*, 577–592.

Bakker, A. B., & Demerouti, E. (2007). The job demands-resources model: State of the art. *Journal of Managerial Psychology, 22*, 309–328.

Bakker, A. B., Demerouti, E., & Euwema, M. C. (2005). Job resources buffer the impact of job demands on burnout. *Journal of Occupational Health Psychology, 10*, 170–180.

Berkman, H., & Neider, L. (1987). *The human relations of organizations*. Boston: Kent Publishing Company.

Berrouiguet, S., Baca-García, E., Brandt, S., Walter, M., & Courtet, P. (2016). Fundamentals for future mobile-health (mHealth): A systematic review of mobile phone and web-based text messaging in mental health. *Journal of Medical Internet Research, 18*(6). Retrieved from https://www.ncbi.nlm.nih.gov/pmc/articles/PMC4920962/

Bozeman, B., Reed, P. N., & Scott, P. (1992). Red tape and task delays in public and private organizations. *Administration and Society, 24*, 290–322.

Brough, P., & O'Driscoll, M. (2005). Work-family conflict and stress. In A. Antoniou & C. Cooper (Eds.), *Research companion to organizational health psychology* (pp. 346–365). Cheltenham: Edward Elgar Publisher.

Brough, P., & Williams, J. (2007). Managing occupational stress in a high-risk industry: Measuring the job demands of correctional officers. *Criminal Justice and Behavior, 34*, 555–567.

Bureau of Labor Statistics. (2012). *Nonfatal occupational injuries and illnesses requiring days away from work, 2011*. Retrieved from https://www.bls.gov/news.release/archives/osh2_11082012.pdf

Bureau of Labor Statistics. (2017). *Occupational employment and wages, May 2016: 33-3012 Correctional officers and jailers*. Retrieved from https://www.bls.gov/oes/current/oes333012.htm

Byrd, T. G., Cochran, J. K., Silverman, I. J., & Blount, W. R. (2000). Behind bars: An assessment of the effects of job satisfaction, job-related stress, and anxiety of jail employees inclinations to quit. *Journal of Crime and Criminal Justice, 23*, 69–89.

Camp, S. D., & Gaes, G. G. (2002). Growth and quality of U.S. private prisons: Evidence from a national survey. *Criminology and Public Policy, 1*, 427–450.

Carissoli, C., Villani, D., & Riva, G. (2015). Does a meditation protocol supported by a mobile application help people reduce stress? Suggestions from a controlled pragmatic trial. *Cyberpsychology, Behavior, and Social Networking, 18*, 46–53.

Carson, E. A. (2015). *Prisoners in 2014*. Washington, DC: U.S. Department of Justice. Retrieved from https://www.bjs.gov/content/pub/pdf/p14.pdf

Center for Promotion of Health in the New England Workplace. (2015). *Using the CPH-NEW IDEAS Tool to reduce stress in the workplace: A step by step guide for design teams and steering committees*. Retrieved from https://www.uml.edu/docs/CPH-NEW_JobStressInterventionGuide%20pdf_tcm18-197848.pdf

Cheek, F., & Howard, R. (1984). *Stress management for correctional officers and their families* (Vol. 106). College Park, MD: American Correctional Association.

Cheek, F. E., & Miller, M. D. S. (1983). The experience of stress for correction officers: A double-bind theory of correctional stress. *Journal of Criminal Justice, 11*, 105–120.

Cullen, F. T., Link, B. G., Wolfe, N. T., & Frank, J. (1985). The social dimensions of correctional officer stress. *Justice Quarterly, 2*, 505–533.

Daft, R. L. (1986). *Organization theory and design* (2nd ed.). New York: Cengage.

Demerouti, E., & Bakker, A. B. (2011). The job demands-resources model: Challenges for future research. *SA Journal of Industrial Psychology, 37*(2), 1–9.

Demerouti, E., Bakker, A. B., Nachreiner, F., & Schaufeli, W. B. (2001). The job demands-resources model of burnout. *Journal of Applied Psychology, 86*, 499–512.

Dowden, C., & Tellier, C. (2004). Predicting work-related stress in correctional officers: A meta-analysis. *Journal of Criminal Justice, 32*, 31–47.

Eisenberger, R., Huntington, R., Hutchison, S., & Sowa, D. (1986). Perceived organizational support. *Journal of Applied Psychology, 71*, 500–507.

Finn, P. (1998). Correctional officer stress: A cause for concern and additional help. *Federal Probation, 62*(2), 65–74.

Finn, P. (2000). *Addressing correctional officer stress: Programs and strategies*. Washington, DC: U.S. Department of Justice.

Garland, B., Hogan, N. L., & Lambert, E. G. (2013). Antecedents of role stress among correctional staff: A replication and expansion. *Criminal Justice Policy Review, 24*, 527–550.

Garner, B. R., Knight, K., & Simpson, D. D. (2007). Burnout among corrections-based drug treatment staff: Impact of individual and organizational factors. *International Journal of Offender Therapy and Comparative Criminology, 51*, 510–522.

Gordon, J., & Baker, T. (2017). Examining correctional officers' fear of victimization by inmates: The influence of fear facilitators and fear inhibitors. *Criminal Justice Policy Review, 28*, 462–487.

Greenhaus, J. H., & Beutell, N. J. (1985). Sources of conflict between work and family roles. *Academy of Management Review, 10*, 76–88.

Griffin, M. L. (2006). Gender and stress: A comparative assessment of sources of stress among correctional officers. *Journal of Contemporary Criminal Justice, 22*, 4–25.

Griffin, M. L., Hogan, N. L., & Lambert, E. G. (2012). Doing "people work" in the prison setting: An examination of the job characteristics model and correctional staff burnout. *Criminal Justice and Behavior, 39,* 1131–1147.

Grossi, E. L., Keil, T. J., & Vito, G. F. (1996). Surviving 'the joint': Mitigating factors of correctional officer stress. *Journal of Crime and Justice, 19,* 103–120.

Hall, G. B., Dollard, M. F., Tuckey, M. R., Winefield, A. H., & Thompson, B. M. (2010). Job demands, work-family conflict, and emotional exhaustion in police officers: A longitudinal test of competing theories. *Journal of Occupational and Organizational Psychology, 83,* 237–250.

Higgins, G. E., Tewksbury, R., & Denney, A. S. (2013). Validating a measure of work stress for correctional staff: A structural equation modeling approach. *Criminal Justice Policy Review, 24,* 338–352.

Hobfoll, S. E. (1989). Conservation of resources: A new attempt at conceptualizing stress. *American Psychologist, 44,* 513–524.

Hobfoll, S. E. (2001). The influence of culture, community, and the nested-self in the stress process: Advancing conservation of resources theory. *Applied Psychology: An International Review, 50,* 337–421.

Hobfoll, S. E. (2002). Social and psychological resources and adaptation. *Review of General Psychology, 6,* 307–324.

Hogan, N. L., Lambert, E. G., & Griffin, M. L. (2013). Loyalty, love, and investments: The impact of job outcomes on the organizational commitment of correctional staff. *Criminal Justice and Behavior, 40,* 355–375.

Hogan, N. L., Lambert, E. G., Jenkins, M., & Hall, D. E. (2009). The impact of job characteristics on private prison staff: Why management should care. *American Journal of Criminal Justice, 34,* 151–165.

Hu, Q., Schaufeli, W. B., & Taris, T. W. (2011). The job demands–resources model: An analysis of additive and joint effects of demands and resources. *Journal of Vocational Behavior, 79,* 181–190.

Ivancevich, J. M., & Matteson, M. T. (1980). *Stress and work: A managerial perspective.* Glenview, IL: Scott Foresman and Company.

Johnson, S., Cooper, C., Cartright, S., Donald, I., Taylor, P., & Millet, C. (2005). The experience of work-related stress across occupations. *Journal of Managerial Psychology, 20,* 178–187.

Kahn, R. L. (1987). Work stress in the 1980s: Research and practice. In J. Quick, R. Bhagat, J. Dalton, & J. Quick (Eds.), *Work stress: Health care systems in the workplace* (pp. 311–320). New York: Praeger.

Karasek, R. A. (1979). Job demands, job decision latitude and mental strain: Implications for job redesign. *Administrative Science Quarterly, 24,* 285–308.

Keinan, G., & Malach-Pines, A. (2007). Stress and burnout among prison personnel: Sources, outcomes, and intervention strategies. *Criminal Justice and Behavior, 34,* 380–398.

Kiely, J., & Hodgson, G. (1990). Stress in the prison service: The benefits of exercise programs. *Human Relations, 43,* 551–572.

Kincade, B. (2016). *The economics of the American prison system.* Retrieved from https://smartasset.com/insights/the-economics-of-the-american-prison-system

Konda, S., Tiesman, H., Reichard, A., & Hartley, D. (2013). U.S. correctional officers killed or injured on the job. *Corrections Today, 75*(5), 122–123 Retrieved from http://www.ncbi.nlm.nih.gov/pmc/articles/PMC4699466/

Lambert, E. G. (2001). To stay or quit: A review of the literature on correctional staff turnover. *American Journal of Criminal Justice, 26,* 61–76.

Lambert, E. (2003). The impact of organizational justice on correctional staff. *Journal of Criminal Justice, 31,* 155–168.

Lambert, E. G. (2004). The impact of job characteristics on correctional staff. *The Prison Journal, 84,* 208–227.

Lambert, E. G., Cluse-Tolar, T., & Hogan, N. L. (2007). This job is killing me: The impact of job characteristics on correctional staff job stress. *Applied Psychology in Criminal Justice, 3*(2), 117–142.

Lambert, E. G., Edwards, C., Camp, S. D., & Saylor, W. G. (2005). Here today, gone tomorrow, back again the next day: Antecedents of correctional absenteeism. *Journal of Criminal Justice, 33*, 165–175.

Lambert, E. G., Gordon, J., Paoline, E. A., & Hogan, N. L. (2018). Workplace demands and resources as antecedents of jail officer perceived danger at work. *Journal of Crime and Justice, 41*, 98–118.

Lambert, E., & Hogan, N. (2009a). Creating a positive workplace experience: The issue of support from supervisors and management in shaping the job stress, job satisfaction, and organizational commitment of private correctional staff. *Journal of Applied Security Research, 4*, 462–482.

Lambert, E., & Hogan, N. (2009b). The importance of job satisfaction and organizational commitment in shaping turnover intent. *Criminal Justice Review, 34*, 96–118.

Lambert, E. G., & Hogan, N. L. (2010). Wanting change: The relationship of perceptions of organizational innovation with correctional staff job stress, job satisfaction, and organizational commitment. *Criminal Justice Policy Review, 21*, 160–184.

Lambert, E. G., Hogan, N. L., & Allen, R. I. (2006). Correlates of correctional officer job stress: The impact of organizational structure. *American Journal of Criminal Justice, 30*, 227–246.

Lambert, E. G., Hogan, N. L., & Altheimer, I. (2010). An exploratory examination of the consequences of burnout in terms of life satisfaction, turnover intent, and absenteeism among private correctional staff. *The Prison Journal, 90*, 94–114.

Lambert, E. G., Hogan, N. L., Altheimer, I., & Wareham, J. (2010). The effects of different aspects of supervision among female and male correctional staff: A preliminary study. *Criminal Justice Review, 35*, 492–513.

Lambert, E., Hogan, N. L., Barton, S., & Clarke, A. (2002). The impact of instrumental communication and integration on correctional staff. *The Justice Professional, 15*, 181–193.

Lambert, E. G., Hogan, N. L., Camp, S. D., & Ventura, L. A. (2006). The impact of work-family conflict on correctional staff: A preliminary study. *Criminology and Criminal Justice, 6*, 371–387.

Lambert, E. G., Hogan, N. L., & Griffin, M. L. (2007). The impact of distributive and procedural justice on correctional staff job stress, job satisfaction, and organizational commitment. *Journal of Criminal Justice, 35*, 644–656.

Lambert, E. G., Hogan, N. L., & Jiang, S. (2010). A preliminary examination of the relationship between organizational structure and emotional burnout among correctional staff. *The Howard Journal of Criminal Justice, 49*, 125–146.

Lambert, E. G., Hogan, N. L., Moore, B., Tucker, K., Jenkins, M., Stevenson, M., & Jiang, S. (2009). The impact of the work environment on prison staff: The issue of consideration, structure, job variety, and training. *American Journal of Criminal Justice, 34*, 166–180.

Lambert, E. G., Hogan, N. L., Paoline, E. A., & Baker, D. N. (2005). The good life: The impact of job satisfaction and occupational stressors on prison staff life satisfaction—An exploratory study. *Journal of Crime and Justice, 28*, 1–26.

Lambert, E. G., Hogan, N. L., Paoline, E. A., & Clarke, A. (2005). The impact of role stressors on job stress, job satisfaction, and organizational commitment among private prison staff. *Security Journal, 18*(4), 33–50.

Lambert, E. G., Hogan, N. L., Paoline, E. A., & Stevenson, M. T. (2008). I want to know and I want to be part of it: The impact of instrumental communication and integration on private prison staff. *Journal of Applied Security Research, 3*, 205–229.

Lambert, E. G., Hogan, N. L., & Tucker, K. A. (2009). Problems at work: Exploring the correlates of role stress among correctional staff. *The Prison Journal, 89*, 460–481.

Lambert, E. G., Minor, K. I., Gordon, J., Wells, J. B., & Hogan, N. L. (2016). Exploring the correlates of perceived job dangerousness among correctional staff at a maximum security prison. *Criminal Justice Policy Review*. Online first at http://journals.sagepub.com/doi/full/10.1177/0887403415623618

Lambert, E. G., Minor, K. I., Wells, J. B., & Hogan, N. L. (2016). Social support's relationship to correctional staff job stress, job involvement, job satisfaction, and organizational commitment. *The Social Science Journal, 53*, 22–32.

Lambert, E. G., & Paoline, E. A. (2005). The impact of medical issues on the job stress and job satisfaction of jail staff. *Punishment and Society, 7*, 259–275.

Lambert, E. G., & Paoline, E. A. (2008). The influence of individual, job, and organizational characteristics on correctional staff job stress, job satisfaction, and organizational commitment. *Criminal Justice Review, 33*, 541–564.

Lambert, E. G., Paoline, E. A., & Hogan, N. L. (2006). The impact of centralization and formalization on correctional staff job satisfaction and organizational commitment: An exploratory study. *Criminal Justice Studies: A Critical Journal of Crime, Law and Society, 19*, 23–44.

Lee, R. T., & Ashforth, B. E. (1996). A meta-analytic examination of the correlates of the three dimensions of job burnout. *Journal of Applied Psychology, 81*, 123–133.

Levinson, M. (2011). *Stress management: Better living through technology.* Retrieved from https://www.cio.com/article/2403343/careers-staffing/stress-management%2D%2Dbetter-living-through-technology.html

Liou, K. T. (1995). Role stress and job stress among detention care workers. *Criminal Justice and Behavior, 22*, 425–436.

Liu, J., Lambert, E. G., Jiang, S., & Zhang, J. (2017). A research note on the association between work-family conflict and job stress among Chinese prison staff. *Psychology, Crime and Law, 23*, 633–646.

Matteson, M. T., & Ivancevich, J. M. (1987). *Controlling work stress: Effective human resource and management strategies.* San Francisco: Jossey-Bass.

Mauno, S., Kinnunen, U., & Ruokolainen, M. (2006). Exploring work- and organization-based resources as moderators between work-family conflict, well-being, and job attitudes. *Work and Stress, 20*, 210–233.

McCraty, R., Atkinson, M., Lipsenthal, L., & Arguelles, L. (2009). New hope for correctional officers: An innovative program for reducing stress and health risks. *Applied Psychopysiol Biofeedback, 34*, 251–272.

McCraty, R., Atkinson, M., & Tomasino, D. (2003). Impact of a workplace stress reduction program on blood pressure and emotional health in hypertensive employees. *The Journal of Alternative and Complementary Medicine, 9*, 355–369.

Morris, M. E., Kathawala, Q., Leen, T. K., Gorenstein, E. E., Guilak, F., Labhard, M., Deleeuw, W. (2010). Mobile therapy: Case study evaluations of a cell phone application for emotional self-awareness. *Journal of Medical Internet Research, 12*(2). Retrieved from https://www.ncbi.nlm.nih.gov/pmc/articles/PMC2885784/

Neel, J. (2016). *Work can be a stressful and dangerous place for many.* Retrieved from http://www.npr.org/sections/health-shots/2016/07/11/484917853/work-can-be-a-stressful-and-dangerous-place-for-many

Netemeyer, R. G., Boles, J. S., & McMurrian, R. (1996). Development and validation of work-family conflict and family-work conflict scales. *Journal of Applied Psychology, 81*, 400–410.

O'Driscoll, M., Brough, P., & Kalliath, T. (2006). Work-family conflict and facilitation. In F. Jones, R. J. Burke, & M. Westman (Eds.), *Work-life balance: A psychological perspective* (pp. 117–142). Hove: Psychology Press.

Pandey, S. K., & Scott, P. G. (2002). Red tape: A review and assessment of concepts and measures. *Journal of Public Administration Research and Theory, 12*, 553–580.

Poole, E., & Pogrebin, M. (1991). Changing jail organization and management: Toward improved employee utilization. In J. Thompson & G. Mayo (Eds.), *American jails: Public policy issues* (pp. 163–179). Chicago: Nelson-Hall Publishers.

Robinson, D., Porporino, F. J., & Simourd, L. (1997). The influence of educational attainment on the attitudes and job performance of correctional officers. *Crime and Delinquency, 43*, 60–77.

Schaufeli, W. B., & Taris, T. W. (2014). A critical review of the job demands-resources model: Implications for improving work and health. In G. Bauer & O. Hammig (Eds.), *Bridging occupational, organizational and public health* (pp. 43–68). London: Springer.

Segal, J., Smith, M., Robinson, L., & Segal, R. (2017). *Stress in the workplace: Managing job and workplace stress.* Retrieved from https://www.helpguide.org/articles/stress/stress-in-the-workplace.htm?pdf=true

Selye, H. (1936). A syndrome produced by diverse nocuous agents. *Nature, 138*, 32.

Selye, H. (1950). *The physiology and pathology of exposure to stress.* Montreal: Acta.

Senol-Durak, E., Durak, M., & Gençöz, T. (2006). Development of work stress scale for correctional officers. *Journal of Occupational Rehabilitation, 16*, 153–164.

Slate, R. N., & Vogel, R. E. (1997). Participative management and correctional personnel: A study of perceived atmosphere for participation in correctional decision-making and its impact on employee stress and thoughts about quitting. *Journal of Criminal Justice, 25*, 397–408.

Stack, S. J., & Tsoudis, O. (1997). Suicide risk among correctional officers: A logistic regression analysis. *Archives of Suicide Research, 3*, 183–186.

Stohr, M. K., Lovrich, N. P., & Wilson, G. L. (1994). Staff stress in contemporary jails: Assessing problem severity and type of progressive personnel practices. *Journal of Criminal Justice, 22*, 313–327.

Taggart, W. A., & Mays, G. L. (1987). Organizational centralization in court administration: An empirical assessment. *American Journal of Criminal Justice, 11*, 180–198.

Tewksbury, R., & Higgins, G. E. (2006). Prison staff and work stress: The role of organizational and emotional influences. *American Journal of Criminal Justice, 30*, 247–266.

Thibaut, J. W., & Walker, L. (1975). *Procedural justice: A psychological analysis.* New York: Erlbaum/Halstead.

Tracy, S. J. (2004). The construction of correctional officers: Layers of emotionality behind bars. *Qualitative Inquiry, 10*, 509–533.

Triplett, R., Mullings, J. L., & Scarborough, K. E. (1996). Work-related stress and coping among correctional officers: Implications from organizational literature. *Journal of Criminal Justice, 24*, 291–308.

Wall, T., Jackson, P. R., Mullarkey, S., & Parker, S. K. (1996). The job demands-control model of job strain: A more specific test. *Journal of Occupational and Organizational Psychology, 69*, 153–166.

Whitehead, J. (1989). *Burnout in probation and corrections.* New York: Praeger.

Woodruff, L. (1993). Occupational stress for correctional personnel. *American Jails, 7*(4), 15–20.

World Prison Brief. (2017). *World prison population list.* Retrieved from http://www.prisonstudies.org/research-publications?shs_term_node_tid_depth=27

Chapter 13
Approaching Correctional Treatment from a Programmatic Standpoint: Risk-Need-Responsivity and Beyond

Ashley B. Batastini, Joshua B. Hill, Alexandra Repke, Laura M. Gulledge, and Zoe K. Livengood

Understanding best practices in correctional psychology is imperative, as successful programming has significant implications for the individual offender, the criminal justice system as a whole, and the broader community. Thus far, previous chapters have outlined best practices in the assessment and treatment of various subpopulations of offenders ranging from those with severe mental illnesses to arguably the most hardened type of criminal—those with psychopathic personality traits. It is clear that competent correctional psychologists must arm themselves with a substantial clinical toolbox if they hope to make an impact in their work with the diverse range of offenders who enter into their facilities on a day to day basis.

Not only is there the challenge of knowing what to do with unique offender populations, but as Fagan and Ax describe in their 2011 guidebook, correctional treatment is also relevant across all stages of the adjudication process from booking to community release (known as the sequential intercept model). This leaves both frontline providers, administrators, and policy-makers to figure out who needs what and how can it be provided given constraints in time and resources. The focus of this concluding chapter is on the implementation of correctional psychology from a broader, programmatic standpoint. We center this discussion on the most researched and generally accepted atheoretical model of offender rehabilitation from the seminal work of Don Andrews and James Bonta, but argue for a more comprehensive approach that moves beyond the three prongs of Risk-Needs-Responsivity to account for severe mental illness and systematic issues, and to make room for

A. B. Batastini (✉) · A. Repke
School of Psychology, University of Southern Mississippi, Hattiesburg, MS, USA
e-mail: ashley.batastini@usm.edu; alexandra.repke@usm.edu

J. B. Hill · L. M. Gulledge · Z. K. Livengood
School of Criminal Justice, University of Southern Mississippi, Hattiesburg, MS, USA
e-mail: joshua.b.hill@usm.edu; laura.gulledge@usm.edu; zoe.levengood@usm.edu

© Springer Nature Switzerland AG 2018
M. Ternes et al. (eds.), *The Practice of Correctional Psychology*,
https://doi.org/10.1007/978-3-030-00452-1_13

283

technological advances. We end by offering correctional psychologists and other providers recommendations for selecting and implementing appropriate services that accommodate offenders and the system responsible for their care.

13.1 The Nature and Prevalence of Correctional Psychology Services

Correctional mental health staff are often tasked with providing a continuum of services ranging from brief crisis interventions for acute mental health symptomology to intensive treatments for high-risk offenders with long-standing criminal justice involvement. This creates a need to better understand how to systematically identify and treat offenders with primarily mental health risk factors, primarily criminogenic risk factors, and those with both mental health and criminogenic factors contributing to continued involvement in the criminal justice system. The latter two of these groups make up the majority of the incarcerated population.

As previous chapters in this book have discussed, the overrepresentation of mental illness within the criminal justice system has been widely acknowledged for decades (Lamb & Weinberger, 1998; Prins, 2014; Torrey, Kennard, Eslinger, Lamb, & Pavle, 2010). This alone sets the stage for an on-going need to provide correctional psychological services. Additionally, a number of correctional researchers have also shown (e.g., Morgan et al., 2012; Skeem, Steadman, & Manchak, 2015; Wolff, Morgan, Shi, Fisher, & Huening, 2011), inmates with serious psychiatric disorders tend to share criminogenic risk factors, such as similar patterns of antisocial thinking, with non-psychiatric inmates. Thus, alleviating mental health symptoms alone is not enough to reduce recidivism in many cases. Despite this evidence, many correctional mental health departments view the mentally ill strictly as psychiatric patients. In a national survey of 230 providers across 165 institutions, Bewley and Morgan (2011) identified six primary goals of psychological services provided to male offenders with mental illnesses. Their findings suggested that mental illness recovery, institutional adjustment, and personal growth were viewed as more essential to service provision than addressing criminogenic risks. Further, providers reported feeling the most effective in their ability to reduce symptoms of mental illness. As Peterson and colleagues (2010) warn, it is false to assume that untreated mental illness is the primary source of criminal behavior among this group, and that providing psychiatric services will reduce recidivism. In fact, a mentally healthier offender may also be a higher risk offender. Taken together, not only do correctional institutions struggle to provide mental health services that address the more intuitive mental health side, but they are also either unaware of the need to treat the criminal side or are untrained in doing so.

Regarding the treatment of offenders in general, many of whom meet criteria for serious psychiatric disorders, the literature is quite clear: there are a number of successful approaches for reducing re-offense risk that target known criminogenic factors associated with continued criminal activity. Specifically, programs adhering to principles of the Risk-Need-Responsivity model (RNR) have reduced offender recidivism rates by up to 35% (Andrews & Bonta, 2012).

Andrews and Bonta's RNR model (2010) is arguably the reining paradigm in correctional treatment today. RNR suggests that higher risk offenders should receive more intensive services than lower risk offenders (*Risk*), that interventions should address known dynamic/changeable risk factors (i.e., criminogenic needs) associated with continued criminal behavior (*Need*), and that these interventions should be consistent with offenders' developmental, cognitive, or physical abilities and resources (*Responsivity*). Several risk factors have been empirically identified as the strongest predictors of criminal re-offense. These factors have dubbed these the "Central Eight" (2010) and they include:

1. Criminal history
2. Antisocial personality disorder or traits
3. *Criminal/antisocial cognitions*
4. *Criminal/antisocial peer influence*
5. *Poor work or educational achievement*
6. *Substance use*
7. *Family or relationship discord*
8. *Unproductive leisure time and recreation*

The first of these four factors are associated with the greatest predictability for future criminal behavior. Of the Central Eight, numbers 3 through 8 can become the focus of treatment. Criminal history and personality disorder (though manageable) are generally considered unchangeable (i.e., static factors). Thus, the *Risk* principle helps answer the questions of (1) "how *much* treatment is needed for this offender?" and (2) "what should treatment look like?" The latter of which forms the basis of the *Needs* principle. It should be noted that an offender's needs are intended to map onto an individually tailored treatment plan. For example, drug and alcohol treatment should only be delivered to offenders who have an identified need related to substance use. Determining an offender's risk level, and subsequent treatment need, is best achieved via structured, pre-treatment assessment. Examples of such instruments include the Level of Service Inventory-Revised (LSI-R; Andrews & Bonta, 1995), The Historical-Clinical-Risk Version 3 (HCR-20[v3]; Douglas, Hart, Webster, & Belfrage, 2013) and the Ohio Risk Assessment System, Misdemeanor Assessment Tool and Misdemeanor Screening Tool (ORAS-MAT; ORAS-MST; Latessa, Lovins, & Lux, 2014).

Not only do correctional programs that adhere to the RNR principles have better outcomes across a variety of offender populations (e.g., Dowden & Andrews, 1999, 2000; Gendreau & Goggin, 2013; Hanson, Bourgon, Helmus, & Hodgson, 2009; Stewart, Gabora, Kropp, & Lee, 2014), but RNR-based interventions have also been associated with reduced costs compared to other, less effective intervention models (Romani, Morgan, Gross, & McDonald, 2012). Unfortunately, familiarity with RNR is not as wide-spread in correctional practice as one might think. As an example from the first author's experience training several groups of senior staff from multiple correctional sites, none of the attendees had ever heard of the RNR principles and were surprised (as well as excited) to hear about the data supporting their application to programming. Of course, this is an anecdotal example, but it nonetheless illustrates the slow pace with which many departments of correction learn about the empirical state of correctional treatment.

The sections that follow in this concluding chapter are generally organized around the overarching RNR framework and summarize existing assessment and "off the self" interventions that target (either directly or indirectly) the six crimino-genic risk factors associated with the needs listed above. Failing to address empirically-supported criminogenic factors, or only focusing on a select few, limits the degree to which change can be effected. For purposes of this paper, interventions that target antisocial peers, family/marital problems, and poor leisure/recreation are grouped under "Interpersonal and Relationship Skills," and educational and vocational programming are under the single heading of "Educational and Vocational skills."

However, for correctional institutions to truly serve a wider range of offenders thereby effecting change behind and beyond prison walls, programmatic efforts must expand on the three basic prongs of RNR. For example, while mental illness is not itself a criminogenic risk factor, when mental illness is present, psychiatric interventions must be included. Morgan and colleagues (Morgan, Kroner, & Mills, 2018) have labeled the need to address dual mental health and criminal risks as the Bi-Adaptive approach. In addition, we discuss other factors associated with increased accessibility and effectiveness of correctional treatment programs that are less explicit in the RNR model, such as the use of telehealth. The chapter concludes with practical recommendations and policy implications for correctional systems seeking to implement more research-driven assessment and intervention into their routine treatment of adult offender populations.

13.2 What Helps in Correctional Treatment: Mapping Services onto Known Risks

13.2.1 Treatment for Criminal/Antisocial Cognitions

Criminal or antisocial cognitions is not only part of the Central Eight dynamic risk factors, but it is among the top four most predictive of continued criminal conduct (Andrews & Bonta, 2010). It is important to first understand that criminal thinking does not mean thinking specifically about crime or planning one; rather, these patterns contain "thinking errors" that are supportive of a criminal lifestyle (Yochelson & Samenow, 1976, p. 359). In other words, these thoughts provide justification for engaging in crime. Thinking errors are typically not recognized by the offender, but nonetheless lead to behavioral problems and often undesirable outcomes. The goal interventions is to help offenders better recognize these maladaptive thinking patterns and adjust their decision-making.

Because of the widespread focus within correctional psychology on criminal cognitions, several assessment tools have been created to better identify these thinking patterns. One of the most widely used of these tools is the Psychological Inventory of Criminal Thinking Styles (PICTS; Walters, 2013). Examples of thinking styles measured by the PICTS include entitlement, superoptimism (i.e., a belief that one can "get away with it"), and doing a good deed to make up for a harmful one. Other assessment tools, such as the Measure of Criminogenic Thinking Styles (MOCTS; Mandracchia, 2017) and the TCU Criminal Thinking Scales (TCU CTS; Knight, Garner, Simpson, Morey, & Flynn, 2006) are also available and validated. Using criminal thinking measures and sharing the results with inmate clients may serve as an effective intervention in and of itself. Linking significantly elevated problematic thinking patterns to real-life, personalized examples can help offenders better appreciate how this risk factor applies to them and emphasizes the need for change.

Altering criminal thinking patterns is fortunately one of the most common targets of correctional treatment programs. Various treatment modalities aimed at reducing criminal cognitions exist, ranging from intensive in-person sessions that span a number of years, to shorter-term, self-administered treatments. Among the most widely used, and most positively evaluated, interventions to address criminal cognitions follow a cognitive behavioral therapy (CBT) framework (Clark, 2011; Landenberger & Lipsey, 2005; Lipsey, Landenberger, and Wilson, 2007; Lipsey, Chapman, & Landenberger, 2001; McGuire et al., 2008; Wilson, Bouffard, & MacKenzie, 2005). CBT-based programs of this nature focus on identifying maladaptive criminal cognitions and replacing them with adaptive, prosocial cognitions that reduce the likelihood of risky behavior. Many correctional treatments fall under the CBT umbrella, including those that address other dynamic factors (e.g., gambling, substance use; see Chap. 3 for a more detailed review). Most of these programs are delivered in a group-format.

A popular CBT program aimed at antisocial cognitions is *Thinking for a Change* (TFC), developed by Bush, Glick, and Taymans (1997). This program teaches offenders prosocial skills and attitudes through the use of problem-solving techniques. TFC consists of 22 lessons that include social skills practice exercises such as active listening, evaluating behaviors that lead to offending, and understanding how others feel (Lowenkamp, Hubbard, Makarios, & Latessa, 2009). A meta-analysis on the effectiveness of TFC found a recidivism rate of 23% for treatment participants compared to 36% for controls (Lowenkamp et al., 2009). When controlling for confounding factors, an even larger treatment effect was found, with a 15% difference between treatment and comparison groups (Lowenkamp et al., 2009). Other well-known and efficacious programs that target criminal cognitions include *Reason and Rehabilitation* (R&R; Ross, Fabiano, & Diemer-Ewles, 1988; Tong & Farrington, 2006) and *Moral Reconation Therapy* (MRT; Ferguson & Wormith, 2012; Little, 2005; Little & Robinson, 1988). Additionally, there are a number of available programs that incorporate techniques for reducing problematic thinking used to justify crime (e.g., see discussion of CLCO and SUSO below).

Existing research shows that CBT programs focused on criminal cognitions, regardless of brand name, can reduce recidivism by about 20% to as high as 55% compared to control groups (Landenberger & Lipsey, 2005; Lipsey et al., 2001; Lipsey, Landenberger, & Wilson, 2007; Wilson et al., 2005), outperforming other forms of treatment (not simply a non-treatment control). Despite the current gold standard approach to reducing antisocial thought processes, CBT is most effective when combined with other programs, such as supervision, employment, mental health counseling, education, and vocational training (Clark, 2011). This is consistent with the general idea that multiple risk factors, like those included in the RNR model, must be addressed if the ultimate goal is to decrease re-offending.

13.2.2 Interpersonal and Relationship Skills Programming

Treatment approaches related to three of the remaining dynamic risk factors will be discussed in this section: (1) antisocial peer associations (i.e., family and friends who also engage in crime), (2) family/marital tension, and (3) unproductive or unstructured leisure time. These factors are combined here because they share a primary focus on interpersonal and/or intrapersonal issues, and treatment efforts aimed at reducing these factors may overlap. For example, interventions that improve engagement with prosocial activities may also address negative peer associations because "participation in prosocial activities … [could] increase the number of positive associates" (Timko et al., 2014, p. 624). Currently, treatment interventions that are specifically designed to address these risk factors are lacking. That is, unlike the structured brand-name programs that target criminal cognitions (e.g., *Thinking for a Change*), there are no known programs of a similar nature for skills such as making better friends or overcoming boredom. However, existing interventions that directly address certain criminogenic risk factors may indirectly address others. We are also aware of at least two treatment programs for mentally ill offenders that has embedded modules related to both antisocial associates and poor use of leisure time (*Changing Lives, Changing Outcomes*; Morgan et al., 2018 and *Stepping Up, Stepping Out*; Batastini, Morgan, Kroner, & Mills, 2016). Given the significant predictive power of criminal peers within the Central Eight, interventions related to this factor should be integrated into the broader structure of offender treatment in some capacity.

It has long been recognized that, when offenders leave the social group that supports criminal behavior and instead attach to a social group that rejects criminal behavior, positive change is likely to occur and sustain (Cressey, 1955). Research on interventions for deviant peer association predominately involves juveniles, since vulnerability to peer influence peaks during early adolescence and diminishes with age (Cauffman & Steinberg, 2012; e.g., *Prepare Curriculum*, Goldstein, Nensen, Daleflod, & Kalt, 2004). For adults, general social skill training may be beneficial when attempting to educate offenders on how to both obtain and maintain friendships with prosocial peers. As an example, the *Social Problem-Solving Skills* (SPSS) approach teaches participants a variety of prosocial skills, including appropriate verbal and nonverbal behaviors, as well as the delivery of speech (Bourke & Van Hasselt, 2001). The combination of these skillsets not only prepares offenders to cultivate positive friendships, but also provides them with tools to disengage from poor peer influences. In their *Changing Lives, Changing Outcomes* program, Morgan et al. (2018) include a 10-session module on associates in which participants evaluate the pattern and quality of their relationship with family and friends, practice basic communication skills, and discuss strategies for moving away from antisocial peers and integrating into a prosocial peer network. The *Stepping Up, Stepping Out* program is based on a similar framework, but addresses more immediate interpersonal conflicts that inmates in administrative segregation may face, such as tumultuous relations with staff and avoiding predatory or rule-violating others (e.g., gang members).

Inmates with significant others and/or children face a unique set of challenges. For instance, married offenders will likely experience marital conflict while incarcerated and are more likely than non-offenders to divorce (Apel, Blokland, Nieuwbeerta, & Schellen, 2010; Lopoo & Western, 2005). These outcomes are problematic considering that healthy partner relationships seem necessary for successful community reentry (Cobbina, Huebner, & Berg, 2012). The *Creating Lasting Family Connections Marriage Enhancement Program* (CLFCMEP) attempts to increase couple connectedness by replacing maladaptive thought patterns with empathetic perspectives; the CLFCMEP also provides skill training in conflict resolution and communication (Shamblen, Arnold, McKiernan, Collins, & Strader, 2013). The CLFCMEP has yielded positive results when used with inmates and their spouses, with both partners showing significant gains in communication abilities and allegiance to each other (Shamblen et al., 2013).

Another program that appears helpful for couples with an incarcerated partner is the *Prevention and Relationship Enhancement Program* (PREP). A 2008 study used PREP with inmates and several of their partners. After completing PREP, individuals showed significant improvements across several relational domains, including communication, relationship satisfaction, and commitment to their partners (Einhorn et al., 2008). While both Einhorn et al. (2008) and Shamblen et al. (2013) respectively speculated that PREP and CLFCMEP can also mitigate some of the negative impacts of incarceration on inmates' children, the *Parenting from Prison* (PFP) curriculum has been associated with improvements in communication specifically between incarcerated parents and their children (Wilson, Gonzalez, Romero, Henry, & Cerbana, 2010). This finding has particular significance, as incarceration has been linked to poor communication between incarcerated parents and their children (Nesmith & Ruhland, 2008). Moreover, PFP's positive findings were not dependent on parents' genders, indicating that both mothers and fathers experienced approximately equal gains in parenting skills after participating in PFP (Wilson et al., 2010).

Too much or poor use of free time places offenders at risk for continued offending for obvious reasons. Planned prosocial activities can replace criminal activity as a means of preventing boredom, as well as provide an excuse to avoid criminal opportunities when they arise (e.g., through peer solicitation). Morgan et al. (2018) also introduce several strategies aimed at leisure. For example, participants are explained the link between leisure and crime, asked to calculate how much spare time they have in a week, take an inventory of prosocial hobbies they would like to pursue, and role play social engagement in these activities. Other programs that educate inmates on healthy ways to spend their free time, like the leisure time management program template developed by McMay and Cotronea (2015), could also be beneficial. In addition to information-based programs, research supports the notion that sport-based programs in correctional facilities can lead to better free time management by participating adult inmates (Gallant, Sherry, & Nicholson, 2015). Effective sport-based intervention programs have included offenders participating in a wide array of physical activity, such as football, hiking, soccer, softball, and yoga (Woods, Breslin, & Hassan, 2017). In addition to modeling an appropriate use of free time, sport-based programs function as an effective psychosocial intervention for youths (Draper, Errington, Omar, & Makhita, 2013; Parker, Meek, & Lewis, 2014). Although these programs were not focused on adults, it suggests that sport-based programs not only aptly occupy inmates' time, but they can also act as a catalyst for prosocial interactions. That is, by implementing these types of programs, inmates experience a prosocial recreational activity first-hand, allowing for the formation of constructive leisure habits, and perhaps secondarily, more adaptive social skills and positive mood. Whenever possible, it appears most beneficial to combine information-based programs with sport-based programs (or other structured hobbies).

13.2.3   Educational and Vocational Skills

Literature focusing on educational and vocational programs also lends valuable insight into what helps in correctional treatment. American prison administrators have long relied upon educational and vocational programming as a way to rehabilitate offenders (Jancic, 1998). One of the main goals of these programs is to positively affect post-release community adjustment and ultimately reduce recidivism. Despite the limiting of offender educational opportunities over the years due to budgetary issues, studies generally support that these programs do reduce the chance that offenders will return to prison (Batiuk, Lahm, McKeever, Wilcox, & Wilcox, 2005; Brazell, Crayton, Mukamal, Solomon, & Lindahl, 2009; Hull, Forrester, Brown, Jobe, & McCullen, 2000; Steurer, Smith, & Tracy, 2001; Vacca, 2004). Overall, it has been concluded that participants in education, vocation, and work programs are less likely to recidivate after release as compared to non-participants. Moreover, recidivism rates tend to be lower for those who participate in education programs than for those who participate only in vocational or work programs (Wilson, Gallagher, & MacKenzie, 2000). It is also important to note that successful completion in post-secondary correctional education is a stronger predictor of decreased recidivism than participation without successful completion (Chappell, 2004).

While the majority of evidence seems to support the assertion that correctional education has value in recidivism reduction, many of the studies are limited methodologically as they do not distinguish between different forms of correctional education. Other studies tend to investigate effects of correctional education on recidivism by focusing on the effects of only one type of program. Keeping this in mind, a brief discussion of the main types of correctional education programming is warranted. *Pre-college programs* in correctional education include high school classes, Adult Basic Education (ABE), and general equivalency diploma (GED) programs. Some of the studies that have assessed outcomes related to pre-college programs concluded that earning a GED was strongly associated with lower rates of recidivism (Anderson, 1995; Brewster & Sharp, 2002). Other components of pre-college programs, such as ABE, were found to have little or no effect on recidivism reduction (Anderson, 1995). *Post-secondary programs* were implemented with increased frequency following the Second Chance Act of 2007 and have a moderate body of literature supporting their relationship to lower rates of recidivism. Indeed, many individual studies, as well as a handful of meta-analyses, have examined the relationship between post-release outcomes and post-secondary education (Burke & Vivian, 2001; Chappell, 2004; Steurer et al., 2001). In one of the few studies that distinguished between various correctional education programs in its analysis, Batiuk et al. (2005) found that college participation reduced recidivism above the effects of other types of correctional education programming (e.g., vocational education, high school, and GED). It has been suggested that post-secondary programs have a greater impact than other types of correctional education programming because they increase the knowledge and cognitive functioning of the participant and are able to affect thoughts, values, and behaviors in ways that pre-college or vocational programs cannot (Batiuk et al., 2005; Wilson et al., 2000).

Vocational education programs, which focus on teaching offenders job-specific skills (e.g., welding, automechanics, cosmetology), were once considered by many policy makers as one of the best ways to reduce recidivism among offenders (Schlossman & Spillane, 1995). Many studies have shown that participation in vocational programs is positively associated with reductions in recidivism and/or other beneficial post-release outcomes such as higher rates of employment (Adams et al., 1994; Gerber & Fritsch, 1995). However, the literature regarding vocational trade programs and its effectiveness is far from conclusive. In their meta-analysis, Wilson et al. (2000) reported that, although vocational education appeared to reduce recidivism, reductions were greater for academic-type programs than correctional work programs. Still others have found no relationship between vocational training and recidivism (Brewster & Sharp, 2002), once again supporting the notion that multiple risk factors must be targetted. Teaching job skills is not enough. It has been suggested, however, that greater effectiveness will be observed if vocational programs are combined with an academic component (Wilson, 1994).

In addition to vocational training and trade programs, the field of vocational psychology (or career counseling) has relevance for offender treatment and post-incarceration success (Varghese, 2012). A primary goal of vocational psychology is to help individuals make meaningful career choices based on their interests, skills, and personality traits (Jackson & Verdino, 2012). Career counseling often begins with an assessment of individual strengths and interests (e.g., O*Net Interest Profile, Strong Interest Inventory, Myers-Briggs; Kennedy & Kennedy, 2004; Luzzo & Day, 1999; Peterson et al., 2001). Career choices are then evaluated based on individuals assessment results and their level of training and education (or motivation to obtain the necessary training and education). Another assumption of career counseling is that people will be more satisfied in their job if it is integrated into their sense of self; that is, work is seen as a life role, not simply a means to an end. Other factors that are unique to offenders may also be important to address in career counseling or career readiness programs. One study of parolee experiences, for example, suggested that having social supports who endorse legitimate employment, embracing a prosocial work identity, and learning how to cope with the stigma associated with an ex-offender status can help community-released offenders find and maintain employment (Cherney & Fitzgerald, 2016). Johnson (2013) proposed a model of career counseling for offenders that focuses on identifying environmental barriers to employment, fostering feelings of self-efficacy in managing those environmental barriers, building a connection with positive community support systems, developing realistic outcome expectations, and setting clear goals for finding a job. While vocational psychology concepts may be indirectly addressed through other intervention modalities, there are currently no known comprehensive programs specifically designed with these issues in mind. Notably, Bewley and Morgan (2011) confirmed a lack of psychological treatment efforts focusing on vocational issues, which is unfortunate considering that occupational functioning is a significant predictor of re-offense. Thus, we encourage treatment developers to explore ways in which career counseling interventions, perhaps grounded in Johnson's model, could be formulated into a structured treatment protocol for correctional populations. One possibility is to expose offenders to such an intervention as a prerequisite for vocational trade or work release programs.

13.2.4   Substance Abuse Treatments

Similar to programs aimed at reducing criminal cognitions, correctional agencies tend to place appropriate emphasis on providing adequate substance use interventions. The high prevalence of comorbidity between substance abuse and criminal behavior is well documented in both the criminological and psychological literature (Fazel, Bains, & Doll, 2006). A substantial proportion of incarcerated populations within the United States is attributable to drug use and related offenses. This comorbidity occurs not only because many substances are by themselves illegal, but also because substance use often increases impulsivity and risk-taking behaviors. Therefore, treatment for drug and alcohol use can substantially impact both substance use behavior as well as recidivism beyond substance abuse (Inciardi, Martin, & Butzin, 2004). For a more detailed review of correctional interventions for substance abuse, readers are directed to Chap. 3 (Ternes, Goodwin, & Hyland, 2018).

13.2.5 Mental Illness

Despite the absence of mental illness from the Central Eight, it is relevant to discuss given the burden these inmates place on the criminal justice system, and in particular, the frontline staff who interact with them. Yet, as noted earlier in this chapter, correctional agencies and departments looking to effect programmatic changes would be remiss to focus on mental illness outside the context of RNR. For offenders with mental illness, there is an obvious twofold problem. Mental health professionals and administrators working in corrections must come to view these individuals as both psychiatric patients and criminals, and consider failure to manage mental illness as an additive risk factor in the RNR model. For example, Morgan et al. (2018) argue that psychotropic medication non-compliance (when medication is indicated) exemplifies criminal thinking, as it shows a lack of responsibility for one's behaviors and disregard for the well-being of others. Assuming that mental illness is the root of someone's criminal behavior, and that recidivism will be reduced if mental functioning improves, is false in most cases. A higher functioning offender may be a better offender! *Changing Lives, Changing Outcomes* (Morgan et al., 2018) and *Stepping Up, Stepping Out* (tailored for inmates in restricted housing; Batastini et al., 2016) are examples of two existing programs that were designed to dually target serious mental illnesses, criminal behaviors, and the intersection between the two. For a more comprehensive discussion of assessment and treatment options for inmates with mental illnesses, readers are directed to Chap. 2 (Nicholls et al., 2018).

13.3 Technology and Innovation

Often in correctional mental health, disconnections occur between service need and accessibility, as well as the continuity of service provision across placements (e.g., transfer from one unit to another or across facilities, transition from incarceration to community release). There are several innovative ways in which correctional agencies have already begun to integrate technology into the services and care they provide to offenders. In the healthcare sector, "telehealth" has been used to describe a collection of services delivered remotely using technology. About 20% of all telehealth applications are estimated to involve justice-involved clients (Lowes, 2001), and interventions that target the needs of mentally ill inmates are one of the most frequently cited uses in correctional settings (Ax et al., 2007). In mental health sectors more generally, the use of technology (i.e., telepsychology) is projected to expand substantially in the coming years (Norcross, Pfund, & Prochaska, 2013). The potential benefits and applications, as well as practical and ethical considerations, of telepsychology to corrections will be reviewed next.

13.3.1   Benefits and Effectiveness of Telepsychology

From a programmatic standpoint, the ability to provide and receive psychological services remotely has a number of potential benefits including lower costs, better access to services, and increased institutional safety. It has been estimated that the average cost of telehealth consultations is approximately 40% less than in-person consultations (National Institute of Justice, 1999). Integrating technology into correctional service provision may also create more seamless connections between differing stages of treatment and incarceration (Magaletta, Fagan, & Peyrot, 2000), or between multidisciplinary interventions and the people delivering them. Inmates who are being discharged from a forensic mental health hospital to a secure correctional facility could have their first few sessions with continuing care providers while still at the hospital. Correctional psychologists helping inmates prepare for community release could facilitate virtual face-to-face meetings between inmates and community corrections officers or potential employers. Special needs cases requiring highly scheduled care that combines psychological and medical services (e.g., substance abuse treatment and infectious disease specialists for HIV-positive inmates) can also be more easily accommodated through live two-way interactions and remote patient monitoring. For incarcerated offenders, telepsychology has the ability to not only involve outside providers in an inmate's treatment, but also family and prosocial others who cannot readily travel to correctional institutions.

In addition to expanding options for addressing the Central Eight dynamic risk factors, telepsychology is directly related to the responsivity principle of RNR, as it may help deliver treatments in a way that is better received, and therefore, better applied. For example, technologies can incorporate audio-recorded information or voice dictations features for individuals with below-average reading and writing skills. And, with the widespread commercial use of remote communication and information sharing services (e.g., Skype, FaceTime), the application of such technologies in corrections simply aligns with existing social norms.

While the use of telepsychology in corrections has a newer literature base, a 2016 meta-analysis of mental health services for substance abuse and offender populations—which included both assessment and intervention—found that videoconferencing was at least comparable with in-person services across outcome variables measuring mental health symptoms, therapeutic processes, program engagement, program performance, and service satisfaction (Batastini, King, Morgan, & McDaniel, 2016). Telehealth may even be useful in the most secure units of a facility in one study (Batastini & Morgan, 2016), inmates who participated in group counseling through a live action video monitor (protected by Plexiglas) showed no appreciable differences across treatment outcomes when compared to an in-person group.

13.3.2   Practical and Ethical Considerations

Given its potential for cost-savings and increased continuity and accessibility of care, there is an obvious a place for technology in correctional psychology. However, there are several practical and ethical considerations when using remote or other electronic service delivery methods. First, software and devices typically need to be compliant with the Health Insurance Portability and Accountability Act (HIPAA) to protect client privacy and provide data security. Thus, information must be shared using secure transmission consistent with this policy. Second, most states now have specialized legislation pertaining to remote psychological and general healthcare practices that providers are expected to know and follow. Third, providers must have the training and required competencies to use whatever technologies they plan to employ, including how to manage interruptions or delays in service and what to do in crisis situations when connection is lost or the offender is explicitly saying or doing something to suggest imminent harm. Fourth, offenders should be assessed for their level of comfort and ability to use the specific technology, as well as any risks they may pose. Fifth, informed consent procedures should include aspects relevant to the technology, such as how it will be used, who will have access to the information, and who to contact for technological assistance. As a final consideration, technology should—whenever possible—be applied as an adjunct to more comprehensive, in-person approaches rather than a replacement. Readers are encouraged to consult the *Guidelines for the Practice of Telepsychology* (2013) and relevant federal and state laws prior to implementing any technology-based intervention.

13.4   Making Programmatic Improvements

This book has summarized the prevalence of, assessment and intervention options for, and innovative responses to a number of common offender types that rotate through the criminal justice system. However, effecting long-standing change is not as simple as selecting one of these name-brand programs and implementing it. Not only must selected interventions be evaluated for their appropriateness, but more sweeping, systematic changes must also occur. Yet, with so many moving parts involved in correctional mental health care, rolling out a new set of programmatic policies may seem challenging. In this last section, we highlight factors beyond RNR that increase the likelihood of positive outcomes regardless of the chosen intervention or for whom it is intended.

13.4.1 General Recommendations for the Practice of Correctional Psychology

The following recommendations are more generic to correctional programming and should be considered prior to adopting specific evidence-based programs. First, correctional systems must treat assessment and intervention as two essential, interlocking steps of the same process. Empirically-driven baseline assessment and treatment referral, follow-through (i.e., actual service delivery), and post-treatment evaluation are critical. Far too often assessments are not correctly linked to treatment. This breakdown may occur because interventions never follow from the initial assessment, interventions follow from improper assessments, or interventions do not match assessment results. Correctional psychologists must work to improve the interconnection between these two aspects (DeMatteo, Hunt, Batastini, & LaDuke, 2010).

Second, while RNR was intended to be atheoretical, research consistently supports CBT approaches as the most efficacious. This makes sense given that a primary risk factor in the Central Eight is criminal thinking—a faulty, maladaptive pattern of thinking about the world that perpetuates an antisocial lifestyle. In fact, most of the name-brand programs discussed in this chapter and elsewhere work within a cognitive-behavioral framework.

Third, and consistent with the Risk Principle of RNR, programs targeting high-risk offenders need to be intensive. Research suggests that intensity is related to duration of programming. Shorter sessions that occur over a longer period of time tend to be more effective in reducing relapse and recidivism than longer sessions occurring over a shorter period of time (Burdon, Messina, & Prendergast, 2004; Hiller, Knight, & Simpson, 2006; Lipsey et al., 2007). This is because offenders, and anyone learning a new set of life skills, need repetition and continued, monitored practice. Fourth, the timing of treatment also matters (Lipsey et al., 2007). For example, offenders who are eligible for community release, but who complete programming too far ahead of their release date are at risk of losing important treatment gains. Therefore, it is recommended that programming either be continual (at least with occasional booster sessions) or more intensive services should be planned out in accordance with offenders' release dates.

Fifth, staff must be properly trained and qualified in assessment procedures and the subject matter of the intervention. While this seems obvious, it is not uncommon for jails and prisons to have correctional officers run mental health groups. Such a practice is ethically questionable. Educational programs require educators, mental health programs require mental health professionals (licensed counselors, psychologists), and so forth. Even for programs that allow correctional officers or other security staff to serve as facilitators, appropriate training is still requisite. Facilities lacking staff with adequate training or credentials may consider inviting professionals in the community to give workshops or lectures on special topics. Webinars are another common, and usually low cost, option. Relatedly, educating and training legal decision-makers (e.g., judges, attorneys) who make referrals at the front end is necessary for preventing misclassification of offenders or falling into a one-size-fits-all approach where services are provided to offenders regardless of individualized need. In many cases, for example, offenders are mandated to programs based more on the gut-instincts of legal decision-makers rather than the results of a well-validated risk assessment.

Sixth, correctional agencies should look for opportunities to collaborate with educators and researchers at local colleges and universities. Many post-secondary educational programs in prisons rely on support and connections with community colleges or state universities. Behavioral science researchers also have interests that align with correctional psychology; yet, they are a resource that institutions do not readily tap into. A 2017 article in *Corrections Today* highlighted the mutual advantages of this type of collaboration for program development, implementation, and evaluation (Hallundbaek, 2017). The degree to which researchers are involved in treatment implementation can even impact the outcome of interventions. Studies have shown that CBT programs implemented specifically for research purposes are associated with larger treatment effects than those that have not (Landenberger & Lipsey, 2005). This outcome is likely due to better monitoring of offender participation and treatment fidelity, and the use of practitioners thoroughly trained in mental health. Researchers are generally open to sharing their expertise and resources in exchange for de-identified data that can be published and/or practical opportunities for their students. In return, correctional systems gain valuable information about their current practices and where improvements are needed. Furthermore, many psychology graduate students are eager to gain applied experience in correctional settings and can provide high-quality supervised services for less or no pay (students receive course credit toward their degree instead).

Seventh, correctional systems should continue to explore and be open to areas of treatment that are currently under-developed but hold promise. For example, while the principles of vocational psychology and career counseling are not new, their application to correctional populations has been surprisingly limited despite the struggle ex-offenders routinely experience in finding and maintaining employment. Vocational counseling services that focus on preparing offenders for work and exploring interests within the scope of available jobs could be offered alongside trade programs and basic job skills training. Telepsychology is another newer practice in corrections that has far-reaching possibilities. Whenever novel innovations are introduced, efforts must be made to evaluate its effectiveness in producing desired outcomes.

The eighth and final recommendation echoes and underscores the general message throughout this chapter: addressing risk factors in isolation is inefficient and ineffective. Following appropriate assessment, offenders need to be plugged into whatever services or programs target their identified risks. Failure to take a wholistic approach can be problematic. Take, for example, one study that found higher rates of recidivism after a 5 year period for offenders who earned their GED compared to offenders who had not (Stevenson, 1992). This finding is seemingly contradictory—if poor educational achievement is a risk factor for crime, earning a GED should help reduce re-offense. Yet, it is possible offenders in this study received few other programs, or participated in programs that did not match their criminogenic needs. For the sake of continuity and to help new knowledge and skills "stick," it may also be beneficial for institutions to standardized (to the extent possible) the language, heuristics, and general techniques used across various programs. Automatic thoughts—a common term in CBT—could be used to discuss instances of criminal thinking, thoughts that precede substance use, or thoughts rooted in a mental health issue.

These recommendations are by no means exhaustive, but they nonetheless encompass a number of strategies that may help correctional agencies implement changes aimed at improving the broader institutional milieu and making communities safer. The eight recommendations are summarized below:

1. Develop individualized treatment plans that directly follow from empirically-driven assessments and actually implement them.
2. Select interventions that follow a cognitive-behavioral framework.
3. Plan for shorter treatment sessions that take place over a longer period of time (at least 4–6 months).
4. Engage offenders in treatment throughout their incarceration and/or wait to apply more intensive interventions closer to their expected release date.
5. Ensure that all persons involved in assessment, referral, and treatment delivery are appropriately trained and qualified to do so.
6. Collaborate with local universities that can assist with program evaluation and/or provide graduate-level trainees to delivery services.
7. Explore novel and innovative theories and practices that may be useful in corrections, but not yet widely applied.
8. Refer offenders to multiple programs based on need and attempt to standardized the vernacular across programs to enhance learning.

13.4.2 Recognizing the Role of Policy

By now, it should be clear that identifying programs and practices meeting the dynamic needs specified in the RNR model, as well as incorporating other important factors, is essential for reducing recidivism. However, it is not uncommon for policy and legislation to dictate the standards of correctional programming. Unfortunately, these standards may not align well with the "what works" literature detailed in this chapter and elsewhere. An example of this that was mentioned earlier is when judges or attorneys assign offenders carte blanche to programs without considering individualized risk and associated needs. In some jurisdictions, there are also legislative mandates that set the level of evidence required for a program to be offered within a state correctional facility (Pew-MacArthur, 2015). To complicate matters further, program implementation costs money (e.g., purchasing materials, hiring or training staff, building space) that many departments do not have. Thus, any programmatic changes must be viewed in the broader context of what is possible and allowable under these policies.

13.5 Conclusions

There are a number of effective approaches for reducing recidivism that rely on empirical evidence. By-in-large, these map onto the dynamic risk factors identified in the RNR model (Andrews & Bonta, 2010). Successful programs that independently address criminal cognitions, educational and employment challenges, social factors, and substance use are represented in the literature, even though they may fall below the high legislative bar for permissible practices set by many state governments (Pew-MacArthur, 2015). While there are no empirically-supported or even evidence-based programs that can function as "off-the-shelf" curricula to address all of the risk factors as a one-stop-shop, many of the extant programs can be adapted to run along-side one another to address the full range of criminogenic and, when relevant, psychiatric risk factors. Of course, individualized assessment remains important to avoid wastefully exposing offenders to interventions that are not applicable to their needs. While RNR is a clearly supported model for structuring programs with offender populations, correctional administrators and providers must look beyond its three prongs if treatments are to be effective in producing change.

References

Adams, K., Bennett, K. J., Flanagan, T. J., Marquart, J. W., Cuvelier, S. J., Fritsch, E., ... Burton, V. S., Jr. (1994). A large-scale multidimensional test of the effect of prison education programs on offenders' behavior. *The Prison Journal, 74*(4), 433–449.

Anderson, S. V. (1995). *Evaluation of the impact of correctional education programs on recidivism*. Columbus, OH: Office of Management Information Systems Bureau of Planning and Evaluation, Ohio Department of Rehabilitation and Correction.

Andrews, D. A., & Bonta, J. (1995). *The level of service inventory—Revised (LSI-R)*. Toronto: Multi-Health Systems.

Andrews, D. A., & Bonta, J. (2010). Rehabilitating criminal justice policy and practice. *Psychology, Public Policy, and Law, 16*(1), 39–55. https://doi.org/10.1037/a0018362

Andrews, D., & Bonta, J. (2012). Viewing offender assessment and rehabilitation through the lens of the risk-needs-responsivity model. In F. McNeill, P. Raynor, & C. Trotter (Eds.), *Offender supervision: New directions in theory, research and practice* (pp. 19–40). New York: Routledge.

Apel, R., Blokland, A., Nieuwbeerta, P., & Schellen, M. V. (2010). The impact of first-time imprisonment on marriage and divorce: A risk set matching approach. *Journal of Quantitative Criminology, 26*(2), 269–300.

Ax, R. K., Fagan, T. J., Magaletta, P. R., Morgan, R. D., Nussbaum, D., & White, T. W. (2007). Innovations in correctional assessment and treatment. *Criminal Justice and Behavior, 34*, 893–905. https://doi.org/10.1177/0093854807301555

Batastini, A. B., King, C. M., Morgan, R. D., & McDaniel, B. (2016). Telepsychological services with criminal justice and substance abuse clients: A systematic review and meta-analysis. *Psychological Services, 13*(1), 20–30.

Batastini, A. B., & Morgan, R. D. (2016). Connecting the disconnected: Preliminary results and lessons learned from a telepsychology initiative with special management inmates. *Psychological Services, 13*(3), 283–291.

Batastini, A. B., Morgan, R. D., Kroner, D. G., & Mills, J. F. (2016). *Stepping Up, Stepping Out: A Mental Health Treatment Program for Inmates Detained in Restrictive Housing*. Under contract with Routledge Taylor & Francis Group.

Batiuk, M. E., Lahm, K. F., McKeever, M., Wilcox, N., & Wilcox, P. (2005). Disentanglinmg the effects of correctional education: Are current policies misguided? An event history analysis. *Criminal Justice, 5*(1), 55–74.

Bewley, M. T., & Morgan, R. D. (2011). A national survey of mental health services available to offenders with mental illness: Who is doing what? *Law and Human Behavior, 35*(5), 351–363. https://doi.org/10.1007/s10979-010-9242-4

Bourke, M. L., & Van Hasselt, V. B. (2001). Social problem-solving skills training for incarcerated offenders: A treatment manual. *Behavior Modification, 25*(2), 163–188.

Brazell, D., Crayton, A., Mukamal, D. A., Solomon, A. L., & Lindahl, N. (2009). *From the classroom to the community: Exploring the role of education during incarceration and reentry*. Washington, DC: The Urban Institute: Justice Policy Center.

Brewster, D. R., & Sharp, S. F. (2002). Educational programs and recidivism in Oklahoma: Another look. *The Prison Journal, 82*(3), 314–334.

Burdon, W. M., Messina, N. P., & Prendergast, M. L. (2004). The california treatment expansion initiative: Aftercare participation, recidivism, and predictors of outcomes. *The Prison Journal, 84*(1), 61–80. Retrieved from http://journals.sagepub.com/doi/pdf/10.1177/0032885503262455

Burke, L. O., & Vivian, J. E. (2001). The effect of college programming on recidivism rates at the Hampton County House of Correction: A 5-year study. *Journal of Correctional Education, 52*(4), 160–162.

Bush, J., Glick, B., & Taymans, J. (1997). *Thinking for a change: Integrated cognitive behavior change program. National Institute of Corrections*. Washington, DC: U.S. Department of Justice.

Cauffman, E., & Steinberg, L. (2012). Emerging findings from research on adolescent development and juvenile justice. *Victims and Offenders, 7*(4), 428–449.

Chappell, C. (2004). Post-secondary correctional education and recidivism: A meta-analysis of research conducted 1990–1999. *The Journal of Correctional Education, 55*(2), 148–169.

Cherney, A., & Fitzgerald, R. (2016). Finding and keeping a job: The value and meaning of employment for parolees. *International Journal of Offender Therapy and Comparative Criminology, 60*(1), 21–37. https://doi.org/10.1177/0306624X14548858

Clark, P. M. (2011). An evidence-based intervention for offenders. *Corrections Today, 73*(1), 62–64.

Cobbina, J. E., Huebner, B. M., & Berg, M. T. (2012). Men, women, and postrelease offending: An examination of the nature of the link between relational ties and recidivism. *Crime and Delinquency, 58*(3), 331–361.

Cressey, D. R. (1955). Changing criminals: The application of the theory of differential association. *American Journal of Sociology, 61*(2), 116–120.

DeMatteo, D., Hunt, E., Batastini, A., & LaDuke, C. (2010). The disconnect between assessment and intervention in the risk management of criminal offenders. *Open Access Journal of Forensic Psychology, 2*, 59–74.

Douglas, K. S., Hart, S. D., Webster, C. D., & Belfrage, H. (2013). *HCR-20V3: Assessing risk of violence—User guide*. Burnaby: Mental Health, Law, and Policy Institute, Simon Fraser University.

Dowden, C., & Andrews, D. A. (1999). What works for female offenders: A meta-analytic review. *NCCD News, 45*(4), 438–452.

Dowden, C., & Andrews, D. A. (2000). Effective correctional treatment and violent reoffending: A meta-analysis. *Canadian Journal of Criminology, 42*, 449–467.

Draper, C. E., Errington, S., Omar, S., & Makhita, S. (2013). The therapeutic benefits of sport in the rehabilitation of young sexual offenders: A qualitative evaluation of the Fight with Insight programme. *Psychology of Sport and Exercise, 14*(4), 519–530.

Einhorn, L., Williams, T., Stanley, S., Wunderlin, N., Markman, H., & Eason, J. (2008). PREP inside and out: Marriage education for inmates. *Family Process, 47*(3), 341–356.

Fagan, T. J., & Ax, R. K. (Eds.). (2011). *Correctional mental health: From theory to best practice.* Thousand Oaks, CA: Sage Publications.

Fazel, S., Bains, P., & Doll, H. (2006). Substance abuse and dependence in prisoners: A systematic review. *Addiction, 101*(2), 181–191.

Ferguson, L. M., & Wormith, J. S. (2012). A meta-analysis of Moral Reconation Therapy. *International Journal of Offender Therapy and Comparative Criminology, 57*(9), 1076–1106.

Gallant, D., Sherry, E., & Nicholson, M. (2015). Recreation or rehabilitation? Managing sport for development programs with prison populations. *Sport Management Review, 18*(1), 45–56.

Gendreau, P., & Goggin, C. (2013). *Practicing psychology in correctional settings.* In I. B. Weiner & R. K. Otto (Eds.), *Handbook of forensic psychology* (4th ed., pp. 759–794). Hoboken, NJ: Wiley.

Gerber, J., & Fritsch, E. J. (1995). Adult academic and vocational correctional education programs: A review of recent research. *Journal of Offender Rehabilitation, 22*(1/2), 119–142.

Goldstein, A. P., Nensen, R., Daleflod, B., & Kalt, M. (Eds.). (2004). *New perspectives on aggression replacement training: Practice, research, and application.* Chichester: Wiley.

Hallundbaek, H. (2017). Art for a change: Innovative reentry program shows off practical implications. *Corrections Today, 79*(1), 56–61.

Hanson, R. K., Bourgon, G., Helmus, L., & Hodgson, S. (2009). The principles of effective correctional treatment also apply to sexual offenders: A meta-analysis. *Criminal Justice and Behavior, 36*(9), 865–891. https://doi.org/10.1177/0093854809338545

Hiller, M. L., Knight, K., & Simpson, D. D. (2006). Recidivism following mandated residential substance abuse treatment for felony probationers. *The Prison Journal, 86*(2), 230–241.

Hull, K., Forrester, S., Brown, J., Jobe, D., & McCullen, C. (2000). Analysis of recidivism rates for participants of the academic/vocational/transition education programs offered by the Virginia Department of Correctional Education. *Journal of Correctional Education, 51*(2), 256–261.

Inciardi, J. A., Martin, S. S., & Butzin, C. A. (2004). Five-year outcomes of therapeutic community treatment of drug-involved offenders after release from prison. *Crime and Delinquency, 50*(1), 88–107.

Jackson, M. A., & Verdino, J. R. (2012). Vocational psychology. *Encyclopedia of the History of Psychological Theories,* 1157–1158. https://doi.org/10.1007/978-1-4419-0463-8_304

Jancic, M. (1998). Does correctional education have an effect on recidivism? *The Journal of Correctional Education, 49*(4), 152–161.

Johnson, K. F. (2013). Preparing ex-offenders for work: Applying self-determination theory to social cognitive career counseling. *Journal of Employment Counseling, 50,* 83–93. https://doi.org/10.1177/0306624X14548858

Kennedy, R. B., & Kennedy, D. A. (2004). Using the myers-briggs type indicator® in career counseling. *Journal of Employment Counseling, 41*(1), 38–43.

Knight, K., Garner, B. R., Simpson, D. D., Morey, J. T., & Flynn, P. M. (2006). An assessment for criminal thinking. *Crime and Delinquency, 52,* 159–177.

Lamb, H. R., & Weinberger, L. E. (1998). Persons with severe mental illness in jails and prisons: A review. *Psychiatric Services, 49*(4), 483–492. https://doi.org/10.1176/ps.49.4.483

Landenberger, N. A., & Lipsey, M. W. (2005). The positive effects of cognitive-behavioral programs for offenders: A meta-analysis of factors associated with effective treatment. *Journal of Experimental Criminology, 1,* 451–476.

Latessa, E., Lovins, B., & Lux, J. (2014). *The Ohio risk Assessment System, Misdemeanor Assessment Tool (ORAS-MAT) and Misdemeanor Screening Tool (ORAS-MST).* Cincinnati, OH: University of Cincinnati Center for Criminal Justice Research.

Lipsey, M. W., Chapman, G. L., & Landenberger, N. A. (2001). Cognitive-behavioral programs for offenders. *The Annals of the American Academy, 578,* 144–157.

Lipsey, M. W., Landenberger, N. A., & Wilson, S. J. (2007). *Effects of cognitive-behavioral programs for criminal offenders.* Oslo: The Campbell Collaboration.

Little, G. L. (2005). Meta-analysis of Moral Reconation Therapy: Recidivism results from probation and parole implementations. *Cognitive-Behavioral Treatment Review, 14*(1/2), 14–16.

Little, G. L., & Robinson, K. D. (1988). Moral Reconation Therapy: A systematic step-by-step treatment system for treatment resistant clients. *Psychological Reports, 62*(1), 135–151.

Lopoo, L. M., & Western, B. (2005). Incarceration and the formation and stability of marital unions. *Journal of Marriage and Family, 67*(3), 721–734.

Lowenkamp, C. T., Hubbard, D., Makarios, M. D., & Latessa, E. J. (2009). A quasi-experimental evaluation of Thinking for a Change: A "real world" application. *Criminal Justice and Behavior, 36*(2), 137–146.

Lowes, R. (2001). Telemedicine. *Medical Economics, 78*, 24.

Luzzo, D. A., & Day, M. A. (1999). Effects of Strong Interest Inventory feedback on career decision-making self-efficacy and social cognitive career beliefs. *Journal of Career Assessment, 7*(1), 1–17.

Magaletta, P. R., Fagan, T. J., & Peyrot, M. F. (2000). Telehealth in the federal bureau of prisons: Inmates' perceptions. *Professional Psychology: Research and Practice, 31*, 497–502. https://doi.org/10.1037//0735-7028.31.5.497

Mandracchia, J. T. (2017). *Measure of Criminogenic Thinking Styles (MOCTS) manual.* Unpublished manual and user guide.

McGuire, J., Bilby, C. A. L., Hatcher, R. M., Hollin, C. R., Hounsome, J., & Palmer, E. J. (2008). Evaluation of structured cognitive-behavioral treatment programmes in reducing criminal recidivism. *Journal of Experimental Criminology, 4*, 21–40.

McMay, D., & Cotronea, M. (2015). Developing a leisure time management program to aid successful transition to community: A program template with recommendations for practitioners. *The Prison Journal, 95*(2), 264–284.

Morgan, R. D., Flora, D. B., Kroner, D. G., Mills, J. F., Varghese, F., & Steffan, J. S. (2012). Treating offenders with mental illness: A research synthesis. *Law and Human Behavior, 36*(1), 37–50. https://doi.org/10.1037/h0093964

Morgan, R. D., Kroner, D. G., & Mills, J. F. (2018). *A treatment manual for justice involved persons with mental illness: Changing lives and changing outcomes.* New York: Routledge.

National Institute of Justice. (1999, March). *Telemedicine can reduce correctional health care costs: An evaluation of a prison telemedicine network.* Retrieved February 10, 2011 from www.ncjrs.gov/pdffiles1/175040.pdf

Nesmith, A., & Ruhland, E. (2008). Children of incarcerated parents: Challenges and resiliency, in their own words. *Children and Youth Services Review, 30*(10), 1119–1130.

Nicholls, T. L., Butler, A., Kendrick-Koch, L., Brink, J., Jones, R., & Simpson, A. I. F. (2018). Assessing and treating offenders with mental illness. In M. W. Patry, M. Ternes, & P. Magaletta (Eds.), *The practice of correctional psychology.* Cham: Springer.

Norcross, J. C., Pfund, R. A., & Prochaska, J. O. (2013). Psychotherapy in 2022: A Delphi poll on its future. *Professional Psychology: Research and Practice, 44*(5), 363.

Parker, A., Meek, R., & Lewis, G. (2014). Sport in a youth prison: Male young offenders' experiences of a sporting intervention. *Journal of Youth Studies, 17*(3), 381–396.

Peterson, N. G., Mumford, M. D., Borman, W. C., Jeanneret, P. R., Fleishman, E. A., Levin, K. Y., … Gowing, M. K. (2001). Understanding work using the Occupational Information Network (O* NET): Implications for practice and research. *Personnel Psychology, 54*(2), 451–492.

Peterson, J., Skeem, J. L., Hart, E., Vidal, S., & Keith, F. (2010). Analyzing offense patterns as a function of mental illness to test the criminalization hypothesis. *Psychiatric Services, 61*(12), 1217–1222. https://doi.org/10.1176/ps.2010.61.12.1217

Pew-MacArthur Results First Initiative. (2015). Legislating evidence-based policymaking: A look at state laws that support data-driven decision-making. *Issue Brief.* Retrieved from http://www.pewtrusts.org/~/media/assets/2015/03/legislationresultsfirstbriefmarch2015.pdf

Prins, S. J. (2014). Prevalence of mental illnesses in U.S. state prisons: A systematic review. *Psychiatric Services, 65*(7), 862–872. https://doi.org/10.1176/appi.ps.201300166

Romani, C. J., Morgan, R. D., Gross, N. R., & McDonald, B. R. (2012). Treating criminal behavior: Is the bang worth the buck? *Psychology, Public Policy, and Law, 18*(1), 14165. http://dx.doi.org.lynx.lib.usm.edu/10.1037/a0024714

Ross, R. R., Fabiano, E. A., & Diemer-Ewles, C. (1988). Reasoning and rehabilitation. *International Journal of Offender Therapy and Comparative Criminology, 32*, 29–35.

Schlossman, S., & Spillane, J. (1995). *Bright hopes, dim realities: Vocational innovation in American correctional education*. Santa Monica, CA: Rand.

Shamblen, S. R., Arnold, B. B., McKiernan, P., Collins, D. A., & Strader, T. N. (2013). Applying the Creating Lasting Family Connections Marriage Enhancement Program to marriages affected by prison reentry. *Family Process, 52*(3), 477–498.

Skeem, J. L., Steadman, H. J., & Manchak, S. M. (2015). Applicability of the risk-need responsivity model to persons with mental illness involved in the criminal justice system. *Psychiatric Services, 66*(9), 916–922. https://doi.org/10.1176/appi.ps.201400448

Steurer, S., Smith, L., & Tracy, A. (2001). *OCE/OCA Three state recidivism study*. Lanham, MD: Correctional Education Association.

Stevenson, D. R. (1992). Rehabilitation effects of earning a general education development (GED) while in total jail confinement as measured by recidivism activity. *Dissertation Abstracts International, 42*. Ann Arbor, MI: University Microfilms.

Stewart, L. A., Gabora, N., Kropp, P. R., & Lee, Z. (2014). Effectiveness of risk-needs responsivity-based family violence programs with male offenders. *Journal of Family Violence, 29*(2), 151–164. https://doi.org/10.1007/s10896-013-9575-0

Ternes, M., Goodwin, S., & Hyland, K. (2018). Substance use disorders in correctional population. In M. W. Patry, M. Ternes, & P. Magaletta (Eds.), *The practice of correctional psychology* (pp. 39–60). Cham: Springer.

Timko, C., Midboe, A. M., Maisel, N. C., Blodgett, J. C., Asch, S. M., Rosenthal, J., & Blonigen, D. M. (2014). Treatments for recidivism risk among justice-involved veterans. *Journal of Offender Rehabilitation, 53*(8), 620–640.

Tong, L. S. J., & Farrington, D. P. (2006). How effective is the "Reasoning and Rehabilitation" programme in reducing reoffending? A meta-analysis of evaluations in four countries. *Psychology, Crime, and Law, 12*(1), 3–24.

Torrey, E. F., Kennard, A. D., Eslinger, D., Lamb, R., & Pavle, J. (2010). *More mentally ill persons are in jails and prisons than hospitals: A survey of the states*. Arlington, VA: Treatment Advocacy Center. Retrieved from http://tulare.networkofcare.org/library/final_jails_v_hospitals_study1.pdf

Vacca, J. S. (2004). Educated prisoners are less likely to return to prison. *Journal of Correctional Education, 55*(4), 297–305.

Varghese, F. P. (2012). Vocational interventions with offenders. *The Counseling Psychologist, 41*(7), 1011–1039. https://doi.org/10.1177/0011000012462369

Walters, G. D. (2013). *The Psychological Inventory of Criminal Thinking Styles (PICTS) professional manual*. Allentown, PA: Center for Lifestyle Studies.

Wilson, P. R. (1994). Recidivism and vocational education. *Journal of Correctional Education, 45*(4), 158–163.

Wilson, D. B., Bouffard, L. A., & MacKenzie, D. L. (2005). A quantitative review of structured, group-oriented, cognitive-behavioral programs for offenders. *Criminal Justice and Behavior, 32*(2), 172–204.

Wilson, D. B., Gallager, C. A., & MacKenzie, D. L. (2000). A meta-analysis of corrections-based education, vocation, and work programs for adults offenders. *Journal of Research in Crime and Delinquency, 37*(4), 347–368.

Wilson, K., Gonzalez, P., Romero, T., Henry, K., & Cerbana, C. (2010). The effectiveness of parent education for incarcerated parents: An evaluation of Parenting from Prison. *Journal of Correctional Education, 61*(2), 114–132.

Wolff, N., Morgan, R. D., Shi, J., Fisher, W., & Huening, J. (2011). Comparative analysis of thinking styles and emotional states of male and female inmates with and without mental disorders. *Psychiatric Services, 62*, 1485–1493.

Woods, D., Breslin, G., & Hassan, D. (2017). A systematic review of the impact of sport-based interventions on the psychological well-being of people in prison. *Mental Health and Physical Activity, 12*, 50–61.

Yochelson, S., & Samenow, S. E. (1976). *The criminal personality: Volume I: A profile for change* (1st ed.). New York: Jason Aronson.

Index

© Springer Nature Switzerland AG 2018
M. Ternes et al. (eds.), *The Practice of Correctional Psychology*,
https://doi.org/10.1007/978-3-030-00452-1

305

Psychopathic personality, 173, 283
Psychopathy, 148, 155, 173, 174, 177–183,
    185–190, 203, 221
Psychopharmacological treatment, *see*
    Pharmacotherapy

R
Radicalization, 219, 220, 222, 223,
    225, 226, 228
Radicalized offenders, 3, 219–230
Readiness to change, 45, 46, 51, 154
Rehabilitation, 23, 56, 74, 93, 116, 129, 138,
    150–152, 156, 157, 206, 207, 220,
    221, 223, 226, 228, 261, 287
Reintegration, 11, 15, 22–24, 76, 89, 91, 113,
    115, 118, 119, 159, 160, 163, 167,
    220, 223, 226–229
Relapse prevention (RP), 19, 27, 46, 58, 75,
    88, 89, 152–154, 181–183, 208, 248
Relational theory, 106, 107, 115, 118
Research, 1, 13, 39, 71, 103, 127, 143, 176,
    198, 219, 235, 260
Risk assessment, *see* Assessment
Risk management, 24, 76, 89, 149, 150,
    204–206
Risk-need-responsivity model (RNR), 15, 18,
    24, 45, 46, 75, 78, 88, 89, 105–107,
    115, 117, 118, 131, 132, 134–136,
    139, 143, 145, 146, 151, 153–155,
    157, 158, 164–166, 206, 207, 211,
    224, 227, 283–299
Role stressors, 263, 265, 267–269,
    271, 272

S
Screening, 11, 46, 49, 50, 111, 112, 174,
    243–245, 250
Screening, triage, assessment, intervention and
    reintegration (STAIR) model, 10,
    11, 15–19, 21–24, 29
Self-medication model, 43
Self-Regulation Pathways (SRP) Model, 78,
    88, 177, 178
Self-report assessments, *see* Assessments
Service delivery, 4, 39, 41–46, 71, 105–108,
    113, 114, 116, 118, 131–133, 137,
    143, 145, 146, 149, 150, 155, 167,
    206, 207, 221–223, 237–241, 262,
    263, 295, 296
Sexual offending/sexual violence, 3, 78, 79,
    83, 88, 89, 153, 197, 198, 201, 204,
    205, 207, 211
Sexual preoccupation, 199–203, 209

The Significance quest model of
    radicalization, 222
Social learning model (SLM), 41–43,
    52, 53, 56
Standards of care, 13, 14
Stress-diathesis theory, 238
Substance use disorders (SUD), 1–3, 5, 11, 18,
    25, 39–60, 110, 147, 148
Support, Occupation, Accommodation and
    Programs (SOAPP) model, 89

T
Technological advances, 59, 119, 235, 284
Telehealth/telepsychology, 118, 286,
    293, 294, 297
Terrorism, 220, 222
Training, 1, 4, 6, 20, 23, 24, 85–88, 91,
    116–118, 137, 152, 153, 160, 162,
    164, 165, 167, 187, 188, 210, 211,
    226, 229, 243, 246–249, 267, 270,
    271, 275, 285, 288, 289, 291,
    295–298
Transtheoretical model (TTM), 41, 44,
    45, 51, 55
Trauma informed therapy, 160, 161
Treatment
    aggression replacement therapy, 152
    animal assisted interventions (AAI), 152,
        160
    cognitive behavioral therapy (CBT),
        20–22, 25, 52, 53, 59, 85–88, 107,
        155, 161, 208, 246, 287
    comprehensive, multi-intervention
        programs, 152, 156
    interpersonal and relationship skills
        programs, 286, 288–290
    moral reconation therapy (MRT), 152, 156,
        157, 287
    opioid substitution therapy (OST), 54, 55,
        58, 59
    reasoning and rehabilitation therapy, 152,
        157, 287
    therapeutic communities, 52–54, 57, 152,
        160, 162, 163
    treatment for psychopathy, 173, 180–183,
        185, 187–190
    treatment for sexual offending, 197, 207, 208
    twelve-step approaches, 56, 57
    violent offender treatment, 143,
        152, 153, 165
Treatment outcomes, 28, 116, 151, 153, 167,
    183, 184, 295
Triage, 11, 16, 17, 228
Tripartite conceptual model, 41, 43, 44

CPSIA information can be obtained
at www.ICGtesting.com
Printed in the USA
LVHW081258050819
626548LV00009B/144/P